Mad, Bad & Dangerous to Know

RANULPH FIENNES

Mad, Bad & Dangerous to Know

HODDER &
STOUGHTON

Copyright © 1987, 2007 by Ranulph Fiennes

Parts of the text first published as LIVING DANGEROUSLY in Great Britain in 1987 by
Macmillan
This edition published in 2007 by Hodder & Stoughton
A division of Hodder Headline

The right of Ranulph Fiennes to be identified as the Author of the Work has been asserted by
him in accordance with the Copyright, Designs and Patents Act 1988.

A Hodder & Stoughton book

10

A CIP catalogue record for this title is available from the British Library

Hardback ISBN 978 0 340 95168 2
Trade paperback ISBN 978 0 340 95183 5

Typeset in Sabon by M Rules
Map of Southern Oman by Raymond Turvey
Printed and bound by Clays Ltd, St Ives plc

Hodder Headline's policy is to use papers that are natural, renewable and recyclable products
and made from wood grown in sustainable forests. The logging and manufacturing processes
are expected to conform to the environmental regulations of the country of origin.

Hodder & Stoughton Ltd
A division of Hodder Headline
338 Euston Road
London NW1 3BH

To my surviving sister
Gill
with love and many happy memories

Acknowledgments

My thanks to my late wife Ginny for a lifetime of love, friendship and inspiration. To my late mother and my late sisters, Sue and Celia, for being my loving family for sixty years. This book is dedicated to my surviving sister Gill. To our good friends for all the happiness and excitements we've shared.

To all fellow expedition co-travellers, sponsors and advisors, including those in Appendix 2 on page 356.

Also, for their help with this book, Gill Allen, Professor Gianni Angelini, Ian Bannister, Anton Bowring, Tom Briggs, Bob Brown, Tony Brown, Kenton Cool, John Costello, Dr Tim Cripps, Monty Don, Norman Dunroy, Simon Gault, Nick Holder, Gill Hoult, Morag Howell, Peter James, Mike Kobold, Andrey Kosenko, Arabella McIntyre Brown, Mac Mackenney, John Muir, Ian Parnell, Donald Sammut, Lord Saye & Sele, Steven Seaton, Ski Sharp, Neal Short, David Smith, Mike Stroud, Paul Sykes, Judy Tarring, Dr Gordon Thomas, Gary Tompsett, Yiannis Tridimus, Giles Whittell, Simon Wilde, Arabella Williams and John Yates.

Also, for the production of this book, my thanks to Ed Victor, Rupert Lancaster, Jill Firman, Maggie Body (my oft-times editor since 1968!), my wife Louise, stepson Alexander and daughter Elizabeth (for their patience), and to all those individuals mentioned in the text who went with me down the long years to 'the limits and beyond'.

Ranulph Fiennes
2007

Contents

Maps

1

At First

The *Guinness Book of Records* described me as 'the youngest posthumous baronet'. This unwanted claim to fame came about because my father, another Ranulph, was killed during the Italian Campaign in the Second World War four months before my birth. In June 1943 he came home on leave and I was conceived. When he left, my mother was never to see him again. He commanded the Royal Scots Greys at Salerno and, reconnoitring a bridge over the Pescara River unarmed and alone, he surprised three Germans in a cave and took them prisoner at the point of his briar pipe. Not far from Naples, checking out a possible route of advance, my father trod on a German S-type mine and died in a Naples hospital. My mother never remarried. From childhood I wanted to be as he was. Especially I wanted to command the Royal Scots Greys.

My grandmother, Florrie, had lost her elder son in the First World War, now she had lost her younger son, and her husband had also died. She had nothing left to keep her in Sunningdale, so as soon as the war was over she decided to return to her own family in South Africa and my mother, three elder sisters and I were wafted along in her wake. We arrived in Table Bay in January 1947. I was two and a half. A cousin came to meet us and welcome us to our new country. Turning to me, he asked Granny: 'And what is her name?' Granny exploded, for she was very proud of her only grandson. 'But,' protested the cousin, 'how can you blame anyone for mistaking his sex when you doll his curly hair up with these long blue ribbons?' My ribbons, the height of Sunningdale kiddies' fashion, were removed that very evening, never to be worn again.

There were thirty-three cousins in Granny's family, the Rathfelders, most of whom lived in happy harmony in Constantia, the Valley of the Vines, in the shadow of Table Mountain, which was an idyllic place for a small boy to grow up. There were no white children of my age in the valley except cousin Bella who cried all the time. Soon the coloured boys took me to their homes and showed me how to play their version of Pooh-sticks under the plank-bridge by their stream. Over the next four years our little gang often roamed the valley, avoiding the forest with its baboons and packs of wild dogs. Bamboo spears and short leather straps to whip the dirt were *de rigueur* and I became co-leader of the gang along with a one-armed lad named Archie. My mother, meanwhile, became fervently involved with a then relatively docile anti-apartheid movement known as Black Sash and drove about collecting signatures on behalf of coloured people's rights.

In October 1950 Granny Florrie suffered a stroke. She died quietly in the house she loved and was mourned by everyone in the valley. The funeral was held in the Anglican church in Constantia, although our normal place of worship was St Saviour's in Claremont, where Canon Wade had two skinny little daughters. The younger, Virginia, later became an English tennis star who won the Women's Singles at Wimbledon.

At prep school the severe-faced headmaster who beat me from time to time for good reason, awarded me the Divinity Prize. I decided briefly to become a priest, until Pathé News showed the first ascent of Everest. Somehow I was left with the muddled impression that Mr Hillary and a Chinese friend had been sent up this great mountain, higher even than Table Mountain, as a wedding present for the English Queen. I, too, would become a climber of mountains and stick the British flag into fierce features of far-flung landscapes; but only after being colonel of the Royal Scots Greys.

My mother had been brought up in another era and in different circumstances. She had married at nineteen and left her protected family environment without even knowing how to boil an egg or iron a shirt. When Granny Florrie died, she was on her own for the first time, with nobody to turn to for advice. Eventually, in 1954 she decided we should return to England. I promised, on saying goodbye, to write to Archie and the gang, but I don't think I ever did.

While Mother house-hunted, I was packed off to my new English prep school in purple blazer and cap and grey flannels. After sobbing into my pillow for the first week I came to enjoy Sandroyd School in Wiltshire as it transformed itself from a hostile planet into an exciting playground. My sisters and I had all developed the Afrikaaner way with English vowels, but English schooling soon eradicated this and in the dormitory I discovered my South African years were an unsuspected asset when it came to spinning 'tales of the jungle'. I only told my stories on Saturday nights, mainly because we were given our weekly chocolate bars on Saturday afternoon. I charged a square of chocolate from each listener.

About the time of my twelfth birthday my mother purchased St Peter's Well, a long, low house that had once been three cottages on the edge of the village of Lodsworth in Sussex. Right across the front garden wall, as far as the eye could see, stretched a paradise of fields, valleys and forest. The River Lod ran along the bottom of our valley and one day my sister Gill – then seventeen – and I canoed down past where it joined the Rother, paddling through the domain of dragonfly, swan and kingfisher, until we passed through a cleft in the South Downs and reached the Arun and, at length, the sea. Mother collected us and the canoe in her bull-nosed Morris Minor. She owned this car for twenty years and to the best of my knowledge never once exceeded thirty miles per hour, probably causing numerous crashes by frustrated speedsters.

A month before our own arrival, a family of five settled in the hamlet of River, a mile from Lodsworth. Mr Pepper ran a chalk pit at Amberley. There were two sons about my age and a daughter of nine, three years my junior. We were invited to tea.

'You must put shoes on, Ranulph,' my mother said sharply. 'People do not expect visitors with bare feet, especially on first acquaintance.'

'I don't want to go to tea with two boring boys and a silly girl. Can't I go down to the river this afternoon?'

Exasperated, my mother was firm. 'They are our neighbours. We can't be rude, and how do you know they are boring or silly since you've never met them?'

So we went to tea at the Peppers. There were excellent cakes which made up for lost time by the river, and the boys were not boring. In the attic they had an elaborate electric train set, the working of which they were happy to explain to me.

After a while a pin pricked my knee under the table and I knelt to spot the cause. I had quite forgotten the boys' sister, Virginia. Her brothers ignored her in a pointed fashion so I had done likewise. Now I saw that she had been playing all along underneath the table and had fired a spring-loaded toy cannon at me.

'Stop it. That hurt,' I told her.

She screwed up her nose at me.

I went back to the trains, rather hoping that she might fire another pin. But she didn't. I had noticed that her eyes were very blue, almost violet, and that her eyelashes were long. Soon afterwards, I returned to school. Common entrance exams came and went. I passed with just sufficient marks to make it into Eton. My mother was proud and delighted and so was I, for luckily I could not foresee the immediate future.

My great misfortune was to be a pretty little boy. I can hardly blame Eton for that, yet my memories of the place are tarnished because of it.

My mother drove me to Mr Parr's House at Eton, the Morris Minor laden with suitcases, a colourful rug and two framed prints of spaniels. Accustomed to Sandroyd with its hundred pupils, I was awed by the thought of over 1,000 boys, many of them eight-een-year-olds and over six feet tall. Some, I was told, used razors.

At Sandroyd my baronetcy and my South African background had proved to be good for my street cred. Here there were numer-ous ex-colonials, and baronets were trashy nonentities eclipsed by a welter of earls, lords and viscounts. At first the customs, the col-loquialisms and local geography left me bemused. Those first weeks were like an attempt to gain a set of daily changing objec-tives blindfolded in a swamp, with a host of hostile custodians shouting instructions in a weird language.

The fagging system was an ever-present bane of my existence. The six senior boys in each House had only to stand at their doors and scream '*Boyyyy!*' for every faggable boy within earshot to drop whatever he was doing and head at maximum speed to the source of the scream. He who arrived last was fagged. Trying to come to terms with this amazing new world, I had little time to be homesick and even less for leisure. But I did find myself attracted to the Drawing Schools where the senior master was a kindly soul named Wilfrid Blunt whose younger brother Anthony was in charge of the Queen's paintings and pursued other activities we knew nothing about at the time.

Quite when and how the horror started is now lost to me since the mind does its best to heal the deepest sores. But I believe I had been at Eton about a month when two older boys entered my room just before lunchtime.

'They say you're a tart, Fiennes. Did you know?'

'What,' I asked them, 'is a tart?' But they giggled together with much uplifting of eyebrows and wouldn't tell me. Eventually I dis-covered that in Eton slang a tart is a boy who sells himself for sexual activities in return for favours, be they in cash or kind. There could be no lower form of life. I must prove my innocence at once.

'I am not a tart,' I would protest. I did not realise that any pretty boy at Eton is going to be labelled a tart and that gossip is based not on what actually happens but on what the gossipers would like to think has happened.

Perhaps if some male relative had warned me of the impending problems adolescence at Eton would involve, I might somehow have forearmed myself. But I had no brothers, no uncles and no father. My tormentors were unremitting. I seriously contemplated throwing myself off the bridge over the Thames between Eton and Windsor, only restrained by the thought of making my mother suffer. Instead I decided to cultivate a perpetual scowl and join the school boxing team. I also enlisted my mother's support to allow me to switch early from the the bum-freezer, the short cutaway jackets worn by Etonians under five feet four, to the less provocative tailcoat of the bigger boys. But neither the new tailcoats that hung protectively over my backside, nor my well-practised scowl, nor even a gradually growing reputation as a pugilist could alter my girlish face. Boys had crushes on me and the verbal torment continued.

Fortunately, time was on my side. Each term brought a fresh crop of pretty faces to distract the gossips. Slowly, I began to enjoy one or two aspects of Eton life. History was my favourite subject, especially the study of British naval heroes and explorers. But one attempt to show off rebounded when I shot my hand up to the master's question: 'What did Stanley say at his famous jungle meeting?' My instant reply, 'Kiss me, Livingstone,' was greeted with the derision it deserved. At that time an attempt to complete the crossing of Antarctica was in progress, led by Sir Vivian Fuchs and my Everest hero Sir Edmund Hillary. Our history master traced the course of the expedition on an ancient chart of the frozen continent.

German, with a new master, David Cornwell, had taken on a new lease of life. He kept the language interesting and the lessons enjoyable. But he left Eton quite soon, sadly for us but profitably from his point of view, when his income rocketed thanks to the books which he wrote under the name of John le Carré.

I had always found making friends at Eton difficult and I only began to enjoy life at school after meeting Michael Denny who was 'in the Library' (i.e. a prefect) at Mr Crusoe's House, the House nearest to Eton's tallest and most imposing building, School Hall.

Since neither Denny nor I was an experienced climber it is difficult to conjure up quite why we began to climb together, but somehow the partnership was formed and, as a result, my last eighteen months at Eton included a good deal of nocturnal excitement.

There is nothing new about stegophily, the dictionary term for the practice of climbing buildings by night. It has nothing to do with the more normal sport of rock-climbing. Indeed, since I had no head for heights and easily succumbed to vertigo, daytime climbing was anathema to me. The beauty of night-climbing is that the thrill of danger is present without the full visual impact of the drop below. Denny and I hoisted assorted dustbins or lavatory seats onto various prized pinnacles and watched with secret pleasure while steeplejacks with ropes and long ladders brought them down again. In some of our activities we were aided and abetted by Chris Cazenove, already an aspiring actor with the Eton Dramatic Society and adept at putting on an innocent face under questioning.

As my time at Eton drew to a close I had to decide on my future. But there had really only ever been one career choice. One day I would be commanding officer of the Royal Scots Greys, like my father. That was the summit of my ambitions and to that end I had joined the Eton College Corps and enjoyed every moment of the training. There were still officers and men in the Royal Scots Greys who had served with my father eighteen years before and remembered him by his nickname, 'Colonel Lugs', on account of his slightly prominent ears. But family connections were no longer a pass into the Army. Now, to enter the Royal Military Academy, Sandhurst, you needed at least two General Certificates of Education at Advanced Level, including mathematics or physics, and five certificates at Ordinary Level. This precluded any chance of my becoming a professional officer by the normal route. But there was a possible alternative: to obtain a short-service commission through Mons Officer Cadet School and, once in the Army on a two-year commission, to try to extend. Even for Mons, however, I would need a minimum of five Ordinary Level passes and nearly five years of Eton had only gained me four. After consultation with my house master, my mother told me the wonderful news that I could leave Eton at the end of the summer term and enrol in a specialist crammer abroad.

And so I became an Old Etonian. I wonder if I would be a different sort of person now if I had missed out on those early years of hell. In one sense it proved the perfect preparation for the trickier vicissitudes of life, since nothing would ever be so bad again. I arrived at Eton full of self-assurance, buoyant from happy days at Sandroyd. Public school and three long years of remorseless nastiness squeezed every last trace of confidence from me. It would take a long time to get back to a balanced state. I still find myself overly sensitive to the least criticism, a direct hangover from Eton days.

To summarise my old school: location hard to beat; facilities excellent; staff above average. My only complaint was the nature of some of my fellow inmates but all schools have their share of nasty little boys. The acid test must be: if I had a son, would I send him there? I cannot honestly say that I would not.

2

Young Love and the SAS

The Eton College Corps held an annual fourteen-day summer camp and, although I had left the school, I was eligible to attend. The Norwegian Army training base at Kvamskogen, north of Bergen, was deep in mountainous country. The captain of Parr's House, Neville Howard, led the enemy patrol and lived rough in the mountains throughout our fortnight at Kvamskogen. He was to become commanding officer of the SAS in later years. Sodden clothing and bruised bodies helped all 300 fledgling officers decide whether or not to plump for careers in khaki.

Rather than return to England with the rest, I hitchhiked back with another boy as far as Copenhagen. There we squandered dwindling funds at Tivoli, sat in sunny parks staring with longing at the abundance of leggy blondes, and wound up on the Tuborg lager factory guided tour. There were two types of tour ticket, one for German nationals and one for the rest of the world. Our non-Teuton group went first and polished off the bountiful supplies of free lager. These were not replenished for the Germans: war-time memories were still bitter.

Unable to cope with the lashings of alcohol, I misplaced my equally befuddled companion and did not see him again for several months. I continued alone through Denmark and Germany. That was my first expedition and, as I explained to my mother back in Lodsworth, its success proved I was quite ready to face

9

whatever challenges awaited me in the language cramming university I was to be sent to in Aix-en-Provence.

The challenge of the opposite sex still remained to be cracked. My first cousin, Greville 'Gubbie' Napier, lived in nearby Midhurst where he managed an antique shop called Keil's. Being five years my senior, he was worldly wise about those very beings my male-only public school had hidden from me but which now loomed enormous on my seventeen-year-old horizon – girls.

'France is *the* place,' he told me one day, sipping tea in the cluttered backroom of Keil's. 'French girls cannot say no or even *non*. They are unrivalled in both beauty and naughtiness.'

We determined to launch an invasion of Paris without delay.

'How do we get there?' I asked. 'I have £15 in the world.'

Gubbie waved his tin of Keil's Beeswax in the air. 'Absolutely no problem. You are the expert on hitchhiking and I am an expert on seventeenth- and eighteenth-century French furniture. We will have a wonderful time.'

The hitching went well as far as Dieppe. Thereafter, despite or because of the Union Jacks on our packs, our thumbs prodded the air in vain. Nobody stopped. We set down our packs in the steady French drizzle and applied ourselves to Plan B. We had been taught about the old Franco-Scottish *entente cordiale* at school, so we produced kilts from our packs and donned these. But the French truck drivers had not received the same history lessons and continued to roar past. This is where Gubbie's brilliance came into play. Another rummage in our packs produced scarves which we wound cunningly round our heads and necks so that from behind, if not examined too closely through windscreen wipers, we just might be taken for girls. It worked. A lorry stopped. The driver was from Yorkshire and before he had time to realise his mistake, we had swarmed aboard and were overwhelming him with gratitude.

And so, eventually, we got to Paris where we ogled the street ladies but declined their offers on the grounds that our exchequer was down to the bread-line. Gubbie, born and brought up in

Scotland, decided we would recoup funds by singing Scottish dit-
ties in cafés, wearing our kilts of course. We made just enough to
travel by bus back to Dieppe, where we called upon the British
consul for a £10 loan to get us back to Sussex. He agreed, providing we told him a dirty joke. Amazing though it now seems,
neither of us in our hour of need could remember a single joke,
clean or dirty, but the consul relented and we were able to buy
ferry tickets.

At home in Lodsworth I had long since made friends with Peter
Tooth, son of the local chief woodsman. Together we roamed the
countryside on our bicycles and also indulged in local roof-climbing
between Lodsworth and Midhurst. We never read books or listened
to music and we didn't have television. A favourite wet-weather
wargame took place in the 'gallery' at home where my mother had
hung Granny Florrie's portraits of Fiennes ancestors. One day my
aim was poor and an arrow sped past Peter's ear, burying itself in
the left cheek of Gregory Fiennes, the 14th Lord Saye and Sele.
Today he hangs in our sitting room on Exmoor and I much regret
his patched-up port jowl. Peter found instructions in some magazine
for making explosives. I studied these for several days and experimented with growing quantities of granulated sugar and weedkiller
until our activities were brought to a halt after I had blown up my
mother's best brass flower vase and terrified the neighbours.

One Saturday, while still at Eton, I went to the Lodsworth
Village Flower Show where my mother had great hopes for her
marrow entries. The village hall was full, so I wandered off to see
if Peter was about. He wasn't, but I noticed a slim girl of about
thirteen wearing a blue and white skirt and a sports shirt with
short sleeves. I was sure God had never designed any girl so perfectly. I sat on an onion display and watched her.

'Isn't it wonderful?' It was my mother.

'Oh, yes,' I said with enormous feeling. My mother looked at
me surprised and pleased, for I did not normally enthuse over her
vegetables. She had won a prize and so, both elated, we headed

back to the Morris Minor. She stopped in the carpark to chat with the occupant of the next car, an Aston Martin. It was Mrs Pepper from River and beside her sat the vision.

'This is Virginia, remember her?' Mrs Pepper said. 'She's back from Eastbourne for half-term.' The girl smiled politely at my mother and looked briefly at me with total unconcern. That evening I told Peter about her.

'Does she like you?'

'I think she couldn't care less. I might have been a concrete gnome from the look she gave me.'

'Ah,' said Peter, knowingly. 'That is an excellent sign. They get taught at school nowadays that the best way to attract the man they want is to ignore him.'

The passport to success in adolescent society at that time was the ability to twist and knowing how to kiss. I achieved the former. The latter was a mystery. A life of kissing sisters and mother out of family love interfered with my zeal to kiss out of desire. Then some senior lady with little patience at a barbecue in Hook prised my teeth apart with her tongue and, after the initial shock, I learned what was required.

A fortnight after returning from France, Gubbie had involved himself with a fuzzy-haired beauty with long legs so I went alone to a Liss party on the Vespa scooter my mother had given me for Christmas. Two of the girls decided to raid their old school, a nearby mansion where Dame Margaret Rutherford had recently filmed *The Happiest Days of Your Life*. The entire party, armed with fireworks and smoke bombs, drove an assortment of motor-bikes, sports cars and old bangers to Bycylla School for young ladies. The raid was a noisy success but my girlfriend of the evening was a bad scooter passenger and, by the time we tailed the escaping cavalcade to the gates, the lodge-keeper had collected his wits and taken my number.

Two days later the police called at Lodsworth. The evidence, they said, was irrefutable and I was to be prosecuted for 'malicious damage resulting in costs of £8 3/6d'. None of the other raiders was caught and, at the Midhurst Court Sessions the proceedings were dropped after I had apologised to the headmistress and paid her £8 3/6d to replace an eiderdown burned by a smoke bomb. However the national newspapers were hard up for news and made tasty headlines out of the mixture of Bomber Baronet, Screaming Young Girls in Nightdresses and Margaret Rutherford.

My mother was at her wits' end, ashamed of her only son, and wondering where it would all lead. I was a liability and not to be trusted in England. What might I not get up to if let loose in France? She decided to find a language school rather nearer home than Aix and enrolled me, aged seventeen, at a crammer in Hove.

It was the time of the mini skirt or pussy pelmet and the place was full of sexy foreign girls. This impeded my concentration. I took a quiet English girl called Maggie to the cinema and afterwards down to the beach at nearby Climping Sands but I did not kiss her because she was too well mannered to look as though she expected to be kissed. So my sexual frustrations grew. To let off steam I introduced some of the crammer students to the delights of climbing buildings by night. I still hated heights but darkness meant that nasty drops were unseen. Over the next twelve months, the Sussex newspapers reported a rash of flagged spires. My finest climb was the lofty spire of Hove Town Hall which housed the police station.

Virginia Pepper kept two ponies at her father's chalk quarry at Amberley and one of my sisters got Mrs Pepper's permission for me to help exercise them. Ginny and I rode by way of woodland paths and long fallow fields which we both knew well. One day, before we rode back I gave Ginny a scarf I had bought especially for her in Paris. I watched as she opened the wrapping and, when I saw her smile, the whole world danced. She liked it. We left the ponies in the paddock and went in for tea. I learned that Ginny was going back to school in Eastbourne the following day so nonchalantly offered her a lift on the Vespa. To my surprise and delight her mother agreed. Her father would have been furious.

Ginny had a school suitcase which fitted on my rear seat when she kept well forward. I felt her pressed against my back and her hands lightly around me. I was definitely in heaven. In fact, if heaven is half as good as I felt that day, it will be worth the struggle to attain.

All went well as far as the school where we dropped off her case. She had agreed to have tea with me in town but on our way back I swerved to avoid a bicyclist. I do not remember the accident, nor the next fifteen hours. But when I woke up in hospital the nurse told me my passenger was in her bed at her school, my scooter was in good nick and the bicyclist, whose fault it had been, was unharmed. Apart from concussion and abrasions I, too, was undamaged. Ginny came to see me the following day with a bunch of flowers and I was fined £4 for riding a scooter without L-plates and carrying an unlicensed passenger. Ginny's father, who had never liked me, was volcanic and forbade her to see me again.

Thus encouraged, we agreed to meet by night in a bathroom at the school. For two hours I sat in the bath and Ginny, in her nightdress, sat on the loo. My cautious suggestion that we could perhaps make ourselves more comfortable were discouraged and I was determined not to risk alarming her. Towards the end of term, and daringly by day, I waited for Ginny with a bunch of other girls on their way back from lacrosse. She recognised me, despite the scooter helmet and goggles and dropped behind the others. We hid in a patch of rhododendrons.

'You are wicked,' she laughed. She was breathless. We kissed for the first time and I felt that I would love her for ever.

The following term I perfected a drainpipe approach to Ginny's new fourth-floor dormitory but was intercepted on the flat roof by a history mistress on night duty. I explained that I had been passing on my scooter and thought I had seen a fire on the roof, so had climbed up to extinguish it, only to find there was no fire . . .

The mistress nodded wisely. 'In that case, I might as well let you back down and out, don't you think?'

I never got my language A-levels (due to the mini skirts) but I did net a German O-level which brought my tally up to five and qualified me to attempt the Army's Regular Commissions Board, where I was put through a series of aptitude tests more taxing on the imagination and physique than the intellect. To my delight I passed. The next step was Mons Officer Cadet School at Aldershot. Day after day we learned drill movements with and without .303 rifle, submachine-gun or sword; how to attack machine-gun nests head-on under cover of smoke; and the enthusiastic application of brasso and blanco.

I discovered a fellow night-climber in the Honourable Richard Wrottesly, known to all as Rotters, who wore a monocle at all times and drove an E-type Jaguar. He proposed we scale the west wing of nearby Heathfield Girls' School which he said was a challenging climb. Three-quarters of the way up we were disturbed by a clamour from below. Rotters, above me on the same drainpipe, looked downwards and the beam of a powerful torch flashed off his monocle.

'We've been spotted,' Rotters hissed and, gaining the horizontal guttering, he swung himself across to a fire ladder that disappeared around the back of the building. But there was no escape. When we reached the ground a uniformed officer and the school bursar, a hefty man in his sixties, frogmarched us towards the main entrance. Without warning Rotters lashed backwards with the rope coil and shouted, 'Break.' I ran straight for the nearest rhododendrons, scaled the fence with wings of fear and sped to Rotters' car. I found it locked and decided to hitchhike back to Mons. First parade at 7.00 a.m. could not be missed.

The first car that stopped for me was a police van and I decided to play innocent. They took me to Ascot Police Station and there I found Rotters demanding his rights and complaining about police harassment of an innocent ornithologist. He showed no signs of recognising me so I responded likewise.

The police officer from the patrol van looked me up and down. 'Sir,' he said with heavy irony, 'you are wearing black Army gym shoes, red Army PT shirt and you have the haircut which can nowadays only be found on young Sandhurst cadets. Our bird-watching friend over there whom you have never seen before is wearing identical clothing with the sole exception of a monocle. He has a similar hairstyle . . . Do us a favour and tell us what you were both up to at the girls' school.'

An hour later the van dropped us off at Mons. Heathfield had agreed with our commandant that charges would not be pressed, providing we were suitably dealt with. Rotters, who had physically assaulted the bursar, was given the boot. I was awarded fifty-six days of Restrictions of Privileges, which was two days longer than I was meant to remain at Mons. I still don't know how I scraped through the exams. My platoon commander informed me unofficially that he suspected the authorities were not prepared to risk my presence for another five months while I redid the course.

Now there were four free months before I had to report to tank-training camp. A chance to see the world. An old school friend, Simon Gault, agreed to accompany me to Norway for a canoeing expedition. The only problem was the lack of a canoe. The cheapest suitable model cost £80, so I set to work to earn the money by doing three jobs in rotation, exercising polo ponies in the afternoon, washing dishes at a hotel in the evening and, after snatching a nap on cousin Gubbie's floor for a few hours, I would get up to hose down Southdown double-decker buses at 4.00 a.m. In three weeks I had the money and ordered the canoe. Maggie, whom I'd omitted to kiss on Climping Sands, came too. We arrived at Jotunheim with my double canoe and Simon's single kayak. For three miles we negotiated minor rapids with ease. Then the river dropped into a canyon, so I asked the other two to wait while I went ahead to film them in the rough stuff. The film, which I still possess, shows my hard-earned canoe hitting a rock and splitting in two. Maggie was caught underneath a spar but Simon rescued her further down the gorge. The canoe was not insured. We returned to England the same week. I had learned two lessons: the value of reconnaissance in unknown places and the futility of paying for expeditions from one's own pocket.

The tank gunnery school at Lulworth is carefully situated so that even the stupidest officers cannot knock off Dorset villages with wrongly aimed high-explosive shells. I remember one gunnery sergeant explaining that a reasonably proficient Centurion tank crew should be able to destroy three Soviet tanks 1,000 metres away within ten seconds of sighting. My own range results indicated that any number of Soviet tanks could safely picnic 600 yards away. Despite this I passed the course eight weeks later: I suspect no one is ever failed.

In February 1963 I made my way to Germany to join the Royal Scots Greys. I was eighteen and had just bought my first car, an elderly Peugeot 403, for £150. As in my father's day, the lion's share of the officers were Scotsmen, as were over 90 per cent of the troopers and NCOs. Only two Greys remained who remembered Colonel Lugs, but the fact that he had been the CO and that Fiennes, pronounced Feens by all the Jocks, was thought to be a Scottish name, saved me from most of the mickey-taking suffered by a number of the more obviously English. I grew to love the Greys as much as I had loathed public school.

Immediately after the war tank-training in Germany was conducted in a cavalier fashion, with little respect for the vanquished farmers whose crops were often crushed and barns destroyed. By the 1950s 'Huns' were being referred to more often as 'German citizens' and, after the Berlin airlift, as 'our German allies'. Year by year damage-causing training rights were curtailed until for brigade or divisional exercises a complex scale of compensation was laid down and upgraded each year. Slight damage to a twenty-year-old pine tree could earn its owner £100 and a crushed gate-post £50. Often smiling farmers would stand by open gates waving invitingly to oncoming tank commanders. A poor crop could be turned into a small fortune if a British tank could be persuaded to drive over it once or twice.

When no tank exercises were anticipated there was an Army budget available for adventure training and on the strength of this I received permission to train the regimental langlauf (cross-country) ski team and form a canoe club, taking groups of Jocks down different European rivers. It all went wrong when I organised a large-scale training exercise canoeing on the Kiel Canal, where officially we shouldn't have been in the first place, but it was night-time so I thought our trespass would go unnoticed. Being crafty, some of the canoeists waited for a merchant ship or tanker to pass, then, braving the powerful backwash between hull and canal bank, they would tuck in behind their chosen vessel which sucked them along, making for less work and good camouflage from my watchers on the bank. Unfortunately, a corporal on my staff accidentally landed a red phosphorus flare on a ship's rear deck. He could not have chosen a worse target, for it was a Soviet tanker with a liquid chemical cargo so volatile that the crewmen wore rubber soles so as not to risk causing a single spark. A klaxon and red light system installed along the canal began to honk and flash as though World War Three was about to erupt. All canal traffic across Europe stopped for five hours and I was later heavily fined by my brigade commander.

During my annual leaves Ginny and I contrived to meet, openly when her father lifted his embargo, discreetly in the back of the Peugeot when he did not. In 1965, my third year in Germany, we spent four precious days together at a hotel in Dartmouth where I signed in under a false name. But by then her father was growing paranoid, made her a ward of court and hired a Securicor agent whose enquiries among the chambermaids, a snoopy bunch, soon established what had been going on. Mr Pepper telephoned my commanding officer in Germany to reveal the extent of my iniquity. Since Ginny was by this time well over the age of consent, my colonel clucked soothing noises at him and delivered me a mild scolding, during which he was unable to keep the twinkle from his eye.

In the autumn I was sent to Berlin for a month with my troop to man three tanks which, in the event of hostilities, were intended to repel the Warsaw Pact from Hitler's Olympic Stadium. While my tanks swivelled their guns about defiantly outside the giant arena, I sneaked into the empty Olympic swimming hall and, attempting, as I was periodically wont, to confront my horrible fear of heights, jumped off the high competition board, scaring myself silly in the process.

I was about to apply for a one-year extension to my short-service commission, when I spotted a three-line advertisement in regimental orders. 'Officers wishing to apply for secondment to the 22nd Special Air Service should obtain the relevant form from the Orderly Office.' Only a week before I had listened spellbound to a Mess story of SAS patrols in Borneo, the only war zone where the British Army was still in action. Here was an open invitation to a three-year secondment with this then little known but élite regiment. I consulted the only Scots Grey I knew who had served in the SAS, a sadistic corporal called Jones who had been to Bavaria on one of my ski courses. From him I discovered that map-reading and extreme fitness with a heavy backpack were important. He added, 'In Bavaria, you told me you hated heights. You're not going to be much use parachuting then, are you?'

By chance a two-week course in parachuting happened to be available in the south of France and the colonel let me go at short notice. The parachute school was at Pau, near Lourdes. A fellow student explained that this was no accident. 'You see, those men who are crippled here at Pau can seek speedy recovery in the holy waters just up the road.'

I was the only non-Frenchman in a class of eighty. The first jump, from a Nord Atlas transport plane, was by day. I tried to cure my terror of heights by the simple method of keeping my eyes firmly closed as I threw myself into space. A few seconds after exit, my parachute opened and tugged my body harness up sharply between my legs, jamming my family jewels in a painful position. But at least the canopy had opened. I looked up, expecting to see a neat array of rigging lines running away from my shoulders to the periphery of my chute. Instead there was a single knotted tangle which met in a bunch behind my neck. I experienced instant panic. The ground was already uncomfortably close.

In fact I was merely experiencing a common problem called 'twists', usually caused by a poor exit from the aircraft. The instructors had probably explained '*les twistes*', but I had failed to comprehend what they were saying. The normal process of elasticity slowly unwound the tangle, but I was spinning like a top on landing and hit the ground with a wallop.

I left the Royal Scots Greys in December, assuring my friends that I would be back in three years' time. After spending Christmas at home, I went to Dartmoor and the Brecon Beacons and trained alone with a forty-pound pack and Ordnance Survey map. Then, in February, I drove to Bradbury Lines in Hereford and through a security gate to the SAS barracks, a battered huddle of low huts or 'spiders'.

Altogether 124 would-be troopers and twelve other officers congregated in the barracks for the selection month. For the first week, officers were tested separately. The first night's activities included a naked swim across the River Wye in temperatures below freezing. There was a great deal of map-reading and fast cross-country movement and very little sleep. Our packs weighed only thirty pounds, but this was soon to be increased.

SAS staff with binoculars seemed to be everywhere. Any form of cheating led to dismissal from the course. Two officers twisted their ankles on the third day and one decided he was not cut out for the SAS. Then there were ten of us. On the fourth day another fell by the wayside. I was selfishly delighted with each new dropout for we all knew that more than 90 per cent of applicants would be failed by the end of the month.

After a night in wet clothes tramping through woods without torches, we were ushered into a classroom and doled out question sheets involving complex military problems. I never discovered how I fared at this test – which is perhaps just as well. That evening we missed tea and went, feeling famished, on a fifteen-mile night march to reconnoitre an isolated reservoir. Back in the classroom, both hungry and tired, we were questioned one at a time by an intimidating group of veterans. Fortunately my short-term memory was good and I remembered every detail of the reservoir, down to water-height, construction materials and the nature of surrounding countryside.

At 10.00 a.m. on the sixth day, I returned from a twenty-mile trudge over the Black Mountains to find a brown envelope on my bed – instructions to carry out a theoretical but detailed raid on a specific bank in Hereford and to brief the SAS staff on its execution by 6.00 p.m. that evening. I gauged that there were two hours in hand to grab some precious sleep, set my alarm and crashed out.

The alarm failed to rouse me and the other candidates, each detailed to a different Hereford bank raid, naturally avoided waking me since their own chances of success would improve with my failure. I woke at 2.00 p.m. and rushed down to the relevant bank. Too late, for it had closed an hour before. I knocked on a side window and shouted at the young woman who appeared that I had an appointment with the manager. She must have decided my short haircut and tweed coat looked harmless, for she opened up and took me to the manager.

Thirty minutes later, after checking my passport, military ID, German bank account and SAS course papers, as well as phoning my London bank manager, he accepted that I genuinely wished to open an account. The only untrue frill that I added was the large amount of family silver I wished to store with him. He was quick to assure me how secure his bank was and thoughtfully explained the excellent alarm system. Thanking the manager for his help, I left to make detailed plans for the robbery, including a scale drawing of the offices and security devices I had been shown. The paper was ready on time and handed in to the staff.

That evening was the only free period of the week so three of us drove to a nearby town for a mammoth meal. I had kept a carbon copy of the bank raid plans and this somehow slipped from my coat pocket in the restaurant. Later the Italian restaurateur found it and called the police.

The first I knew of this turn of events was upon reading the headlines of the national newspapers the following day. These included 'Big Bank Raid Mystery' and 'Ministry Enquiry into Bank Raid Scare'. Two days later the headlines had changed to the

Daily Mail's 'Army Initiative Upsets Police' and comments in *The Times* that 'the Services are letting their zeal outrun their discretion'. A weekend-long security operation had stopped all police leave because every bank in Herefordshire had been surrounded, owing to the lack of a specific address on my plans.

I was summoned before the SAS adjutant. It was instantly clear to me that he thought I had planted the plans in the restaurant out of misplaced mischief. This appealed to the SAS sense of humour so I only received a warning. Had they known the plans had been genuinely mislaid, I would have been sent packing.

SAS selection courses no longer involve theoretical bank raids.

By the end of the first week, at which point candidates of all ranks came together, seventy men and six officers remained. Week two saw the departure of forty more men and two officers. I was still around, a lot thinner and craftier. The final test of the third week was known as Long Drag. This was a forty-five-mile cross-country bash carrying a fifty-pound pack, twelve-pound belt kit and eighteen-pound rifle without a sling. During most of the selection course I moved alone for greater speed but on Long Drag I set out with Captain Fleming, one of the three other officer survivors. We decided that the only way we could beat the clock on this last dreadful test was to hire the services of a local farmer with a black Ford Anglia.

At Pen-y-Fan we were lying sixth, about a mile behind a Scots Guards officer, the son of Britain's Chief Scout. We needed to maintain that position to avoid suspicion so, with adroit use of the Ford, binoculars and mist cover, we managed to arrive at isolated checkpoints, some of them several miles from the nearest feasible access point, almost a mile behind Lieutenant MacLean.

I felt guilty afterwards but not badly so, since subterfuge was very much an SAS tactic. I passed the selection but, sadly, Fleming, who finished Long Drag alongside me, was failed. In late February 1966 the SAS CO, Lieutenant-Colonel Mike Wingate Gray awarded three officers and twelve men their buff-coloured SAS berets and sea-blue stable-belts. Since all SAS officers are ranked captain or above, I missed out the rank of first lieutenant and became the youngest captain in the Army at that time. But not for long. 'Pride came,' in the words of my CO, 'before a bloody great fall.'

'You are not in yet,' Staff Sergeant Brummy Burnett warned us, 'so don't get cocky.' He was understating the facts. The selection course proved merely a warm-up to the next four months of intensive training, during which we picked up eight personal skills basic to any beginner sent out to join his first SAS unit: fast response shooting-to-kill, static line parachuting in six-man sticks, demolition, signals using Morse, resistance to interrogation, CQB (close-quarter battle), field medicine and survival techniques.

The CQB included self-defence against an assailant with knife, pistol or blunt instrument and in each case we learned a two-step response again and again until our movements were karate quick. Field medicine was not my favourite subject as I become squeamish easily. Some of the lecturers were fresh back from Borneo and taught us practical tips: 'When your mate's shot, treat him for shock. Give him liquid if you have it, except when the bullet enters between nipple and knee. Don't forget that, 'cos a bullet going in above the knee might end up in the stomach and the poor feller won't want liquid inside then, will he now?' Signals training began in sound booths until we were Morse proficient to five words per minute. Morse was no longer in use in most of the Army but with the tiny but primitive SAS gear we could transmit quick bursts of coded message thousands of miles with little likelihood of hostile direction-finding equipment locating our position.

Brummy himself supervised shoot-to-kill and other sergeants taught us demolition, from the mathematics of fuse-burning rates to the tensile strengths of suspension bridge targets. We demolished old buildings, steel girders, railway tracks and pear trees, and by the end of three weeks I possessed a boot-full of detonators, fuse wire and plastic explosive, the result of demolishing my set targets with less than the issued amounts. I should have returned this volatile booty to the stores but I did not. My motives were acquisitive rather than criminal. I did not intend to blow up anything in particular but fancied the notion that I had the capacity to do so, given a suitable target.

Survival skills were taught by a tiny Welsh corporal who slit the throat of a sheep on our classroom table and watched over us as we skinned the animal, dug out its entrails and boiled the mutton. None of the meat was wasted and he stressed that no sign or scent of the butchery must remain. Theft from farms in winter, leaving no trace of our visit, or making it appear that our hen coop depredations were the work of foxes, were dealt with in minute detail. At the end of the Welshman's week, I felt confident of surviving anywhere short of the Gobi Desert.

At Abingdon airfield I discovered for the first time just how many things could go fatally wrong with a parachute jump, facts I had been protected from in Pau by the limitations of my O-level French. But I also found out I had glandular fever. I was despatched home to recover.

Ginny's father, an artist at blowing hot and cold, now decided Ginny could officially see me again and she appeared at my bedside in a light summer frock with a fashionably high hemline which can't have been good for my swollen glands.

'I picked these for you in the wood.' She gave me a bunch of late spring daffodils. Ginny was no longer just the little girl I had loved for so long. At nineteen she was tall, shapely and much sought after by a number of eligible West Sussex suitors. While in Hereford I had kept wary tabs on my competitors through Gubbie.

Later that summer I ran into an old Eton friend, William Knight, who wanted to register a protest at the way 20th Century Fox was desecrating a trout stream that ran through the picturesque village of Castle Combe in order to film Rex Harrison and Samantha Eggar in *The Adventures of Dr Dolittle*. William, then a wine salesman in the area, had learned about local anger whilst in the village pub. With my opportune supply of explosives, I was to mount the diversion which would draw away the security patrol and I was also to alert a friendly journalist to cover the story. The diversionary flares did their stuff but my tame journalist shopped us to the *Daily Mirror* who in turn informed the police who were lying in wait. The result was a pandemonium of excited cries and canine joy. Having but recently learned all there is to know about evading capture by various types of hound, I made good my escape by jumping into the stream which was the centre of all the fuss and submerging all but mouth and nostrils. But I was the only one of the conspirators to return to where we had parked our cars. It so happened that my fifth-hand Jaguar would not at that time start without a tow, so I changed into smart clothes, dried my hair and waited in the bushes for William to return for his Mini. He did not turn up but a police car did, sliding quietly and without lights into a corner of the park. After twenty minutes with no William and no movement from the police I decided I must make a move as I was due to fly out to Malaya for SAS jungle training the next morning and it would not do to miss the plane.

Retiring up the lane some distance, I reapproached the carpark whistling and, after surveying the dimly lit cars, spotted the police and went over to them. There were two officers and, when I hailed them, one put a finger to his lips. In a low voice I explained my car would not start and could they kindly give me a tow-start.

'Which car is yours, sir?' the driver asked. I pointed at my Jaguar.

'You must be Captain Fiennes, then.' It was a statement not a query. They must have been told my car's registration. 'I think you had better come with us.'

Considering I could have gone to gaol for seven years, the fine of £500, plus costs and legal fees at the subsequent court case, was an intense relief. But I was immediately expelled from the SAS and I realised that I would no longer achieve my dearest wish, for the Royal Scots Greys might not want a convicted arsonist for their commanding officer.

Ginny was another casualty of the Castle Combe affair, for her father, believing she had obtained my explosives from his Sussex chalk quarry, immediately packed her off to stay with cousins in Spain, which had no police extradition agreement with Britain. He warned her under no circumstances to contaminate herself further by even telephoning me. I was, he snorted, mad, bad and dangerous to know.

As for me, I was recalled to Germany and the tank troop. Here I was encouraged to channel my energies back into the canoe club, the langlauf ski team and boxing and in the summer I set up another Norwegian journey following an ancient cattle trail over Europe's largest glacier, the Jostedalsbre in Central Jotunheim, and then a canoe run down the glacial waste waters. These proved too rough for our canoes but on that journey I learned to lead by physical example rather than rhetoric and also to choose for challenging endeavours a selection of chiefs and Indians, not merely a gaggle of the former.

The langlauf Greys that year were better than ever. I was not to know it but the months of dedicated ski-training for the Greys were to serve me well for the future, just as the years of preparation in battle tanks subsequently proved about as useful as learning Latin, due to Gorbachev, Reagan and Thatcher interfering with and eventually closing down the whole Cold War set-up. During our final week of ski-training in Bavaria Ginny came over from England. We skied together and drank hot chocolate by log fires. We laughed and talked, threw snowballs, and Ginny learned to langlauf.

By now I realised that my Whitehall file was marked in indelible red for caution. I might wriggle my way up to major over the years but I would go no further. I had no wish to mark time in khaki mediocrity and so made up my mind to call it a day as soon as my three years' contracted service were up. Such was my state of mind when my Greys friend Major Richard John suggested I volunteer to serve in Oman in the Sultan's Armed Forces. Postings lasted two years for seconded officers and the pay was marginally better than in Germany. More important, there was sun, sand and excitement aplenty. My CO approved my application without delay, in fact with indecent haste.

My old world was breaking up. I felt no urgency to marry and settle down. Far from it. I had a powerful urge to do and see things and to be free as I had never truly been before. I thought not at all of married life, but a great deal about Ginny. I knew I could have easily lost her after Castle Combe and, soldiering in remote Oman, might risk her again. Sitting in Ginny's battered Mini van in a Midhurst side street, the tarmac shining from a summer shower, I asked her to marry me. By then I had loved her for twelve years.

At the end of June I left England for Arabia.

3

Fighting for the Arabs

In the late 1960s few people had heard of Oman or knew of its links with Britain. So long as Britain had held neighbouring Aden, the Omani Sultans were able to keep their country together, but the British withdrew from Aden in 1967. Marxism then had a firm base in Arabia, and Dhofar, the impoverished southern sector of Oman, was a natural Soviet target. Oman was also all that blocked the way between Aden, now the People's Republic of Southern Yemen, and the Straits of Hormuz, gateway to the Persian Gulf, through which two-thirds of the free world's oil needs were daily tankered. The aged Sultan of Oman did nothing to prepare for the impending storm. At the time I joined the Sultan's Army there were but 200 fighting men in Dhofar under a dozen British officers and their standard weapons were bolt-action rifles dating back to the Second World War.

With seven other officers I flew out to Muscat via Bahrain where we were marooned for eight days by a BOAC strike back home. It was here I learned that a British officer had just been flown out from Muscat with one shoulder and a portion of his chest shot away by the Communists, and I was told, 'They say he was on a stretcher in the mountains for ten hours before they evacuated him. Your Sultan uses mules instead of helicopters. What a place to volunteer for!'

I asked the officer's name. It was Richard John, my only friend in Oman.

28

The vintage Fokker to Muscat staged via Sharjah where we took on our first real-life mercenary. The Sultan hired freelance officers as well as seconded Brits as insurance against the British government getting cold feet. The new arrival, Captain David Bayley, was from Hove, so we had common ground.

More to the point he had recently spent three interesting years fighting for royalist guerrillas in the mountains of North Yemen. Nerve gas attacks by Egyptian aircraft on his cave headquarters, he explained, were the most dreaded events.

I was destined to command a reconnaissance platoon in Dhofar. The men were a mix of Omanis and Baluchis who cordially hated each other, so I had to be doubly careful to appear even-handed at all times. The enemy were the *adoo*, and a large part of our task was to ambush them before they could target us. The *adoo*, well trained and armed in the Soviet Union, knew all the tricks of night warfare without benefit of Hereford.

My immediate priority before we went south was to nurse our meagre equipment up to combat condition. Weapons were cleaned and oiled. Some were in a filthy state and the two-inch mortar had gone missing altogether, a fact which in the British Army would have involved a major enquiry and heads would have rolled. I set out to find a replacement mortar. Richard John was still away recovering from his wounds and there was no other British officer in his company at the time, so I 'borrowed' a mortar and, for good measure, a machine-gun from his armoury. Over the next two years neither was missed by its previous owner and both weapons saved our lives more than once.

On our patrols we were sometimes offered coffee, even in remote cave dwellings. This was always poured to guests in order of importance. Sometimes I came after all the others for, being a Nasrani or Christian, I rated lower than the poorest Muslim.

Sick people would come to our vehicles. We had first-aid satchels but no medical orderly. The population was riddled with eye trouble and our aspirin and Optrex dispensing seemed starkly inadequate.

'Hundreds of our people go blind each year,' said my staff sergeant, Abdullah. 'There is nothing to be done about it. To God be the praise.'

There were three hospitals in all Oman and eight out of every ten babies born died within a year. The Sultan would not allow foreign units such as Save the Children Fund into his country. He seemed determined, as far as I could make out, to perpetuate his country's backwardness and poverty. When I cross-questioned Abdullah about the lack of medical care he was not impressed. 'The government has little money. We are not a wealthy country. There are more pressing matters. Anyway this southern region is a poor area with miserable people. Illness comes to those who sin.'

My conscience was increasingly ill at ease: I was clearly a part of the military machine that upheld the Sultan in denying 800,000 Omanis their rightful inheritance. Away from the large towns of the north the people did not know what they were missing but ownership of cheap transistor radios was spreading and discontent increased alongside awareness.

All around us the Arab world was in ferment – from Egypt to Jordan, from the Sudan to the Yemen. Oil revenue was changing lifestyles radically for our nearest neighbours along the Persian Gulf, known to the Omanis as the Arabian Gulf. I listened in to Aden Radio because it was good for my Arabic and heard the People's Republic of Yemen urging the Omanis: 'Throw off the harness of British imperialism. Take back the wealth that is yours but is stolen by the Sultan.'

Before heading the 500 miles south to the Dhofar war zone with my own men, I was sent there without them for a familiarisation month's secondment to the Northern Frontier Regiment. At B Company headquarters in Umm al Ghawarif David Bayley and I were issued camouflaged clothing and headcloth, three blankets, 100 bullets and a bolt-action Mark 5 .303 rifle. Also a set of maps of the mountains on a weird scale I had never seen before, 0.36 inches to the mile. There were few place-names and many of the existing ones had the words 'position approximate' in brackets beside them. We were each given command of a platoon.

Our work at first was simple and unpleasant. We were to scour the wadis and cave-riddled cliffs and arrest every able-bodied male who might conceivably be an *adoo*. The policy was to subdue the people of the plain and the foothills into refusing food supplies to the guerrillas. Arrests, harassment and interrogations would in theory cow the locals. In practice our patrols served only to increase their hatred of Army, government and Sultan. It was only fear of being branded a coward that prevented me from resigning from the Sultan's forces as the *adoo* regrouped in force and threatened the major towns of Salalah and Marbat.

Back in the north again after my first taste of Dhofar, I confided my doubts about the efficacy of what we were doing to Staff-sergeant Abdullah. But he was adamant that the British were better than the Communist alternative.

'You must not feel the British do wrong here, sahib. They do not meddle with our way of life or our religion. Listen to me.' He lowered his voice. 'It is said in the sooq that Qaboos, the son of the Sultan, will rule before long. With oil money, he will give us those very things the Communists are promising, but without taking away our religion, as they will do. If you British leave before that can happen, then the Communists will take over without a doubt. They will force us to denounce Islam or they will kill us.'

I was impressed by Abdullah's sincerity but unconvinced. It was several days later that I finally came to justify my own role without misgivings.

Captain Tim Landon, from whom I had taken over the Recce Platoon, had returned briefly from an intelligence course to see old friends before going to a different part of Oman. He had, I knew, a special relationship with Qaboos bin Said, the Sultan's son. They had been at Sandhurst together but then had gone to separate regiments in the British Army, Tim with a cavalry regiment and Qaboos to a Scottish infantry unit. In due course Qaboos was ordered back to Salalah by his father. Because their family history included an unhealthy number of inter-familial coups and even murders, Qaboos was kept by his father under a sort of loving paternal house-arrest for seven years in the Salalah palace. To keep him happy, the Sultan allowed him a weekly visit from his old Sandhurst friend Tim Landon. This seemed harmless enough to the old Sultan who was unaware that they were plotting a coup to oust him. I knew nothing of this, of course, but recognised Tim's extensive knowledge of Oman and the current crisis. After talking to him I felt reassured with our role in fighting Marxism.

Change was inevitable in Oman. Either the Sultan must use his new oil revenue for progress or a more enlightened ruler must take over. The critical period was now. Unless the British ensured the status quo during this dangerous time, the Communists would, via Dhofar, take over all of south-eastern Arabia. Once Dhofar fell, the rest of Oman would follow. If Dhofaris were not soon given at least basic proof of support by their existing government, they would continue to swell the ranks of the *adoo*, or to use their official title, the People's Front for the Liberation of the Occupied Arabian Gulf (PFLOAG).

From Tim Landon's summary it was clear to me that I must stay and do all in my power to help keep PFLOAG at bay, at least for as long as it took Tim and others to remove the Sultan and replace him with Qaboos.

Weekly reports signalled from Dhofar indicated that newly trained *adoo* bands with modern weapons had arrived in many regions of the Jebel. Their tactics were imaginative, their firepower impressive and their shooting accurate. I was given eight weeks to prepare Recce Platoon for operations there.

My five years with Centurion tanks had done little to prepare me for an infantry Recce Platoon, but I did find my SAS training useful. One of the few hard and fast Hereford rules was movement by night whenever feasible and my previous brief visit to Dhofar led me to apply this maxim. In the SAS four men form a basic operational group, not two dozen, so I had to work on my own system of control by night. The resulting drills were not to be found in any textbook but they emphasised speed, simplicity, silence and common sense. All our training involved live ammunition and advances over broken ground by night, with frequent switches from single file to line abreast and back to file, practised time after time, along with twenty simple hand signals.

I took my six weeks annual leave while my platoon transferred to Dhofar's safer northern zone, and when I caught up with them again they were operating from the desert base of Thamarit. As the plane taxied in the men rushed out from the shade of the huts to grab my bags and gun and pump my right hand in greeting. I felt moved by this unexpected welcome. I knew all thirty men by name now and they called me Bachait bin Shemtot bin Samra, for reasons which I never discovered. The nearest English equivalent is John, Son of Rags, Son of the Thorntree.

For weeks I trained with the men in the gravel wastes outside our Thamarit base. Searing hot winds from the Empty Quarter blew sand through the air day after day. The camp, a long-deserted oil prospectors' base, was beside a well where bedu of the Bait Kathiri called with their thirsty camels. I went to greet each new arrival and we gave out flour or aspirins in exchange for information about the *adoo*. It was a one-way trade: all aspirins and no information.

From Thamarit the CO ordered me to the Yemen frontier to verify a suspected *adoo* infiltration route by locating camel tracks. This was at the time approaching Ramadan, the month of fasting, when the men were excited about a proper sighting of the new moon which would signal Ramadan's beginning. In Muscat it was already in force.

'In Pakistan,' muttered one of the Baluchis, 'three chief *qadis* fly up in an aeroplane to see the moon arrive. Once they report by radio, it is Ramadan for all.'

When our 'local' moon arrived a sigh came from the men and all of them knelt to pray. I remained standing but I also prayed since it felt appropriate. I prayed for my mother and sisters and Ginny.

For two days we pushed south, shedding broken-down vehicles

and their men to fix their own repairs since we had too little water to wait for them. Huge boulders blocked our way and the wadi narrowed to a winding corridor as dark as a Manhattan alleyway. The men began to complain. The Army had never been in these parts before. It was Ramadan, no time to be pushing heavy vehicles through soft sand until the forehead veins bulged. The Baluchi mullah was especially vociferous but I told him we must obey orders. I too had scrupulously drunk and eaten only during the sunless hours so my argument did not seem unfair.

We came to the high, bald escarpment of Deefa, not far from the Yemen border, the farthest west that we could travel without risking certain cut-off in enemy-held territory. The *adoo* grip on Dhofar was tightening and we returned to Salalah to be briefed on further ambushes.

Once we were scaling a hillside when we encountered a herd of cows. In the dark we listened to the sharp tac-tac of the herdsman's stick. Then someone halted above us and there came the falsetto cry much used by Dhofari herders. One of my men whispered, 'They heard the Land Rovers and sent the cowman to find us. Those men move their cows only by day. We must be more careful. He smelled us, sahib. We must cover ourselves.' We smeared the liquid green spattering of the cows on our shirts and trousers and smelled satisfactorily unpleasant, but it took another day holed up in a cave before we could make good our retreat undetected. We became skilled at the game of cat and mouse in the mountains. Ambush or be ambushed.

To stop the flow of heavy weapons from the Yemen into central Dhofar, our colonel devised the Leopard Line – a loose blockade running north from the coast to the sands of the Empty Quarter. Our company manned the line on the plain and in the foothills. To cover such a vast region with only five Land Rovers meant nonstop patrolling and recognising *adoo* signs when we chanced upon them. For this our bedu guide was invaluable. Water points dictated the route of camel travel and he knew the location of most of the springs in the Nejd, a narrow band of steppe country between the monsoon belt and the true desert. By kneeling beside the prints of a lone camel he could glean a mine of information. Sometimes he knew the name of the camel's owner by the shape of the hoof, where and when it had last drunk by the amount and frequency of its droppings and, by their texture, in which wadi it had last eaten.

Early in 1969 I was referred to patrol the ancient Dehedoba camel trails in the rugged country immediately north of the Qara mountains and up to the Yemeni border. For months we lived on the move in the scorching, gravel deserts, dodging enemy traps, suffering ulcerating desert sores, straying many miles over the Yemeni border and never developing a routine. The key was always to respect the enemy, but never to allow that respect to overawe and blunt the scope of our own strategy.

In the Sands we were more at ease. The men talked into the small hours, squatting with fingers sieving the pure sand or simply watching the stars. They never spoke derisively of one another or tried to score over a neighbour as British soldiers are wont to do. Each man had his say and the Baluchis sat at peace among the Arabs. The months of shared dangers had dissolved previous hostility. They were happy to talk for the pleasure of communicating, and needed no alcoholic stimulus nor swearwords to help express themselves. I thought of other nights by other fires: of the Jocks in Germany, the clatter of beer cans, the filthy language with every sentence and the crude laughter as someone rose to urinate into the fire. I felt happy and at one with these Muslim soldiers in a way I had never felt in Germany or with the SAS.

We did one night mission for Tim Landon deep into enemy-held territory to intercept some important *adoo* we had been told about by an informer. We had to scale steep cliffs and the men were jittery as we jogged from cover to cover, racing the dawn. Then we waited through the heat of the day, burrowed into a thorn bush and observing, a few hundred metres below our tiny hide, the movements of our enemy building stone sangars in defensive positions. A narrow goat trail ran between our thicket and the top of a steep grassy slope. Two tall men were approaching along it. I saw their dark clothes and the glint of weapons in their hands. The second *adoo* wore a shiny red badge in his cap, not the Mao button badge worn by many of the militia, but the hexagonal red star of a political commissar. These were our men. I was sure of it. There was no time to think. They were fifteen yards away. The first man stopped abruptly, appearing to sniff the air. His face was scarred, his hair closely shaven. I watched his fully automatic Kalashnikov, its round magazine cradled in his elbow, swing round as he turned to face us. Inch by inch I lifted my rifle. The sun out-lined the man. He peered directly at me now. I remember thinking, he has seen us. He is weighing his chances.

My voice seemed to come of its own volition. 'Drop your weapons or we kill you.'

The big man moved with speed, twisting at the knee and bring-ing his Kalashnikov to bear in a single movement. I squeezed my trigger. He was slammed back as though caught in the chest by a sledgehammer. His limbs spread out like those of a puppet and he cartwheeled out of sight. Behind him the commissar paused for an instant, unsure what to do. I noticed his face beneath the jungle cap. He looked sad and faintly surprised. His rifle was already pointing at my stomach when a flurry of shots rang out from either side of me. The man's face crumpled into red horror, the nose and eyes smashed back into the brain. Further bullets tore through his ribs and a pretty flowering shrub caught his body at the top of the grassy slope.

One of my men cautiously retrieved from the commissar's body a leather satchel stuffed with documents. He handed it to me and crawled back to place a grenade with the pin removed under the commissar. I hissed at him, 'Forget it, Said. Come back.' I knew we were deep inside enemy territory, many miles from our own scattered troops and with no helicopter support in all Oman. We would be surrounded and cut off in minutes. I whispered the retreat. '*Rooch feesa. Guldi. Guldi.*' Mixed Omani Baluchi slang for instant withdrawal north to the desert and our Land Rovers.

Later in camp I found sleep elusive. I had often shot at people hundreds of yards away, vague shapes behind rocks who were busy shooting back. But never before had I seen a man's soul in his eyes, sensed his vitality as a fellow human being, and then watched his body torn apart at the pressure of my finger. A part of me that was still young and uncynical died with him and his comrade the commissar, spreadeagled on a thorn bush with his red badge glinting in the hot Dhofar sun.

In 1970 a palace coup, orchestrated largely by my friend Tim Landon, replaced the elderly and ineffectual Sultan with his son Qaboos who was himself half Dhofari and the amnesty he immediately declared triggered a trickle of *adoo* deserters that soon became a flood. By 1975, with ongoing help from Britain, as well as Egypt, Jordan and Iran, the tide was turned and the Marxist threat removed from Dhofar. The old Sultan, exiled to the Dorchester Hotel in London with a group of retainers, died there in 1972, a sad but charming old man. In three short years, Qaboos heaved Oman from the Middle Ages into the twentieth century. He used his blossoming oil revenues to the benefit of his country and in doing so whipped the propaganda carpet from under the feet of the revolutionaries.

By the year 2007 Qaboos still reigned supreme in twenty-first-century Oman, popular with his people who, being Ibadhi Mulims, were uninvolved in Shia and Sunni strife and were not infected by the innate hatred of most Arabs for their biblical brethren, the Israelites.

On 2 March 1970, the day that Ian Smith proclaimed Rhodesia a republic ruled by whites, I flew back to England. I was twenty-six and my chosen career was ended. I must find a new civilian life that suited my startling lack of qualifications.

4

The Fastest River

In my absence Ginny had been busy on my behalf and signed me up with George Greenfield, the best literary agent in the adventure business who, seeing something interesting in her if not yet in me, procured an advance of £400 from Hodder & Stoughton for me to write a book about an expedition I had made up the Nile during my six weeks annual leave the previous year. Five of us had travelled by Land Rover and hovercraft, the latter then being a novel means of transport in Egypt so it removed barriers that might otherwise have cut our travels short in that volatile part of the world.

I was thankful to both Ginny and George and set to work on my first book. I also joined Foyles lecture agency and started to go round the lunch club circuit earning £25 a talk and selling my own book at the same time. *A Talent For Trouble* earned under £600 but it did seem I might be able to make a basic living if I could plan and execute an expedition every year between June and October and then write and lecture about it from November until May.

From a sofa in Ginny's London flat, shared with three other girls (the flat, not the sofa), I set about organising my next project, an unambitious summer journey in central Norway. My only firm business rules were to spend no money on mounting an expedition. Everything must be sponsored. And, should any income result from an expedition through lecturing, writing or photography, this must be mine and mine alone. To this end I would take on no one who did not fully and happily accept this principle before signing on. After a lifetime of school and army, I was now on my own for the first time, with no capital, no income and no academic qualifications.

I had no itch to become wealthy – which was just as well – and absolutely no desire to marry and settle down. It never occurred to me to ask myself why on earth I had proposed to Ginny two years before if I never intended marrying anyone, not even her whom I adored. I can only assume that, dog-in-the-manger-wise, I had selfishly staked my claim on her with a diamond ring to warn off the competition. But Ginny was not someone to be misused. If I was not prepared to set a date for our wedding, even a distant date, now that I had left the Army, what was the point of remaining engaged? Did I really love her? Did I want children by her? As I listened to her, I felt like the worm that I was. I was truly ashamed but could not bring myself to accept the dreaded state of wedlock. Ginny made up her mind. If I would not promise her marriage, she would return her engagement ring and go away. She left for Scotland the following week and I returned to my mother's home in Lodsworth.

My mother had grown attached to Ginny and was sorry to hear of our break-up. As usual she was comfortingly fatalistic: 'Life must go on. You won't find another Ginny but it's not the end of the world.' I immersed myself in organising the Norwegian expedition and tried to forget that Ginny was no longer a part of my life.

The general purpose of the expedition was to tackle a physically difficult task and to succeed, so that subsequent more ambitious schemes would more readily gain sponsorship. The specific purpose was to survey the Fabergstolsbre Glacier on behalf of the Norwegian Hydrological Department to see whether or not it was receding. Today global warming has made this kind of research a top priority but in 1970 we were merely considered an economical way of picking up a dropped thread. In 1966 the Hydrological Department had made a comprehensive survey of the twenty-eight glaciers flowing off the 10,000-foot Jostedal Ice-cap to compare with their 1955 survey. But the Fabergstolsbre had eluded them due to an error with the aerial dye-bomb markers. A land-based survey party like us would mop up the omission at no cost to the Norwegian tax payer.

We planned to be parachuted on to the ice-cap, but once the survey work was done we would have to descend on foot with the expensive and delicate loaned survey gear. The simplest route appeared to be straight down a glacial tongue and from there to the nearest roadhead via a glacial river in light boats. This would mean that all the team members must know or learn how to parachute, ski, river-boat and climb. Assembling such assorted talents took some time.

At weekends I jogged in the Welsh mountains with a sixty-pound backpack and a compass. For four years I had brooded about my time with the SAS, not my sacking which I had deserved, but the fact that I had only passed the final hurdle of the 1965 selection course with the help of a taxi. On applying to join the Territorial Army soon after returning from Dhofar, I discovered there was a curious anomaly known as Reserve Squadron, 22nd SAS Regiment, which was neither regular nor Territorial, but whose role was to provide reinforcements for the regular SAS in time of war. Applicants to join R Squadron had to pass the regular SAS selection course. Here was my chance to banish a ghost. Thanks to my Welsh jogging stints, I found no difficulty in keeping ahead of the hundred or so regular Army applicants. I passed into R Squadron, but only as a trooper. No matter. I had completed Long Drag without motorised help.

The sergeant-major in charge of my new unit turned out to be my old SAS training sergeant, Brummy Burnett. After six months with R Squadron, desirous of more pay, I asked Brummy if I might get a commission to captain. He looked down at me. 'If you're very lucky, Fiennes, you might make corporal in five years. But no promises. Pigs might fly.'

Many of the older SAS sergeants, though not I think Brummy

himself, still held a grudge against me for my indiscretions of 1966 because I had caused a shaft of public scrutiny to fall on a unit with an obsession for secrecy and obscurity. In years to come the SAS was to be used as a public relations tool in the struggle against IRA terrorism, but my own peccadillos occurred when, to most people, SAS still merely meant Scandinavian Airlines System.

Norwegian preparations were all in order and I was living off my earnings from SAS weekends when I learned via the grapevine that Ginny, at work with the Scottish National Trust, had become good friends with the son of the Lord Lieutenant of Ross-shire. With no precise plan in mind, but aware that I must not let Ginny get too involved with this most eligible Scotsman, I decided to go to visit her on her birthday.

I owned a Triumph Tiger motorbike at the time and decided to ride all the way to Ginny on it. Proof surely of my devotion. By the time I reached London I was soaked through, so the Tiger and I used British Rail to Inverness before riding the last two hours to Ginny.

The Trust caravan where Ginny lived was parked close to Loch Torridon. Not stopping to think what I would say, I knocked on the door. When Ginny's little face peered, startled, through the misted window, I saw quite clearly that I must marry her: if necessary that very week in Torridon kirk.

I revved the Tiger's throttle. 'Hello,' I said. I did not mention British Rail.

'Why have you come?'

'I brought you a birthday card for next week.'

'Couldn't you have posted it?'

Gradually, over the next two days she thawed out a bit. On her birthday she drove me in her Mini to Applecross and we walked along the deserted coast which looks west to Skye. She let me hold her hand as we walked along the white beaches to the cry of gulls. But when I tried to kiss her and tell her I could not exist without her, there were bitter tears and she said I must leave and stay away for ever.

I promised to go the next day and that night, when it rained, Ginny let me into the caravan where I slept on the floor beside her narrow bunk. Before leaving for Inverness I asked if she would drive down to Newcastle in early August to see me off on the ship to Norway.

'Maybe,' she said.

A month later she was there. I told Ginny that if she would only agree to marry me, we would hold the wedding within ten days of my return from Norway. She looked happy but shook her head and refused to give me an answer. I confided in one of the team, Patrick Brook, an Army friend of many years, that she had turned me down and later saw him speaking to her urgently with much gesticulation. As I kissed her goodbye at the gangplank she whispered 'Yes', the most precious single word in my life.

'What did you say to Ginny in Newcastle?' I asked Patrick later.

'Oh, only that if you were to fall down a crevasse in Norway – which is quite likely – she would never forgive herself for having said no.'

The likelihood of intimacy with a crevasse arrived soon enough when, in Bergen, we boarded a Cessna sea-plane after we had been taught, in theory, how to jump off its floats. As the engines roared, I licked my lips. My stomach felt furry-lined as squadrons of butterflies free-fell within it. I would be first to jump and did not relish the idea. *The Sunday Times* described the occasion as 'The World's Toughest Jump', but they had paid £1,000 for coverage rights and wanted their money's worth. I looked down 6,000 feet at the slits of crevasses big enough to swallow a regiment of parachutists without leaving a trace. I fought back the rising panic of vertigo.

Awkwardly, we levered ourselves into kneeling positions facing the door. The rough hand of our instructor, ex-SAS Don Hughes, shook my shoulder as he prodded meaningfully at the exit. But something was wrong. I had been waiting for the sound of the engines cutting back, the necessary preliminary to any free-fall jump. The Cessna was still at maximum speed. I pointed at the pilot, but Don's 'shove off' gesture was repeated. I forced one arm through the slipstream and grasped the wing strut as we had been instructed. Then I lunged my legs outwards, aiming for the float. As my boots scrabbled for a foothold my hands lost their grip on the strut and I was sucked bodily into space. Out of control, I passed close by the fuselage and struck the side of the float with the back of my hand.

'One thousand and one. One thousand and two . . .' I heard my voice inside my helmet churning out the seconds and I opened my eyes. I will freeze solid in this ridiculous position, I thought, for coldness was the first sensation. Then came fear as I recognised the early signs of body-spin. Without warning I began to keel forward into a nose-dive. My arms snapped inwards to locate my ripcord but a camera had come loose inside my anorak and lodged itself against the ripcord bar. Grovelling in the folds I found the red handle and ripped it outwards. Then I snapped both arms back to the star position to arrest a rapidly materialising somersault. A second or two later, with a whipcrack sound and a breathtaking jerk, my orange canopy deployed fully. Two crevasse fields passed beneath my boots. The ice surface provided no perspective. I braced my legs, knees bent for impact. When it came I hardly knew it, as my landing was cushioned by the softness of a snow-bridge spanning an old crevasse. Four of the others landed close by, followed by our gear.

After some initial confusion as to which glacier we had actually landed on, and after a torrential storm, the survey work began in earnest as we liaised by radio with our ground party below. The work was cold and boring but allowed no lapses in concentration since even the slightest mathematical slip could render the whole project a failure. Geoff Holder, a Royal Engineers captain and our surveyor in chief, finally announced that the survey was complete. The paperwork was evacuated and we were free to look forward to the next stage of our enterprise, the descent of the Briksdalsbre Glacier. For this we had hired two of the Norwegian Tourist

Board's top guides. But we were in for a shock. The guides were unwilling to take us in dangerously thick mist on the forty-kilometre ice-cap journey to the top of the Briksdalsbre. On skis with light packs they could do the trip in eight hours. Pulling over-loaded sledges, they reckoned we would take two days, if indeed we could get that far.

At length we reached a compromise. They would ski along the ridge for thirty kilometres, at which point they would leave one of our ice-axes pointing in the direction of the Briksdalsbre. They would then veer north to descend a different route. It took us eleven hours of non-stop hauling to reach the ice-axe marker. As it grew dark we entered our first crevasse field and gingerly threaded a maze-like route through wicked-looking fissures. We knew we should be roped up but were too tired and cold. Each new chasm forced us off our chosen bearing. From every side came the booming echoes of avalanches. With numb fingers we erected two tents and pegged their guy-ropes to ski sticks.

Next morning the mist cleared at dawn and we saw the first ice-fall of the Briksdalsbre Glacier directly below us. The descent was sudden and, in minutes, one of our laden sledges slid out of con-trol and cartwheeled down into a crevasse. Alarmed, we donned helmets and roped up. About a hundred yards further down the yawning incline our second sledge turned turtle, dragging Roger Chapman and Patrick Brook behind it. Using a sawtooth sheath-knife, Roger slashed through the harnesses and saved both their lives. The pulk disappeared down a crevasse. All our skis were lost and our only remaining gear was in our backpacks, including one two-man tent between the five of us.

I winced at the thought of thousands of pounds' worth of lost gear, of angry sponsors and the effect on my future expeditions. But there were more immediate worries to hand: 3,000 feet of near sheer ice, and none of us were climbers. At noon we were con-templating an unstable causeway of ice-blocks which we would have to cross to reach the main descent line. It looked lethally inse-cure. We sought radio advice from the boss of our Land Rover mobile base in the valley below, and were not comforted to learn that of the twenty-eight glacier tongues that pour off the Jostedalsbre, this was the only one still unclimbed by Norway's ace glacier specialists. I edged warily over the causeway. In places only thin wedges spanned the gap and twice I froze as lumps of ice, disturbed by my passing, fell away like rotten planks from a footbridge. Once across, I made the rope firm and one by one the others joined me. I noticed blood on the ice and discovered that my fingers were bleeding. There was no pain, for my hands were numb. The others found the blood-trail a help when we passed through labyrinthine piles of loose ice boulders.

A twelve-foot crack that stretched across the entire glacier finally foxed us, forcing us back on to the rockface deep inside the bergschrund. Streams of icy water ran down our backs and a knife-like wind whistled down the dark cranny. Subterranean torrents roared below us in the nether regions and I prayed I would not slip from my fragile holds on the wet rock. When we emerged from the cavern we had bypassed the crack but evening stars were already visible and we were forced to camp for the night, all five of us in our two-man tent. Next day we survived the perils of avalanche rubble and two 400-foot abseils to the glacial lake where our base team awaited us in an inflatable boat.

Ten days after returning to England, and with Gubbie as best man, I married Ginny in Tillington church, a mile to the east of Lodsworth and her River home where we had met as children.

I did not marry Ginny because I had decided she was more important than my freedom, but because I considered it should be possible to have both. The early days of our marriage were to test this bland assumption sorely, starting from day one. I did not consult Ginny about our honeymoon programme since my understanding of tradition was that bridegrooms do not interfere with wedding arrangements nor brides with honeymoon details. Unfortunately, she did not find the prospect of a tour through Eastern Europe only two years after Soviet tanks had crushed

Dubcek's Czechoslovakia as intriguing as I did. She also complained at not getting a turn to drive my MG and nearly abandoned me in Munich. Things did not improve. In eastern Yugoslavia the exhaust pipe fell off. The officials at both ends of Czechoslovakia were painstakingly unpleasant, the Bulgarian and Hungarian police hounded us, due to our noisy exhaust, and the East Germans screwed every pfennig from us at the obligatory campsites. As a last straw, when we reached Vienna, I went off to find us a couple of ice creams, leaving Ginny in the queue for the Opera House, but I didn't manage to find my way back to where she was waiting before the last on-the-day ticket had been sold. To make amends I told Ginny we would visit Vienna's famous Lipizzaner Riding School. Only to discover that the wonderful white horses were all away in Spain on holiday.

After this inauspicious start, we settled temporarily in a rented cottage in Wester Ross where I buckled down to meet my deadline on a book about Norway and Ginny went for long walks in between dishing up Irish stew or scrambled eggs, the extent of her cookery repertoire. I never complained, since I liked both. We were both strong characters in our late twenties who had long practised doing our own thing. We were in love and had yearned for each other, despite powerful paternal opposition, for over a decade. But the institution of marriage closed about us like a cage and we began to fight like chained tigers. Having no money and no job did not help.

One day out of the blue I received a telegram from the William Morris Agency asking me to go to London to audition for the part of James Bond. Sean Connery had retired, his successor George Lazenby had been pensioned off, and the prime mover of the Bond films, Mr Cubby Broccoli, was on the lookout for a new 007. Mr Broccoli, I was told over the phone, was looking for 'an English gentleman who really does these things'.

'What things?' I asked.

'Shoot rapids, climb drainpipes, parachute, kill people, you know . . .'

The fact that I couldn't act seemed irrelevant, and it was an expenses-paid trip to London so I went down. The final interview after all the screen tests lasted all of ten minutes, sufficient for Mr Broccoli to decide I was too young, most un-Bond-like and facially more like a farmhand than an English gentleman. He settled on Roger Moore instead, so the cinema-going world had to wait for my cousins Ralph and Joseph to come along before the Fiennes name made it on to the silver screen.

In the new year we moved back south to Sussex, which didn't make Ginny any happier, and I got taken on as a captain by the 21st SAS Regiment (Territorial) in London and spent most weekends with my new unit, very grateful for the pay packet. Then in February, a letter arrived from the Royal Scots Greys, on whose list of reserve officers I still figured. They had an expedition for me to lead.

In 1971 British Columbia was celebrating the centenary of its joining the Canadian Confederation and wished to commemorate the early pioneers, most of whom had been Scots who had explored their impenetrable territory by river. The centenary committee in Vancouver had suggested a river journey by Scotsmen from their northern border with the Yukon to the United States border on the 49th parallel would be a feat to match those of their forebears. If successful, it would also be the first recorded north-south transnavigation of British Columbia. The route, along nine interconnecting water systems, ran deep through the Rocky Mountains and included some of the roughest rivers in the world. The Canadians approached the Ministry of Defence and they passed the suggestion on to the Greys, who liked the idea, especially since in June they were due to lose their identity and their famous grey berets through regimental amalgamation. The expedition would be a fine last fling but, as they had no regular officers available to lead it, my name came up. I was told the regiment would provide 'two or three soldiers and some supplies'.

Ginny agreed to join as road party leader and radio operator,

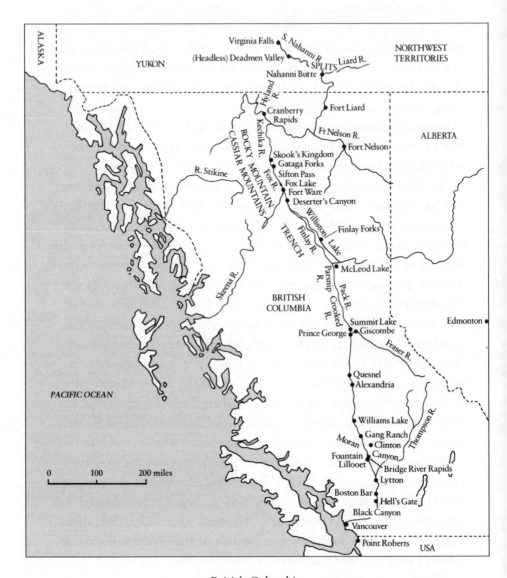

British Columbia

and when two of my old langlauf team volunteered I accepted both at once. One was an ex-butcher's apprentice from Edinburgh called Joseph Skibinski (we used to call him an Oatmeal Pole); the other, Jack McConnell, was a skilled radio operator. My last acquisition was a tank mechanic called Stanley Cribbett who, though short in size, could, according to Skibinski, repair anything from a clock to a sputnik. *The Observer* sent their top photographer, Bryn Campbell, and the BBC *World About Us* supplied a two-man film team and a Yorkshire policeman, Ben Usher, with lifeboat experience was recruited to steer for them.

An RAF Hercules flew us to Edmonton from where we drove our sponsored Land Rover and a four-ton lorry lent by the Canadian Army north-west to Fort Nelson. Here the plan was for the three boats to undertake a 400-mile trial journey before committing ourselves to the main expedition and attendant publicity. This seemed sensible since our UK training had only been on the Thames and none of us had wild water boating know-how. The trial goal was to reach the little known Virginia Falls, twice the height of Niagara, and 110 miles up the South Nahanni River. American river-runner and author Colonel Snyder, not given to understatement, described the South Nahanni as 'the fastest river in North America and the most dangerous in five continents'. To reach the Nahanni itself involved a further 290 miles of river travel. It would be a fair test.

We Royal Scots Greys wore our grey berets with their silver eagle badges as we left Fort Nelson. This was out of respect for our famous regiment which four days previously had ceased to exist after 300 years as Scotland's own cavalry regiment. My father during World War Two had seen the last of the grey horses in the 1940s; I wore the last grey beret in the seventies.

The three boats slid away, edging into the current as we gathered speed. A Mountie, two Indians and a group of press from Vancouver waved us off. Ginny stood alone on the bank, small and forlorn in her dusty jeans, soon a fading blur in the willows.

The river was 300 yards wide, both banks were thickly wooded and the world passed by quite silently but for the rush of water, the soft plunk of paddles and the sudden boil of converging eddies. An hour from Fort Nelson things changed with a vengeance.

'The current's racing along,' Bryn mused, 'as though there's a waterfall ahead.'

'There's no rapid on this river,' I assured him.

From up ahead I heard a sound as of breakers lashing a shingle beach; the same dull double boom and the rushing hiss of under-tow. The channel ahead curved right but the local current sucked us left. The other boats were out of sight.

Along the left-hand bank fallen trees rose and fell in the water. Torn down by the force of the floods upon the elbow of the river's curve, their gnarled roots clung to the bank and their trapped trunks threshed to the pulse of the rushing water. If a boat was sucked into this chaos of tangled roots, the tubing would be torn and punctured. We stabbed deep with our paddles, straining to move into mid-river. Before Stan could reach the outboard, a branch lashed across and cut his face. A splintered root dug into the hull behind Bryn and ripped it open. The port air tube wrin-kled and subsided and the boat shuddered as we struck a grounded log. We bounced off. If the boat had been of wood, we would probably have foundered and been sucked beneath the mass of heaving vegetation.

For a moment we were free, spun away from the bank by an eddy. This was merely a brief respite, for the shock of our narrow escape was soon eclipsed by the horror of the scene ahead. Now we could see the source of the earlier wind-borne roar, an island in mid-river on which, it seemed, every log borne downriver by recent floods was impaled. The whole force of the current, channelled by the acute bend, ran full tilt against the upstream apex of the island, and every piece of flotsam, from floating stumps of juniper to eighty-foot logs, was ensnared where the current split in two against the island.

We could not go left because that channel was a moving mass of tangled debris. So we swung right, sweating over the paddles.

Stanley wrestled with our outboard, swung its drive-shaft down until it locked vertically and tugged hard on the ignition cord. Again and again he pulled and twice the engine spluttered hopefully. Bryn stopped paddling to look over his shoulder, distracted by the shocking sound of log crashing onto log.

The water about us was disturbed now by back eddies surging around the jam. We were sucked inexorably backwards to where the river rushed under the sieve of logs. I thought to myself: 2,000 miles to go and here we are drowning on the first day. Then we smashed into the logs, sharp branches whipped at us and the boat up-ended. Someone screamed and a heavy object rammed my chest. I felt a branch rip down my back and the shock of cold water.

For a moment the boat was held by a branch and I scrabbled up from the floor to the mid-tubing. The branch broke and our bows disappeared, sucked inch by inch under the churning debris. Water poured over the bagged gear and the lashed fuel drums.

A branch flailed at Bryn and tore him away. He disappeared underwater, his hands clawing the air as he went.

The boat was about to go under. We must get on to the logs while there was a chance or we would all drown. I shouted to warn Stan and tried to scramble on to the nearest log above us. But it was too large and too slimy to grip. Then the boat shuddered and I fell back among the fuel drums. Stan shouted with excitement. He had started the engine. All this time he had single-mindedly tugged at the cord, not noticing the disappearance of Bryn. Now he engaged gear and the forty-horsepower engine roared in reverse cavitation.

There was hope. We both jumped up and down on the half-submerged craft to vibrate the trapped bows loose. A lashing line snapped, a ten-gallon drum broke loose and the bows shot free. Stanley grabbed the tiller and, with painful slowness, we edged away from the log jam.

Then I saw Bryn, or rather his mop of black hair. An under-water surge had spewed him up further down the log jam and his smart denim 'ranger' jacket was caught up on a branch. As we watched, his head sank a few inches. The full force of the undertow was dragging at him from the waist down.

We donned life-jackets and Stanley nosed the boat as near as possible to the downstream end of the log. I jumped on to it and edged along its bucking length towards Bryn. Sometimes the tree spun through half a turn. Reaching Bryn, I held his jacket scruff firmly and, with our combined strength, he came clear of the water. He was white, cold and shaken, but managed a rueful grin. His frail stature and normally immaculate garb belied a tough and resilient spirit.

The other crews both managed to keep clear of the great jam. We learned our lesson about the danger of snags and thereafter warmed our engine for a while each morning and started it at the first sign of any likely threat.

At Fort Liard we stopped to visit the Hudson's Bay Company store with the sign outside which proclaimed 'HBC 1886'. The Scotsman who ran it told us the locals said this stood for 'Here Before Christ'. He warned us the mosquitoes would be far worse in Nahanni country. 'The upriver Indians say the air is so thick with them, you canna starve. Simply keep breathing with your mouth open and you will get your daily meat ration.'

More practical was the advice of the local French priest who indulged in a fit of Gallic shrugs on inspecting our three inflatables and urged us, as he doled out moose stew and carrots, to get a flat-bottom river boat like his.

I followed his advice as soon as we reached Nahanni Butte, the point where the South Nahanni River joined the Liard. Here I hired from a local Indian a thirty-two-foot river boat for $50 and a bottle of our sponsored Black & White whisky. It would make a more solid platform for the BBC crew and would also enable us to carry extra fuel for the two inflatables.

Next day we entered the first canyon of the Nahanni. The towering walls acted as an echo chamber to every gush and twirl of the current, the sky above narrowed to a faraway strip of blue and we shivered in deep shadow, three waterbeetles struggling against the flow in a sheer-sided drain. The wiles of the river had to be watched at all times. There was no time to relax and enjoy the incredible scenery. To do so would be as suicidal as studying the Arc de Triomphe while driving round it.

High above us soared sheer red walls with successive pine-clad tiers of rock teetering atop the lower cliffs. The sun seldom touched us as we inched along the gloomy corridors of the canyon. Elsewhere, fighting for every inch of progress, we had to tug the river boat upstream on tow-lines with the eight of us hauling knee-deep in icy shallows. Policeman Ben, the strongest of us, was built like an Aberdeen Angus bull and, when he slipped, we all went under. The rope ripped away, tearing free of my numbed grip. On our next attempt we lined her, the jockey-light Stanley stayed aboard and cleverly nosed the boat upstream as we took in slack on the ropes.

Eventually we entered a region much favoured by the Canadian press due to its macabre associations. In Deadmen Valley, tucked between the Headless Mountains and the Funeral Range, three headless skeletons were found in the early 1900s. Canadian newspapers had been clocking up the unexplained deaths score in the area ever since and put the toll as high as thirty-two, but Ginny's research at the Royal Geographical Society and the Royal Canadian Mounted Police records confirmed only seventeen unexplained deaths or disappearances. Which might be considered enough. We did not add to those statistics and left Deadmen Valley with our heads intact.

In less than a hundred miles we had climbed over 1,000 feet. The final canyon was an impressive display of water force. A pocket of converging currents very nearly defeated us. We inched up the wall of water in the eddy-trap and water poured out of the butterfly valves in our boat bilges. Stanley zigged the tiller of our boat, shouting with relief as we crested the last rapid in an explosion of spray. Then the roar of pounding water intensified to an overall boom and from the heavens, or so it seemed from river-level, there appeared a waterfall of Olympian grandeur beneath a halo of high-flung spray. We had reached the Virginia Falls. Even the dour features of Constable Ben softened with pleasure at the majesty of the place.

The current whisked us back to Nahanni Butte where Bryn and the film team caught a bush plane to Fort Nelson to film firefighting in British Columbia. The trial journey was over. We drove north-west to the Yukon border ready to launch the boats on our 1,500-mile attempt to transnavigate British Columbia.

No sooner had we been rejoined by the BBC film crew than I sensed an overtly hostile atmosphere. Earlier they had fretted about not having a more definite timetable and again about not having enough time to sort out their gear at the end of the day. But I had been able to ignore that. Now I could tell I was in for trouble.

The Hyland River took us gently over the Yukon border into the Liard River and all went well as far as the Cranberry Rapids, where the Jocks overturned and Stanley ripped our own boat open on a snag. Jack's morale was dented by the experience, for he was sucked below by undercurrents, despite his life-jacket, and battered against submerged rocks.

Not far beyond the Cranberry Rapids and above the Rapids of the Drowned, we entered the mouth of the Kechika (or Big Muddy) River. This tributary of the Liard was sourced from a high swamp in the Rocky Mountain Trench known as the Sifton Pass and every authority I had consulted assured me our inflatables would not penetrate very far upriver. When we could get no farther I planned to canoe or to walk with rucksacks and had brought from England two portable canoes which, when dismantled, would be divided between our four backpacks. The point at which we would have to give up on our inflatables was probably going to be a spot known as Skook's ranch. This was the kingdom of Skook Davidson, *skookum* being the local Indian for The Tough One.

Skook ran a camp for big-game hunters, all his clients, guides and stores being flown in by float-plane. When the film crew learned that Skook had pack-horses for hire they approached me with the, to them, reasonable-sounding proposal that they hire these for their heavy camera gear. They could not see my view that the ethics of the expedition precluded outside support. Either we travelled the river or, where we ran out of waterways, we walked. Ever since my use of a taxi on the SAS Long Drag I had developed a fixation about cheating. But as far as the BBC crew were concerned I was being wilfully obstructive for no good reason. From that moment my fate was sealed. I would be the villain in their documentary film.

Skook was over eighty. Leaving Scotland as a teenager with £10 to his name, he became the finest rodeo rider in British Columbia and settled in his valley in 1939. Now he looked after twenty big-game hunters a year, specialising in grizzlies, bighorn sheep, cougars and mountain rams. The great man welcomed us from his bed, an old gnarled pioneer crippled by arthritis. He fumbled to light a candle. 'Sit down, darn you,' he barked. 'You folk from the old country never seem to know what the Lord gave you asses for.' Candlelight revealed a row of medals nailed to a log. Skook had done a stint as a sniper in the 29th Vancouver Battalion during the First World War.

From Skook's the boats went back downstream with Ginny, and the film team flew south to meet up with us at Fort Ware.

I asked Skook about the country to the south.

'When you can canoe no further,' he advised, 'you'll find my old trail beside the river, all the way to Sifton Pass.'

The Rocky Mountain Trench and the Kechika both lie north-south and, on the far side of the Sifton Pass, a new river, the Tochika or Fox, flows south all the way to Fort Ware. Skook's memories of his trail from thirty years ago were difficult to check and I found it ominous that a surveyor whose book I had studied described the trail, only six months after Skook had made it, as 'requiring much work every season if it is to be kept open, due to washouts, rapid growth and windfalls'. I consulted a local Indian guide. 'You'll be all right,' he said, 'so long as you don't follow a game trail by mistake. They're all over the place.' When asked how we were to recognise the real trail from the game trail, he replied:

'Why, you just do.' Then as an afterthought he warned us to watch out for bears. 'You surprise a grizzly on the trail with her kids and she can get real mean.'

We ran out of waterway at Gataga Forks where the river became too narrow and too powerful, so we collapsed the canoes we were then using, lashed them to our 110-pound packs and started following a trail blazed with old tree slashes. Jack fell off a tree-bridge into a thorn thicket and lay pinioned by the weight of his rucksack until rescued. Little Stanley Cribbett, not much larger than his pack, stumbled along, his face pale as he winced from a spasm of coughing and spat blood. Joe fell off a log and wrenched his back. Unable to carry his load, he had tried hauling it on a two-pole 'sled' but fallen trees made this impractical. Reluctantly, but unanimously, we agreed that Stanley and Joe should return to Skook's ranch, our last point of contact with civilisation, and radio for a plane to take them south to Fort Ware to rest and recover.

This left Jack and me. Things only got worse. Jack sprained his ankle and we lost all signs of any trail to the south. Rations were running out and eventually the only course was to return to Skook's and start again. Skook could not understand how we had missed the trail, but it was a long time since he had been on it. We set out again, but Jack's ankle was worse than before. Crying with frustration, he agreed he too had to give up. He gave me his pistol and we shook hands.

Route-finding continued to be a nightmare. I was ready to throw in the towel myself until the possibility occurred to me that the local Sikanee Indians might have moved Skook's trail across the river. I waded across and six hours later picked up the clearly marked triple slash which indicated their traplines. Forgetting sores, hunger and blisters, I covered the next twenty miles in two days to the headwaters of the Kechika, high on the flats of the Sifton Pass, a cheerful place of flowering plants and berry bushes. This was good trapping country, flush with beaver, marten, mink and otter. Now the Indian trail became easy to see, no longer a will-o'-the-wisp passage through undergrowth but a trodden path with blaze marks every few yards.

Late in the afternoon after crossing the pass I rounded a bend to find Jack and Joe hunting squirrels and they led me down to their camp at Fox Lake where the film crew were also installed.

Everyone seemed rather subdued. There was no welcome for me. Jack brought me tea and a pot of stew and, when the others were out of hearing, told me what was going on. 'The Beeb are out to get yoo's, Ran,' summed up the situation. He explained how the film team had been passing the waiting time prompting Stanley and Joe to complain about their treatment on tape. They had pictures of the diminutive Stanley staggering about under the weight of his pack. They had film of Joe declaring that 'Ran couldna' organise a piss-up in a brewery', and by way of proof that I was an egomaniac glory-seeker, the suggestion that I had encouraged the others to drop out so I could cross the Rocky Mountain Trench all by myself. On top of everything else I was plainly a lousy navigator. All that was now needed was for the journey to fail somewhere along the miles of violent rivers to our south. Then the BBC could make a fascinating in-depth study of leadership failure.

To select the perfect expeditionary team, in my opinion, is nearly impossible. There is no foolproof selection process and the longer, the more ambitious the endeavour, the more time there is for each person's failings to rise to the surface. The most I hope for is to find at least one true companion on each journey. In Canada I was lucky. Jack became a loyal lifelong friend, a man I would ask again on any expedition and trust whatever the stresses.

We launched ourselves back on the river at Fort Ware then followed the boisterous Finlay, the log-jammed, storm-tossed Williston lake, the mosquito and black-fly-infested Parsnip, Pack and Crookford Rivers until at last we reached Summit Lake. One night Ginny, waiting to contact us in a thickly forested swamp beside the river, was surprised by a black bear. She lost her nerve and screamed. The bear came closer and she pulled her .38 Smith and Wesson out of her anorak pocket. Somehow she pressed the trigger before the gun was clear and a bullet passed through the outside welt of her rubber boot, within a couple of millimetres of her foot. The bear departed and so did a terrified Ginny. Next time I met her she was furious. Why had I not made the rendezvous? Why did she have to wander through stinking woods and portage heavy gear? Nobody ever thanked or acknowledged her. I did, I pointed out.

'No, you don't. You just use me. You couldn't care less what happens to me so long as I'm in the right place at the right time.'

I did not try to argue as, by that time in our marriage, I knew that would be useless. Instead I thought of my favourite quote from Albert Einstein: 'Some men spend a lifetime in an attempt to comprehend the complexities of women. Others preoccupy themselves with simpler tasks such as understanding the theory of relativity.'

All the rivers we had travelled prior to reaching Summit Lake had flowed to an Arctic destination. Summit Lake was a dead-end, a high-altitude source of this Arctic watershed. To continue south we carried our boats nine miles along the ancient Giscombe Portage trail, over the Intercontinental Divide and down to the Pacific watershed and the biggest river of British Columbia, named after the great Scots explorer Simon Fraser.

We launched the boats on to the Fraser River late on 20 September and within minutes swept over the Giscombe Rapids wearing black frogsuits and life-jackets. From Giscombe, the river, the lifeline but also grave of so many pioneers, flowed for 850 tempestuous miles to Vancouver and the sea. Between Prince George, British Columbia's most northerly city, and the Fraser-side town of Lytton the river drops 1,200 feet, four times the height of Niagara Falls. Seventy miles south of Prince George it penetrates a deep trough many hundreds of feet below the surrounding land mass. The uncertainty of not knowing the state of the river in the boiling canyons ahead wore at all our nerves. When we attempted to glean local knowledge along the way we were met by the universal response that nobody knew what 'the river does down there'.

We entered the Moran Canyon, a rushing, roiling cauldron squeezed between black walls 1,000 feet high. The underplay of currents was impressive. Huge surface boils, bubbling like hot water in a saucepan, twice turned us about completely and thrust us chaff-like against the granite walls. By nightfall we stopped a mile above the great killer rapid of the Bridge River confluence. The press were waiting in Lillooet below the Bridge River Falls, licking their lips.

When the time came to run the falls, Stanley climbed on to our boat as though it were a tumbrel. The film team waved from a high boulder. I pushed the boat off and sprang aboard. Plucked from the bank like a feather we plunged into the white water. A roar like the thunder of doom rushed at us as we shot downwards. For a while I could see nothing. We were awash within a cartwheeling tunnel. The craft keeled over, forced to the side of a monster wave by centrifugal force. It was a wall of death on the horizontal plane and our hull clung to the inner side of the spinning liquid tube. At the lower end the boat was gripped by an undertow, dragged around and around, then spat out into a whirlpool. Our outboard roared frantically as we swung around the sinkhole and the cliffs of the river disappeared as we sank deep within the river's bowels. Then the sinkhole closed and regurgitated us towards the left-hand cliff. Stanley, water gushing from his helmet, tried to steer away from the rocks. He failed and we dashed against a boulder. The hull screamed in rubbery protest and crumpled along one side as the tube split open. But we were through. We shook hands and felt on top of the world. Our second boat also managed to defy the Bridge River Rapids.

After repairing the boats we continued south as the river flowed fast and furious through the Coastal Range and the Fraser's final monster rapid, Hell's Gate. Four days later we passed through the suburbs of Vancouver and navigated with care into a Pacific sea fog until a police launch met us with a bullhorn. 'This is it, folks. You're in Yank territory now.'

The two BBC films that were made from this expedition led their sixteen million-strong British audience to believe I was a cruel and incompetent publicity-seeker. The innuendoes which helped paint this picture certainly added spice and colour to the films, but did surprisingly little to discourage my sponsors in the future and helped me in a small way to develop a tougher skin when later expeditions were laid open to public scrutiny and criticism in the future.

Jack and Stanley left the Army a year after the expedition and emigrated to Western Canada where they both married. Jack called one of his sons Ranulph.

5

Ginny's Idea

Early in 1972, Ginny was stirring the stew when she came up with a weird suggestion. 'Why don't we go around the world?' She had mooted the idea once before in Scotland, and I had ignored it as impractical because what she envisaged was a longitudinal route – through the Poles – which was, I knew, neither physically nor administratively possible. A year passed and with no other projects on hand, we visited the Royal Geographical Society's map vaults and, grudgingly, I began to accept that her idea might after all be feasible. We could follow the Greenwich Meridian around the world's axis. We could start at Greenwich and head south to Antarctica, then up the other side of the planet, over the North Pole and back to Greenwich. A simple plan on the face of it.

For the next seven years we worked non-stop and unpaid to launch the endeavour, during which we often despaired of eventual success. Luck and hard work saw us through. At the weekends and on free evenings we lectured in civic centres, borstals, ladies' luncheon clubs and men's associations. We attacked the problem with total dedication and a determination that every item of equipment, every last shoelace and drawing pin, must be sponsored. We opened no bank account and possessed no chequebook, so there was no danger of the expedition overspending.

In the beginning I approached my 21st SAS Regiment CO to see whether the SAS group of regiments would sponsor the expedition.

But the Director of the SAS, a brigadier, at first refused to consider the idea because of my involvement with the Castle Combe raid. 'This expedition,' the brigadier expostulated to our CO, 'is unbelievably complex and ambitious. That Fiennes is not a responsible person. I can tell you straightaway that the SAS will not attach their good name to a plan such as this under a fellow like Fiennes.'

We were disappointed to hear the CO's account of his meeting. But a week later he summoned us to his office. They had evolved a workable solution. Brigadier Mike Wingate Gray, who, as CO of the regular SAS seven years before, had sent me packing after the Castle Combe incident, was appointed overall boss of the Transglobe Expedition. If I accepted his loose supervision, then the SAS group would nominally sponsor the whole venture and provide us with office space in the Duke of York's Barracks just off the King's Road, Chelsea. We were in business.

Over the next two years our new office, a high attic which had earlier served as the 21 SAS rifle range, filled with sponsored equipment and its walls became papered with maps showing the more remote stretches of our proposed 52,000-mile journey. There was no telephone in the attic, but a friend who was a telephone engineer and Territorial trooper fixed up a phone one night which he clipped into the rooftop Ministry of Defence line. This was critical, since no phone meant no contact with sponsors. The expedition aim was that a core group of our team must travel over the entire surface of the world via both Poles without flying one yard of the way.

Early in 1975 Ginny, who was to be chief radio operator and mobile base leader, joined the Women's Royal Army Corps to learn about radios, antenna theory and speedy Morse operation. Oliver Shepard, a 21 SAS lieutenant, applied to join us. He looked overweight. I remembered him vaguely from Eton and had decided he was definitely not Transglobe material. By then we had a system of testing all volunteers in North Wales. Each weekend that winter and over the next two years, the Territorial SAS provided army trucks and rations for me to train a mountain racing team in

Snowdonia and, from the team hopefuls, about sixty SAS men in all, I would pick the three best ones for the expedition. Oliver Shepard joined the Welsh training weekends and proved to be more determined than he looked. He resigned his job and slept on a floor in the barracks, breakfasting on expedition rations and working evenings in a nearby pub, the Admiral Codrington. Oliver introduced me to an out-of-work friend named Charlie Burton, who had spent four years as a private soldier in an infantry regiment. His rugged face bore a pattern of rugby and boxing scars. Charlie passed the Territorial SAS selection course and joined our Welsh mountain training sessions. So too did Geoff Newman, who gave up his career with a printing firm. Finally, a part-time secretary, Mary Gibbs, joined us as nurse and generator mechanic. The six of us seemed to work well together, despite the strain of the tiny office and single telephone. By the autumn of 1975 we were sponsored by over 800 companies.

Andrew Croft, an Arctic explorer of note, advised me: 'Three men is a good number if you all get on. Two men is relatively suicidal. Four men can create cliques of two. In extremis, with three men, two can gang up against the leader. My advice is that you should decide whether to have two or three companions only after you have seen your potential colleagues in action during trials in the Arctic.'

From the moment Ginny and I started our joint struggle to launch Transglobe, we began to grow together. Our continued dedication to the venture survived even our total lack of know-how in all polar matters, the assurance of experts that our plans were impossibly ambitious and the long morale-sapping years of negative responses. For four or five years the British Antarctic Survey and the Royal Geographical Society (without whose blessing it would have been impossible, short of being a millionaire, to enter Antarctica) genuinely believed the projected journey to be hopelessly ambitious and probably impossible. Our prospects were summed up by one of Britain's polar godfathers, Sir Miles Clifford, an ex-director of the Falkland Islands Dependencies

Survey. 'You are saying, Fiennes, that your group will, in the course of a single journey, complete the greatest journeys of Scott, Amundsen, Nansen, Peary, Franklin and many others. You must understand that this sounds a touch presumptuous, if not indeed far-fetched.'

Sir Vivian Fuchs advised me that we could not hope to achieve Transglobe without polar training, so I began to plan two separate trial journeys. The first, to the Greenland Ice-cap in 1976, would train us for similar terrain in Antarctica. Next, in 1977, as there was nowhere suitable merely to simulate the Arctic, we would try to reach the North Pole itself.

Ginny's painstaking lobbying with the Ministry of Defence gained us permission for our first polar training and after four years in our barracks office, the RAF flew us to Greenland in July 1976 with 30,000 pounds of equipment. We landed at a US forces airbase in the north-west of the great ice-bound island. Along with two similar sites, one at Fylingdales in Yorkshire and the other at Clear in Alaska, this base formed part of a Soviet missile-spotting radar screen across the top of the world. Hills of grey gravel enfolded the base and eight miles inland we could see the rim of the ice-cap which covers all of Greenland save for the rock-girt fringes.

The redoubtable polar traveller Wally Herbert had advised me that fur parkas are unbeatable for Arctic winter travel. He also recommended that the ice-covered parts of our journey would best be attempted by some sort of machine rather than by dog teams, since we did not have time for the couple of years he considered essential for intensive dog-handling training. The snowcats we were going to use, which we called Groundhogs, were fitted with home-made buoyancy bags, and would float, swim and steer reasonably well between the cruising islands of pack-ice. Each towed two 1,000-pound sledge-loads separated by long safety lines.

During our first week on the Greenland Ice-cap a two-day bliz-zard kept us tent-bound and we learned simple lessons which would have been second nature to seasoned polar travellers: which way not to position the tent's entrance; how not to leave anything anywhere except on a Groundhog or inside the tent; how to string the radio's antenna wires to ski sticks rather than laying them along the snow surface where, after a blow, they became hard to dig out without damage. We quickly determined that snow for melting for drinks would come from one side of the tent foyer and the 'loo' would be on the other.

The Groundhogs, which started easily at temperatures down to −10°C, thereafter revolted and, on our first −20°C day they failed to respond to the electric circuit or the manual crank until Oliver poured the two Thermos flasks of hot chocolate, prepared for the day's travel, over the starter motors, whereupon the engines roared into life. Over the next months these machines caused non-stop trouble. The vehicle manuals were all in German which did not help, being beyond the scope of my hard-won O-level in that language.

I learned that neither my jungle nor my desert experience helped me much as ice-cap navigator, for the cold made my hand compass frustratingly slow to settle, while all manner of new problems cropped up to confuse and hinder accurate use of the theodolite. My first computed theodolite position in Greenland, following altitude shots of the sun at noon, was wrong by some sixty-two nautical miles. As our Groundhogs twisted their way through narrow snow valleys beneath the coastal mountains I used obvious features for compass backbearings. Later we climbed on to the inner ice-fields of the Hayes Peninsula, passing between heavily crevassed slopes. Blizzards pinned us down, inclines overturned the heavy sledges, throttles jammed, carburettors blocked, fuel lines leaked, a gearbox gasket blew and sprocket tyres shot off, landing up to sixty feet away. Finally we ran into serious trouble when both Groundhogs plunged into crevasses at the same time. We spent three precarious days tunnelling down to and under the stricken machines to retrieve them with pulleys and aluminium ramps.

But by the end of our ordeal we were working well together. Oliver's mechanical procedures were slick and we could strike or break camp in under an hour, compared with six hours a month before. Although no polar veterans, we had mastered deep snow ice-cap travel in temperatures of −20°C. The next step, a different game in every sense, was apprenticeship to Arctic Ocean ice-floe travel in temperatures of −40°C.

I arrived back in London from Greenland weighing thirteen stone. Over the next three 'office-bound' months I lost sixteen pounds and grew my first grey hairs as every possible political hurdle that might hinder our Arctic Ocean training plans was raised by the authorities. With limitless funds, we could have bought our way around most obstacles but we were, in Oliver's words, 'skint as squirrels'. In desperation I explained our immediate requirement − £60,000 to charter a ski-plane − to my old Dhofar contact, Tim Landon, and he introduced me to a wealthy Omani businessman, Dr Omar Zawawi, whose company agreed to sponsor the cost. In February 1977 a chartered DC6 flew the six of us into the polar darkness to try for the Pole.

Alert Camp, the world's most northerly settlement, is supplied only by air since there are no roads for hundreds of miles and all sea access is permanently frozen over. Sixty Canadian soldiers and scientists known as the Chosen Frozen manned the base in six-month stints. On the day of our arrival the temperature was −48°C and the night was pitch black. There would be no sign of the sun for a month. Our own camp, a deserted huddle of four wooden shacks, was perched along the very shore of the frozen sea a mile or so north of the Army camp. Between our huts and the North Pole lay nothing but 425 nautical miles of jumbled ice and black sea-smoke emanating from seams of open sea.

Oliver and Charlie prepared our new snow machines called skidoos. Much lighter than the Groundhogs, they were powered by 640cc two-stroke engines and steered by way of handlebars controlling a single short front ski. Skidoos are the snow traveller's motorbike: they provide scant protection from the elements.

I practised with my theodolite in a twenty-eight-knot wind at temperatures of −45°C, fairly average conditions for the time of year. One night the shooting of a single star took an hour and fifty minutes. In England I would have shot a dozen in twenty-five minutes. My eyelashes stuck to the metal of the scope and my nose cracked with the first symptoms of frosting. If I carelessly directed my breath on to the scope, even for a second, it froze; if I then wiped its lens with my bare finger, ungloved for even just a few seconds, this brought on circulation problems. Each time I tried to turn my head my beard hairs were tugged by the ice that meshed them, my eyes watered and more ice formed on my lashes which then froze together. But I persevered, for my ability to keep track of our position on the moving ice of the Arctic Ocean, whether by the sun or stars, would be key to our survival. An error of four seconds would put my position wrong by a mile.

We set out on 1 March, a few days before there is any glimpse of the sun at that latitude, and travelled five miles along the shoreline west of our camp before driving on to the sea-ice. A mile later we camped at −51°C, two men to a tent. Geoff tried to send a message back to Ginny, but his Morse key froze up and his breath simply froze on the inside of the fine wire mesh of his microphone. Then the main co-axial power line cable cracked when he tried to straighten it out. Next morning, after an unforgettably evil night, none of the skidoos would start.

During the two months of our North Pole attempt our chartered Twin Otter ski-plane visited us eight times. But there were other days when the pilot did not manage to spot us and returned to Ginny with a glum face and a negative report. Ginny sat at her radios for ten hours a day, often longer, knowing we were passing through areas of unstable breaking ice. She never missed a schedule and at times of major ionospheric disturbance, when even the major Canadian radio stations were blacked out, Ginny would tirelessly change antennae on her high masts, hop from frequency to frequency and tap out or yell out her identification sign hour after hour in the hope we might pick up her call. Out on the ice we were dependent on her ability. In the the tent, hearing her faint Morse signal or, in good conditions, her voice was the happiest moment of any day.

We never tried to drive skidoos and sledges north until we had first prepared a lane with our axes, work we dreaded because of the body sweat it caused which turned to ice particles inside our clothing. A typical stint of axe-work would last nine to eleven hours and clear a skidoo lane of between 500 and 3,000 yards. At first, aware of the dangers of polar bears, we each carried a rifle, but soon dropped the practice through sheer exhaustion. Slipping, sliding and falling into drifts made it difficult enough to manage a shovel and axe without worrying about a rifle as well.

Geoff and Oliver in particular suffered from frost-nipped finger ends. For long minutes in the dark I thought of nothing but my eyes. The eye-pain was a living thing. With a wind chill factor of −120°C the natural liquid in our eyes kept congealing. It was difficult to avoid outbursts of temper and hours of silent hostility in such conditions. For three years in London and four months in comparatively temperate Greenland, relations between us had been idyllic. But the Arctic put an end to the harmony. Any outside observer would have thought we were a close-knit group, but the new level of strain was beginning to get to us. Apsley Cherry-Garrard, describing Scott's winter party, wrote: 'The loss of a biscuit crumb left a sense of injury which lasted for a week. The greatest friends were so much on one another's nerves that they did not speak for days for fear of quarrelling.'

Over the weeks we inched north until the pressure ridges were no longer an unbroken mass. We began to find flat icefloe pancakes where travel was easy and quick flashes of hope, even elation, would then upset my determined cocoon of caution. I experienced exhilaration as the ice flashed by, my sledge leaping like a live thing but settling back on its runners instead of overturning.

Ginny's Idea

During the second week of April the pack-ice showed the first symptoms of break-up. The temperature soared to −36°C and nights of creaking, rumbling thunder gave way to mornings of black or brown steam-mist, a sure sign of newly opened water-leads. For days we crossed open canals and lakes of *nilas*, which is newly formed dark grey sludge-ice. Winds picked up surface snow and filled the air with the glint of freezing ice particles. White-out conditions resulted when clouds blocked the sun and then we travelled slowly, for navigation was awkward without shadow or perspective. No hole in the ice was visible until you fell into it; no hummock or thirty-foot wall evident until you collided with it. One of us would walk ahead with a prod before the skidoos slowly followed.

Open water, being black, was clearly visible but new ice, mere centimetres thick, was quickly covered by spindrift and formed traps for the unsuspecting. Conventional wisdom has it that white ice is thick and grey thin. I discovered that this was not always true while gingerly exploring a recently fractured ice-pan. The ice felt spongy underfoot at first, then more like rubber. Suddenly the surface began to move beneath my boots, a crack opened up and black water gushed rapidly over the floe, rushing over my boots and weighing down on the fragile new ice. As the water rose to my knees, the crust under my feet cracked apart. I sank quickly but my head could not have been submerged for more than a second since the air trapped under my wolfskin acted as a life-jacket.

The nearest solid floe was thirty yards away. I shouted for the others, but there was no one in earshot. Each time I tried to heave myself up on to a section of the submerged crust, I broke it again. I crawled and clawed and shouted. Under my threshing feet was a drop of 17,000 watery feet down to the canyons of the Lomonosov Ridge. Sailors in the world wars, I recalled, survived one minute on average in the North Sea. I began to tire. My toes felt numb and there was no sensation inside my mitts. My chin, inside the parka, sank lower as my clothes became heavier. I began to panic.

After four, perhaps five minutes, my escape efforts had weakened to a feeble pawing movement when, ecstatic moment, one arm slapped down on to a solid ice chunk and I levered my chest on to a skein of old ice. Then on my thighs and knees. I lay gasping for a few seconds, thanking God, but once out of the water, the cold and the wind bit into me. My trousers crackled as they froze. I tried to exercise my limbs but they were concrete-heavy in the sodden, freezing parka. I trudged robot-like via a solid route back to my skidoo which I could not start. For fifteen minutes I plodded round and round. My mitts were frozen and the individual fingers would not move.

Oliver came along my tracks. He reacted quickly, erecting a tent, starting a cooker, and cutting off my parka, mitts and boots with his knife. Twenty-four hours later, with me in spare clothes and a man-made duvet, we were on our way again. I was lucky to be alive. Few go for a long swim in the Arctic Ocean and survive.

During the latter half of April we pushed hard to squeeze northerly mileage out of each hour's travel. Only three teams in history had indisputably succeeded in reaching farther north towards the Pole – Plaisted, Herbert and Monzino. By 20 April we had exceeded the records of all previous travellers but these three. On 5 May we passed 87° North, a mere 180 miles from the Pole. The transpolar drift was what stopped us. The two major currents of the Arctic, the Beaufort Gyral and the Trans-Siberian Drift, meet and diverge somewhere between 87° and 88° of latitude, causing surface chaos, tearing floes apart in places and jumbling others up to heights of thirty feet. On 7 May there were wide canals and slush pools every few hundred yards. The entire region was in motion.

At this point the engine of my skidoo blew a head gasket and we could not progress without a re-supply drop. By the time Ginny had cajoled a ski-plane into dropping a new part we had drifted sixty miles to the south and east and a six-mile belt of sludge surrounded us. We waited for a further week, hoping for a freak temperature drop, but on 15 May, with temperatures rising to 0°C, I decided to call it a day.

Our funds ran out with the flight that extricated us from the floe and took us back to Alert. There Ginny gave me a radio message from London: Prince Charles had agreed to become patron of the main Transglobe Expedition.

The Arctic journey confirmed that the main expedition would have to have its own dedicated Twin Otter ski-plane and crew for re-supply purposes. I spent three years and numerous interviews with big company bosses before finally persuading Lord Hayter of Chubb Fire to sponsor us with the three-year loan of a Twin Otter with skis.

Back in the London office we carried on much as before. But the Arctic journey had humbled me, my first expedition failure. Soon afterwards Mary and Geoff were married and left the expedition. Mary's place as Ginny's base camp companion was taken by a young Cumbrian named Simon Grimes. A scruffy-looking man with a black beard, Anton Bowring, applied to join up as a ship's deck-hand. He was quiet and unflappable. He listened impassively when I explained there was no ship as yet for him to be a deck-hand on. But his first job, to keep him busy, could be to find one. It must be an ice-breaker and free of charge. A year later he located a thirty-year-old ice-strengthened vessel and persuaded the insurance brokers, C.T. Bowring, once owned by his family, to buy her on our behalf. This they did, with an eye to the fact that they had sponsored Captain Scott seventy years previously with his ship, the *Terra Nova*. Anton recruited sixteen unsalaried but qualified crewmen for his ship which he christened the *Benjamin Bowring*, after an adventurous ancestor. I was meanwhile lucky enough to obtain the services of Britain's most skilled Twin Otter polar pilot, Captain Giles Kershaw. The British Army loaned the expedition the services of Gerry Nicholson, an electrical and mechanical engineer specialising in Twin Otter maintenance who had spent time in Antarctica with the British Antarctic Survey.

By the end of 1978, after six years of unpaid full-time work, we had 1,900 sponsors from eighteen countries, £29 million worth of goods and services support and a team of fifty-two unpaid individuals giving their time and expertise towards Ginny's dream of the first circumpolar journey round earth.

One summer weekend Ginny's pet terrier drowned in a slurry pit. For weeks she was inconsolable until a friend turned up with a Jack Russell puppy with which she instantly fell in love. We called him Bothie in honour of his donor whose surname was Booth, and Ginny informed me she was not coming on Transglobe without him.

At Farnborough, in the spring of 1979, Prince Charles opened the Transglobe's press launch, arriving at the controls of our Twin Otter. He announced that he was supporting the expedition 'because it is a mad and suitably British enterprise'. Late in the afternoon of 2 September 1979 the *Benjamin Bowring* left Greenwich with Prince Charles at the helm. He wore a black tie because his uncle, Lord Mountbatten, had been killed three days before by the IRA. There were many people lining the pier. I spotted Geoff who was shouting rude messages at Oliver, and Mary, smiling through her tears. At the end of the jetty Gubbie held up one of his daughters who, with misplaced priorities, was busily waving her arm at the nearby *Cutty Sark*.

6

The Bottom of the World

On the day we set out from England, Prince Charles commented, 'Transglobe is one of the most ambitious undertakings of its kind ever attempted, the scope of its requirements monumental.' *The New York Times* editorial column, under the heading 'Glory', stated, 'the British aren't so weary as they're sometimes said to be. The Transglobe Expedition, seven years in the planning, leaves England on a journey of such daring that it makes one wonder how the sun ever set on the Empire.'

Our initial plans were mundane enough. With three Land Rovers we would cross Europe, the Sahara and West Africa. The ship would take us from Spain to Algeria and again from the Ivory Coast to Cape Town. Departure from Cape Town had to be timed precisely in order to enter Antarctic waters in mid-summer, when the ice-pack should be at its loosest. This was the reason we left England in early September and why we had to leave South Africa by late December.

Anton Bowring's crew of volunteers were a wonderful bunch, professional at their posts but fairly wild when off duty. They included Quaker, Buddhist, Jew, Christian and atheist, black, white and Asian. They came from Austria, America, both ends of Ireland, South Africa, India, Denmark, Britain, Canada, Fiji and New Zealand. Most of the crew were Merchant Navy men who gave up promising careers, at a time of growing unemployment, to join a three-year voyage with no wage packet. Paul Anderson from Denmark, who had signed on as a deck-hand, had worked with us for a year in the office and on the ship but died of a heart problem just before we left England.

Ginny was not the only female aboard, for Anton had selected an attractive redhead, Jill McNicol, as ship's cook. She soon gained a number of ardent admirers from among the crew.

In Algiers the port officials showed ominous interest in our three-year supply of sponsored spirits and cigarettes. When the first wave of officers departed, promising a second visit in an hour, our skipper decided to make a run for it and quickly unloaded our vehicles and gear. As the crew waved us goodbye, the *Benjamin Bowring's* thirty-year-old variable pitch control jammed itself in reverse. So the vessel retreated out of the harbour and out of sight steaming backwards.

In our three sponsored Land Rovers we drove through Algeria to the sand-dunes of El Golea, a sticky-hot hell-hole dubbed 'El Gonorrhoea' by Oliver. We were pleased to leave the sweltering sands and head south to the Hoggar Mountains. At 8,000 feet we reached the Pass of Asekrem, the haunt of French monks. We savoured views of vast mountain ranges disappearing to Chad and the centre of Africa. From Tamanrasset we rattled down ever-worsening trails to lonely Tit and thence over trackless miles of sand and scrub to Tim-Missao and the Touareg lands of the Adrar des Iforas. Wide starry nights and wind-blown dunes brought back memories of the Dhofari Nejd and desert days long past.

From the Forest of Tombouctou to Goundam on the Niger we roared and skidded over dunes of thirty-foot-high sand in low gear to the cheer of barefoot donkeymen in sampan hats driving cavalcades of pint-size mules along the same trail.

At Niafounke we learned that extensive flooding barred our planned route to the Ivory Coast, but a 700-kilometre westerly detour took us at length to Loulouni and the Ivorian border at Ouangolodougou. For a week we camped in thick jungle beside the Bandama Rouge River, an excellent collection point for bilharzia-bearing water-snails, one of Oliver's tasks for the Natural History Museum, then south to the lush and hilly coastline. In Abidjan harbour, we were met by the *Benjamin Bowring*. Simon and two members of the crew were weak from malarial fever but we pressed on and sailed across the Equator close by the Greenwich Meridian.

Somewhere off the Namib coast, the Benguela Current coincided with a Force Seven storm. The electrical system of the stern refrigerator room broke down and a ton of sponsored mackerel turned putrescent. Brave hands volunteered to go below and clean up the mess, slipping about, as the ship rolled and heaved, in a soup of bloody fish bits. They fought their way up the ladders and tossed the sloppy bundles of rotten fish overboard. Then a forklift truck burst its lashings, crushed valuable gear and spattered battery acid about the cargo hold. Nowhere on the bucking ship, from cabins to fo'c'sle, could we escape the fumes of acid and mackerel. We were in the tropics and there was no air-conditioning system. This was, after all, a ship designed for work at polar temperatures. With each roll to port our cabin porthole spat jets of sea-water on to our bunks. All night the clash of steel on steel and the groan of hemp under stress sounded from the cargo holds.

The old ship struggled on at a stately eight knots and delivered us, slightly dazed, to Saldanha Bay, near Cape Town, on 3 December. Jackass penguins squawked from the rocky shoreline, hundreds of thousands of them, as we anchored to take on fresh water.

We stayed two weeks in Cape Town to mount an export sales-orientated exhibition of our equipment, one of eight such events to be held during the course of the voyage. On a free evening I drove to Constantia with Ginny and visited our old house, built by Granny Florrie thirty-four years before. Nothing was as I remembered it. The valley was no longer the wild and wonderful place of my dreams. Residential expansion had tamed and suburbanised the woods and vineyards. The vlei where I had roamed with Archie and the gang was now a row of neat bungalows for foreign embassy staff. Our own house, Broughton, was a transitory post for US Marines on leave and nobody had tended the garden in years. There was no longer a view of the valley, for Granny Florrie's

The Transglobe Expedition, 1979–82

shrubs had flourished unchecked and the four little palm trees named after my sisters and me were now roof-high.

We wandered in silence through the old vegetable patch. No trace remained of the summerhouse, a place of bewitching memories. My mother's rockery, tended with so much care and love, had run amok. Up the valley, beside a building lot where caterpillar trucks were at work, we called on my cousin Googi Marais, whose rifle bullets passing over the roof at night had once caused our English nanny to pack her bags and flee. Googi was now crippled with arthritis, but he and his wife gave us tea and filled

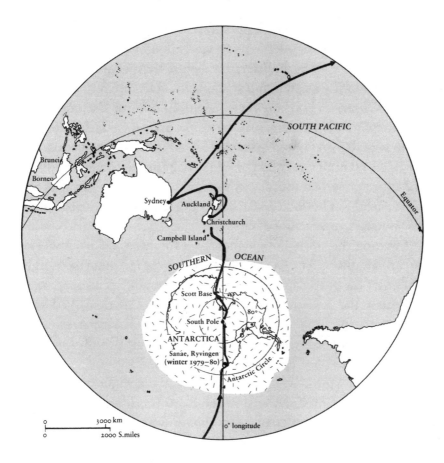

me in on the past quarter century of happenings in our valley.

Over the next ten days I was reunited with twenty-two other cousins, one of whom, an alderman of Cape Town, showed me a family tree which proved he and I shared a close relationship with Karl Marx. I regret not having taken away a copy to shock the family back in England.

We left South Africa three days before Christmas, passing by Cape Agulhas, the last land for 2,400 miles, and set a course south to Antarctica.

77

Bothie, our Jack Russell, appointed himself ship's mascot and, respecting no privacy, left calling-cards in all cabins. Ginny tried hard to remove all his indiscretions before they were discovered by the crew but it was an uphill struggle.

The Observer, covering the expedition, sent Bryn Campbell to Antarctica with us to record the ship's arrival. A four-man film team was also on board – provided by millionaire octogenarian Dr Armand Hammer, a friend of Prince Charles – intending to film the entire three-year journey by joining the team in the more accessible areas. The actor Richard Burton was to provide a background commentary.

Swelling the ship's complement still further were a number of oceanographers. At certain stages of the voyage there were eight scientists on board and at all times our own resident boffins, an Irishman and a Cape Town University researcher, worked with their bathythermographs and nets to study current patterns and the interaction of water bodies at sub-tropical and Antarctic convergences.

Christmas spirits were dampened by a Force Eight storm which tore away the Christmas tree lashed to our mast and made eating rich festive fare a risky business. Giant Southern Ocean rollers forced the ship to list 47° both ways and, fearing the worst, I asked Anton if the ship could cope. His eyes glinted evilly and he proceeded to tell me a number of Antarctic shipwreck horror stories.

As the old year slid away, we entered pack-ice and the sea slowly settled. Anton reflected that Scott and Shackleton had been active in these waters less than seventy years before. The skipper sent a lookout up to the crow's nest to shout directions to the fo'c'sle through the antiquated intercom. The loose pack-ice yielded to our steel-clad bows and only once did we need to halt and slowly ram a new path through the floes.

On 4 January 1980, we sighted the ice-cliffs of Antarctica and the same day gouged ourselves out a nest at Sanae, in the thin bay-ice of Polarbjorn Bite, where we could climb straight down a ladder on to the ice. The unloading of over 100 tons of mixed cargo, including 2,000 numbered boxes and 1,600 fuel drums, began at once.

To ensure that the ship could leave before the pack solidified and cut off her escape, we raced to carry every item two miles inland to more solid ice. Everyone helped, even the film team. Our sole tow-machine apart from skidoos was a Groundhog rescued from Greenland but, in only eleven days, the complex operation was complete.

Halfway through the unloading a storm broke up the ice and I watched from the bridge as eight drums of precious aircraft fuel sailed north on a floe. It was as if the bay-ice all about the ship were pieces of a jigsaw all coming apart at the same moment.

Our steward Dan Hicks, a permanently merry character, drank too much whisky and fell off the gangplank, floating belly-up between the hull and the ice-edge, in imminent danger of being crushed, until someone hauled him out on a boathook. One of the engineers slipped and broke three ribs and Bothie lost a fight with an angry chinstrap penguin. The chief engineer, who had hoisted his Honda motorbike on to the ice for a quick ride, lost the machine for ever during a storm. Otherwise the unloading went well and those of us who were to stay behind waved goodbye to the ship and crew on 15 January. All being well, they would pick us up again in a year or so, 2,000 miles away on the far side of the frozen continent.

Ten days later, in conditions of nil visibility, Ollie, Charlie and I took our skidoos and laden sledges on a 370-kilometre journey inland to set up a base on the high polar plateau in which to spend the next eight months of polar winter and the long disappearance of the sun. The base-site beneath Ryvingen Mountain was chosen because of its height above sea-level and its distance inland, the furthest which the Twin Otter could be expected to reach carrying a 2,000-pound cargo load. We hoped, by wintering at 6,000 feet, to become acclimatised to the bitter conditions before the main crossing journey the following summer, when the average height would be 10,000 feet above sea-level. Until we reached our winter site we would be simple travellers. But once south of our camp, we would become true explorers of one of earth's last untrodden regions. For 900 miles we would pass through terrain neither seen nor touched by mankind. Oliver would be mapping this whole unexplored area using an aneroid barometer, as he had been trained to do by the British Antarctic Survey.

The Twin Otter flew in Ginny, Bothie and four cardboard huts Ginny had designed, and the race began to prepare our camp for the long winter. The Twin Otter crew completed their seventy-eighth ferry flight from Sanae to Ryvingen and we wished them a safe flight back to Britain via the Falkland Islands and Argentina.

The weather clamped down on the ice-fields, travel for any distance became impossible and we were soon cut off from the outside world. We were 400 miles from and unreachable by the nearest humans, the twelve South African scientists in their snow-buried seaside hut at Sanae. For eight months we must survive through our own common sense. Should anyone be hurt or sick there could be no evacuation and no medical assistance. We must daily handle heavy batteries, generator power lines and heavy steel drums, but avoid the hazards of acid in the eye, serious tooth trouble, appendicitis, cold burns, fuel burns or deep electrical burns. Temperatures would plunge to −50°C and below. Winds would exceed ninety knots and the chill factor would reach −84°C. For 240 days and nights we must live cautiously and mostly without sunlight.

After a few days the huts disappeared under snow drifts, and all exits were blocked. So I dug tunnels under the snow and stored all our equipment inside them. In two months I completed a 200-yard network of spacious tunnels with side corridors, a loo alcove, a thirty-foot-deep slop-pit and a garage with pillars and archways of ice.

Since our huts were made of cardboard with wooden struts and bunks and our heaters burned kerosene we were apprehensive of fire. A Russian base, 500 miles away, had been burnt out the previous winter and all eight occupants were found asphyxiated in an escape tunnel with blocked hatches.

Katabatic winds blasted our camp and snuffed out our fires through chimney back-blow. We experimented with valves, flaps and crooked chimneys, but the stronger gusts confounded all our efforts. The drip-feed pipe of a heater would continue to deliver fuel after a blow-out and this could cause a flash-fire unless great care was taken on re-lighting the heater.

Generator exhaust pipes tended to melt out sub-snow caverns which spread sideways and downwards. One day Oliver discovered a fifteen-foot-deep cave underneath the floor of his generator hut. He moved his exhaust system time and again but nearly died of carbon monoxide poisoning three times despite being alert for the symptoms.

Without power from the generators, Ginny's radios would not work, so our weather reports, which Oliver must send out every six hours, could not be fed into the World Meteorological System, nor could Ginny's complex, very low frequency (VLF) recording experiments for Sheffield University and the British Antarctic Survey be undertaken. So we fought hard against snow accumulation in certain key areas of the camp.

At night in the main living hut we turned the heater low to save fuel. We slept on wooden slats in the apex of the hut roof and in the mornings there was a difference of 14° between bed level and floor temperature, the latter averaging −15°C.

Ginny and I slept together on a single slat at one end of the hut, Oliver and Charlie occupied bachelor slats down the other end and Bothie slept in a cavity behind the heater. The long black nights with the roar of the wind so close and the linger of tallow in the dark are now a memory which I treasure.

There was of course friction between us. Forced togetherness breeds dissension and even hatred between individuals and groups. After four years at work together our person-to-person chemistry was still undergoing constant change. Some days, without a word being spoken, I knew that I disliked one or both of the other men and that the feeling was mutual. At other times, without actually going so far as to admit affection, I felt distinctly warm towards them. When I felt positive antagonism towards the others I could let off steam with Ginny, who would listen patiently. Or else I could spit out vituperative prose in my diary. Diaries on expeditions are often minefields of over-reaction.

Each of us nursed apprehensions about the future. The thought of leaving the security of our cardboard huts for the huge unknown that stretched away behind Ryvingen Mountain was not something on which I allowed my thoughts to dwell.

On 2 May the wind chill factor dropped to −79°C. Windstorms from the polar plateau blasted through the camp with no warning. Visiting Ginny's VLF recording hut one morning, I was knocked flat by a gust, although a second earlier there had not been a zephyr of wind. A minute later, picking myself up, I was struck on the back by the plastic windshield ripped off my parked skidoo.

Even in thirty-knot wind conditions we found it dangerous to move outside our huts and tunnels except by way of the staked safety lines which we had positioned all around the camp and from hut to hut. Charlie and I both lost the safety lines one day when an eighty-knot wind hurled ice-needles horizontally through the white-out. We groped separately and blindly in circles until we blundered into a safety line and so found our way to the nearest hut's hatchway. That same day the parachute canopy covering the sunken area of Ginny's antennae-tuning units was ripped off, and by nightfall two tons of snow had filled in her entire work area.

Before the sun disappeared I taught Oliver and Charlie the rudiments of langlauf skiing, for I knew, if we succeeded in crossing Antarctica, that we would meet many regions in the Arctic where only skis would be practical.

On a fine autumn day we left camp with laden sledges for a quick sixteen-kilometre manhaul trip to a nearby *nunatak*, a lonely rock outcrop. A storm caught us on the return journey and, within minutes, the wind had burned every patch of exposed skin and frostnipped our fingers inside their light ski mitts. At the time we were each moving at our separate speeds with a mile or so between us. This was not acceptable by current mountain safety practices but it was a system encouraged on all SAS training courses. The fewer individuals in a group, the faster the majority will reach their goal. This presupposes that the weakest link can look after himself. Oliver was last to arrive back at camp, his face and neck bloated with frostnip. For a week he took antibiotics until his sores stopped weeping.

Ginny's problems were mostly connected with her radio work. Conducting low-frequency experiments with faraway Cove Radio Station in Hampshire, she worked a 1.5 kva generator in the foyer to her hut. A freak wind once blew carbon monoxide fumes under her door. By chance I called her on a walkie-talkie and, receiving no reply, rushed along the tunnels and down to her shack. I found her puce-faced and staggering about dazed. I dragged her out into the fresh −49°C air and told the Cove Radio operator what had happened. Next day we received a worried message from their controller, Squadron Leader Jack Willes.

Even in a comfortable environment the operation of electrical radio components is a hazardous operation. In your location the dangers are considerably increased . . . Remember that as little as thirty mA can kill. Never wear rings or watches when apparatus is live. Beware of snow from boots melting on the floor . . . Your one kilowatt transmitter can produce very serious radio frequency burns . . . Static charges will build up to several thousand volts in an aerial. Toxic berillium is employed in some of the components . . .

Only four days later, with all her sets switched off and no mains power, Ginny touched the co-ax cable leading to her forty-watt set and was stunned by a violent shock that travelled up her right arm and 'felt like an explosion in my lungs'. The cause was static, built up by wind-blown snow.

Not being a technical expert, Ginny used common sense to repair her sets, replace tiny diodes and solder cold-damaged flex.

When a one-kilowatt resistor blew and she had no spares, she thought of cutting a boiling ring out of our Baby Belling cooker. She then wired the cannibalised coil to the innards of her stricken radio and soon had everything working again, the home-made resistor glowing red-hot on an asbestos mat on the floor. The chief back at Cove Radio described her as 'an amazing communicator'.

To keep our little community happy, Ginny listened to the BBC World Service and produced *The Ryvingen Observer*. On 6 May we learned that the bodies of US airmen were being flown out of Iran following an abortive attempt to rescue American hostages, that Tito's funeral was imminent, that SAS soldiers had killed some terrorists at the Iranian Embassy in London and that food in British motorway cafés had been summed up in a government report as greasy and tasteless.

Bothie spent his days following Ginny from hut to hut. She kept old bones for him in each shack and dressed him in a modified pullover when the winds were high. I fought a non-stop battle with the terrier for eight months, trying to teach him that 'outside' meant right outside the tunnels as well as the hut. I lost the struggle.

Charlie, in charge of our food, rationed all goodies with iron discipline. Nobody could steal from the food tunnels without his say-so, a law that was obeyed by all but Bothie. Our eggs, originally sponsored in London, were some eight or nine months old by mid-winter and, although frozen much of that time, they had passed through the tropics en route. To an outsider they tasted bad – indeed evil – but we had grown used to them over the months and Bothie was addicted. However hard Charlie tried to conceal his egg store, Bothie invariably outwitted him and stole a frozen egg a day, sometimes more.

The months of June, July and August saw an increasing workload in the camp, due both to the scientific programme and our preparations for departure in October. The sun first came back to Ryvingen, for four minutes only, on 5 August, a miserably cold day. Down at our coastal Sanae base hut, Simon, overwintering with one other Transglober, Anto Birkbeck, recorded a windspeed in excess of 100 miles per hour. July 30 was our coldest day. With the wind steady at forty-two knots and a temperature of −42°C, our prevailing chill factor was −131°C, at which temperature any exposed flesh freezes in under fifteen seconds.

In August Ginny had to complete a complex research task which involved working with two other remote Antarctic bases, Sanae and Halley Bay, to pick up Very Low Frequency signals emanating from the Arctic. All pick-up times (once every four minutes) had to be exactly synchronised between the three bases. But Ginny discovered the oscillation unit in her VLF time-code generator had failed due to the cold. To complete the VLF experiment without the instrument meant manually pressing a recording button every four minutes for unbroken twenty-four-hour periods. Wrapped in blankets in the isolated VLF hut she kept awake night after night with flasks of black coffee. By October she was dog-tired and hallucinating but determined to complete the three-month experiment.

As the sunlit hours grew longer, the ice-fields reacted. Explosions sounded in the valleys, rebounding as echoes from the peaks all about us. Avalanches or imploding snow-bridges? There was no way of knowing.

With departure imminent, I realised how much I had grown to love the simplicity of our life at Ryvingen, a crude but peaceful existence during which, imperceptibly, Ginny and I had grown closer together than during the bustle of our normal London lives. Now I felt pangs of regret that it was ending. Also tremors of apprehension. As the days slipped by my stomach tightened with that long-dormant feeling of dread − once so familiar during school holidays as the next term-time approached.

'I wish you weren't leaving,' Ginny said.

In the last week of October it should be warm in the −40s°C and light enough to travel at 10,000 feet above sea-level. Then we would attempt the longest crossing of the Antarctic continent, the first crossing attempt to use vehicles with no protective cabs for the drivers and the first to travel from side to side, rather than split-teams approaching the Pole from both sides. The frozen land mass we must cross was bigger than Europe, the USA and Mexico combined, than India and China together, and far larger than Australia. The ice-sheet was five kilometres thick in places and covered 99 per cent of the entire continent. Four days before we set out, a news release through Reuters quoted the New Zealand Antarctic Division boss as criticising our intended journey as under-equipped and our skidoos as under-powered. The official view was that we would fail: it was 'too far, too high and too cold'.

On 29 October we left Ginny and Bothie in a drifted-over camp and headed south. The wind blew into our masked faces at twenty knots and the thermometer held steady at −50°C.

Clinging to a straight bearing of 187°, we crossed the sixty-four kilometres to the Penck Escarpment, a steep rise of several hundred feet of sheet ice. Spotting the curve of a slight re-entrant, I tugged my throttle to full bore and began the climb, trying to will the skidoo on with its 1,200-pound load – a heavy burden for a 640cc two-stroke engine operating at 7,000 feet above sea-level. The rubber tracks often failed to grip on smooth ice, but always reached rough patches again before too much momentum was lost. Renewed grip and more power then carried me on – just – to the next too-smooth section. The ascent seemed interminable. Then came an easing of the gradient, two final rises, and at last the ridgeline. Fifteen hundred feet above our winter camp and forty miles from it I stopped and looked back. The peaks of the Borga Massif seemed like mere pimples in the snow, Ryvingen itself just a shadow.

We pressed south and by dusk there was no single rock feature in any direction. Only endless fields of snow. Nothing to navigate by but clouds and soon – once we left the weather-making features of sea and mountain behind us – there would not even be clouds.

On the second day, at −53°C, we climbed slowly into the teeth of high winds and a white-out, the true plateau still 4,000 feet above us. After four hours Oliver staggered off his skidoo and lurched

My father, Palestine 1940.

With my mother, 1944.

Me at 11; Ginny (left) and family. Her father (right) was the man who described me as 'Mad, bad and dangerous to know' – perhaps with some justification, given the newspaper coverage below.

Not even her father could stop us getting engaged –
even though I nearly missed my opportunity.

On patrol in the Omani southern deserts, 1969.

Training with the SAS (Territorials): this was a good way of keeping fit when I was no longer part of the regular army.

Parachute training prior to the glacier drop, 1970.

The first recorded descent of the highest glacier in Norway, 1970, the author third from left.

Even in those days my hands caused me problems.

The majesty and beauty of ice has always captivated me –
the Jostedals Glacier, 1970.

The Headless Valley Expedition, 1971: the Virginia Falls,
twice the height of Niagara.

Ginny sometimes had to resupply our boats in thick forest and
once had a seriously close encounter with a black bear.

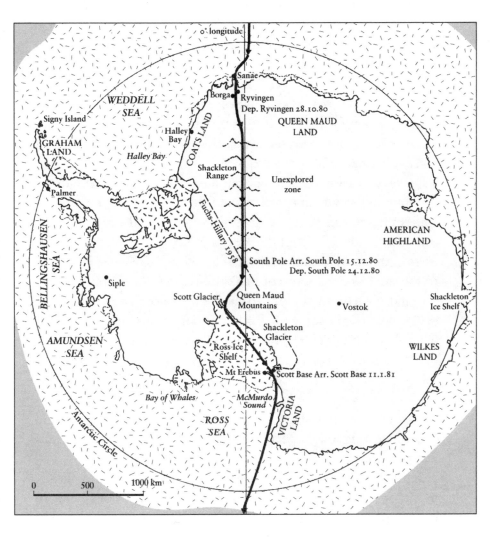

The Transglobe Expedition's route across Antarctica

over to me, his speech slurred. 'Must stop. I'm getting exposure.' We boiled water and gave him tea. He was physically the toughest of us and wore five layers of polar clothing. But the cold was cruel and wore us down hour after hour. We travelled for between ten and twelve hours a day.

That night Oliver wrote: 'Very bad weather. I think we should have stayed in the tent.' I saw his point but Greenland five years earlier had taught me that we could travel in high wind and white-out and every hour of progress, however slow, helped our slim chances of success. We had 2,200 miles to go, 900 of them unexplored.

I took a bearing check every ten minutes against the clouds: as these moved slowly and maintained their silhouettes for quite a while, they served me well. At times when partial white-outs hid sun and clouds, all I could do was aim my compass at imperfections in the snow ahead. When the sun shone I navigated by means of the shadows of a series of penknife-scratched lines on the plastic windshield of my skidoo. To check on the accuracy of this crude system and to put some life back into our frozen limbs, I stopped for five minutes in every hour. We always maintained a space of a mile between each of us so, as soon as I stopped, a backbearing on the two specks back along my trail provided a good check on the angle of travel.

For four days and nights the temperature hovered around −50°C, creating weird effects such as haloes, sun pillars, mock suns and parhelia.

In the mornings the skidoos were difficult to start. Any wrong move or out-of-sequence action caused long delays. Try to engage gear too soon and the drive belt shattered into rubber fragments. Turn the ignition key a touch too hard and it snapped off in the lock. Set the choke wrong and the plugs fouled up. Changing plugs at −50°C in a strong wind was a bitter chore which no one fancied.

Often the whole day would pass without a word spoken between us. Our routine was slick and included, after camping, the drill of ice-core samples at every degree of latitude, a full coded weather report by radio to the World Meteorological Organisation, and the taking of urine samples as part of our calorific intake programme.

Back at Sanae, our coastal base, Giles and Gerry had returned from England with the Twin Otter and took Simon up to help Ginny at Ryvingen. Every 300 or 400 miles we would run out of fuel and Giles would have to locate us from my theodolite position. In ten days' travel we were 404 nautical miles from Ryvingen with a suspected major crevasse field just to our south. Since no man had been there before us, we had only satellite photographs from which to try to detect such obstacles.

On 9 November we ran into our first bad field of sastrugi, ridges of ice cut by the wind and resembling parallel lines of concrete tanktraps. Due to the prevalence of east-west winds, these furrows were diagonal to our southerly direction of travel. The sastrugi were from eighteen inches to four feet high and, being perpendicular, they often impeded any advance until we axed out a through-lane. They buckled our springs, bogey wheels and skis. Oliver struggled to improvise repairs.

At 80° South we camped in one spot for seventeen days to allow Giles to set up a fuel dump halfway between the coast and the Pole.

For weeks our progress was painfully slow. Sledges with smashed oak spars were abandoned, frequent overturns caused minor injuries, axe-work through sastrugi fields progressed sometimes at a mere 800 yards in five hours, and the ever-present fear of crevasses gnawed at our morale. One morning, stopping on an apparently harmless slope, Charlie stepped off his skidoo to stretch his legs and promptly disappeared up to his thighs. He was parked right over an unseen cavern, with less than two inches of snow cover between him and oblivion.

Close to 85° South, in a high sastrugi field, we had stopped for repairs when we heard from Ginny that a team of South African scientists, operating at the rim of the coastal mountains near Sanae, were in trouble. One of their heavy snow tractors had plunged sixty feet down a crevasse together with its one-ton fuel sledge. One man then fell ninety feet down another crevasse and broke his neck and their rescue party, returning to their coastal base, became lost in the ice-fields. They had, by the time Ginny contacted us, already been missing with minimal gear for five days. Already short of fuel and with a recurring engine start-up problem, highly hazardous in Antarctica, Giles nonetheless flew over 1,000 miles to search for, and eventually locate, the missing South African scientists. This saved their lives.

From 85° South we struggled on, detouring east to avoid a mammoth crevasse field and running into total white-out conditions. Navigation became critical and on 14 December, after nine hours of travel in thick mist, I stopped where I estimated the Pole should be. There was no sign of life, although a sixteen-man crew of US scientists worked in a domed base beside the Pole. We camped and l radioed the Pole's duty signaller.

'You are three miles away,' replied a Texan twang. 'We have you on radar . . . Come on in.'

He gave us a bearing and, an hour later, the dome loomed up a few yards to my front. At 4.35 a.m. on 15 December, 900 miles south of Ryvingen and seven weeks ahead of our schedule, we had reached the bottom of the world.

Giles flew Ginny, Bothie and Simon to the Pole, complete with the radio station stripped from Ryvingen. The temptation to spend Christmas Day with Ginny at the Pole was powerful, but we had to press on. With each passing day the crevasse systems between the polar plateau and the coast were growing more rotten, snow-bridges accumulated from drifts the previous winter were daily sagging and collapsing.

For five years I had tried to discover a straight-line descent route from the polar plateau to the coastal ice-shelf. The Scott Glacier appeared to be the straightest, but no one knew anything about it and I only had an aerial map to go by. This showed extensive crevassing at the glacier's crest some 9,000 feet up, fractures in belts down its course and massed around its mouth where the ice debouched on to the ice-shelf 500 feet above sea-level.

We left the Pole on 23 December. I thought of Captain Scott, whose team had reached the Pole sixty-nine years earlier. 'All day-dreams must go,' he had written, for his Norwegian rivals had arrived there first. 'It will be a wearisome return.' They never made it back.

From the Pole we steered north. Every direction was of course northerly but my compass setting was 261° for 180 miles. There were no sastrugi all the way and no crevasses, so we reached the plateau edge in only two days. At 5.00 p.m. on Christmas Day I stopped on a small rise and saw far ahead the summit of Mount Howe, guardian of the Scott Glacier Valley and the first natural feature we had seen in well over 1,000 miles. It made an excellent Christmas present. That night there was an air of apprehension in the tent, not in anticipation of Christmas stockings but through fear of the impending descent.

My map dotted Scott Glacier with vaguely delineated rashes of crevasse belts, an artist's impression rather than an exact record from which an optimum compass course could be set. I decided to play Scott Glacier by ear rather than compass. Oliver changed all our carburettor jet settings for the lower altitudes and we swapped our one-metre sledge tow-lines for six-metre safety lines.

A series of east-west pressure swellings heralded the first obstacle. We breathed in as we passed over huge crevasses but all were bridged well enough to take the minimal ground pressure of our skidoos. The narrower fissures, from four to twenty feet wide, were the greater danger, for many were spanned by sagging snow-bridges that collapsed under the slightest weight.

Each time I crossed a relatively weak bridge, my sledge, heavier by far than my skidoo in terms of ground pressure, broke through, partially, plunging a cascade of snow down into the fissure below. Only forward momentum saved the day at such times. Charlie, behind me, would have to find himself another crossing-point. So too, later, would Oliver.

The La Gorse range for which I was headed was soon obscured by mist, as were all other features, so we camped in the centre of a wide crevasse field. Next morning the white-out was still clamped about us and, impatient, I decided we should move on. This was perhaps a rash decision.

From about this period of the expedition Charlie underwent a subtle change that I cannot, to this day, explain. He radiated a muted hostility which never broke out into rage. Instead it simmered away month after month, nursing itself quietly.

After six years of working together with two men for whom I had no prior affection or common ground – save for the single desire to achieve Transglobe – the vicissitudes of our common experiences had slowly led me to grow fond of Oliver and to dislike Charlie. I disliked being disliked. Hostility bred hostility. I was fully aware that the major part of the expedition, and by far the more hazardous sector, lay ahead and that one of my two companions and I were silently at loggerheads. Since this situation was only known to the two of us and it was never openly acknowledged, I saw no reason why it should impair our chance of success, which was, after all, all that mattered. The fact remained that we worked well together and there were no arguments.

Our nightmare trail down the glacier led us into a cul-de-sac, surrounded by open crevasses. We retraced our tracks and tried again via another narrow corridor between blue ice-walls. A maze of sunken lanes beset with hidden falls finally released us, shaken but unhurt, close by the Gardner Ridge and 6,000 feet above our ice-shelf goal. In forty-knot winds and thick mist, we followed the Klein Glacier for twelve miles until forced along a narrow ice-spit between two giant pressure fields, a chaos of gleaming ice-blocks.

I knelt to study the map to find a way through, but the wind tore it away. I carried one spare chart with my navigation gear and, using it, plotted a course to the eastern side of the valley. Halfway through the smaller pressure field, a sudden drop revealed the lower reaches of Scott Glacier, a breathtaking show of mountain and ice-flow, rock and sky, dropping 600 metres to the far horizon and the pinnacles of the Organ Pipe Peaks. A crevasse field five miles deep crossed the entire valley from cliff to cliff and halted us short of Mount Russell, so we detoured east over a 1,000-foot-high pass and, three hours later, re-entered Scott Glacier – beyond the crevasse field – by way of a wicked ravine. We had travelled for fourteen hours and covered five days' worth of scheduled progress. The next day our mad journey continued. More ice-walls and skidding, out-of-control sledges. At the foot of Mount Ruth we cat-footed along the ceiling of an active pressure lane as rotten as worm-eaten wood.

The last concentrated nightmare, south-west of Mount Zanuck, was a series of swollen icy waves pocked by broken seams.

Beyond the powerful in-flow of the Albanus Glacier the dangers lessened hour by hour until, at the final rock outcrop of Durham Point, there was nothing ahead but flat ice and the Pacific. We had reached the Ross Ice-shelf. Dog-tired, we camped after fifteen hours of travel and awoke next day to Oliver shouting, 'Welcome to the tropics! It's *plus* 1° on the thermometer.'

For nine further days I held to a bearing of 183°, which took us well north of the disturbed zone known as the Stagshead Crevasses. On the seventh day we crossed the 180° meridian which, at that point, is also the International Date Line. I experienced a zany temptation to zigzag north along it singing, 'Monday, Tuesday, Monday, Tuesday.'

On the ninth day, passing the region where Oates groped his frostbitten way to a lonely but honourable death, we first saw the mushroom steam-cloud of Mount Erebus, a hundred miles distant but marker to our destination. Beneath the 13,000-foot volcano lies Scott Base where, on 11 January, we arrived at 6.00 p.m. We had crossed Antarctica in sixty-seven days.

Much of our strength, despite our lack of polar experience, lay in our collective ability – remove any one of us and the other two became a far less capable entity. Unfortunately, that is precisely what happened. Oliver's wife Rebecca, from whom he had been separated – then re-united for the past few years – had grown sick with worry during the Antarctic crossing. Oliver was faced with the cruel choice of wife or Transglobe. He took the long-term option because he loved Rebecca more than his six-year-long ambition to achieve Transglobe's goals.

Oliver's loss caused wider problems than the mere mechanics of food supplies and weights to be carried in the Arctic. Back in London the committee who represented the expedition, including ex-SAS Brigadier Mike Wingate Gray, decided it would be irresponsible for us to attempt the northern hemisphere with a team of only two. They were solidly in favour of a third man, probably from the Royal Marines or SAS, being recruited to replace Oliver. A committee deputation to decide the issue of the third man was to be sent to meet us in New Zealand after the *Benjamin Bowring* penetrated the pack-ice again and removed us from Antarctica.

7

Full Circle

On arrival at Christchurch, New Zealand, I received a warning message from Anthony Preston, the ex-RAF man in charge of our London office. He had discovered that an American, Walt Pedersen – one of the 1968 team that reached the North Pole under Ralph Plaisted – was all set to sledge to the South Pole early next year. Determined to become the first man in the world to reach both Poles overland, he had spent twelve years getting his act together. It looked as though he would beat us to the double by four months, since the earliest we could hope to reach the North Pole would be April 1982. I reflected that virtually none of our Antarctic experience was applicable to our coming Arctic struggle. The two places were as alike as chalk and cheese.

Mike Wingate Gray, our chairman, Sir Vivian Fuchs and other key members of our London committee, held long meetings with Ginny, Charlie and me, but we could not agree to the recruiting of a third man. I resolved to put the final decision to our patron, Prince Charles, and at Sydney, where he opened our trade fair, I explained the whole problem to him in the skipper's cabin. I was as firmly against taking on a replacement for Oliver as the committee were in favour of the idea. I quoted Wally Herbert who during his pioneering Arctic crossing stated: 'As a two-man party we would travel harder, faster and more efficiently than as a three-man unit.' I stressed to Prince Charles that Charlie and I had already spent six years together, including travel in Greenland, the

Arctic Ocean and Antarctica. We knew each other's limitations and strong points. We had worked out a mutually acceptable *modus vivendi*. Should a third man be forced on us, his very presence, no matter how we interacted with him, might undermine our own mutual compatibility for the Arctic crossing which we knew would be far more testing than Antarctica. The upshot of the various discussions was that Charlie and I should carry on alone, but Sir Vivian Fuchs warned me that if things should go wrong, the blame would be entirely mine.

On the *Benjamin Bowring*'s boat deck we gave Prince Charles three cheers and a miniature silver globe, marked with our route, to congratulate him on his engagement to Lady Diana Spencer. Bothie joined the cheering, yapping aggressively until Prince Charles patted and spoke to him.

While we were in Sydney, Charlie married the girl that he loved and Anton married Jill, our ship's cook. The *Benjamin Bowring* was becoming quite a family ship. All in all the expedition was to witness seventeen marriages of its members to each other or to outsiders. One *Daily Mail* headline talked of 'The Love Boat'.

From Sydney we steamed north over the Equator to Los Angeles, where President Reagan had kindly agreed to open our trade exhibition. Sadly, someone took a shot at him just beforehand so he sent us a message instead, acclaiming our 'can-do' spirit.

Our final exhibition, in Vancouver, was completed on schedule and we followed the coastline north to the mouth of the Yukon River in Alaska.

If the ship had been able to continue north through the Bering Strait – between Russia's eastern tip and Alaska – she would have sailed on to the North Pole, over the top and back to England via Spitsbergen. But because the Arctic Ocean is full of moving ice the best the *Benjamin Bowring* could do was to drop Charlie and me overboard with two 12-foot long rubber boats in the Bering Strait, as close as she could get to the mouth of the Yukon.

Eight years earlier we had scheduled our arrival off the Yukon for the first week of June because, in a bad year, that is the latest time when the northern rivers shed their load of ice and become navigable. All being well we would now ascend the Yukon for 1,000 miles, then descend the Mackenzie River to its mouth in the Arctic Ocean at the Inuit settlement of Tuktoyaktuk. From there we would make a 3,000-mile dash east through the fabled North-West Passage and north up the Canadian archipelago to Ellesmere Island and Alert, our old stamping-ground. It was imperative to complete the entire boat journey from the Bering Strait to Alert within the three short summer months when the Arctic Ocean ice-pack should be at its loosest. We had to reach Alert by the end of September or risk being cut off by freezing seas and twenty-four-hour darkness.

Fewer than a dozen expeditions had ever successfully navigated this passage in either direction. Those few all used boats with protection from the elements and took an average of three years to get through, due to blockage by pack-ice en route.

The *Benjamin Bowring*'s skipper tried hard to close with the Yukon mouth but, when still fourteen miles away in heavy seas, the echo sounder showed only six to eight feet clearance below the hull, with a ten-knot offshore wind making the ship's position highly risky.

Our two twelve-foot dinghies slammed up and down in the lee of the ship as we loaded them. Bryn Campbell of *The Observer* was to accompany Charlie and me as far as Tuktoyaktuk and he clambered atop the fuel drums on Charlie's madly tossing boat. I experienced a sudden flashback to the very first day of that other Canadian boat journey, ten years before, when Bryn had come within an ace of drowning. Bryn's diary on leaving the *Benjamin Bowring*:

We waved until the ship was out of sight. Soon the waves were breaking over us, hitting us hard from behind. Often we were completely awash . . . As we watched Ran's boat pounded by the sea and disappearing in the ten-foot troughs, we had all too vivid an image of how vulnerable we were. I turned to talk to Charlie and saw him lifted bodily by a surge of water and thrown clean over my head. As the boat capsized, I tugged my feet free of the fuel lines and jumped as far away from the propeller as I could. Then the hull crashed down on me.

I was attempting to keep to a compass bearing despite the silt-laden water smashing on to my boat, stinging my eyes and covering the compass glass. At the top of a breaker I risked a quick glance backwards and to my horror saw Charlie's boat upside-down with no sign of either passenger.

It was a while before I could try to turn round. The secret of survival in such shallow riotous waters was to remain totally alert and keep the bow at all times into the next breaker. In just such rubber boats we had come safely through far worse conditions on the rivers of British Columbia. It was a matter of aim and balance. After a big wave, I whipped the tiller round and the boat sped through 180° in time to face the next attack. In a while I saw Charlie crawl on to his boat's bottom and then haul Bryn up by his hood. I breathed out with relief. They began to try to right their inflatable using the hull hand-grips, but they were too exhausted. I flung a rope across to Charlie but a wave ripped the line's fixture point away from my hull. With my propeller blades threshing only inches from their prancing rubber tubing, I flung the rope over again. Timing the arrival of the next big wave, we succeeded in flipping the boat back over. I slowly towed the stricken boat with its waterlogged outboard back towards the distant silhouette of our ship.

Charlie had lost only his rifle, but Bryn's cameras had sunk and he was decidedly unhappy. Overnight, back on the *Benjamin Bowring*, a Force Seven gale blew up and the hull began to strike the sea floor in the heavy swell. The skipper weighed anchor at once and we headed 200 miles north to another mouth of the Yukon, known as the Apoon Pass. With 120 miles to go and off a dangerous lee shore, one of the main tie-bolts – which hold the ship's engine in place – sheared. This had happened before and the engineers had only one set of replacement bolts. After eight hours of toil below decks and anxiety above, the engines restarted and we reached Apoon.

Seventy cold, wet miles in the inflatable boats followed before we came to the river village of Kotlik where we bedded down in the local gaol. The Kotlik sheriff warned us that the summer winds could turn certain stretches of the Yukon into no-go areas.

At Kravaksavak we joined the brown and powerful Kwikpak River, which is the main arm of the Yukon. The banks were thickly forested but we saw fox, bear and river birds. Continuing through half the moonlit night we covered 150 miles to the village of Marshall. The river then narrowed and for days we fought an eight-knot current.

Fifteen miles short of the village of Holy Cross we noticed dust-storms raging on both banks. With little warning the river erupted into a cauldron which caught us in mid-stream. Pine trees crashed down into the river and whole sections of the banks collapsed. The forest swayed towards the river, its upper canopy pressed flat by the force of the wind. There was no question of trying to land in such conditions. In mid-stream we battled through five-foot-high waves which followed one upon the other with hardly a breathing space for recovery. Once or twice my bows failed to rise from a plunge and the next wave swamped the boat. I thanked the Lord for positive buoyancy chambers. Then the river twisted to the east and the storm subsided. My long-nurtured idea of the Yukon as a gentle Thames-like river had been shattered. At Holy Cross, the keeper of the travel-lodge told us we were lucky to be alive. We had been travelling north, he said, in the first big southerly blow of the year, with winds exceeding seventy knots. Local river men stayed land-side on such days.

For long days of glare and heat we moved on across the face of Alaska towards Yukon Territory and the Canadian border. On 15 July we reached the only river-bridge anywhere from the sea to Dawson City, having boated over 1,000 river miles. Ginny and

Bothie met us in their Land Rover, on to which we lashed our deflated boats and gear. She drove us 500 kilometres up the recently opened Dempster Highway. Floods held us up for four days where this dirt highway was washed out but, a hundred miles from the sea, we reached the end of the road at Inuvik on the Mackenzie River.

Simon awaited us at Inuvik airstrip with a sixteen-foot open fibreglass whaler boat. Ex-Scots Greys Jack McConnell of the 1970 Headless Valley expedition, now a Canadian citizen, joined us for the journey to Tuktoyaktuk. He took the helm of Bryn's boat while the rest of us squeezed aboard the whaler and set out for the mouth of the Mackenzie.

The little whaler was a last-minute idea which had come to me back at Kotlik. I had used the sheriff's radio phone to ask Ginny to obtain one from a sponsor. Somehow she had, after phone calls to Hong Kong, London and New York, obtained the boat, outboards and a cargo plane flight from Vancouver to Inuvik, all free of charge. While we boated upriver she had worked at a motel outside Dawson as a waitress – in return for free telephone calls and a bedroom. Ginny was not just a pretty face and lovely legs.

On the afternoon of 24 July, back on our tight schedule, we entered the harbour of Tuktoyaktuk in the North-West Passage. Jack and Bryn flew south. Ginny and Simon set up a radio base and Charlie and I loaded the whaler for our 3,000-mile journey through the passage.

Worried about navigation, I visited a local barge skipper with sixteen years of experience. I was planning to navigate the passage by magnetic hand compass plus my watch and the sun. The skipper said simply, 'You are mad.'

'But I have good charts and a hand-made balanced prismatic compass,' I assured him.

'Throw it away,' he muttered.

'What do you use?' I asked him.

He pointed at his sturdy barge-towing tug. 'She has everything. She goes in the dark, out in the deep channels. Radar beacon responders, MF and DF, the works.' He shook his head dismissively. 'You must hug the coastline to escape storms so you will hit shoals, thousands of shoals. Also you cannot go across deep bays for fear of wind and big waves so you must hug the coastline which is like crazy pavement. You have to use more gas and take extra days. Most of the time there will be thick fog. No sun means you use your compass. Yes?'

I nodded.

He flung his hands up. 'Ah, but you cannot use a compass. Look . . .' He prodded his desk chart of the passage and I saw the heavily printed warning 'MAGNETIC COMPASS USELESS IN THIS AREA'.

'Too near the magnetic Pole, you see. You stay here in Tuk. Have a holiday.'

On 26 July we headed out into the choppy bay of Tuktoyaktuk. In thirty-five days we must not only complete the 3,000 miles of the passage, which traditionally takes three years, but also cover an additional 500 miles further north, attaining some point within skiing distance of our intended winter quarters at Alert before the sea froze, forcing us to abandon the whaler.

Four or five isolated Inuit settlements and eight Defence Early Warning camps were the sole inhabited points along our route. Five years previously I had set up a complex arrangement with the air company which supplied the bases, to take our ration boxes and fuel cans to these outlying sites. To cover the intermediate distances was just possible (given the maximum fuel load capacity of our whaler), providing I made no navigating errors en route.

The coastline, on leaving Tuktoyaktuk, was flat as a board and quite invisible whenever shallow water forced us out to sea. The treeless tundra of the Tuk Peninsula might just as well not have been there. Fortunately the sun was out to give us direction, so we headed due east until the glint of breakers off Cape Dalhousie showed like silver froth on the horizon. A conical hill, or pingo, stood proud from the otherwise unseen coastline, giving me a rough indicator of our position.

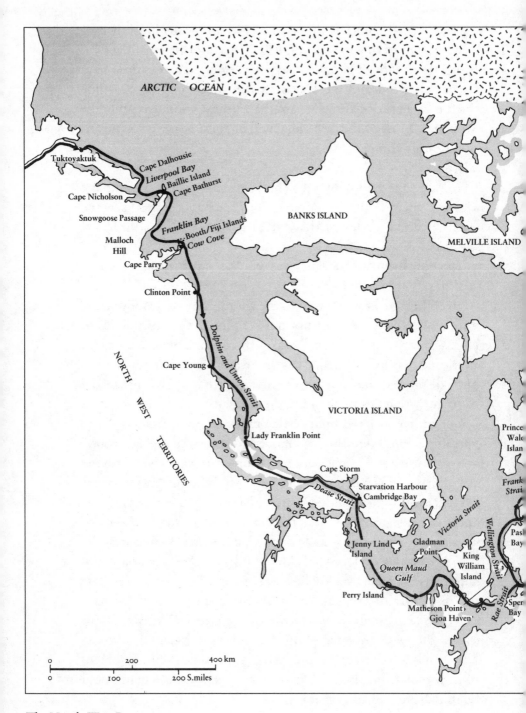

The North-West Passage

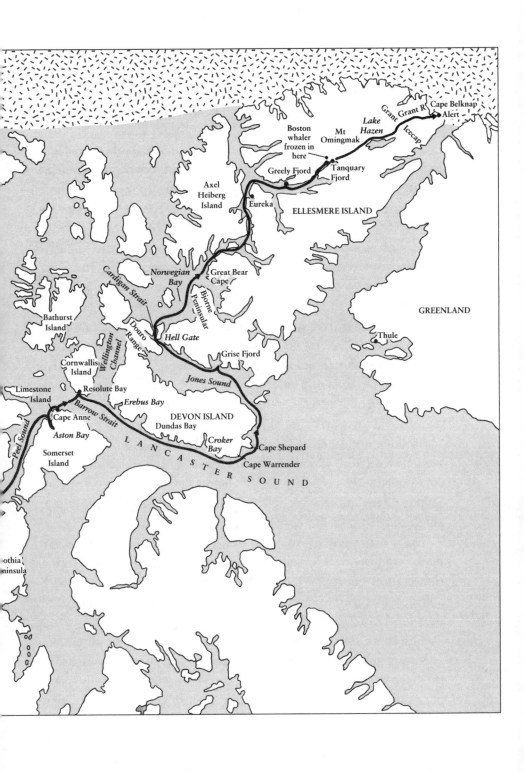

East of the cape we bucked forty miles through a rising sea which soaked us anew at every crest. A flat tongue of shingle south of Baillie Island was the cache-point agreed a year previously with a government helicopter pilot, then in the area, for two drums of fuel.

The sea was too rough on both sides of the spit to allow a beaching. So Charlie dropped our light anchor overboard and I waded through the surf, back and forth with twelve jerry cans. Three hours later, re-fuelled, we entered Snowgoose Passage via a vicious tide-rip toothed by shoals. Once in Franklin Bay the full force of wind and wave struck us and for fifty miles we ran the gauntlet between fourteen-foot breakers and the wave-pounded cliffs to our west. We were soaked and our teeth chattered in unison. Each wave that broke over the whaler showered us. Salt-water poured down the neck-holes of our survival suits, running down back and chest and legs to collect in slowly rising pools inside our waterproof boots. Our underclothes were salty and sodden. Time and again we were forced to swing off our course to face into rolling waves which raced at us from the flank. Once the boat hung almost on its side as a green wall of water surged by in a rush of power.

As dusk approached I saw fires ahead and, an hour later, we passed a section of low cliffs wherein the mineral components smouldered and gave off an acrid chemical odour. Dante's Inferno. Sulphur deposits glowing red and yellow, for ever burning. Yellow smoke curled up from deep rock crevices.

The storm grew in intensity but, by a piece of good luck, we penetrated the beach breakers via a ten-foot-wide channel into a tiny lagoon beneath Malloch Hill. Next morning, shaking with cold, we marched up and down the beach in our wet clothes until the blood ran again. Then we set out east into thick mist.

'Surely we should head further to the right?' Charlie shouted.

Knowing how easy it is to be tempted to distrust the compass at the best of times, I closed my mind to his suggestion: 'The compass says this way,' I shouted back, 'so just keep aiming for that darker patch of sky.'

I had a local error of 43° set on the compass, with five more degrees added to cope with the effect of the boat's engine and metal fittings. How great the magnetic Pole's influence was I could not tell but I had, over twenty years of navigating, developed a certain faith in the compass.

To our great relief, after two hours of nothingness and our first chunks of floating ice, Rabbit Island loomed close ahead and, an hour later, we stopped in Cow Cove, a leeward beach. A flat stretch a hundred metres from the beach-anchored boat provided our camp spot. The next morning we returned with our camp-kit to the boat to find the wind had boxed through 180° and the whaler, now on an unprotected shore, was full of water and being pounded by breakers.

For two days we drained the fuel system and dried our gear; then, in a twenty-knot wind and the usual fog, we entered the narrows of Dolphin and Union Strait. For thirty-six hours without a break we ploughed east. We grew very tired and had to shout and sing to force our brains to stay alert. We determined not to stop, for there was no beach with a stitch of cover from the surf. The evenings, when the mists rolled back, were full of wild beauty which faded from red dusk to purple dawn with no darkness between. But winter menaced us unseen like some Damoclean sword. Already the sun at midnight caressed the silent surface of the sea.

For 340 miles we stood in the narrow bucking space between helm and fuel cans until at last, dodging a rash of inlets, we crossed a narrow channel to Victoria Island and left the mainland coast for the first time. We spent the night at Lady Franklin where I set up the radio. Ginny came through clearly from Tuktoyaktuk. She and Simon were watching live coverage of Prince Charles's wedding. The previous night a storm had sunk many of the local Inuit boats, complete with outboard engines and fishing gear, so she had been worried about us.

Over the next four days we were delayed by outboard troubles 130 miles east of Lady Franklin but limped on through rain and high winds. Wild storms lashed our passage across the mouths of bays, one wider than the English Channel, and past forlorn capes of twisted red lava domes. There was no shelter, no landing beach until we reached Cambridge Bay Inuit settlement.

Because Ginny was losing radio contact with us, she and Simon moved their base to Resolute Bay on Cornwallis Island. On their way north they had stopped in at Cambridge Bay and I noticed a black dog, smaller than Bothie, in Ginny's kit-bag.

'What,' I asked, 'is this?'

'Ah,' she said. 'This is Tugaluk. Two months old and a good dog.'

'Whose is she?' I pressed. Ginny blustered and I knew she was feeling maternal. If she had left the dog in Tuktoyaktuk, she said, it would have been shot as a stray. Bothie had fallen in love, she added, but he would doubtless get over it in Resolute and then Ginny would give the puppy to a new owner. The matter was closed, Ginny was clearly intimating, but the very fact that she had given the dog a name struck me as sinister.

Ginny and the others flew on and, a day later, we too left Cambridge Bay.

Originally I had planned to strike east across Queen Maud Gulf by way of Jenny Lind Island, but a tongue of pack-ice had recently slid down in a northerly wind and blocked off this entire route, so we detoured south an extra 200 miles to creep around the pack. The navigation was complex and only possible with total concentration. All day a mist obscured the coastline. We passed through corridors between nameless islands filled with shoals where the sea boiled between gaunt stacks of dripping rock. Hour after hour I strained my eyes through the misty glare to recognise some feature but there were islands of all shapes and sizes and the coastline was so heavily indented with fjords, bays and islets that the fog made it easy to mistake a through-channel for a dangerous cul-de-sac.

After 130 miles of nerve-racking progress between these shoals, a storm came at us from the west and threw great rolling waves over the reefs. I deemed it too risky to continue and we camped on

Perry Island in a sheltered cove. After twenty-four hours the storm showed signs of abating so, impatient, we ploughed on east for ten hours, often out of sight of land.

Since the compass was useless and the sun made no appearance all day I kept my nose glued to the charts. At dusk the storm renewed its attack and we plunged through cresting breakers. I prayed we would not strike a reef in the dark.

Close to midnight, a break in the cloudbanks revealed a low gap along the dim silhouette of the cliff-line. Nosing inland, we were rewarded with a sheltered islet where we spent the remaining four hours until dawn. We shivered uncontrollably in the tent and agreed to broach a bottle of whisky. By dawn the bottle was empty and we were shivering less.

With the first streaks of eastern light we squelched back into the survival suits, our thighs red-raw from the long days of salty chafing. For nineteen hours we weaved our way through innumerable gravel islands, a task made easier when the sun decided to show itself weakly through the post-storm haze.

At Gjoa Haven settlement, the Inuit warned us that pack-ice blocked the Humboldt Channel and the Wellington Strait to the north, my planned route, and we would be crazy to attempt to travel to Resolute Bay without first calling at the last Inuit settlement in the region, Spence Bay, to hire boat guides. I eagerly concurred and, after crossing Rae Strait in fine weather, we entered Spence Bay – the halfway point on our voyage to Alert.

Here we obtained the services of an Inuit hunter with an unrivalled knowledge of the area. He was accompanied by the local Mountie and three Inuit boatmen. We followed our guides whose boats, like ours, were some sixteen feet long and outboard-powered. An hour or two north of Spence Bay the Inuit turned inland and shelved their craft on a beach. We hovered offshore. 'What's wrong?' I shouted.

'There's a storm coming,' the Mountie shouted, 'a bad one. Our friends will go no further and advise you to stop here or head back to the village.'

The sky looked clear and my overall fear of winter catching us in the passage overrode any suspicion that the Inuit might be right. I was also suffering from the delusion that I knew better than the Inuit. There was no apparent danger, so why waste precious time?

For a hundred miles we moved north until the storm caught us. The coastline was not blessed with a single nook or cove where we could seek shelter. Committed, and caught between heavy pack-ice and a hostile lee shore, we had no choice but to struggle on. After six hours of drenching with ice-cold water our eyes were inflamed and our fingers ached with cold. Thankfully, we reached a keyhole-cove named Parsley Bay and turned east – directly away from the wind – to gain shelter.

But the next two miles proved the wisdom of the Inuit and only luck saved us from a watery end. The bay was a boat-trap. Waves followed one another, steep and close, so that our bows plunged off one six-foot wall, down its front and into, not over, the next. The whaler was awash. Waves smashed on to the prow and filled the cockpit. Visibility was difficult. As soon as we opened our salt-filled eyes, more water would cascade over our heads. Surf pounded against the beach when we finally made the crossing, but we located the mouth of a small river and the boat was flung into the safety of its estuary on a surge of flying foam. Next day the sea was down to an angry but manageable swell outside the bay and we clung to the coastline to avoid the ever-increasing presence of ice.

A day later, some miles past the vertiginous cliffs of Limestone Island, a strong northerly wind sprang up and set the entire ice-pack of Barrow Strait on the move. It became painfully obvious that, inching along a north-facing coastline with no likely place of shelter, we stood in grave danger of being crushed. Much to Charlie's annoyance I decided to retreat until conditions were safer. This involved back-tracking twenty miles to a shallow bay for protection.

On the morning of our third day in this cove a skein of new ice sheened the surface of the bay, a nasty reminder of the approaching freeze-up. Next day the wind changed and we threaded our way out of the cove, now all but beset by crowding bergs. Later we crossed Barrow Strait, forty miles wide, and nudged past pack-ice into the cove of Resolute Bay, capital city of the archipelago.

Resolute is home to over 200 Inuit and a number of transient Canadians, mostly technicians and scientists. Ginny was housed in a tiny shack with her radio beside her bunk, Simon lived in the main scientists' accommodation. The black dog from Tuktoyaktuk had grown to almost twice Bothie's size and Ginny was plainly infatuated. Our boating outlook from Resolute to Alert, Ginny warned us, looked bleak. In a week or so the sea would almost certainly undergo a general freeze-up, stranding us *in situ*.

The Resolute meteorological station commander proved to me by way of his ice-charts that we were all but blocked into Resolute for the year. The strait east of Bathurst Island was frozen, as was the northern end of Lancaster Sound. All routes to the west and north-west were already solidly iced. We could still attempt a 600-mile detour round Devon Island but its eastern coast was storm-bound and a maze of icebergs. I thanked him and opted for the last course through lack of a positive alternative.

For four days our whaler, very nearly crushed in one overnight ice-surge, was blocked inside Resolute Bay. Then, on 25 August, a southerly wind allowed us to escape east along the coastline of Cornwallis Island. The seas were rough and high for hundreds of miles and the coast to our north was either teetering cliff or glacier, pounding surf or disintegrating icebergs. With over 1,000 miles to Alert and under a week before freeze-up, we slept little.

With high waves breaking violently upon icebergs all about us, we were caught ten miles short of any shelter at nightfall. Two propeller blades broke against chunks of growler ice. Straining my eyes up at the mountain tops silhouetted against the moonless night sky was not easy, for the boat bucked and danced in the waves. Charlie fought the tiller to avoid icebergs visible only at the last moment. By weak torch battery and wet chart I guessed at the location of Dundas Bay and we nosed cautiously past cliffs against which waves smashed twenty feet high, luminous in the darkness. The mouth of the bay was crammed with grinding bergs and only lack of choice made us risk pressing on. Once past the outer ring of clashing icebergs a huge swell took over from the breakers. Soaked to the skin and numb-handed, we secured the boat between two grounded bergs and camped in a long-deserted Inuit hut. For an hour before sleeping we let the tension unwind as we lay on the floor propped up by our elbows, sipping tea by candlelight and chatting of Army days long ago in Arabia. Charlie's not such a bad old sod after all, I thought to myself.

The next five days are etched on my memory. I remember a blur of danger, a race against the dropping thermometer and constant cold. The nastier the elements, the further the natural barrier of restraint between Charlie and me dissipated. Our latent antagonism disappeared altogether once the predicament of the moment entered the danger level and became positively unpleasant.

Glacial valleys draining enormous ice-fields created bergs larger than cathedrals, which sailed seaborne from their dark spawning valleys to collect off the coast. Battered ceaselessly by waves containing broken ice-chunks, these bergs disintegrated bit by bit. A course running parallel to the cliffs and mere yards offshore seemed the least dangerous.

Waves smashed against cliffs and icebergs in a welter of thundering surf. Our port propeller's shearpin split against a growler, a half-submerged chunk of ice, entailing a repair job only possible at anchor. We prayed the second engine would keep going or we would soon be fibreglass matchwood, ground to pieces by rock or ice.

Eventually we found a deep inlet between cliffs. At the only possible landing point a large polar bear sat watching us, so we stopped in rocky shallows and fought to steady the craft among basking beluga whales. I stood in the sea holding the stern as still as I could while Charlie worked as fast as he could on the propeller. The bear dived into the sea and swam around us. We kept the rifle to hand but only the animal's nose and eyes remained above water as it swam.

After 300 miles we rounded the north-eastern tip of Devon Island and aimed across Jones Sound for Ellesmere Island. At Grise Fjord, the most northerly Inuit village in Canada, we beached the boat in a safe cove and rested for twenty-four hours. Our skin was the texture of etiolated bacon, our faces burned dark by the wind and the glare. We had lost a good deal of weight and various parts of our bodies, especially our crutches, thighs and armpits, were suffering from open sores and boils. The sea was due to freeze over in two or three days, should the winds drop and flatten the water.

Back in Resolute, Ginny, fully aware of the dangers of Devon Island's east coast, had awaited my radio call for twenty-eight hours. At Grise Fjord I fixed up an antenna between Inuit drying frames and, although her voice sounded faint and faraway, I could detect Ginny's happiness that we had reached Ellesmere Island.

With forty-eight hours to go and 500 sea miles to cover to the most northerly point we could hope to reach, Tanquary Fjord, we slid into our damp survival suits after emptying the last of our foot powder down the leggings.

The journey to Hell's Gate Channel was a blur of black cliff, freezing spray and increasing pack-ice. The channel was blocked with bergy bits but, through good fortune, the only alternative corridor, Cardigan Strait, was partially open and we edged into it beneath the great mountains which guard the western gateway of Jones Sound.

The long detour had paid off, but that same evening the surface of the sea began to freeze, congealing silently and quickly. Twenty miles south of Great Bear Cape we were caught between pack-ice and newly forming frazil ice, a paper-thin crystalline cover.

Forcing our way back south through the new crust, we spent an anxious night camped at the edge of Norwegian Bay and Ginny promised to obtain aerial guidance if she could. At noon on 29 August, Russ Bomberry, a Mohawk chief and one of the best bush pilots in the Arctic, flew his Twin Otter overhead for two hours to guide us, by a labyrinthine route, through sixty miles of loose pack to Great Bear Cape. When Russ flew away back to Resolute, we broached our last bottle of whisky. We slept five hours over the next two days and prayed for once that the wind would continue to blow. It did and the surface grease ice did not settle thickly enough to prevent us ascending Greely Fjord, Canon Fjord and finally the dark narrows of Tanquary Fjord, a cul-de-sac deep within glacier-cut mountains.

Tiers of snow-capped peaks rimmed the winter sky as we snaked into a twilit world of silence. Wolves stared from shadowed lava beaches but nothing moved except ourselves to sunder in our wash the mirror images of the darkened valley walls. Twelve minutes before midnight on 30 August we came to the end of the fjord. The sea journey was over. Within a week the seas behind and all about us were frozen.

Alert camp lay 150 miles to the north-east of Tanquary Fjord. With the temperature dropping daily and sunlight hours fleeing over the polar horizon, we needed to reach Alert within three weeks. The eastern heights of the main United States Range and the Grant Ice-cap block a straightforward overland route. We planned to use skis and snowshoes, rucksacks and light fibreglass sledges to cross the ice barrier, carrying fourteen days' food and cooking fuel from Tanquary Fjord where we abandoned the boat.

Charlie carried his bear-gun and I packed a .44 Ruger revolver into my eighty-pound rucksack. We followed a series of riverain valleys, trudging slowly, for we were weak from the months of boat travel and many salt-chafed sores that rubbed as we walked. In one narrow valley a huge ice-tongue, an offshoot from the ice-cap, tumbled into the canyon blocking our advance. Summer floods had cut a long tunnel through this icy barrier so, with heads bent and rucksacks dragged, we crept underneath the glacier and through the dripping culvert.

Charlie slipped on ice and his forehead struck a rock. Hearing him shout, I dropped my pack and ran back, thinking a bear had attacked him. Blood filled one of his eyes and covered one side of his face and neck. He felt sick and faint. An hour later, bandaged and dizzy, he carried on. That night we checked his feet and found broken, weeping blisters covering both his soles and most of his toes. He said he ached all over.

Charlie and I seldom walked together. Sometimes we were separated by an hour or more. In a film made later of the expedition, Charlie said: 'Ran is always pushing himself. He can't do it the easy way. I don't know what drives him but he always pushes himself. I'm not that way inclined. I'm a slow plodder. If I tried to keep up with him, I wasn't going to make it.'

Each time I stopped to wait for Charlie, I became cold and impatient and swore at him. If I had moved at his pace I could have avoided this, and I did try once or twice to do so. But I just could not maintain such a desultory amble.

On the third morning ice crystals lined our tent, although we were merely 1,000 feet above sea-level. Snow covered the land and walking was difficult. Skis were not practical due to long stretches of ice and rock. Charlie's left eye was quite closed and puffed up like a yellow fungus. His back and his knees and his blistered feet all hurt him. The blister wounds had gone septic and walking must have been purgatory for him.

In mid-September we passed Omingmak Mountain and Charlie could go no further without a rest. His groin glands were swollen with poison and his knees with fluid. But winter was coming and I urged him to keep going, for we had to complete the journey over the high ice-caps before polar sundown. There seemed little point anyway in waiting for new skin to replace the open sores on Charlie's feet since the first few miles on snowshoes would soon re-open them.

We emptied the contents of our rucksacks on to our light portable sledges and, strapping on snowshoes, set out in a cuttingly cold wind. The temperature fell to −18°C as we passed Lake Hazen. North of the lake I tried to follow a bearing of 130° but the compass was sluggish. Musk-oxen snorted and stampeded as we loomed through the freezing fog.

There were no distinguishing landmarks. At 2,200 feet above

sea-level we camped in a frozen gulley at –20°C, a temperature which remained steady for three days' hauling through deep snow-fields where the stillness was immense. No musk-oxen now. Nothing and nobody.

Over the rim of the Grant Ice-cap, spurred on by increasing cold, we limped at last to the edge of the high plateau beneath the twin glaciers of Mount Wood, dwarfed by the blue ice-falls which rose to the sky. A wary hush presided below these 2,000-foot ice-formations. A cataclysmic event seemed imminent. Craning my neck back to ease my knotted shoulder muscles, I glanced up and felt momentary unease as the sky-high ice-falls above seemed to teeter on the verge of collapse.

Towards dusk we found the narrow entry-point to the upper canyon of Grant River, a winding ravine that falls thirty miles to the sea. The canyon kinked, snaked and was blocked by black boulders, so that often we manhandled the sledges over solid rock for hundreds of yards.

On 26 September, towards noon, the river-bed plunged thirty feet down a frozen waterfall. From the top of this cleft we could see the Arctic Ocean, a jagged vista of contorted pack-ice stretching away to the polar horizon. Nine hours' travel along the edge of the frozen sea, dreaming of warmth and comfort, brought us to Cape Belknap and, by dusk, to the four little huts that we knew so well, the most northern habitation on earth.

We had travelled around the polar axis of the world for 314° of latitude in 750 days. Only 46° to go but, looking north at the chaotic ice-rubble and remembering our failure in 1978, we knew that the journey to date had been easy compared with what lay ahead.

Five days before our arrival at Alert, Ginny had flown in with winter equipment, our old Antarctic skidoos and the two dogs. The three of us spent the next four months of permanent darkness in the Alert huts preparing equipment, completing a new series of scientific research tasks and training on the local pack-ice.

In mid-January the Alert met-man warned me that his sea-ice recordings showed a thickness of 87cm, thinner than that of any previous January on record, the average being 105cm. The true cold, which crackles the nose and ears like parchment, congeals the blood in fingers and toes like rapidly setting glue and fixes the sea-ice slowly into a precarious platform to the Pole, finally came in late January. Better late than never. The camp thermometer hovered around −51°C with a fresh ten-knot breeze. One night a fox outside the hut awoke me and I noticed Ginny's hot-water bottle lying in between her bed-sock'd feet – frozen solid.

We received a radio message from a Californian friend. Walt Pedersen, the American aiming to reach both Poles, had given up his impending attempt on the South Pole due to stonewalling by the US National Science Foundation. We could still become the first people in history to reach both Poles. Prince Charles radioed through to Ginny and mentioned that he had heard rumours of a Norwegian team racing us to cross the Arctic. 'No racing,' he said to me with a stern edge to his voice.

By the last day of January I must decide when to set out to cross the Arctic. To start prior to the first appearance of the sun would be to lay myself open to accusations of irresponsibility. On the other hand it was imperative that we reach the North Pole before the annual summer break-up. Once at the Pole we would at least be in the zone of currents which float their ice-cover in the general direction of Spitsbergen or Russia. If we delayed our departure from Alert until after sun-up in March, as in 1977, we would again risk falling short of our target. Whenever we set out we could not be certain that success was attainable, for the simple reason that no man had ever crossed the Arctic Ocean in a single season.

On 13 February 1982 I said a quick goodbye to Ginny. We had spent the previous night in our hut closing our minds bit by bit to reality. Over the years we had found it better that way. The wrench of departure was worse than in Antarctica for we both knew the southern crossing was a mere nursery slope compared with the Arctic.

The weather was clear, although the day was as dark as night, when we pulled away from the huts. I glanced back and saw Ginny clutching her two dogs closely and looking up at the passage of darkness by which we had left.

Charlie and I sat astride the open, heavily laden skidoos, each towing 600 pounds of fuel and gear. Our beards and eyelashes were ice-laden within minutes, for the chill factor was −90°C when stationary, increasing with the speed of our advance. We followed a wild zigzag way along the dark and ice-girt coast. I remembered the 1977 travels which helped me not to get lost, although that year we had of course travelled in daylight. Crossing a high pass somewhere on the Fielden Peninsula, Charlie turned his sledge over on a steep slope above sheer cliffs. He managed to extricate himself some yards from a long drop into the dark.

On 17 February we came in twilight to a canal of newly open water from which emanated dark clouds of frost-smoke. In the depths of winter, long before sunrise and at a point of maximum coastal pressure, this was an ominous sign. We had not expected open water so early. With extra care we skirted the canal and entered a narrow corridor of blue ice, emerging a short distance east of Cape Columbia, that coastal point off which the southerly sea currents split west and east. This makes the cape a sensible jumping-off point from land-ice to sea-ice. After axing ourselves a ramp of ice-blocks we took the skidoos for a twenty-foot slide over the tide-crack. We were now 'afloat' at sea.

We camped 300 yards out from the coast in a field of broken ice. In a way I was glad of the darkness for it prevented a wider and therefore more depressing view of our route north. I pressed a mitt to the raw end of my nose and was silent as a host of vignettes flooded my mind, memories of what had passed last time we tried to pit our wits against the power of the Arctic pack. We had learned a lot of lessons then about what not to do.

During the first day of twilit labour with our axes we cleared 800 yards of highway through the pressure rubble. Our axed lane was precisely the width of a skidoo and it followed the line of least

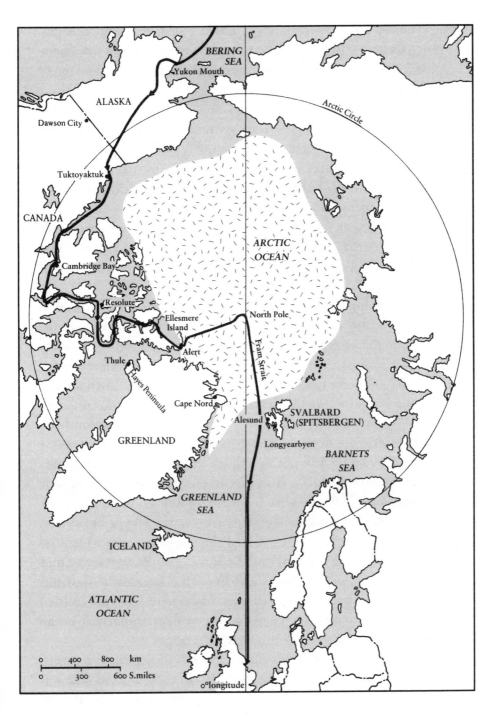

The Transglobe Expedition's route across the Arctic

resistance, which unfortunately added 75 per cent of extra distance to the straight course we would have taken were it not for obstacles. To gain the Pole we must cover 825 miles – then much further again on its far side to reach a potential rendezvous point with the ship.

There were two dangers: failure to reach the Pole – and therefore the Spitsbergen current – by summer floe break-up time, and the subsequent worry of failing to reach the *Benjamin Bowring* before the end of summer when the ship must retreat to more southerly waters. We could not hope to achieve either goal without air re-supply with food and cooker fuel from the Twin Otter which was to fly out from England with Gerry Nicholson and a skilled Arctic pilot called Karl Z'berg, a Swiss Canadian who had flown our chartered Otter in 1977.

We axed our skidoo lane through 200 yards of twelve-foot-high ice-blocks. Damage to equipment was inevitable as the only way to negotiate the switchback lane was at full tilt, bouncing off walls and over iron-hard slabs. On 19 February my drive axle snapped. That did it: I determined to switch to manpower and abandon the skidoos – at least for the first hundred miles where the pressure rubble would be at its worst.

The previous winter at Alert, preparing for this eventuality, I had tested two lightweight eight-foot-long manhaul pulks and it was with these fibreglass sledges, carrying 190 pounds each, that we pushed north on 22 February. After eight hours of haulage, our underwear, socks, facemasks and jackets were soaking wet or frozen, depending on which part of the body they covered and on whether we were resting or pulling at the time. But, by the end of four dark days, we had logged eleven northerly miles. This would not sound very impressive except to someone who has also pulled a load in excess of his own bodyweight over pressure rubble in the dark and at a temperature of −40°C.

Charlie plodded on at his own pace and, unable to slow down, I stopped every hour for twenty minutes or more for him to catch up. I attempted to avoid freezing solid during these long waits by cursing the Arctic in general and Charlie in particular. Sheer exhaustion overcame any fear of bears or indeed of falling into the sea.

Charlie and I saved time daily by never cooking breakfast. We merely drank a mug of coffee from our vacuum flask, heated the night before. This gave us the courage to unzip our bags and climb into our frosted clothes and boots. For seven months we were to remain in precisely the same clothing without washing.

We dragged behind us, man for man, the same weight as Scott and his team. Their aim was to be first to reach the South Pole, ours was to be first to reach both Poles. Like them, we were racing the clock. On 3 March, at −49°C, the blood-red ball of the sun slid briefly along the rim of the sea. Sunlight, although welcome to improve visibility, was our number-one enemy. Ultraviolet rays would now begin to eat at the structure of the pack-ice and, by mid-April, so weaken the ice that the least pressure from the wind would crack up the floes and halt our progress.

At 4.00 a.m. on 4 March, at −40°C, a fire broke out in our stores hut back at Alert. Ginny rushed out with an extinguisher but, 'It was just one big fireball inside with smoke issuing from the seams in the walls and flames filling the windows . . . There were forty-five gallon drums of fuel stacked by the wall. They had been there for years and were frozen into the ice.' While they watched, eight drums of gasoline exploded, as did fusillades of rocket flares and 7.62 FN rifle bullets.

Until that point the world's press had ignored the expedition. Now newspapers and television screens all over the world carried headlines such as 'Conflagration at Polar Base' and 'Polar Expedition in Flames'. After the night of the fire every action we took – and one or two that we didn't – became news from London to Sydney, from Cape Town to Vancouver.

Seven years beforehand Ginny had argued that I should lay an equipment cache at Tanquary Fjord as well as at Alert – just in case. With the generous help of the Canadian Coastguard's ice-breaker two years before, we had done so. This meant that the expedition need not now be abandoned. Spare radios, generators, ice rations and skidoo gear were available for our Twin Otter to collect from Tanquary as soon as the weather allowed. I made a mental note to tell Ginny once again she was not just a pretty face.

With enough food for eight days we digested the news of the fire – about which we could do nothing – and concentrated on northerly progress, yard by painful yard. Our shoulders and hips were raw from the rub of the pulk harnesses. My nose, weeping blood and fluid for the last two weeks, was now frost-nipped as well. The rough and frozen material of my facemask chafed the wound and I could no longer wipe away nose-dribble with the back of my mitts, so a sheen of ice, constantly growing in size, covered the bottom half of my facemask, punctured only by the small hole over my mouth.

At night the act of breathing caused the worst discomfort. Generally speaking, polar travel would be quite pleasant if it was not necessary to breathe. When we tried to snuggle down inside our sleeping bags, our breath formed a thick rime of frost where it met cold air. The resulting frost layers cascaded down our necks whenever we moved. To avoid this I blocked both nostrils up with plugs of Kleenex and tried to position my mouth to breathe out of the bag's hood-hole. This worked well except that my frostbitten nose remained outside the bag's warmth and, unprotected from the tent's average temperature of –40°C, was far colder than a deep-freeze.

A storm blew up and shattered the ice-pack. All about us were vast areas of open sea where, for at least the next two months, the ice should have remained largely solid. On the coast behind us, the five-man expedition of our Norwegian rival Ragnar Thorsketh, which had announced its intention to beat us across the Arctic, were astonished to find open sea and no ice at all in sight. They made camp on the land and waited.

Simon and Karl Z'berg located the two skidoos we had abandoned along the coastline and managed to land the Twin Otter beside them. Later they delivered the skidoos and steel sledges to us on a flat floe. Overjoyed at shrugging off the harnesses, we continued by skidoo and were blessed by a patch of good going.

Still travelling at dusk, I swerved to avoid a sudden canal and drove straight into a trench full of *shuga* porridge-ice. I was flung clear and watched my skidoo sink out of sight within a minute. The steel sledge slowly up-ended but I caught hold of its lashing strap. Charlie ran over in response to my yelling. He attempted to save our tent by removing his mitts in order to undo a lashing buckle. In seconds his fingers began to freeze and, before we could loosen the tent, the sledge disappeared underwater. We saved only our radio and theodolite.

Charlie's hands were in immediate danger. I erected a makeshift shelter from the tarpaulin with which Charlie used to cover the vehicles and started up the cooker. He spent an hour forcing blood slowly back into his hand and so saved his fingers from anything worse than painfully nipped ends. We passed an extremely uncomfortable night at −40°C under the tarpaulin with one sleeping bag between us.

Two days later Karl found a landing floe half a mile from our location and brought in a skidoo, sledge and gear from Tanquary Fjord. 'Don't sink any more skidoos,' he advised. 'That's your last.'

Forty-knot winds battered the pack and we headed north in a semi-white-out. With no visible sun, I followed my compass needle.

On 16 March, with millions of tons of ice on the move all about us, we camped and lay listening to the awe-inspiring boom and crackle of invading floes. The anemometer rose to fifty-five knots and weaker pans fractured all about us, nipped and flaked by their larger jostling neighbours. One crack opened up twenty yards from our tent and cut us off on an island for a day.

Ginny warned me that the press were turning critical. In England the *Daily Mail* stated that the Transglobe sponsors were considering finding a new leader since our chances of success were looking bad. One reporter interviewed the cameraman on our 1970 Canadian expedition, who said the soldiers on that journey had mutinied and threatened me with knives. In Vancouver, a reporter pointed out that SAS members Fiennes and Burton had cleverly cut themselves off in the Arctic beyond all possible recall by their regiment for service in the Falkland Islands war which was raging at the time.

When the storm died away we packed up in conditions of total white-out and moved off into a curtain of brown gloom, a certain sign of open water. Within minutes I narrowly missed driving into the edge of a river of moving sludge. Charlie and I took a deep breath and spent two perilous days pussy-footing through a sludge swamp, often crossing lakes of half-inch-thick ice which writhed under our skidoos and broke under the sharp runners of the sledges. God was good to us on both days. The next two days passed by in a haze. We pushed on our bruised bodies and mutinous minds and craved more sleep.

My chin was numb one evening when I came into the tent. I must have pulled my frozen facemask off too hard. When thawing the garment out over the cooker and picking ice-bits from around the mouthpiece, I found a one-inch swatch of my beard complete with skin implanted in a bloody patch of iced wool. It took a while to detach this from the mask. Where the skin had torn away from my chin, there was an open patch of raw flesh the size of a penny. In a while my chin warmed up and bled. Then it wept liquid matter which froze once the cooker was turned off.

On 22 March I shot the sun with my theodolite and found the loose pack had drifted us many miles too far east. I applied a 15° westerly correction and we moved on at a good rate. My chin throbbed like a tom-tom by nightfall and, running out of antibiotic cream, I applied some pile cream.

'He's got piles on his chin,' Charlie shrieked with mirth. It was lucky we shared a weird sense of humour. Unlike during the latter part of our Antarctic crossing, there was now no tension between us. I hugely respected and admired his ability to suffer and keep going.

For a week we averaged fifteen miles a day, sometimes travelling for sixteen hours at a time in what we called a double-shuffle.

Charlie was frostnipped along the length of his nose and one of my eyelids puffed up with wind-burn. Navigation was becoming more or less instinctive, with or without the sun.

A memorably evil day was 29 March, during which we pushed to the limits of skidoo travel. Streamers of brown vapour wafted through the overall fog and soft squeaking, grinding sounds emanated from the moving sludge banks we passed. To check each apparently weak section, before charging it on my skidoo, I went ahead gingerly on foot with my ice-prod. Charlie advanced halfway between me and the sledges, calling from time to time when I lost sight of him in the gloom.

When we made it at last to solid ice I felt elated. If we can cross that, I thought, we can go anywhere. We stopped at 87°02', within nine miles of our most northerly camp in 1977 but forty days earlier in the season. If our aim had been solely to reach the Pole we could have felt reasonably confident.

As we crept north in early April the movement and noise of the floes increased. It seemed as though we were rushing pell-mell, caught in an unseen tidal race, towards the maw of the world, Poe's maelstrom. For three days the troubled fissure zone of the convergence, the area where the Beaufort Gyral current ends, slowed us to a crawl. For some time we crossed a no-man's-land where floes spun around in limbo, uncertain which way to go. Then the fringe of the transpolar drift began to take hold of all surface matter and we entered a new gyral with a strong north-easterly pull. A great deal of rubble was piled up in pyramidal heaps within this convergence and at 87°48' North we were stopped by the bulkiest wall I had ever seen in the Arctic. Rising to thirty feet high, the barrier was well over 100 yards wide. It took us four hours to axe and four to cross.

After the convergence we entered a sixty-mile region of fissures and high barriers. On 8 April we crossed sixty-two sludge cracks, often by shovelling snow into the water and then ramming the resulting weak bridge before it sank.

Twenty miles short of the Pole the going improved dramatically. At mid-day on 10 April I carefully checked our noon latitude and each subsequent mile until we were at 90° North. I had no wish to overshoot the top of the world. We arrived there at 11.30 p.m. GMT and passed the news to Ginny early on Easter Day 1982. We had become the first men in the world to have travelled the earth's surface to both Poles.

Apprehension about what lay ahead overshadowed any sense of achievement that we may otherwise have felt, for the *Benjamin Bowring* was still many cold months beyond our horizon.

I aimed south along a line some 15° east of the Greenwich Meridian. We changed to a routine of travel by night and sleep by day so that the sun would project my body's shadow ahead and prove a natural sundial.

As we left the Pole, the Transglobe crew steamed from Southampton harbour en route for Spitsbergen.

Over 1,000 miles still separated us from the latitude to which the *Benjamin Bowring* might, with luck, be expected to smash her way when, in August, the pack was at its most penetrable. The *Benjamin Bowring* would not be able to penetrate heavy Arctic pack, being merely an ice-strengthened vessel, but, if we could reach as far down as 81° North, she might – through the skill of her skipper and the eyes of Karl in the Twin Otter – be able to thread her way into the pack's edge.

From the Pole all went well for four days – in reality, nights – during one of which we achieved a distance of thirty-one miles in twelve hours over a freakishly unbroken pan of floes. From 88° down to 86° the conditions deteriorated slowly with an increasing number of open leads. I had grown accustomed to keeping an eye ever open for potential Twin Otter landing strips. But for the last forty miles there had been neither a single floe flat enough for a landing nor a pan solid enough to camp on safely during a storm.

The temperature rose to –20°C and stayed there. New ice no longer congealed over open leads within twenty-four hours, so wide canals with no crossing-points became permanent stoppers, not mere hold-ups. Tedious foot patrols to find crossing-points became increasingly necessary. Following a brief storm on 23 April we axed for two hours through a forest of twelve-foot-high green rafted blocks and reached a series of winding couloirs of new ice packed with black pools of sludge. Alongside this marsh I tripped and fell. My hands shot out to ward off a heavy fall. My axe disappeared and sank. My arms pierced the surface up to the elbows and one leg up to the knee, but the snow-covered sludge held my body weight. Seven miles later seawater cut us off in all directions except back north, so we camped. The wind blew at thirty knots and chunks of ice, floating across pools and along canals, all headed east.

That night I told Charlie I would begin to search for a floe on which to float south. He was horrified, feeling we would never reach the ship if we did not make much more southerly progress before beginning to float. Stop now, he feared, and the expedition would fail. I argued with him that wind and current should take us to 81° before winter, providing we could only locate a solid enough floe to protect us during storm-crush conditions. If we waited one day too long before locating such a floe we could easily be cut off on a rotten pan and then there would be no answer to our predicament. Better safe than sorry. Charlie agreed to disagree. But, he reminded me, in the future – whatever happened – I should remember the decision to risk a float from so far north was mine alone.

Two days later we escaped from the weak pan and managed to progress another five miles south on increasingly thin ice before having to camp. Four days later I thought the river-ice had congealed and attempted to cross by skidoo. To my surprise my sledge runners broke through the sludge at a point where I had safely walked an hour earlier. Thereafter this sludge-river remained at the same tacky consistency, insufficient for sledge weight. The temperature rose towards 0° and we ground to a halt.

Charlie searched for cracks and weak points on the floe we were on and eventually decided upon a line of hummocks along the impact point of an old pressure ridge. We flattened out the top of this high ground with axes and made a camp there.

During the first week of May I asked Ginny to send us two light canoes and rations for a long float. She flew with Karl and Simon from Alert to the north-east corner of Greenland and at remote Cape Nord set up her last radio base. She told me that the remnants of the Norwegian expedition racing us to cross the Arctic had reached the Pole too late to continue and had been evacuated.

On 11 May, without a sound, our floe split apart 500 yards east of our tent and we lost a third of our original real-estate. Bending over the edge of the newly opened canal, I saw that our two-thirds was some five or six feet thick. I had hoped for a minimum of eight feet but – too bad – we were committed to this place.

Our tent floor of axed ice was uneven and daily became more sodden with water as the surface of the floe melted down. Soon, all about our slightly raised platform, the floe became a floating pool of vivid blue salt-water, five feet deep in places.

Late in May two members of our London committee travelled to Spitsbergen to visit the ship. Karl flew them over the pack and, horrified at our overall predicament, they returned to London and warned the committee that our chances of success this summer were minimal. We must be airlifted out at once while such a course was still possible or any subsequent disaster would be on their hands. Ginny queried the committee's follow-up message, a direct evacuation order, and rallied those in London who were against such a course. Only when the order had been softened to a recommendation that we abort the float but that the final decision should be mine, did Ginny inform me.

I felt, and Charlie agreed, that there was still a strong chance of success without risking an international search-and-rescue operation, so we continued to float at the mercy of wind and current. For five days a southerly storm blew us back towards the Pole and for several days our southerly heading veered sharply towards Siberia, but overall we continued south at a steady rate towards Fram Strait, between Greenland and Spitsbergen. Karl managed to land on a rare mist-free day. He dropped us off two tents, two canoes and a two-month supply of rations. He warned us that in another week he would no longer be able to take off from our increasingly soggy floe. We were on our own. On 6 June in thick fog our floe was blown against its northerly neighbour and, where the ice fronts clashed, a fifteen-foot-high wall of broken blocks reared up.

The sense of smell of the polar bear is phenomenal: they can detect a seal from ten miles away. Large males weigh half a ton, reach eight feet tall and tower to twelve feet when standing. They glide over ice quietly, yet can charge at thirty-five miles per hour.

One night in my sleeping bag I was woken by loud snuffling sounds beside my head on the other side of the tent cloth.

'Ran?' Charlie called.

Since his voice came from his own tent I knew with a sinking feeling that he was not snuffling about outside my tent. It must be a bear. Grabbing camera and loaded revolver, I peered outside. So did Charlie, whose eyeballs grew huge as he spotted – behind my tent – a very big bear. I craned my neck and three yards away saw the face of the bear which was licking its lips with a large black tongue. We photographed the fine animal and after a few minutes it shuffled away.

A week later another bear would not leave and showed signs of evil intent. We fired bullets and even a parachute flare over its head but the bear only grew irritable. We agreed to shoot if it approached closer than thirty yards. It did, so I fired a bullet at its leg. The bear hesitated in mid-stride then broke sideways and loped away. There were blood splashes but no sign of a limp. Over the next few weeks many bears crossed our floe and eighteen visited our camp, tripping over our guy-ropes. This kept us from getting bored by our inactive existence.

The uncertainty of our situation, especially at times when communications blacked out, was a great strain on Ginny. She had a long history of migraines and spastic colon attacks and her life at Nord was full of pain and stress. She had no shoulder to cry on and no one from whom to seek advice. She hated this part of the expedition but kept steadily on at her job. Late in June she made contact with the *Benjamin Bowring*. The sooner she could remove us from our floe the better, for the remnant of our floe was fast approaching a danger area known as the Marginal Ice Zone, the ice pulverisation factory of Fram Strait. Two million square miles of the Arctic Ocean are covered by pack-ice and one-third of this load is disgorged every year through Fram Strait. Very soon now our own floe would enter this bottleneck, where currents accelerate by 100 per cent and rush their fragmenting ice burden south at an incredible thirty kilometres a day. Keenly aware of our danger, the skipper and crew agreed to take a risk. Arctic pack-ice is far more hazardous than the Antarctic equivalent.

On 2 July, after a game attempt, the ship was forced back some 150 miles south of our floe. On 10 July the mist cleared at noon long enough for a sun shot. After seventy days on the floe we were at 82° North. That night a chunk of two acres split off our floe. The next-door floe rode up over a forty-yard front and 80 per cent of our pan was covered in slush or water up to seven feet deep. New ridgewalls rose up daily and noisily where we struck our neighbours. Off our seaside edges humpback whales sang at night and huge regattas of ice sailed by before the wind. There was seldom any sign of the sun and the low-hung sky reflected the dark blotches of great expanses of open sea to the south and north of our floating raft.

As we approached nearer to Fram Strait we began to gyrate like scum heading for a drain. To remind us that summer here was short, the surface of our melt-pools began to freeze over.

The *Benjamin Bowring* tried a second time to reach us in mid-July and again they failed, this time putting themselves in considerable danger. Anton recorded: 'hurling the ship at six- to seven-feet thick floes which are breaking without too much difficulty. But the ice is more solid and further to the south than before . . . Evening: We are stuck solid at 82°07′ north, 01°20′ east, 82 miles south of Ran . . . Jimmy has spotted a cracked weld.'

Cleverly the skipper rammed a low floe and managed to lift the damaged bows clear of the sea. Two engineers worked, squatting on the ice, to effect temporary repairs with welding gear.

During the last week of July our floe was daily buffeted and diminished in size. Charlie had chosen our camp spot with great skill, as it was about the only part of the floe still uncracked. But on 29 July he showed me a widening seam close beside his tent. We had been on the floe ninety-five days and our entry into the crushing zone was imminent.

I told Ginny and she spoke to the skipper. They decided to make a final dedicated push northwards. Karl flew Ginny from Greenland to Longyearbyen where she boarded the *Benjamin Bowring*. They set out on the first day of August, our seventh month out on the pack ice, and – within twelve hours of smashing a straight route through medium pack – they reached a point forty-nine miles to our south.

Late on 2 August after a twenty-four-hour fight north-west through heavy ice and thick fog, the skipper reported sinister signs of a wind change. The pack would close about the ship if the wind rose. Throughout the long night the skipper and crew willed the ship north yard by yard in a potentially suicidal bid to reach us.

At 9.00 a.m. on 3 August Ginny spoke on my radio. She sounded tired but excited. 'We are seventeen miles south of your last reported position and jammed solid.'

Charlie and I packed basic survival gear into our two canoes. We had hoped the *Benjamin Bowring* would smash her way to our floe, but this was clearly impossible. For us to attempt to travel from our floe might easily prove disastrous, for everything was in motion about us: great floating blocks colliding in the open channels and wide skeins of porridge-ice marauding the sea lanes. At noon I took a sun shot which put us only twelve miles from the ship. A southerly wind or current could easily widen this gap. We left our bedraggled tents and I took a bearing south-east to the probable current position of the *Benjamin Bowring*. The wind blew at twelve knots as we paddled nervously through the first open lead.

Having lain in our bags with scant exercise for so long, we were unfit. Charlie was nearly sick with the sudden effort. Every so often I filled my water bottle from a melt pool and we both drank deep.

Makeshift skids attached to the canoes snapped off on rough

ice and then we dragged the boats along on their thin metal hulls.

Trying to negotiate a spinning mass of ice-islands in a wide lake, I glanced back and saw two high bergs crunch together with an impact that sent a surge of water towards my canoe. Luckily Charlie had not yet entered the moving corridor and so avoided being crushed.

At 7.00 p.m., climbing a low ridge to scout ahead, I saw an imperfection on the horizon along the line of my bearing. I blinked and it was gone. Then I saw it again – the distant masts of the *Benjamin Bowring*.

I cannot describe the feeling of that moment, the most wonderful of my life. I jumped high in the air, yelling at Charlie. He was out of earshot but I waved like a madman and he must have guessed.

For three years I had always known our chances of overall success were heavily loaded against us. I had never dared allow myself to hope. But now I knew and I felt the strength of ten men. I knelt down on the ice and thanked God.

For three hours we heaved and paddled. Sometimes we lost sight of the masts, but when they re-appeared they were always a little bigger.

At fourteen minutes past midnight on 4 August at 80°31′ North, 00°59′ West, all but astride the Greenwich Meridian, we climbed on board the *Benjamin Bowring*.

Ginny was standing alone by a cargo hatch. We hugged each other as though we would never let go. Her eyes were full of tears, but she was smiling. Between us we had spent twenty years of our lives to reach this point, the fulfilment of her dream.

Revelry lasted well into the night. There was no hurry now, which was just as well because the ship remained stuck fast for twelve days, until the wind changed.

From the lonely islands of Spitsbergen we steamed south through the Greenland Sea and the North Sea. On 29 August Prince Charles joined us on the Thames and brought the ship back to our starting-point at Greenwich, almost three years to the day since we had set out. Ten thousand cheering people lined the banks. Our polar circle around the world was complete.

That night, when all the crew and our friends had gone, Ginny and I slept in our old cabin. I watched as she fell asleep and the lines of stress fell away from her face. I felt as happy as I had ever been.

8

Hammer and Sickle

Three days after returning home I learned that Transglobe had accumulated debts totalling £106,000. We had no funds to pay them off. This was where Anton Bowring appeared in our hour of need to announce that he considered the expedition complete only when all debts were paid. For the next eighteen months he and Ginny worked full-time to that end, a thankless task, but they eventually even turned a modest profit through sales of T-shirts and old Transglobe gear at Camden Lock street market. Anton and his wife Jill, the *Benjamin Bowring*'s cook for three years, became our best friends. Ginny was godmother to their eldest daughter, Mini Ginny, who was conceived during Transglobe. They were to have three daughters, all red-haired like Jill, and collectively known as the Carrots. I meanwhile was writing the expedition book, *To the Ends of the Earth*, which made the *Sunday Times* bestseller list. Bothie achieved fame by nipping TV host Russell Harty and I was decoyed into *This Is Your Life*. Family and friends assembled from all periods of my past, included Chris Cazenove and Jack McConnell, as well as the history mistress who caught me on Ginny's school roof in Eastbourne and the entire Transglobe team. Eamonn Andrews' researchers were put off the military aspects of my life when one asked my former CO in Oman whether he could regurgitate any heart-warming tale of my 'bravely saving someone's life'. The colonel replied with vehemence. 'Saving lives?! Fiennes wasn't out there to save lives. He was there to kill Communists.' Not what we would today describe as PC.

I turned forty in March 1983 and one of my presents was a sweatshirt emblazoned with the words 'I'm over the hill'. But I was discovering what happens to so many polar travellers, the urge to return. As the less comfortable memories of the Transglobe years receded, I increasingly felt the lure of the North. I determined to ignore this mesmeric polar attaction with the same vehemence as a smoker must shun thoughts of tobacco. For a while I was helped by a phone call from Los Angeles at 2.00 a.m.

'Is that Ran Fiennes?' The voice was gravelly and brusque. 'This is Armand Hammer.'

Assured that it was me, the good Dr Hammer continued, 'I want you to work for me in London. You will be my Vice-President of Public Relations in Europe.'

This was my very first offer of a civilian job. The octogenarian head of Occidental Petroleum knew me because, at Prince Charles's behest, he had financed the film-making on the Transglobe expedition and approved of our success. So, aged forty, I experienced the joys of commuting for the first time. I discovered that 'nine to five' actually meant 'seven to seven'. I made after-dinner speeches in French and German on behalf of Dr Hammer at glittering European functions. I tried hard to sell an unwanted oil terminal for him on Canvey Island and saw that his visits to Europe ran without a hitch, despite his penchant for changing his mind and schedule with little warning and requiring a meeting at two days' notice with Prince Charles or Robert Maxwell or Mrs Thatcher. In the same week he had me rushing to Rome with secret papers for the ex-King of Afghanistan (who Dr Hammer was hoping to reinstate) and making a speech to Raisa Gorbachev in Moscow. I learned to chat up airport officials to allow me to meet the doctor's private Boeing 727 with a bevy of rented Rolls-Royces on the airstrip to avoid the tiresome business of customs and immigration. This worked everywhere in the world, including Moscow, Peking and Cardiff, but not Heathrow, where the rules were inflexible and, when I finally gave up trying to buck their system, I felt quite proud to be British!

Amid all this Hammer-inspired rushing about, Oliver Shepard called me one day in 1985 with a proposal for the ultimate polar journey, the grail of the international polar fraternity: to reach the North Pole with no outside support and no air contact. No one had yet achieved it. I found myself reacting with unexpected enthusiasm and realised that, ever since the end of the Transglobe travels, I had without knowing it been yearning to return to the cold white unknown. There is a Danish word, *polarhullar,* an ache for the polar regions, that grips the soul of a traveller so that nowhere else will ever again satisfy his or her appetite for the essence of 'over there and beyond'. A victim of *polarhullar* will forever be drawn back to the very extremities of earth.

Part of my annually renewed contract with Dr Hammer allowed me to go off on expeditions for three months in any year. After the success of Transglobe, sponsorship had become much easier to obtain. Equipment, food, travel and insurance could all be quickly lined up free of charge in return for promises of publicity. To obtain the interest of a major newspaper or television film producer was, however, still no easy business.

I failed to find a documentary film-maker but, since such films are statistically watched only by a maximum of two million TV viewers, I concentrated on the main TV News channels which were watched twice daily by over sixteen million. I had once worked as a TV News reporter for ITN in Oman and so approached them first. This began a great working relationship with their reporter Terry Lloyd who ITN agreed to send north with us that year to the base we would make on Ward Hunt Island in the Canadian Arctic.

In the winter of 1985 Ginny was due to lecture about her Very Low Frequency work in Antarctica to a conference in Chicago. At little extra cost she flew on to Resolute Bay in the North West Territories and hitched a lift on to Ward Hunt Island, a remote former scientific summer camp, in a Twin Otter ski-plane that was positioning sonar buoys in the Arctic pack. Ginny measured the skeletal ribs of one of the long abandoned Ward Hunt huts and a sponsor back home constructed a tough new custom-made hut cover. But after reconnoitring the place for us, Ginny would sadly no longer be our base leader.

Back in England, and thanks to my salary from Dr Hammer, we had found our dream home, a near derelict farm in the wilds of Exmoor. There was no electricity but Ginny had started to build up an organic beef herd around an initial six Aberdeen Angus cows. She was also breeding from Bothie's girlfriend Blackdog, the stray Inuit puppy who had come back with us from Tuktoyaktuk and who Ginny had mated to a Crufts champion black labrador. In 1985 Ginny recommended one of our Transglobe team, Laurence Howell, known as Flo, to take her place in the Arctic as our base leader and radio operator.

Ollie and I completed our winter sledge trial runs and in March 1986 were established at our Ward Hunt base with Flo, preparing to set off. A few days later a Twin Otter brought in the French manhauler, Dr Jean-Louis Etienne. He was aiming to be the first solo traveller to the North Pole. We agreed to show him the best route we had discovered through the chaotic pack-ice that formed a high wall just north of the Ward Hunt ice-shelf. Then we shook hands with the diminutive doctor and watched him disappear into the moonlit icescape.

'I wish we had sledges like his,' Ollie commented. The French sledge weighed a mere four pounds and its load eight. Our own 450-pound loads included seventy pounds of bare sledge. Jean-Louis would be resupplied by air every eighth day and his sledge replaced whenever it was damaged so he could afford to travel light. But if we were to be unassisted this could never be for us. We were finding that even the superior design of our new sledges did little to improve our snail-like performance. We kept paring down equipment to a bare minimum, even shaving the Teflon runners with Stanley knives.

At this moment Ollie had the rug pulled out from under him. He received an ultimatum by radio. Either he returned to London within four weeks or he lost his job, then with Beefeater Gin. He had no alternative but to cry off. This left Ginny back home in England with the task of finding a last-minute replacement from the very small field of fully fit polar sledgers. Polar expert Roger Mear suggested that Ginny call Dr Mike Stroud from Guy's Hospital who had been first reserve for Mear's own and very recent Antarctic journey. He would still be manhaul-fit.

When, a week later, Mike climbed off the Twin Otter at Ward Hunt Island I was shocked at how short he was. Small people, in my book, were not built to drag over 300-pound sledges for hours on end. You needed carthorses. Mike's head came to a level with my shoulder. But, on closer inspection, it became clear that Mike was built like an ox, with the biceps, chest and thighs of a body-builder. He pulled like a husky, digging his boots in and leaning so far forward that his nose seemed to scrape the ice. I was soon to discover he could drag his sledge, more than twice his bodyweight, alongside mine and trudge on relentlessly for hour after hour. So we waved goodbye to Flo Howell and set out north three days after Mike's arrival. I reflected that if a committee had been running this expedition, after the fashion of our Transglobe committee, we would never have resolved things so quickly. I remembered reading that 'a committee is a group of people who individually can do nothing, but as a group decide nothing can be done.'

At the time Mike Stroud arrived on Ward Hunt Island the world record for human travel without support towards the North Pole stood at ninety-eight nautical miles following the near fatal journey of the Simpsons and Roger Tufft in 1968. Subsequent attempts, such as those of David Hempleman-Adams and Clive Johnson in the 1980s, had ended in failure and frostbite less than fifty miles from the Arctic coast. The terrain included some 2,000 walls of ice rubble up to twenty-five feet high, regions of rotten ice that break up and overturn as you try to negotiate them and zones of open waters, sometimes as far as the eye can see, which are often skimmed with a treacherous *shuga* ice layer of porridge-like consistency. Add to these obstacles a temperature that is often lower than a deep-freeze and a northerly wind that cuts into exposed skin like a bayonet and it is no wonder that, despite intense international competition, the challenge had yet to be met.

Some seventy miles from the coastline we were struggling in a field of broken ice-blocks and thin floes. My sledge cannoned off a twelve-foot chunk and knocked me from my hauling position. I broke through the ice and was instantly immersed. Mike was luckily close at hand and dragged me out, but the damage was done, for we could not stop in such a fractured zone. So it was four unpleasant hours later before Mike could erect the tent. By that time my hands were lumps without feeling and I could not help him. More seriously, I had no feeling in my feet. Inside the tent I struggled to remove my sledge jacket, but since both it and my clumsy mitts were encased in a thick film of frozen sea-ice, I had no success. All the while I battered my two boots together in an attempt to force blood to flow.

Mike at last appeared through the tent's tunnel entrance with some four inches of frozen nose mucous stuck to the chin of his balaclava like a gnome's beard. Unlashing the sledge had quickly made him cold. Any pause from the exhausting action of manhauling soon results in a lowered heart rate, so that the blood flow rapidly retreats from the extremities and shivering begins. Sweat caught between layers of clothing turns to ice and there is an urgent need to do one of two things: you can either return to the treadmill of manhauling or, if too tired, erect the tent and eat into the sternly rationed daily quota of fuel to provide life-giving heat.

To cut down cargo weight, our fuel ration allowed only for cooking, not for tent heating or clothes drying, so an immersion like mine caused major problems with the vital fuel supply. This sort of setback could lead to bitterness between team members, since to fall in could be considered the result of stupidity. On all previous expeditions I had gone to considerable lengths to vet every team member but circumstance had obliged me to accept Mike sight unseen. That we proved to be totally compatible was remarkably lucky. There was no strained atmosphere, no recrimination, not even the occasional heated exchange.

Mike managed to remove my mitts and I shoved my hands inside the ski jacket and under my armpits. There was a chance they might return to life, according to Mike's practised eye. More seriously, my boots would not come off, however hard Mike struggled with them. The obvious answer, since it was vital we extricated my toes with minimal delay, would have been to cut through the frozen bootlaces with our pin-nosed pliers. Since the laces were completely encrusted, the actual boot canvas would need cutting too.

'If we cut up the boots,' Mike said, looking at me from beneath a fringe of iced-up eyebrow, 'it will mean the end of the expedition: failure.'

I nodded. We carried no spares. To save weight every item not vital to progress had been jettisoned: and that meant none of those spares normally considered indispensable, such as extra mitts, goggles or bootlaces. We had a choice between dangerously delaying the resuscitation of my feet while thawing the laces out and cutting through the obstacles at once to give my feet a better chance but the expedition none. Ruefully I remembered a day eight years before when I had fallen through Arctic ice and Ollie Shepard had saved my feet by cutting my boots off with the help of an axe.

Reluctantly, I asked Mike, by now shivering with cold himself, to thaw the boots out as quickly as possible. I could feel no sensation at all in either foot. The thawing process seemed to take for ever. Once the boots were off, Mike declared my left foot 'redeemable' since it had remained miraculously dry, except for the toes and the sole.

'Not so good,' he said, shaking his head as he examined my other foot. Three of the toes and an adjoining area of skin were parchment-white and devoid of any feeling. Slowly he warmed up both my feet, expending valuable fuel, before applying dry dressings. Breaking the normal rule against using the cooker merely for damp clothes, he dried out my socks and slipped them over the bandages.

Next day we set out on time. I felt no pain throughout the day and was surprised when, back in the tent, Mike swore aloud on removing the dressing. What appeared to be the outer half of my little toe and a segment of flesh had come away with the bandage. A large area of raw flesh and bone was left exposed which felt, as soon as my foot warmed up and blood returned to the nerve ends, as though it were on fire. For the rest of the journey I dreaded the mornings until, after an hour or so of travel, the foot grew cold enough to deaden the nerves. Likewise the evenings, when the reverse process took place. Nevertheless, despite our heavy loads and my early morning limp, our progress continued to outpace that of the two fully air-supported expeditions to our north. After fifteen days we passed the ninety-eight nautical miles point, the existing unsupported world record, and celebrated with an extra cup of tea.

In bad conditions we craved each tea break, yet at the same time feared the intense cold that accompanied a halt. One evening Mike announced that he had broken one of our two vacuum flasks. Since this cut us down to a single intake of hot liquid a day, I felt distinctly hostile towards him, although I made no comment.

'We have a choice from now on,' Mike said. 'We can use the remaining flask either for tea or for Pre-stress.'

Pre-stress was a specially prepared quick-energy drink that helped to stave off hypothermia and which we normally alternated with tea.

'As a doctor, what do you advise?' I asked Mike.

'We'd better stick to Pre-stress, despite the taste,' he said, giving the reply I had expected.

Two days later Mike was unusually quiet in the tent and after a while broke the news that he had somehow managed to break the second and last vacuum flask. Mike's solution to the problem was that we should use our communal plastic pee-bottle.

'You must be joking,' I replied. 'Are you suggesting peeing into it each night and drinking Pre-stress out of it each day?'

'Why not? We can call it Pee-stress. Urine will do you no harm, after all.'

'*Mine* won't,' I retorted. 'But I can't say I fancy the idea of drinking from a container with your frozen pee stuck to the outside.'

'I never thought of you as fastidious. But I'm happy if you don't wish to share the contents.'

'It's one short step from cannibalism,' I muttered. But the following day I noticed no change in the taste of the Pre-stress.

Some days later the tent was filled with a foul smell when Mike changed my foot bandages. Gangrene. It spelt the end of our attempt for 1986. We found 400 yards of comparative flat surface on a well-weathered floe and marked out an airstrip with coloured ration bags. Then I radioed Flo Howell at Ward Hunt Island. We had passed the record of the previous best unsupported northing by nine miles but we were still over 300 miles from the Pole.

Back home I learned I was to be installed in the *Guinness Book of Records*' World Hall of Fame as the 'World's Greatest Living Explorer' (alongside Paul McCartney for music and Billie Jean King for sport). I hobbled on to the BBC stage to receive my award from David Frost and Norris McWhirter wearing a black sock over the bandages and no shoes. Ginny and I gained more quiet satisfaction from receiving the Polar Medal from the Queen, with unique bars for Antarctica and the Arctic. Ginny was the first woman to receive the medal, and soon afterwards the first woman to become a member of the prestigious Antarctic Club.

Ollie, Mike and I had another try for the Pole in early 1988. Flo Howell was again base leader, this time with his wife Morag manning the radio with her colourful Orcadian accent. This attempt foundered after sixty miles in the face of appalling terrain and weather. The following spring Mike Stroud and I set off yet again from Ward Hunt Island. The conditions were average but we fell well short of the record we had set in 1986 and I opened up a skin graft on my right foot which had been applied after the gangrene episode. As we left Ward Hunt Island for the last time I asked Mike if he would like to try once more, next time from the Siberian side of the Pole.

'Glasnost permitting,' he replied with a grin.

The thawing of relations with Russia had indeed opened the field and in 1990 there were, as well as ourselves, Russians, Canadians and Norwegians all preparing to be the first to make it unaided to the Pole. Although the North Pole is some 100 miles further from Russia than from Canada, the sea currents carry the ice floes towards not away from the Pole which should, we all thought, prove a great help. In Moscow I was delighted that Arctic hero, Dr Dmitry Shparo, was prepared to organise my bid. He warned me of stiff competition from Colonel Vladimir Chukov of the Soviet Special Forces. On the other side of the world the Canadians were led by none other than my old friend Jack McConnell.

From Moscow in the spring of 1990 Mike, Flo, Morag and I were flown to the depths of Siberia and stayed one night in a scientific camp where only a year earlier we would never have been allowed, for the station was the Soviet equivalent of Canada's Defence Early Warning line which Charlie and I had encountered on our 1981 push to Alert. Our Soviet hosts entertained us to dinner at the even remoter station of Golomiany where we were told proudly that we were the first foreigners to visit since the days of the Tsar. One of the six-person station's occupants had been killed the previous month by a polar bear outside their cookhouse. Once the sun arrived along the Siberian coast, Dmitry organised an ex-Afghan gun-ship to fly us north to Cape Arktikiski, the most northern point of land in Severnaya Zemlya. As on our previous Arctic journeys, Terry Lloyd of ITN was on hand to see us off.

On the other side of the world three Norwegian ski champions had declared their intention to reach the Pole first and two separate teams of Soviet skiers were somewhere behind us. Flo and Morag Howell manned our radio base, together with two Russian operators, and through the electronic clutter of our HF radio Morag's voice came and went from a Soviet Army shack on the island of Sredniy, keeping us up to date with the competition as we made our own careful progress north.

'Kagge and his Norwegians are out of the race,' she told us some weeks later. 'One of them has been airlifted to safety with a frostbitten foot. The other two are carrying on but their challenge has obviously been compromised by their air contact.'

Now we had only the Russians to worry about, for Jack McConnell's Canadian team had also withdrawn with frostbite.

'Chukov's men are doing well. We estimate they are less than one hundred miles to the south of you.'

'What about Fyodor Konyukhov?' I asked Morag.

'Also compromised,' Morag replied. 'A Soviet helicopter picked him up. He was in trouble with breaking ice in a bear-infested zone.'

I knew that Vladimir Chukov was ranked high in the lists of Russian polar explorers. He had led two unsupported journeys to the Pole in previous years. Both times he had reached the Pole but death and injury to team members on each occasion had necessitated air contact. Chukov played by the unwritten rules of unsupported polar travel. These stipulated that any contact at all en route to the Pole compromised the attempt. So Chukov was trying again. He had learned many lessons. He knew the hazardous nature of the drifting Russian pack-ice, far looser and more volatile than the corresponding sea-ice on the Canadian side. Here, a single error could quickly lead to death. I knew his team's progress would be slow and methodical.

After about 400 miles Mike and I abandoned our heavy carbon-fibre sledge-boats and continued with basic food, fuel and camp gear carried in rucksacks. These weighed nigh on 100 pounds each and it was all but impossible to stand up unaided after struggling into the harness. Our chances of making the last two degrees of latitude, 120 miles, to the Pole rested on luck and avoidance of hypothermia. Sometimes I skied, sometimes I strapped my skis to the pack and walked. Mike had no option but to walk as one of his ski bindings had broken irreparably only seven days out. This slowed us to the speed of a walking expedition but that we kept going at all was a tribute to Mike's tenacity.

One day on a drifting hummock I spotted the fresh prints of an adult polar bear. I knew I must warn Mike, for bears will usually attack the rear member of any group and we had heard that the Norwegians had had to shoot a large male bear close by their tent. I regretted the fact that only a few days previously we had abandoned our radio and our revolver as being too heavy to keep carrying. I tried to bury negative thoughts but the total concentration necessary for successful navigation in broken pack-ice was absent that morning which was perhaps why I misjudged the width of a canal through the porridge-like slush and fell in. Fettered by my skis and rolled face-down by my heavy rucksack, I struggled in panic until Mike arrived and, lying on his stomach, reached down into the canal. He managed to grasp a loose strap from my sack and, with no means of leverage and with fingers already lacerated from broken blisters, he hauled me to safety through sheer force of willpower.

Over the following weeks we each fell in six or seven times, mercifully not both at the same time. Around 88° North, with 447 miles behind us and within a tantalising eighty-nine miles of the Pole, our strength quite suddenly disappeared as the extreme loss of bodyweight reached the point where we became debilitated. Cold pervaded our bodies and sleep, always difficult on ice that shrieks and shudders, grew impossible lying on thinly padded bones. In addition my eyesight became too poor to navigate. To pull a heavy sledge you must lean forward. Your heavy breathing if wearing a balaclava and goggles will mist up the goggles when below −40°C. So, as navigator, needing constantly to scrutinise the ice ahead, you travel with no goggles, squinting into the glare. Not good for your long-term sight. Though we were only ten days from the Pole we recognised it was time to give up and activated a miniature radio beacon to request our evacuation.

A Soviet helicopter extricated us and took us to their nearest scientific base on an ice-floe. This unfortunately split up in a storm, cutting their landing zone in half, so the Aeroflot plane which commuted scientists weekly to and from the Soviet Union was delayed by ten days awaiting the bulldozing of a new runway. While we waited I experienced a severe kidney stone attack, my third in twenty years, and Mike dosed me with his remaining store of pain-killers. When we eventually returned to Moscow we learned that Chukov's group had also failed to reach the Pole and had been evacuated further south than us. We were given medals and assured by the Russians that we had made the longest and fastest unsupported journey towards the Pole to date. Polar records are seldom without controversy. The Norwegians, Erling Kagge and Børge Ousland, did reach the Pole that season but only after the third member of their party had been airlifted out, so their claim to be wholly unsupported was not recognised by the Russians, the Canadians or the British. To us it was as blatant a piece of assistance as an Olympic athlete taking drugs. I said so in the press. The Norwegians called me a bad sportsman and we left it at that. In 1994 Ousland was at last to achieve a proper record when he made it solo and unsupported to the Pole in fifty-two days.

After the last of these Arctic journeys I went to London's top eye surgeon, Eric Arnott, worried about double vision. He diagnosed that the long weeks of travel with no horizon and no real focus point had made my eyes focus at a distance of one metre ahead of my boots and it took weeks for this 'convergence of the visual axes' to relax.

'You failed again, then?' Dr Hammer growled when I first met him after the Siberian journey.

'Not exactly, Doctor,' I bridled. 'We broke the existing world record by over 300 miles.'

A few months after our group finally abandoned our North Pole attempts, Charlie Burton and Ollie Shepard began to come down with South Pole fever. How about us making an unassisted crossing of Antarctica, they suggested, manhauling sledges just like Scott. It sounded good, but I already had other expedition plans under way at the time, so I listened to them cajoling me persuasively but in vain in the map room of the Royal Geographical Society. *Polarhullar* notwithstanding, I had had enough of frozen climes for a while.

9

The Frankincense Trail

Back in 1968, when I was serving in Dhofar, a bedu guide had told me about a fabulously wealthy city of antiquity which was reputed to be lost in the sands. Over the years, on occasional return visits for other purposes, I had investigated possible sites of this lost city but never with enough time to take things to a conclusion. Now Ginny and I had taken on the planning and mounting of a fully fledged expedition. Some historical sources called the city Ubar, others Irem. My hunch was that the site must be somewhere astride the trade route which carried the precious high-quality Dhofari frankincense to the markets of the north.

On the first maps of the Arabian Peninsula, drawn up by Ptolemy in AD 150, there was a major market town which he located on the southern rim of the region now known as the Empty Quarter, the greatest sand desert of the world. Lawrence of Arabia records being told of ruined castles seen by wandering tribes. Bertram Sidney Thomas, an administrator of Palestine, and financial advisor to the then Sultan of Muscat, received permission in 1925 to attempt a crossing of the Empty Quarter from south to north. The journey took him fifty-eight days. He received the personal congratulations of King George V and the Founder's Medal of the Royal Geographical Society, but the mystery of Ubar remained unsolved.

Our own interest evolved into a joint venture with an old friend, Nick Clapp from Los Angeles, who had edited Dr Hammer's film of the Transglobe expedition. I would liaise with Sultan Qaboos of Oman, organise sponsors and lead the expedition in the field, Nick would do the archaeological research and the filming. His researches led him to NASA in quest of space photographs, hoping these would give us a head start, but all the eventual NASA shuttle photos produced was an L-shaped site way out in the dunes. All the same, the connection between buried biblical cities and space-age technology remained a good talking point for raising sponsorship.

We began with a short reconnaissance trip in July 1990, taking along with us an eminent archaeologist from Missouri called Juris Zarins who had a vaguely reassuring resemblance to Indiana Jones, complete with battered brown trilby. Juris didn't think we had a cat in hell's chance of finding Ubar, if indeed it existed, but he was keen to have a chance to conduct archaeological work in southern Oman and if searching for Ubar provided a pretext, fair enough. Our timing coincided with Saddam Hussein's invasion of Kuwait, but as nobody was expecting the trouble to spread to Dhofar, our visas were duly stamped. Our main guide on the ground would be Major Trevor Henry, my instructor on an SAS jungle course back in the 1970s. He told me bluntly that if there had been any surface ruins in Dhofar they would have been spotted by oil prospectors, talkative bedu or land and air patrols from the Sultan's Armed Forces. But he was happy to help.

First of all we flew by helicopter to inspect the mysterious NASA-provided L-site. On the ground it was as clear as it had been from 160 miles in space, but Juris was quick to dismiss it as merely an ancient lake bed, though he did find the stone patterns of some ancient dwellings and hearths nearby. We then flew to other possible locations that might have a bearing on the frankincense trade. I revisited caves from which I had once spent many days and nights ambushing Marxist soldiers.

Trevor pointed out the spoor of leopards and some aloe trees – 'very good for curing wounds' – and castor-oil trees – 'you know what that's good for'. He led us to Jebel Kasbah, a lofty crag above a spring. Hidden by thorn and mimosa, a tangle of ruined walls puzzled Juris. A large rectangular room, well plastered and hardly damaged over the centuries, had perhaps served as a reservoir for monsoon water. It was reasonable to deduce this was a mountain garrison from which the incense trade was once policed, an interesting fragment in our jigsaw puzzle, but not a clue to Ubar's whereabouts.

After a whirlwind tour of the plain, the mountains and the Nejd, we drove from Thamrait to my earlier Ubar hunting grounds of Shis'r and Fasad on the edge of the Sands. Both places had undergone considerable change. Where in 1968 there was only barren desert at Shis'r and a crumbling *Beau Geste* mud fort, there now flourished cultivated plots of palm, fruit and vegetables. At Shis'r there was also a modern Arab-style housing development not far from the rock cleft waterhole.

Shis'r's very location, so close to the Sands and astride the best aquifer in the region, indicated that ancient camel trains may have watered here en route for Yemen and previous visitors had recorded tracks running west from here to the Sands which our satellite photographs had confirmed. We spent three hours wandering about a heap of rubble and Juris was delighted to find fragments of pottery and various ambiguous mounds, evidence of former springs. He was sure people had lived here longer ago than the 300 years theorised by the only previous archaeologist to have visited Shis'r. There was plenty for Juris to explore, but as to locating Ubar, we were really no further forward. The interim report I eventually submitted to the Sultan and our sponsors made the best of a bad job.

We postponed our main expedition until the autumn of 1991, because of ongoing troubles caused by Saddam Hussein. On the day we set out I discovered that in my rush I had collected the wrong travel bag from our London gear store. Instead of tropical shirts, sun-cream and malaria tablets, I had a duffle bag with snow goggles, balaclava and mitts. I decided not to mention this to the larger party we had now assembled in case it alarmed them as to my administrative efficiency.

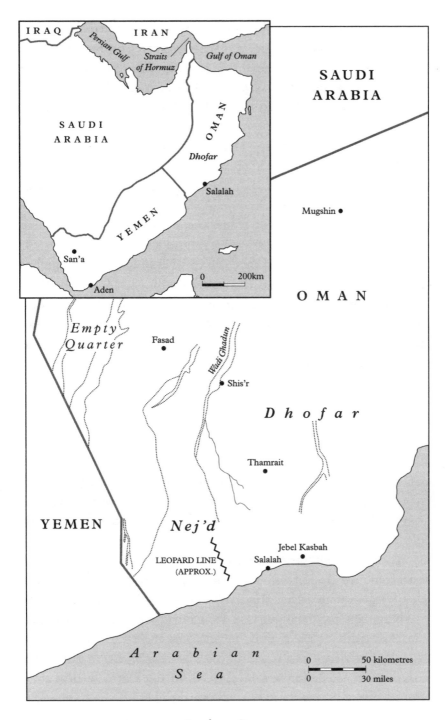

Southern Oman

We based ourselves at Shis'r, where Ginny set up our HF radio base, because it seemed a good place to branch out from. I linked up with desert bedu and mountain folk I had known from the late 1960s who were useful as scouts or advisers, and there were many long and inconclusive debates as to Ubar's likely location between the film director, the explorer, the archaeologist and the Imam of Fasad, through whose home terrain we were hesitantly creeping and who agreed to take us out into the Sands. At least we felt confident that wherever we ended up, he would know the most direct way back.

Terry Lloyd and his ITN cameraman Rob Bowles joined and recorded many of our desert wanderings. I savoured the beauty of the stars at night and read the Qur'an to Ginny: 'It is Allah who makes men laugh and weep, it is He who kills and makes alive . . . He is the Lord of the Dog Star, He who destroyed Ad of yore, and Thamud, and left none of them, and the people of Noah before them. Their cities, he threw them down and there covered them what did cover them.' The Dog Star, I mused, could tell me every secret of the Sands and where to find Ubar, which the Qur'an called Ad.

I knew well from my Arab Army days that there were three main aquifers running north into Dhofar's southern fringe of the Empty Quarter. The existing water sources at Fasad, Shis'r and Mugshin all lay at a latitude through which an incense road hypothesised by Bertram Sidney Thomas might have passed. The water at Fasad is very sulphurous, and at Mugshin highly salty, but Shis'r's water, that of the Wadi Ghadun aquifer, is famous for its sweetness. Though historians had written Shis'r off as a mere 300 years old, we decided to start digging here, for reasons quite unconnected with archaeology.

Three days before Christmas 1991 I overheard the two Omani students, who worked with us on loan from the Ministry of National Heritage and Culture, commenting on the fact that we had been in Shis'r for ten days, that our dig-teams were sitting around doing nothing and that all we seemed to do was film each

Geoff, Charlie and Ollie, 1977: our first experience of travel at minus 50°C.
Even wearing Inuit wolfskin parkas, our learning curve out on the Arctic
Ocean sea-ice was steep - and nearly cost Geoff his fingers.

Antarctica 1980: Ollie is halted by a bank of iron-hard sastrugi ridges.

Easter Day 1982: the first men in history to reach both Poles. But over 1,000 miles of broken ice lay ahead.

The mouth of the Yukon – rough seas and no land in sight.
This photo was taken just before the near fatal capsize.

Arctic man-hauling in early March. Not an activity
to be generally recommended.

Self-taught radio operator Ginny survived near poisoning by carbon monoxide and two hours sleep a night to keep the expedition in touch. She became the first woman to receive Britain's elite Polar Medal.

The crew of the Benjy B forcing a way for our old ship between Arctic ice-floes.

One of my favourite photos: Bothie the dog is fearless in approaching the strange frozen jeans monster. Rygvingen Mountain, the last known feature for 900 unexplored miles, is in the background.

1989: an unusual sight, the author in suit and tie,
working for Dr Armand Hammer . . .

. . . but not for long: searching for the lost city of Ubar,
deep in Arabia's Empty Quarter, 1991.

As epic a natural force as I've seen anywhere in the world:
a sandstorm about to engulf my old base at Thamarit.

The longest track – the first unsupported crossing
of the Antarctic continent, 1992.

other. This seemed a fair summary, but it would not sound good at all in the wrong quarters. On Christmas Eve I had a quiet but urgent word with Juris and suggested he start digging *anywhere* so that the Ministry students could see the action. So he took his dig-team some 200 yards from our camp to the rubble around the old Shis'r well. Desultory work began. Two days later Juris looked smug. He had found a piece of red pottery identical to the style of the Jemdet Nassir period in Uruq, Mesopotamia. If carbon dating proved this to be so it would pre-date previous thinking as to the start of trade between Mesopotamia and south Arabia from 4000 to 5000 BC. He was not yet ready to go out on a limb and say we had discovered Ubar, but he was clear that our Shis'r dig was already proving to be a very important Roman-period site and probably went back at least 4,000 years.

Two months later Juris summed up what we had by then unearthed: 'So far we have walls and towers that are square and round and horseshoe-shaped. There was clearly a central tower, an inner sanctum and an outer wall which had a minimum height of between ten and fifteen feet and a consistent thickness of eighty centimetres. Some of the original rooms, complete with hearths, did not collapse as others did and these have already yielded rich finds for the key periods between the second millennium BC and around AD 300.'

When free time was available, I took a shovel and pickaxe to the site and attacked any area that did not require more delicate atten-tion using trowel and handbrush. But the archaeologists in our team, who were allergic to shovels, would scream and chase me away, so Ginny and I spent more time plodding about in the desert searching for subsidiary camps, rich in axe-heads and Fasad points, arrowheads from between the sixth and fourth millennia BC, places where travellers would have camped within sight of the many-towered citadel that Shis'r had clearly once been.

As we dug down, we found the original building work of our city was excellent, consisting of semi-dressed stone cemented with a white plaster similar to that used in the north of the peninsula by contemporary peoples such as the Nabataeans of Petra. Our archaeologists came across the only ancient chess set ever to be found in south Arabia, six soapstone pieces, each two or three inches high and well polished by the fingers of the players. After a month the diggers were three feet down in places and pottery from Rome, Greece and Syria joined Celadon and Ming pieces from China, glass bracelets of bright clear colours from Aden and Neolithic flint weapons from 5000 BC. But was this Ubar? Was it Irem?

Each new artifact helped to fill in the puzzle which Juris needed to reconstruct about Shis'r's unknown past. Between 8000 and 6000 BC the region was too arid for humans. In 5000 BC, with wetter weather, Neolithic folk from Syria and further east arrived and built hearths. Even then, Juris believed, they traded in incense and travelled the then less arid interior, now the Sands, on foot and, after 4000 BC, by donkey. By the seventh century AD, when the Qur'an and later Islamic writers described the fabled city, the site itself was gone, a place only of fanciful legend. The decline would partly have been due to natural catastrophe, the decline of Rome, the spread of Christianity and the dwindling demand for frankincense.

When I was summoned to report on our finds to Sultan Qaboos in person, and he asked me if our Shis'r excavation was definitely Ubar, I felt able to reply, 'I believe so, Your Majesty. It is difficult to know what else it could be.' There is after all only one Dhofar 'place of trade' marked on Ptolomy's map of Arabia.

The carbon dating tests confirmed Juris's hunch and the world-wide attention aroused by the expedition brought tourists and television teams aplenty to Shis'r. Sultan Qaboos recognised that oil revenues would diminish in time and tourism could offer a lucrative alternative source of income. I like to think that the eventual success of my long search for Ubar has in a small way repaid the people of Oman, the country that has given me some of the best times of my life.

10

The Longest Track

While Ginny and I had been in Oman, I had done nothing about the Antarctic crossing journey originally mooted by Ollie and Charlie, but back in London I heard that Norwegian plans for an Antarctic record-breaking journey were afoot by Erling Kagge, our earlier rival in the north and an exceptionally fine cross-country skier. Without delay I started to raise sponsorship for Antarctica. With Kagge as a rival, speed and endurance would now be a high priority for our team and I was concerned about our collective stamina. I had recently noticed what looked like a paunch on Charlie.

In mid-May 1991 I went to a trade fair at Olympia where Oliver had organised a sales stand for his employers. By chance, Charlie Burton was in charge of security there, so I was able to explain my worries to them both, and suggested that I ask Mike Stroud to join our team.

'He is like a bull terrier,' I stressed, 'small in stature but incredibly powerful.'

'That's great,' Charlie remonstrated, 'but where does that leave us oldies? Surely a team moves at the pace of its slowest member?'

It was agreed that some thought would be given to the idea of inviting Mike along and, not long afterwards, Ollie called me to say that he and Charlie had both decided to change their role in the project. 'We would want to enjoy the experience,' Charlie told me later, 'and I know that, once you get competitive, you take any

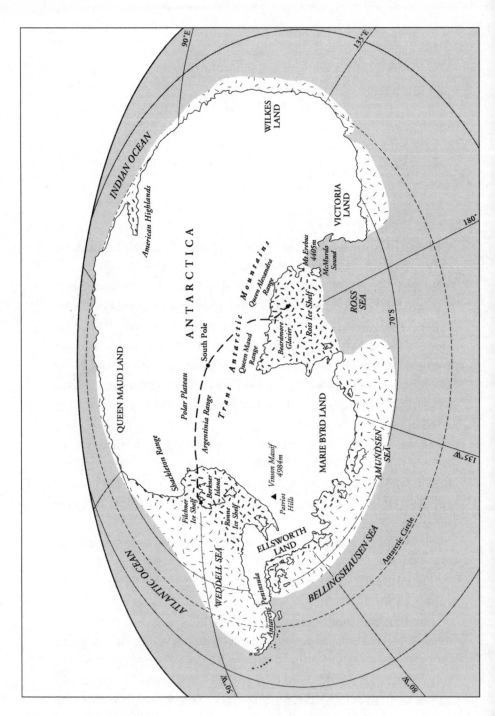

The continent of Antarctica

signs of enjoyment on my part as being tantamount to mutiny and a clear sign that we should be travelling faster.'

So he and Ollie took on the role of organisers from London, and I approached Mike Stroud by telephone.

Usually, the only position that I can tolerate on an expedition is that of team leader. Ollie, Charlie and Mike were totally aware of my peculiarity in this respect, but all three were strong personalities and not yes-men. My policy with everyone on any journey is to follow the democratic route (*when* there is time), of talking about options rather than pronouncing dictatorial and unilateral decisions. If others, whether or not they form a majority, favour an opinion which I believe to be stupid, dangerous or unlikely to help attain the goal of the expedition, then I overrule them, no matter how disaffected this may make them feel. In fact, because most fellow polar travellers know how to progress over snow and ice, we normally all agree on the best way forward, so contretemps are quite rare.

I knew very little in depth about Mike. This may seem strange as he had, by 1990, already come on four of my Arctic expeditions and we had been through a great deal together. To take *friends* on stressful expeditions has always seemed to me to be foolish, since I can think of no easier way of marring a friendship for ever. An expedition's aim is best achieved by individuals who can look after themselves, need little or no directing or nursing and are tough in body and mind. I look for professional or dogged people and treat any friendship resulting from an expedition as an unexpected bonus.

Polar expeditions are well known for causing stress and enmity between participants and quite why Ollie, Charlie, Mike and I had never come to blows, literally or even verbally, during our Arctic journeys remains a mystery to me.

'I know you. You like to lead from the front,' Mike observed. I conceded we would take hourly turns in navigation before he finally agreed to join. He also wrung out of me the agreement that he could conduct an extensive physiological research programme throughout the journey. This was bad news since I hate the sight of blood, especially my own, but it seemed a reasonable penalty in order to secure Mike's participation.

Prince Charles was once more our patron and he asked us to use the expedition to raise funds for multiple sclerosis research. We partly based this on members of the public pledging a penny a mile covered. Since Antarctica is over fifty times the size of Great Britain, a lot of pennies were involved.

Timing, as ever, is crucial when contemplating the Antarctic. Because the Antarctic plateau is so high and so cold, the period when humans can travel over it is severely limited. So is the availability of transport to and from Antarctica. We would be flown in on the Atlantic side and taken off by cruise ship on the Pacific side, which meant walking 1,700 miles between 1 November 1992, the very earliest flight date, and 16 February, the cruise ship's departure date. We would be pulling sledges at least sixteen miles a day for 108 days with loads likely to exceed 350 pounds, well in excess of any manhauling achievements to date.

In 1903 Scott, Shackleton and Wilson hauled loads of 175 pounds. Eight years later, on 'the worst journey in the world', Wilson, Bowers and Cherry-Garrard started out with 253 pounds. Especially unnerving for us were the much more recent observations of Reinhold Messner, the world's greatest mountaineer, and Arved Fuchs, Germany's top polar explorer, during their own crossing attempt. I had serious doubts that Mike and I could outperform such a team. Of his Antarctic journey Messner wrote: 'With sledge-loads of 264lbs, the longest stretch would be murderously strenuous. Perhaps even impossible . . . 264lbs is a load for a horse not a human being.'

By early October the projected weight of our sledge-loads had gone up to 400 pounds. We were entering the realms of the theoretically impossible but it was too late to back out now. To mention 400 pounds per load to anyone with the slightest knowledge of manhauling was to invite ridicule . . . so we didn't. The starting loads finally climbed to 485 pounds each. And that despite paring our gear down to minimal necessities.

On a gusty morning in late October Ginny drove me to Heathrow. We said goodbye in the carpark for there would be many people in the terminal. I waved as she drove off and thanked God for her. I had told myself after many previous journeys that I would never again leave her at our bleak Exmoor home for the long and lonely winter. As she left I felt wretchedly guilty. It occurred to me that *I* had never spent a single night alone at our house on the moor.

As Mike and Morag Howell, again in charge of our communications, chatted on the plane, I idly considered their motives in coming along. I knew Mike's. He had spent two years of his life, seven years earlier, hoping to walk to the South Pole with Swan and Mear but, to his dismay, another man was eventually selected, leaving him merely first reserve. Now, whether or not we managed to cross the whole continent, he knew that he stood a chance of at least making it to the Pole.

When I am asked for my own life motives I openly admit that expedition leadership is quite simply my chosen way of making a living: and under 'occupation' in my passport the entry has always stated 'travel writer'. Mike found my financial motivation upsetting and 'commercial'. His own rationale was more romantic. He talked of stunning landscapes and equated his adventures with a more intense version of the pleasures he had found as a boy from mountaineering, hill-walking and rock-climbing. I am not introspective and find it awkward having to dig within myself to produce replies to journalistic questions about motivation. I liked the response of Jean-Louis Etienne when asked why he went on polar expeditions. He replied: 'Because I like it. You never ask a basketball player why he plays: it is because he enjoys it. It is like asking someone why he likes chocolate.'

The KLM Boeing stopped at Sao Paulo, Montevideo, Santiago, Puerto Montt and finally Punta Arenas on the southern tip of Chile. We were met here by Annie Kershaw of Adventure Network (ANI). Annie was the widow of Giles Kershaw, our Transglobe Twin Otter pilot in Antarctica, who had later died in a gyrocopter accident. Annie had taken over running ANI, his polar air charter business on his death. Her first DC6 passenger flight of the year to her tented camp and ice runway at Patriot Hills in Antarctica was scheduled to depart two days after our arrival in Punta Arenas, South America's most southerly city. Until the Panama Canal replaced the Cape Horn route, Punta Arenas flourished with 138 brothels to cope with visiting sailors. Now it is a strategic Chilean naval base. The 200,000-strong population are mostly descended from nineteenth-century immigrants: Spaniards and Germans just outnumber the descendants of Scottish shepherds and Croatian goldminers. Chilean grannies in fur coats could still be heard speaking English in Scots accents almost as thick as Morag's. Unfortunately, engine problems delayed take off for six days, the first dent in our tight schedule.

We flew south over the South Atlantic and then Antarctica for nine hours. At last, in the endless white sheet below we glimpsed a flash of tiny figures, tents and two Twin Otters. The notorious blue ice airstrip of Patriot Hills flashed beneath us. Twice our Canadian pilot rehearsed his landing to test the cross-wind. Then, with a shattering impact that could not have done any part of the DC6 much good, we struck the ice and bounced, rattling over the rippled blue surface. I do not remember any other landing even half as impressive in thirty years of arriving at remote spots in small aircraft.

Three hours later, Mike and I had transferred to one of the Twin Otters bound for Antarctica's Atlantic coastline. With us were Terry Lloyd, Rob Bowles and our radio base leader, Morag Howell. The Twin Otter ski-plane roared over the ice-front of the Weddell Sea, a vertical cliff forming the seaward face of the Filchner Ice-shelf. Antarctica is composed of two vast ice-sheets divided by a mountan chain. The sheets contain ten million square kilometres of ice which, in places, is four and a half kilometres thick and moves slowly but surely seawards. This huge wilderness provides scientists with a unique playground of volcanoes, fast-flowing glaciers, mobile ice-sheets, katabatic winds of frightening power and a perfectly pure and sterile interior where temperatures in winter can reach −100°C. After several cautious rehearsals, our pilot found a relatively smooth stretch of snow at the point where Berkner Island meets both the ice-shelf and the sea. We were set down at 78°19.8′ South and 43°47′ West on Antarctica's Atlantic seaboard.

Morag helped us unload and wished us well. For the next few months she would attempt to keep radio contact with us from a tent at Patriot Hills and with our UK base which was manned by her husband Flo at their home in Aberdeen. We watched the little aircraft depart until the engine noise was a distant drone and the great silence of Antarctica closed about us.

Months of unspoken apprehension were coming to a head. The key question was whether or not full loads of 485 pounds each, including the hundred days' fuel taken on at Patriot Hills, could be moved by the two of us. The main bulk was rations. These were equally important both to our chances of success and to Mike's physiological research. Each bag was packed to provide two men with twenty-four hours of food at a daily intake of 5,200 calories. This packing system had evolved over a period of sixteen years of polar journeys, beginning with my first North Pole attempt in 1976.

The average daily intake of both Scott's and Amundsen's teams was 4,500 calories per man. This proved enough for the Norwegians who skied unencumbered and with husky power. But to support the hard labour of the British manhaulers, the amount was insufficient and they slowly starved. The first man to weaken and die was Taff Evans, the biggest and heaviest on Scott's team, the man they 'least expected to fail'.

I considered our team's vital statistics. I was eleven years older than Mike and approaching my fiftieth birthday. I was taller by five inches and heavier by three stone. But in terms of sheer strength, especially of the vital lower limb powerbase, Mike was clinically tested as considerably stronger.

At home on our Exmoor farm, Ginny would give me twice her

own food portions, although she worked harder than I did. Over the months ahead I would be consuming exactly the same calorific intake as Mike. I feared that, like the heavily built Evans on Scott's team, my performance would deteriorate first and more markedly than Mike's. I determined from the outset, therefore, to avoid my normal course of forging ahead at maximum output.

As each piece of equipment was loaded we ticked it off in our notebooks, alongside its weight, down to the nearest ounce. The total was, as we had feared, 485 pounds each, constituting far heavier loads than those of any previous polar manhaul journey on record.

We finished loading the sledges and looked at their bulk. Then at each other, and shrugged. The moment of truth had arrived. We adjusted the manhaul harnesses about our stomachs and shoulders. I leaned against the traces with my full bodyweight. The near half-ton sledge paid no attention. I looked back and spotted an eight-inch ice rut across the front of the runners. I tugged again with my left shoulder only, and the sledge, avoiding the rut, moved forward. I will never forget that instant. I *could* pull a 485-pound sledge. Mike was also on the move. The expedition was under way.

After a hundred yards I stopped, out of breath. I was pleased to see, looking back, that Mike was also labouring hard. The thought of pulling my sledge for an entire mile, never mind to the South Pole and beyond, was appalling. The map, or strictly speaking chart (since the sea was beneath us), showed a rash of blue lines, the crevasse symbol, running south along the foot of Berkner Island for some eighty miles.

Should we fix a safety line between us before reaching the first crevasse? I knew this was our agreed drill but the sheer weight of the sledge had already biased me against any action beyond the sheer task of progress. Even though we were descending a gentle incline, the sledge was totally inert. The very instant I stopped pulling, it stopped moving. There was not the least glissade. I conjured up a parallel. If I were to lash together three average-sized adults, each weighing 160 pounds, dump them in a fibreglass bathtub with no legs and then drag them through sand-dunes for 1,700 miles, the difficulties involved would be similar.

My sledge-load soon grew to represent something animate and hostile. I knew the pattern well. First my inner anger would be directed at the weather, the equipment and the ice. Later at my companion. The same would hold good for Mike. I determined never to allow myself to think unnecessarily far ahead. Sufficient unto each day is the mileage thereof . . . providing daily progress tallies with the schedule.

After two hours I felt certain we had reached the ice-shelf. About a mile behind us and to our immediate north was the ice-front, a chaotic jumble of giant ice fragments where shelf met true sea-ice. In every other direction there was nothing but mirage shimmer and the great white glare of Antarctica.

After five and a half hours it was time to halt for we had been awake for twenty-four hours since leaving Punta Arenas. For navigation purposes, we must keep to a carefully timed daily schedule. I intended to use my watch and body shadow to establish direction all the way to the Pole and that meant keeping the sun due north at local midday. There were, I reasoned, only another 1,696 miles to cover and, since we had rations for a hundred days, there was yet time to find a way of increasing the daily average to sixteen miles. There must be absolutely no rest days or we would fail.

Remembering the promise I had made to Mike, I alternated the navigation with him at hourly intervals. I found this increasingly annoying since I had spent well over twenty years leading expeditions from the front and mistrusted anyone else's navigating abilities. Another thing that annoyed me, I reflected as my legs dangled inside my first mini-crevasse of the trip, was the ignorant complacency of journalists who said that of course it was 'different nowadays' with all our technological gadgetry. Crevasses are today, just as in the time of Scott and Mawson, the chief threat to Antarctic travellers and the danger has not lessened one iota over the intervening years.

Up to my armpits in deep soft snow, with my lower torso

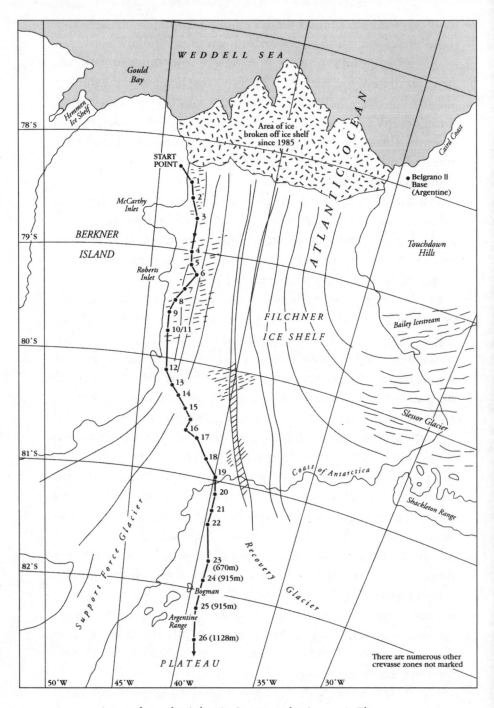

Ascent from the Atlantic Ocean to the Antarctic Plateau

treading air over nothingness, I only wished the gadgetry fallacy had some basis in reality. Too much movement on trying to extricate my body could in an instant collapse the whole snow-bridge. My attempts to look back at my sledge failed, for the hood of my parka and my cotton balaclava prevented sufficient lateral movement of my neck. Furthermore I had breathed into the balaclava as I fell, which had the immediate effect of misting up my goggles and the mist had frozen across the insides of the lens. To all intents and purposes I was blind since I had no hand free to tear off the goggles.

The alloy poles leading back from my body harness to the sledge had snapped close behind me, which actually helped me by allowing sufficient movement for me to wriggle up, inch by inch, until my hips were out of the hole. The rest was easy. I replaced the broken poles with rope traces.

Many of the crevasses we were to negotiate were over a hundred feet wide with sagging bridges. The weakest point was not, as might be expected, in the centre but along the fault-line, where the bridge was joined to the crevasse wall's lip. In the most dangerous cases the whole bridge had already descended a few feet down into the maw before catching on some unseen temporary stopper. New snow had then partially filled the resulting trough.

Hauling the sledges down on to such teetering bridges presented no great physical task since gravity was on our side. If the bridge held under our initial weight, we pulled onwards over the centre span. At this point the going became singularly off-putting because, in order to manhaul our monster loads up the far side of the disintegrating bridge, maximum downward pressure with skis and sticks must be applied to its weakest point. There were moments of sickening apprehension as our straining ski sticks plunged through the crust, or part of a sledge lurched backwards, its prow or stern having broken through. I never grew inured to the crevasse hazard and continued to sweat and silently curse as each new death trap passed beneath us.

Fifteen miles above us was a feature first discovered by the British Antarctic Survey nine years before, the hole in the ozone layer, which is also the nest where man-made pollutants called chlorofluorocarbons come to roost. Stratospheric winds carry these compounds, long used in aerosols and coolants, south, where they mix with high-altitude clouds in the cold and dark of the Antarctic winter. As the sun returns in spring, these frozen chemical clouds react with its rays, releasing chlorine molecules that temporarily dissolve the thin layer of ozone that protects earthbound life from harmful solar radiation. Since we were travelling directly below this hazard, it made sense to cover our skin. But, hauling huge loads in our tight dog harnesses, we needed to breathe deeply, gasping for air without fogging our goggles, so the sun shone day after day on our uncovered lips and noses. Mine deteriorated rapidly. The lip scabs always stuck together overnight and, when I woke, the act of tearing my lips apart in order to speak and drink invariably opened up all the raw places. Breakfast from a communal bowl consisted of porridge oats in a gravy of blood.

Soon our minds churned over the fact that we were not averaging ten miles a day. We had to cut the loads.

'Mike, I'm chucking my duvet jacket. I have hardly worn it all week. We work so hard we will keep warm even when winter comes.'

He nodded. We both knew it was a big decision. The weather was now warm, in polar terms. Maybe we would have second thoughts later. But there would be no later if we could not get a move on now. Next morning we buried the two down-filled jackets along with the empty ration packs. I was later bitterly to regret the decision but it is easy to be wise with hindsight.

At the end of the first week we entered a zone of great instability. Thunderous roars warned us that the whole ice-shelf had entered a hyperactive phase, causing hitherto safe snow-bridges to collapse all around us into their crevasses. No amount of ice lore could keep us out of trouble here. A gaping hole opened up with an explosion of snow spray as we watched. Some ten paces ahead of Mike, and 45 feet wide by 120 feet in length, it lay directly across his intended path. Had it occurred but a few seconds later he and his sledge would have disappeared, along with several tons of plunging snow-bridge. All around us renewed implosions announced further cratering. The sensation was memorably frightening. We must escape at once to a safer area. But where was safer? Only the looming bulk of Berkner Island offered certain stability. We roped up with nervous fingers, fearing that at any moment the snow beneath us would open up and dump us hundreds of feet. The surface of the ice shelf all about us rumbled and reverberated again and again. Geysers of snow dust rose into the air. The feeling was similar to closing on enemy troops when under mortar fire. As each new crump exploded at random, the fear increased that the next catastrophe would have our name on it.

The nylon rope between us was sixty feet in length. We moved as fast as the sledges and the wings of fear allowed. Time stood still. I came to an abrupt halt as a wave of cold air rushed past, accompanied by the loudest and closest of the explosions. I ducked, for the all-engulfing sound seemed to pass both overhead and underfoot.

Immediately between Mike and me an immense crater appeared. One moment the ice-shelf ahead was solid and white. The next a maw like the mouth of the Underworld, steaming with snow vapour, lay across our intended route, wide enough to swallow a double-decker bus. The roaring echoes of imploding snow cascading into the bowels of the ice-shelf returned in successive waves, like shore ripples from an undersea volcano. Although a cold wind scoured the ice-sheet, I sweated with fear. The next hour was a nightmare of apprehension; nowhere was safe. Only pure luck enabled us to escape from this volatile zone.

On the ninth day the ice-shelf showed signs of climbing towards the interior. There were no spot heights on my local chart and my small-scale map of Antarctica showed only that we were about to enter the largest crevasse field on the Filchner Ice-shelf. Mike agreed that we seemed to be climbing but maintained that the undulating series of rising steppes, which I could see through the wafting mists, was in reality only an illusion in our minds caused by the heavy loads and mirage effects. We could not actually see any gradient.

Fortunately the deep drifts of the ice-shelf did not extend to these wind-scoured flanks so the going was easier than at any time since the firm coastal strip. Temperatures of around −15°C were not low enough to coarsen the surface and Mike, when navigating, set a pace that seemed to me as the day went by increasingly and unnecessarily fast.

I resolved to make no comment and at first found no difficulty in keeping hard on his heels. My shoulder blades and lower back screamed at me but the old competitive urge came back. Why let this guy steam ahead? For almost twenty years now I had pulled sledges, in all conditions, faster than any colleague of any age, and on the northern expeditions over the past six years I had out-pulled Mike, day after day, in even the worst of Arctic conditions.

I talked persuasively to myself in this vein but all the time Mike's small but powerful legs pulled on piston-like and I began to realise it was self-defeating for me to keep up such a pace. At thirty-nine Mike was in his prime. In Siberia, when he was thirty-six and I was forty-seven, I had no difficulty keeping well ahead. So, at that stage, his eleven-year advantage made no difference. Something must have happened since.

Like Shackleton, the first man to plan a crossing of Antarctica, I found myself preoccupied with the ageing process. Each new ache of muscle or tendon soon achieved obsession rating and blisters and chafing sores screamed their presence through every long and toilsome day. I swore silently when Mike was leading and moving faster than suited my pace for then I was forced by pride to abandon the rhythm of my polar plod. Self-pity is not an attractive trait and I do not remember indulging in it on previous occasions. As the days struggled by and the stress mounted, we faced increasing tensions between us. We could not ease the pain, the fear, above all the sheer burden of the sledge-loads by kicking our sledges, so we took it out on each other, at first silently, as had been our wont in the Arctic, but then with controlled outbursts.

After only five miles on the seventeenth day Mike's foot blisters became painful and he told me he thought it would be sensible to stop. I said nothing in the interests of diplomacy and we camped four hours early, to my mind a dangerous precedent.

We reached the Antarctic coastline some time during the twentieth morning. We could not actually see where the floating ice-shelf stopped and the continental ice began since the joining point was covered in seamless snow, but once we crossed over we began the true continental crossing journey. At first any uphill gradient was imperceptible but by the afternoon each and every heave on the traces required concentrated mental and physical effort. And then we reached the start of the first sastrugi field, a great rash of iron-hard furrows lying directly across our route. I know no other way to advance when the ice gets nasty than to attack it head-on with every ounce of gristle at your disposal. Tightening my harness and stick-straps, I focused on each successive wall of ice and threw energy conservation to the winds. Towards the end of the day, after eleven hours of uphill hauling, we came to an especially rugged zone of serrated ice and Mike lagged well behind, despite my pauses for him to catch up. At the end of the final hour I had the tent up in time for his arrival and knew at once that he was livid. Mike let rip. I had surged irresponsibly ahead despite the evil terrain and, worse, I had gone straight at the sastrugi instead of taking a sensible indirect route through the worst of it. Fortunately, the hostility we nurtured towards each other on the route almost invariably evaporated once we were in the tent, which saved the journey for both of us from becoming a non-stop nightmare.

That is not to say that our irritations with each other eased. He would surge far ahead and complain at my steady plod, when not attacking sastrugi. I was infuriated when his watch stopped because he had not put in a new battery before leaving England, despite several reminders. This meant I had to let him have mine and shout when it was my turn in front. His blister and diarrhoea stops also outraged me. I was all set to have the whole thing out with him when he announced that the abscess on his heel was so swollen that he had decided to operate. I watched with intense admiration as he gave himself two deep injections of anaesthetic and then plunged a scalpel deep into the swelling with diagonal incisions. Pus poured out and the swelling visibly decreased. Mike then bandaged up his heel and packed away his medical kit. I am not sure whether or not he felt faint but I certainly did. I said nothing more about the early halts or the stricken Rolex.

Over the next three days we climbed to 5,000 feet above sea-level with constant Force Eight winds in our faces. Arriving some distance ahead of Mike one evening, I began to erect the tent by fixing a safety line to my sledge before trying to slot the ten-foot alloy poles into the sleeving. The fourth and last pole was almost positioned when an especially violent blast tore the tent from my mitts and buckled one of the poles. Since I only carried a single eighteen-inch spare pole section for the entire journey, I left the bent pole in place and prayed we would be spared a big katabatic event in the days ahead.

I thought of Ginny back on Exmoor. She had lit an outsize church candle in our kitchen and intended to keep it burning day and night until I returned. It was four feet long but so many hundreds of miles stretched ahead of us I could not help but think the candle would run out long before I came home.

One morning I noticed a black item behind Mike's sledge. It turned out to be a spare battery. Mike looked grim, as well he might, for he had packed the battery deep inside his load and there was no way it could have escaped but through a hole in the hull. We rolled the sledge on to one side and then the other, revealing a ragged split across its entire width. This had been caused by Mike falling twenty feet into a crevasse days earlier. We had done our best to repair it at the time, but not, it now seemed, well enough. We erected the tent as a new gale blew up, unloaded, repaired and reloaded his sledge, then set off again to make mileage over the last four hours of the day.

The following day brought our first true white-out as well as sastrugi. When we camped, after a memorably nasty ten hours lurching over unseen obstacles and crashing into invisible trenches, I found both my cheeks burning and inflamed by UV rays. I had exposed my cheeks to help demist my goggles but it had been a mistake. Mike's eyes, even though he wore goggles for all but two hours, were also affected. Soon after we camped he developed snow blindness symptoms. Only the mildest of attacks, but enough to have him lying back in considerable pain.

Since our overall speed and rate of progress for the first forty days were slightly better than for any previous Antarctic manhauling journey on record, our pace should not theoretically have caused dissension. But we were both under increasing strain and our bodies, under the stress of slow starvation combined with enormous energy expenditure, were altering chemically. Subsequent analysis of our blood samples was to show that our whole enzyme systems, everything that controlled our absorption of fat, were changing and we were recording levels of gut hormones twice as high as were previously known to science. We were adapting to our high-fat rations in a way hitherto unrecognised. Furthermore, with zero remaining body fat, we were losing muscle and weight from our hearts as well as our body mass.

By the fifth week Mike's intermittent surges of speedy sledging were telling on him. He confided to his diary that he was feeling hypoglycaemic. He told me that he could 'feel the weight falling off'. On Christmas Eve we were able to take full advantage for the first time of a wind driving us south and use the sails we had optimistically brought along to attach to our sledges. But on Christmas Day the wind veered again. I was now suffering from haemorrhoids, which at least allowed me to forget the pain in my feet due to the new aggravation. Cherry-Garrard wrote: 'Sometimes it was difficult not to howl.' I understood how he felt.

One day Mike produced from his science pack two small bottles of very expensive water for us to drink in the interest of his urine sample analysis. He told me not to spill any because each bottleful cost hundreds of pounds, and it was like atomic heavy water, but non-radioactive. I never ceased to admire Mike's dedication to his research work. One of his science projects measured our calorific experience. The results were startling: 'When we made the ascent to the plateau, the isotopes gave daily energy expenditure of 10,670 calories in Ran and 11,650 in me. They confirmed the highest maintained energy expenditures ever documented – values that must lie close to the physiological limit.'

On our sixtieth day Mike had a very bad time and told me he must be wrong about the effects of altitude. He was worried within himself about his ability to continue fending off negative thoughts. He wrote: 'Last night I did express to Ran my fears of not being able to hack it if things go badly. Needless to say I got a sort of "we will be tough" type talk rather than true understanding. He gets his strength from "God and family and the whole clan here inside me". All very useful but I know it won't help me if I can see the whole chance of success slipping away and us just slogging on.'

That night I gave Mike two chocolate squares and he seemed to appreciate the gesture. I am not good at being sympathetic. I knew that Mike was agnostic and did not expect him to gain any mental help in that direction. I had hoped, however, that he might be able to invoke his family and the knowledge that they were all gunning for him but he seemed to scoff at this as too contrived a mental aid.

My practice was to hype up my mind during the first hour of every day, when the pain from my feet was at its worst, by simply remembering that I was not alone in facing the dreaded hours ahead. I pictured my grandfather who had trapped in northern Canada and fought for his country all over the world. I thought of my father and uncle who were killed in the two world wars. I pictured my wife, my mother and my sisters and I knew that all of them were right behind me, helping to suppress the ever-lurking urge to put a stop to the pain and the cold by giving up.

The last 200 miles before the Pole involved us in climbing above 10,000 feet. The altitude effects added to our debilitation and the loads were beginning to change us in many subtle ways. Mike reached the end of his tether, grinding to a halt in his tracks, head lolling, as if he were about to succumb to hypothermia. I set up the tent, got the cooker going and he accepted a mug of tepid soup in a trance. My mind was in a turmoil. I had little doubt but that he was pushing himself far too hard. I was doing likewise. We had no alternative. We had to earn our daily ration with the mileage put behind us.

On our sixty-eighth day the wind dropped and the mists cleared. Towards evening there was a *thing* ahead. For the first time in over 700 miles a man-made object was visible in the snow. Could it be the Pole? The item turned out to be a half-buried meteorological balloon. After seven hours' hauling on 16 January, on the eighty-first anniversary of Scott's sad arrival at the same point, we topped the final rise and came to the South Pole. The journey was far from over but we had dragged to the Pole just enough stores to allow us to cross the continent and survive. If our luck held. It was a moment of sheer elation. Especially so for Mike, who had not been selected back in 1985 when Roger Mear was finalising his Pole team.

All the isolation of the past months fell away. The polar site had vastly altered, even in the twelve short years since my last visit. Strangely shaped installations on jacked-up steel legs reared monstrously in every direction from the main black-roofed dome in which over-wintering scientists lived and worked. A small huddle of nine figures had come out to greet us, but we put aside thoughts of the food available in the dome canteen as we forced ourselves to continue north. In all, we paused at the Pole for only eighty minutes.

Only then, beyond the Pole, did we discover the true meaning of *cold*. Our condition in terms of body deterioration, slow starvation, inadequate clothing, wind chill temperature, altitude, and even the day of the year, exactly matched those of Scott and his four companions as they came away from the Pole in 1912.

We learned from Morag that Erling Kagge had reached the Pole before us and had been airlifted out the previous week. The Norwegian press talked of his winning the race, but our sledges were twice as heavy and our journey twice as long so our morale was not too badly dented by this misleading piece of media spin.

I could sense that Mike was in a bad way, despite his continued power surges. I knew that even now he would never recognise

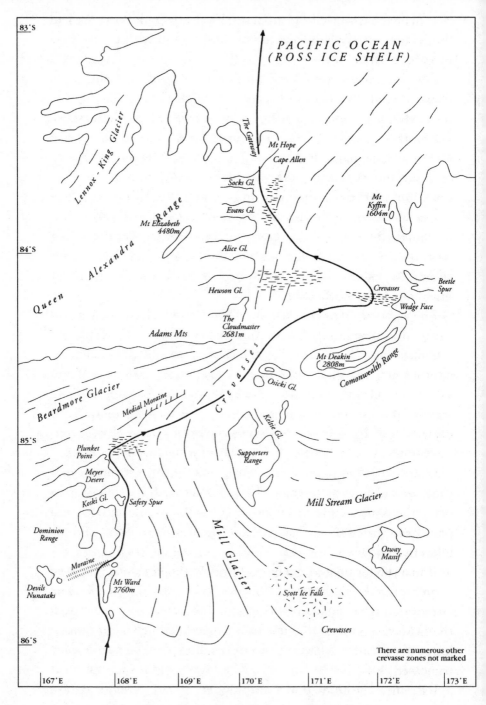

Descent from the Antarctic Plateau to the Pacific Ocean

that his pace was his own worst enemy. I would never be able to 'bully' him into copying my polar plod. I could only try to compromise with him over matters of pace wherever necessary. I had my own mounting problems with harness sores, diarrhoea and haemorrhoids, and the most agonising throbbing pain in my feet. Mike diagnosed possible bone infection and put me on antibiotics. I realised how lucky I had been for fifty years in experiencing little pain. Broken bones and teeth, torn-off digits, frostbite and chronic kidney stones had seemed unpleasant at the time. But now I knew real pain and I feared lest it overwhelm me.

On 30 January we recorded our first barometric descent of a few hundred feet, but this welcome news was balanced by a potentially disastrous discovery. Mike had lost both his ski sticks off his sledge. Trying to share mine and progress with one each was unbalancing, and when Mike again fell behind, I gave him both, but he was once more on the edge of hypothermia and we had to camp early. Our bodily condition was becoming highly suspect. I was not in the business of leading suicide expeditions. We were approaching the edge of our ability to cope safely with very extreme conditions and this was, we both knew, because we were starving, losing ten ounces every day through a deficiency of 3,000 calories each and every day for three months.

The next day Mike began to work out a satisfactory way of forcing his sledge to move with just one stick and I constantly checked the compass for I knew we would need great accuracy to enter the Mill Glacier, the start of the long descent from the plateau to the Pacific coast. Mike and I needed to make no mistakes from now on. We were committed to the 9,000-foot descent as if in a rubber boat at the moment of yielding to the first pull of a great rapid. The horizons which now opened to us were awesome, a sprawling mass of rock and ice in motion. These were the headwaters of a slow-moving ice-river. Huge open chasms leered ahead and standing ice-waves reared up at the base of black truncated cliffs.

I scanned the skies north and saw no clouds. So long as the

good visibility conditions remained, I could find the best route. I felt a God-given confidence and, for the first time on this journey, the warm pleasure of challenge. I knew the rules. Never waste a minute. Pause for nothing. Here there could be no place for my polar plod. So long as the weather held we must go like the wind. This was the region of monster holes described by Cherry-Garrard as 'vast crevasses into which we could have dropped the *Terra Nova* with ease'.

We came at last to where the Mill joins the Beardmore Glacier and another breathtaking vista opened up. Messner and Fuchs, the only others to have attempted our route, had lost their way at this point. We had to cope with more crevasses, interrupted for a while by a field of sharp sastrugi. Unable to cross these with my skis on, I made the fatal error of unclipping and strapping them to my sledge. The very first crevasse bridge I attempted to cross without skis was a minor affair, no more than four feet wide and similar to hundreds we had safely traversed. Because my harness waistband was unfastened the sledge ropes did not restrain me as they should have done and my abrupt plunge into the dark shaft was halted only by the thin webbing strap of my ski stick looped over my right wrist.

I dangled for a moment more surprised than frightened. The fear came as soon as I realised that only my ski stick, wedged above me and still fastened to my wrist, was postponing my imminent demise. Any movement that dislodged the stick was liable to send me downwards. Throwing caution to the winds, I lunged upwards with my free hand, my feet scrabbling against each smooth ice-wall. With my arm strength sapping, I lifted my body high enough to reach the crevasse lip with my mitted hand and then to heave my chest over to safety. For a minute I lay shaking with relief until, with dismay, I realised that my stick and the other mitt in its wrist loop were loose down the hole. I inched to one side until I could squint down, my breath rushing out in a sigh of relief as I spotted the ski stick now loosely lodged some four feet down. Using my boots as grabs, I managed to retrieve both stick and vital mitt.

A few days later we strayed into a treacherous crevasse field, as lethal as any Marxist minefield, but our guardian angels saw us through successive obstacles of a hairy nature. At last we reached a steep slope some 500 feet above the edge of the Ross Ice-shelf and pitched our ninetieth camp. We were within half a mile of having walked over the highest, coldest, most inhospitable continent on earth from Atlantic to Pacific. How much longer did we stand a chance of surviving? Since all our main aims were now achieved, the only practical rationale for continuing must be to reach the ship before its departure in eight days' time.

On our ninety-second travel day, clear of crevasses at last, we hauled for ten and a half hours over the floating Ross Ice-shelf. On 12 February, our ninety-fifth day of travel, the last US aeroplane left Antarctica. In five days our ship would steam out of the Ross Sea. We were still 289 nautical miles from Ross Island. The time for procrastination was over. I radioed the Twin Otter which picked us up from the ice forty miles 'out to sea' on the Pacific Ocean.

Mike wrote in his diary that evening:

While Ran made the radio call for our pick-up, I went and stood outside. Our tent was pitched in the middle of a huge white plain and the sun was shining. To the south, a thin line ran back from where I stood to disappear beyond the horizon, towards mountains and wind-sluiced valleys. There it ran back up the glacier and then due south to the Pole. It continued on – straight for the rest of the plateau, and dropped tortuously through valleys, dune and sastrugi to the ice-shelf on the far side and so to the Atlantic coast. It was the longest unbroken track that any man had ever made.

We will never know how much farther we could have continued over the ice-shelf because there are too many ifs and buts. As it was, our achievement took us into the *Guinness Book of Records* and Mike and I were awarded OBEs. If, like Scott, we had had no option but to battle on, it is my opinion that we would have died short of Ross Island.

Scott's modern detractors make much of his stupidity in championing manhaul travel over the use of dogs. Amundsen's colleague Hanssen is often quoted as concluding: 'What shall one say of Scott and his companions who were their own sledge dogs? Anyone with any experience will take his hat off to Scott's achievement. I do not believe men ever have shown such endurance at any time, nor do I believe there ever will be men to equal it.' All attempts for a century, whether by Norwegians, Russians or Americans, to cross the continent unaided and using snowmachines or dog teams had failed miserably. In hauling our own loads across this area, greater in mass by far than the United States, we have shown that manpower can indeed be superior to dog-power and, in doing so, have partly exonerated Scott's much-abused theories on the matter.

Our record in the *Guinness Book* simply states: 'The longest totally self-supporting polar sledge journey ever made and the first totally unsupported crossing of the Antarctic landmass was achieved by R. Fiennes and M. Stroud. They covered a distance of 2,170 km (1,350 miles).'

A year later various types of kites and para-wings emerged that enabled Antarctica to be crossed with far less effort in a mere fifty days. Now it is possible to traverse both Antarctica and the Arctic Ocean with no outside support by harnessing the wind with lightweight sails. A sledger, using modern kites, can pick up and harness winds from over 180°. Until 1994 the great journeys of Shackleton and his successors, including Mike and me, made use of crude sails which could only run before a directly following wind. Should Mike and I have described our 1993 expedition, or Shackleton's for that matter, as 'unsupported' when we harness the wind, albeit in a minimal way? It is a question of definition, for there is, after all, no polar version of the International Olympic Committee.

11

How Not to Get Old?

The media in Britain reacted to our Antarctic journey in a mostly positive vein, but there are always some who will rattle on about the point of it all. Few people bother to write to counterattack columnists unless they feel very strongly. Several letters bounced back this time, including one from John Hunt, the leader of the first ascent of Mount Everest, who reprimanded *The Independent*'s Margaret Maxwell: 'It ill becomes Ms Maxwell to question the motives underlying this astonishing feat of human endurance and courage . . . Surely at a time when, as never before, we need to develop these qualities in the young generation, this story should be accepted at its face value, as a shining example to Britain's youth.'

Various letters also flurried between the polar pundits as to precisely what had been the previous record. Dr Geoffrey Hattersley-Smith, a great polar traveller of the 1950s, wrote: 'Shackleton's party, without support, covered a distance of 1,215 statute miles. They picked up depots laid by themselves on the outward leg of the same march. It is this record that they have broken. All honour belongs to both Sir Ernest's and Sir Ranulph's parties, men of different eras whose achievements approached the limits of endurance. Comparisons are superfluous if not impossible to make.'

Another aspect which exercised the media was a supposed falling out between Mike and myself. It is as if the press cannot believe two people can survive great dangers together without being at each other's throats with recriminations immediately afterwards. Sometimes it is the newspapers that help bring this state of affairs about. Reinhold Messner and Arved Fuchs completed their supported crossing of Antarctica in a reasonably friendly fashion but *Stern* magazine contrived to portray Fuchs as the quiet hero and Messner the villain which drove a fatal wedge between them. Roger Mear and Robert Swan managed things better. After their 1985 South Pole journey they maintained what Mear called 'an outward pretence of cohesion', but in their joint book they were open and honest about one another's failings and their relationship did not degenerate into a mud-slinging match that would ruin whatever mutual feelings of respect had withstood the journey itself.

For eighteen years of polar expeditions Charlie Burton, Oliver Shepard and I managed to survive these post-expedition strains. Ollie and Charlie were loyal and honourable men. They nursed the odd grudge, as did I, but they kept these to themselves and we remained the most solid of friends as a result and despite constant rumours to the contrary. I can say the same for my good friend of twenty years, Mike Stroud.

The Director of the Scott Polar Research Institute at the time, Dr John Heap, told me that he considered that Mike and I were 'a marriage made in heaven, with your initiative and drive and Mike's scientific ability'. After our return, Mike's sister, Debbie, told a reporter: 'When I heard that Mike nearly died through hypothermia, I didn't know whether to run up to Ran and hug him for saving my brother or whether to shout at him for putting him in that danger in the first place.' Mike told the press that we had got on 'extraordinarily well' together and, when asked if he would consider another expedition with me, replied: 'I can think of nobody I would rather do these things with.' My own responses had been on similar lines.

Five peaceful months after our return from Antarctica, a tabloid reporter produced a full-page article which claimed to be based on

Mike's writings, which began: 'The smiles and mutual backslapping that marked the return of Fiennes and Stroud from their record-breaking Antarctic expedition was a sham and their ninety-five day trek was peppered with bitter arguments.'

Mike phoned me the day that the article appeared, apologised profusely and explained that he was furious with the newspaper which had completely misquoted him. He wrote back to the paper to say they had published 'unadulterated rubbish' and that he hoped to be able to go on another expedition with me before too long. For my part I had no intention of switching from Mike, should another expedition plan crop up.

At this point however I had had enough of polar travels for the time being and found I could be happy and fulfilled just living at home with Ginny and her ever-increasing Aberdeen Angus herd, by that time over a hundred head of cattle. Each animal had a name and Ginny would often ask me to go and check on Gravity or Umberto or Bakhaita or whoever in one of the fields. The farm was situated at 1,300 feet above sea-level in the heart of the Exmoor National Park and attracted fog off the surrounding moors a good deal of the time. Locating a particular cow or bull was never easy, since to me they were all black, furry and identical. Only by their yellow ear tags could I initially identify any individual, although by 1995, after two whole expedition-free and domesticated years on the farm, I had become personally acquainted with the looks and foibles of at least two dozen of the Angus and a good handful of Ginny's Black Welsh Mountain sheep.

There were also her birds, about 200 at the time, ranging free in a fenced-off field with two ponds. Quail, guinea fowl, ornamental ducks, geese and egg-laying bantams rootled, swam and squawked alongside coots, pheasants, mallards and Canada geese. Iridescent Kayuga ducks were Ginny's favourites. In the summer of 1994 Ginny entered her best looking cows at a number of West Country shows and won a great many awards. My job was to lead her bulls around the rings, wearing an NHS doctor's white coat, tweed cap and Aberdeen Angus Society tie. Ollie Shepard was often at the same shows manning the mobile stall of the country clothing outfitters for whom he was working. That year Ginny and I also went to the Chelsea Flower Show, not to check out the exhibits, but to take the mickey out of Charlie Burton who was the head security officer controlling traffic and entry gates in a peaked cap and lapelled police-type jacket. The four of us met up on Exmoor or in London from time to time to yarn or to plan new projects that never left the drawing board.

Ginny's farm activities were profitable, though not hugely so. She did much of the work herself, including calf-delivery, basic husbandry, mucking out, feeding and field maintenance. She was self-taught as she had been in the fields of polar base leading and radio communications. To augment our income I worked for a number of lecture agencies who hired me as speaker for business conferences, dinners and awards ceremonies all over the world.

I had started to lecture about travel back in the early seventies for £18 per talk, mostly in London town halls to audiences of ladies with hats and hearing aids. As many as two or three dozen would turn up but as Ginny, who handled the slide show projector at the back, noted, 'They don't listen to you, Ran. I think they only turn up for the company and the free council cuppas.' By 1994 audiences at some of the events exceeded a thousand and, even after paying the lecture agency's 20 per cent plus 40 per cent to the Inland Revenue, we were able to live well enough and go skiing for a fortnight every December when the lecture season was over.

Ginny made many friends among the people who bought the Black Dog puppies that she bred from the original Arctic Black Dog – one was Monty Don, who later became a famous gardener. We spent a weekend with his family helping to clear some scrub on his property. Taking a rest, I observed, as though in slow motion, Ginny cutting down a fairly large tree. I watched as it fell and saw Monty, right in its path, bending over to start a chainsaw. I tried to scream a last-second warning but it was too late; the tree hit

Monty right across the back of his neck and knocked him flat. Both Ginny and I were sure he was dead. But somehow he wasn't, and he survived to become the Percy Thrower of the 21st century.

We had a good circle of friends, mostly from previous expeditions, my old regiments, or our school days, and we kept in close touch with our families. Ginny's father had died finally approving of our being married, her mother Janet and my own mother still lived in West Sussex and were good friends. My three sisters were all married, respectively to an Army colonel, an American surgeon and a Yorkshire-based farmer, so I had plenty of nephews and nieces who often stayed with us on Exmoor. Ginny's brother Charles had for years exported British-made goods to Asia and the Middle East, so we formed an export company together. I located suitable UK manufacturers, many of which had at some point sponsored our expeditions, and Charles found foreign buyers. We took a small percentage of the resulting sales contracts. Ginny's only sister, Abby, who had helped us with the Transglobe Expedition, moved to Liverpool and started her own publishing business there.

In March 1994 Ginny booked a surprise holiday for my fiftieth birthday. I was still ignorant of our destination when we followed the transit signs at Amsterdam's Schiphol Airport. The Scandinavian Airlines loudspeaker finally gave the game away – Iceland. We hired a Land Rover and spent a second honeymoon touring that weird and wonderful island of sagas, geysers and moonscapes. We had known and loved each other for four decades, we had no children and I knew that, without Ginny, there would be no point to my life.

Back home I had suffered financially due to the Lloyds insurance crash and, more ominously, I had noted an alarming drop in the number of contracts for conference presentations booked for 1995. Since this business had become 90 per cent of our income, I consulted Jeremy Lee, the acknowledged doyen of conference speakers. His advice was simple. You are, as in the movie business, only as good as your *next* project. At the time Maggie Thatcher had just dropped her speaker's fee to £20,000 but was still in great demand, as was ex-England Rugby captain Will Carling at £8,000. Conference agencies want celebrities, and if you have done nothing for a while, your chances of being chosen decrease with alarming speed. There was only one answer: another expedition, and in order to get the necessary sponsorship, it must have attendant media coverage, which in turn meant that its aim must be to complete a 'first'.

I had less than happy memories of the most recent Antarctic trip, so I would have favoured the Arctic for any future polar project. But in the autumn of 1995 I heard from Morag and Flo Howell in Aberdeen that the gossip grapevine in Norway was buzzing again. Not Erling Kagge this time, but his colleague Børge Ousland was planning an attempt to cross Antarctica solo and unsupported in the 1996–97 travel season. Ousland's rationale was clear. All the great polar challenges, north and south, had already been achieved by groups of two or more. All that was left was for an individual to try unaided.

Solo travel had never appealed to me. Half the fun of an expedition is the planning of it and, as with old soldiers, the shared memories afterwards. Also, since I make a living through books and talks about the expeditions, I need good photographs and film, which are difficult to get when by myself. On the plus side, however, a lone traveller can experience fewer frustrations caused by rivalry, discontent and, as with Mike and me, differences of pace.

The Howells warned me that Børge Ousland was an even better skier than Erling Kagge. This was the equivalent of a footballer even more skilled than Pele. Proof of this was not long in coming when, in the spring of 1996, Ousland reached the South Pole unsupported in a staggeringly quick forty-four days. Mike and I had taken sixty-eight days to reach the Pole during our 1993 crossing.

I discussed with Ginny the idea of competing with Ousland for the solo Antarctica crossing laurels. She shrugged and observed, 'You're not very fit.'

This was true. If I was to enter such a race, I had eleven months in which to train hard, for Ousland would start his solo crossing attempt in October 1996. At thirty-four years of age he was at the peak of his ability. At fifty-two I was getting rusty round the edges, but Mike Stroud had the answer – the Eco-Challenge race.

'It lasts for seven days and nights,' he told me, 'and I am entering a team. You need to be super-fit to stand any chance of even finishing the 500-mile course. Join my team.'

Mike explained that Eco-Challenge races occurred only once a year and involved athletes from all over the world. Teams from elite special forces units, physical training instructors from American universities, marathon-runners and orienteering clubs enter every year. Some are sponsored by Nike, Reebok and the like, who pay team members $10,000 each if they win, so the competition is fierce. Participants are usually selected for their supreme fitness and capacity for great endurance. The average age of the contestants is twenty-five. I agreed to sign on.

Mike had decided that his five-person team's make-up would buck the age trend. His idea was to have an age range stretching over five decades, in order to prove that endurance is not the prerogative of the young. Rebecca Stevens, Britain's first woman up Everest, was in her thirties. Mike was himself forty-one, I was fifty-two, Chris Brasher – the man who with Chris Chataway had paced Roger Bannister's first four-minute mile – was in his sixties, and Mike's father, Vic Stroud, a retired businessman and keen fell-walker, was seventy-one. In the end Chris Brasher had to withdraw, to be replaced by David Smith, a forty-four-year-old cardiologist from Exeter.

On day one at 5.00 a.m. in a high mountain pasture near Whistler Mountain in Jasper, British Columbia, seventy-four five-person teams charged away to the echo of the starting gun's signal reverberating through the forests all about us. On every side the broken silhouette of the Rockies reared above us until it was obscured by the dust cloud generated by 370 competitors.

Each team had two mountain ponies for the first twenty-six miles. Vic and Rebecca rode our stocky steeds and the rest of us ran. Then at a checkpoint, we wrapped up our gear in polythene bags and leaped into a raging river, the only way forward. Vic was swept away, and for several agonising moments we feared he would drown, until Mike rescued him. For four days we slogged up and down high mountains, through tangled undergrowth in forests, along streambeds, over crevassed glaciers and down cliffsides. Mike's face was so swollen from hornet bites that he could hardly see; Vic's backside remained badly blistered from the initial pony ride.

By day three we had moved from fifty-sixth position to forty-ninth. People from younger, tougher teams were dropping out. Next came the river section. The five of us crammed into two canoes and paddled hard day and night without pausing to rest, through some of the most beautiful scenery in North America. At the next checkpoint we exchanged the canoes for mountain bikes and, still unrested, pushed on all night and for most of the next day, suffering several falls in the process. Our final position was twenty-ninth.

The event and the previous months of training for it had successfully dragged me back to a reasonable level of fitness, but the solo Antarctic crossing attempt would need a lot more than physical abilities. I needed a support team, nutritional and medical advice, a communications network and the sort of media coverage that would persuade somebody to sponsor the whole project with at least a quarter of a million pounds.

As always before those journeys which Ginny could not join, she was a tower of strength and sound advice, based on her own wide polar experience. She would check my preparations with meticulous care and home in on key items I might have forgotten. She was never keen on my leaving her for an expedition, but she never tried to dissuade me from going. This time she was more worried than usual because I was going solo. I felt guilty and selfish and tried to salve my conscience by repeating to myself that when we married Ginny had been fully aware of how I intended to make a living.

Flo Howell was by 1995 a senior employee of Philips Petroleum in the North Sea oil fields and so was not able to take time off for this Antarctic trip. But he agreed instead to man his own radio station in the garden of his Aberdeen home and keep in contact with Morag who would base herself again at Patriot Hills and attempt to keep in daily contact with me as I crept across the Antarctic icecap. Morag had meanwhile been finding out more about Børge Ousland. The secret of his phenomenal speed, Morag said, was his adept use of the very latest hi-tech wind-chute.

'You mean a kite?' I asked.

'You'd better get one yourself,' Morag nodded, 'and learn how to use it fast.'

I found a kite-maker in South Wales and practised flying it at home on windy Exmoor. At first the string lines became frequently and hopelessly tangled with bushes and heather but I persevered until I had mastered the rudiments of keeping the kite aloft whenever the wind was reasonably strong. Even mild gusts pulled me off my feet and, had I been on skis manhauling a heavy sledge, would surely have pulled me over ice or compact snow at a goodly speed. I was impressed. But my arms were quickly sore, as were muscles in my shoulders and back whose existence I had not previously suspected. I called Brian Welsby of Be-Well Foods in Lincoln who had provided my expeditions with high-nutrition rations for sixteen years. He agreed to devise a complex carbohydrate diet for me to eat for the eleven months prior to the journey. He would also put together, with Mike's advice, special rations for the trip itself, very similar to those Mike and I had eaten in 1993.

As for my sore muscles, which in reality indicated an actual lack of muscles, Brian introduced me to my first ever fitness trainer, Jonathan Beevers, a member of the British Olympic sailing squad's training team at the recent Olympic Games in Atlanta which won more sailing medals than any other nation. I called Jonathan Adolf, for he was a hard taskmaster. In the month before the expedition a single day's programme included a brisk walk with seven-pound weights in each hand carried for two and a half hours, repeated weight exercises in a gym for one hour, pulling lorry tyres cross-country for two hours and a run for one hour and ten minutes.

I sorted out an ongoing, and sometimes incapacitating, back problem by seeing a Harley Street specialist, Bernard Watkin, for deep injections of dextrose, glycerine and phenol solution into the ligaments of my lower back on either side of the spine. This was followed up with a dire exercise regime laid down by Mary Bromiley, our next-door neighbour and famous horse physio, who advised the New Zealand Olympic equine team. She had helped Bernard Watkin keep my back from crippling me over the previous two decades. For manhauling mega-sledgeloads a working spine is fairly critical.

So is a financial sponsor to underwrite an expedition, but past experience had taught me never to waste time seeking one out until I could promise maximum media coverage of the event as a whole and said sponsor's corporate logo in particular. Astute PR reps will often turn their noses up and advise their directors accordingly if I merely promise 'a documentary film and general news reports'. Adventure documentaries, they observe, are statistically watched by a mere 1.5 million viewers at best, and general news reports can never be assumed in advance since they will be easily eclipsed by any 'heavier' news such as ministerial scandal or murder. In 1996 both ITN and *The Times* signed up to cover my solo Antarctica crossing bid, and I came across our sponsor quite by chance.

Ginny's Japanese vacuum cleaner broke down after years of sucking up the considerable output of long black hairs shed by her many Black Dogs and the fallout from her own boots and overalls on her daily return from the cattle shed. She bade me get her a new machine from the retailer in Porlock, our nearest shopping town.

'The Panasonics are still okay,' I was advised by the salesman, 'but would you like to try this new marque, the Dyson, which is bagless? It's been getting rave reviews.' Ever a sucker for clever sales angles, I paid the extra amount for the ultra-modern-looking, bagless model and, unpacking it at home, glanced at the brochure which was stuck to the box. Details of the bagless idea's inventor, James Dyson, were given, stressing that he was British. I phoned him and he agreed to meet up on Exmoor. We went for a run together to Dunkery Beacon and, a fortnight later, he wrote, 'I did enjoy our run and enclose some good running socks. I can also confirm I would be delighted and excited to sponsor your crossing attempt to the tune of £275,000.' He later stipulated that the charity we should work with should be Breakthrough, which concentrated on funding research into finding a cure for breast cancer. Both his parents had died young of cancer, and Breakthrough needed £3 million to start a special clinic at the Royal Marsden Hospital in London, the first such in Europe.

Unlike my previous sponsors, James Dyson took a personal interest in the project. As the *Telegraph* noted, he was clearly 'not a man to throw his money away on a whim'. His research engineers helped with various sledge-haulage gear designs and his graphics boss, a keen parachutist, helped my kite training on the Dyson factory's football ground. This was less than a success. A gust of wind lifted my instructor in the air, he let go, the kite took off for the main road and got run over by a Volvo. Stupidly, I failed to follow up kite-work beyond the basic principles. This was to prove a costly omission. By the time I was ready to go, I had spent eleven months becoming what one newspaper described as 'the fittest 52-year-old in Britain, albeit with defective vision, arthritic hips, lower back pain and chronic piles', but I had only spent a few days attempting to master the complex art of kiting.

Mike Stroud gave me a well thought out container of medicaments, tailor-made for the crossing attempt. He also advised me on exactly what rations I should ask Brian Welsby to provide, aiming at 5,600 calories per day as a result of his analysis of our previous expedition work. Mike was now the senior lecturer on nutrition at Southampton University and the most experienced specialist in survival nutrition in Britain. He also agreed to be spokesman for the expedition, fielding all polar queries from the media.

In the course of my two years at home I had been busy writing books and one of my last obligations before setting off for Antarctica was to complete a nationwide promotion tour for my latest title. *The Sett* was the biography of a Welsh accountant whose wife had been murdered. Unfortunately, the man partly responsible for her murder had himself been shot and killed by a man, then in gaol, who had become my friend in the course of my researching the book. I started to receive threats by telephone and the police advised twenty-four-hour security for Ginny. It could not have happened at a worse moment. James Dyson kindly lent us two ex-Paras whose job was normally to spot and apprehend industrial spies at the Dyson factory. They took turns to patrol our farm and slept there in my absence. As for the book which had landed us in this trouble, *The Times* compared it to Hemingway and it reached number four in their bestseller list. But I was grateful for the brace of ex-Paras all the same.

At the Dyson press conference at Heathrow I was told Børge Ousland was not the only man after the crossing record. The top polar Pole, Marek Kaminski, at six foot five even taller than Ousland, had been on many a fine expedition, including solo to the South Pole the previous year. Of the two, I feared Ousland more, probably due to my long-fought rivalry with the Norwegians. Like football team managers before a match, I thought it diplomatic to play down my own chances, so, when asked what I thought of Ousland, I replied, 'He's very impressive. Tall and well built. When I stand near him I feel small, like a worm.'

Ousland's pre-race tactics, however, were those of a boxer psyching his opponent. He told the press, 'Fiennes's competitors are much, much stronger.'

12

Solo South

An American once wrote that 'nothing is more responsible for the good old days than a bad memory', and on my way back to Antarctica, as long latent memories of gangrene and crutch-rot wormed their way back into my mind, I had to agree with him. Horrid times and subsequent self-promises never to do it again had so often been eclipsed by rose-coloured recollections of journeys past. Now I was at it again. And yet, had I stayed home and watched the news, I would surely have forever regretted letting somebody else grab one of the last remaining polar records without even giving it a go myself.

The trouble with the narrowness of the polar windows of opportunity is that competing expeditionaries do not have much choice but to turn up at the same time in the same place. There's no sidling unnoticed in to Antarctica when you all have to collect in Punta Arenas and await the vagaries of the weather for a flight south to Patriot Hills. I had hoped to set out as early as possible, ideally by 1 November. But blizzards kept me and my rivals champing at the bit throughout October 1996 and well into November. At least it gave Morag and me a chance to eye up the opposition. Incongruously, we did this at a drinks party given by Annie Kershaw who would be responsible for flying all expeditions to their various Antarctic starting-points.

Børge Ousland was tall and well built, with a stern and guarded manner. I was impressed by his professionalism and focused dedication, as well as his youth – he was eighteen years my junior – and obvious physical power. I sensed that our competitive status, or maybe the memory of our row in the Norwegian press in 1990, made him reserved and that, in other circumstances, he would have been friendly enough. Marek Kaminski was thirty-three years old and, in 1995, had travelled by ski to both the South and North Poles, the first person ever to do so in a single year. He was a friendly giant of whom both Morag and I grew quickly fond.

We had all succumbed to Antarctica's magnetic pull. We each wanted to implant at least a part of it in our memories, whatever other personal quests we sought. For a while I had been the only person to cross the continent twice and, on both journeys, had met not a single other human being (apart from at the Pole Station) in a country bigger than China and India joined together. But now there were regular tourist flights in to Antarctica, as well as visiting cruise ships, with around 15,000 people a year visiting the continent. These included groups of the wonderfully named sphenisciphiles or penguin lovers.

A third party, going for the same end goal as us, was Heo Young-ho from South Korea. In fact there were six Heos, each with an identical sledge. All were wreathed in smiles and all professed earnestly to be 'going solo but as a group'. Collectively Morag dubbed them the So-Hos. Small, stocky and bright-eyed like so many Jack Russells, they were in some ways even more impressive than Ousland and Kaminski.

Three members of a team led by Lloyd Scott, an Englishman with leukaemia raising funds by walking to the Pole, arrived when the weather had held us in Punta for two frustrating weeks. One of them, Clive Johnson, was using a para-wing similar to that used by Ousland and Kaminski the previous year, and he showed me how it worked in the nearest flat field, but it was too late for me to beg or borrow one of these state-of-the art models. We left at last on the seven-hour flight by Hercules to Antarctica, three weeks behind our intended start date.

The Hercules landed gently this time and Chilean skidoo drivers ferried our cargo to a nearby Twin Otter ski-plane. Within three hours we were climbing above the Ellsworth Mountains and heading north towards the seaward edge of Berkner Island. I had wanted to reconnoitre the ice-shelf five miles out from Berkner's eastern coast, but the pilot said this would be highly expensive in both fuel and extra dollars. I had to abandon my favoured route and go for a more westerly approach from the edge of the Antarctic ice for the 250-mile haul to the true edge of the continent. Both Ousland and Kaminski had used this western route when, with far lighter loads, they had hauled to the Pole the previous year.

Group by group the rival teams were dropped off at appointed spots along the Antarctic coastline in high winds and thick fog. I waved goodbye to Morag and Terry Lloyd, hitched the sledge's dog harness around my chest, shoulders and waist, set my compass for due south and took the strain of my 495-pound load, enough fuel and food to last me for 110 days.

A fifty-knot wind from the east slammed at me, blasting my goggles. I could see nothing about me and marvelled at the skill of the recently departed ski-plane pilot. Somewhere to my right lay the western flank of Berkner Island, perhaps half a mile away. I must keep clear of its crevasse fields which had caused Mike and me so much trouble. So I allowed myself to veer left in the white-out. After eight hours' stumbling progress the wind speed shown on my hand anemometer was gusting to eighty knots in the howling polar 'night' and I was falling asleep on the move. Erecting my tiny tent took thirty minutes. Later, on the high polar plateau, I knew this job would have to be done in just three or four minutes, with a wind chill factor of −90°C, to avoid hypothermia.

The next day the wind lessened and blew miraculously from the north-north-west, a rare event in that area. So I unfurled my kite and, to my great delight, felt my skis surge forward, hauling me and my 495-pound sledge-load in the approximate direction of the South Pole. Several times gusts slammed the sledge into my legs and I collapsed in a welter of skis, sticks and tangled ropes. One high-speed crash gave me a painful ankle and smashed ski-tip – I bandaged both with industrial tape. This was the learning process. Necessity is the mother of invention and for the first time I began to develop the knack. To my enormous delight, I learned to catch the wind and hold it. But only in the direction which the wind dictated. A GPS check showed that all my wonderful sailing had taken me east of my destination. So I was forced to return to the grind of manhauling: the difference between Formula One racing and carthorse riding. Everything in my tent was wet that night. Both lips wept pus from burns like cold sores which cracked and bled when I ate chocolate.

On 18 November I made weak contact with Morag in her tent at Patriot Hills, more than 300 miles away. She told me that over two days I had gained nearly thirty miles to Ousland's twenty-one. The following day, however, saw the arrival of a steady east wind, enabling Børge to use his para-wing and cover a staggering ninety-nine miles in two days.

Throughout 21–22 November there was no wind, only white-out, and both Ousland and I manhauled due south along our separate routes. He managed nineteen miles; I completed 19.3, despite my 100-pound extra load. Not exactly catching him up, but a good sign for the 500-mile plateau ahead, where manhauling would come into its own. The So-Hos, Morag said, were progressing extremely slowly and were having sledge problems. And Marek Kaminski had been lucky to escape with his life after an accident soon after starting out.

In a high wind and thick fog he had been trying to adjust his sledge harness when a sudden gust knocked him over and concussed him. He came to some time later to find that he had been dragged by his para-wing for an unknown distance but unattached to his sledge and its life-supporting contents. He would die within hours if unable to find his tent and stove. Noticing a small blood-stain, he took a compass bearing on it, since he must have arrived from that direction. After many minutes of desperately retracing his route, with no help from tracks due to blowing snow, he felt overwhelming relief when a dark shape materialised up ahead. His head ached but he was alive! He shrugged and carried on, the Polish flag affixed to his jacket.

My heels developed blisters, so I strapped on foam snippets cut from my bedmat and tried to ignore them. My chin, windburned, became poisoned and swollen, so I lanced it with a scalpel until the swelling subsided. My eyes lost their long-distance focus after a week staring at the glare through goggles. As usual, the lids puffed up with liquid. My eyes became mere slits. I resembled a rabbit with advanced myxomatosis. Every evening I attended to my developing crutch-rot with Canestan powder and applied lengths of industrial sticky tape to raw areas. My back and hips were sore, but not as painful as on previous journeys because my Dyson harness-designers had developed an effective new padding system. For the first time, life was truly bearable, almost enjoyable, on a heavy polar manhaul journey.

The sun provided no relief. It burst through the white-out one day and almost instantly I was hot. I went on dressed just in my underwear. Any bare strip of skin quickly burned purple; the ozone hole was at its worst at that time of year. I fashioned a head cover from a rationbag which covered my neck and shoulders like the flap of a kepi. A day later the white-out returned but I still managed eleven hours of non-stop manhauling. This despite long tiring stretches of pie-crust snow, known to glaciologists as firn or névé, which is fallen snow that is granular but still has aerated cells. Its effect is to hold your footfall for a second prior to collapsing and allowing your foot to sink. This can cause the alarming sensation of a crevasse fall and can sound like a snowquake or mini explosion.

One improvement to my manhaul gear of previous years was in the ski skins department and the superior adhesive mix which glued them to my skis. No longer did they come adrift on uneven ice, so I avoided the frozen fingers caused by repeatedly having to reattach them.

A rare north wind and conditions of good visibility allowed me to try my luck at kiting again. Without stopping for chocolate and taking quick gulps of energy orange from my Thermos, I kited 117 miles in one day. I now thought I was almost certain to succeed in the entire crossing. That evening I was only able to eat my day's 5,600 calorie ration by stuffing myself. I did not *need* more than half the ration for I had not exerted myself, merely steered the kite, braced my legs against occasional rough bumps and slid at speed along Berkner Island's rim. So easy. The exact opposite to manhauling which would use up 8,000 calories in a typical ten-hour day. That night I unloaded and buried eight full days of rations weighing twenty pounds, due to the extra mileage covered.

Before leaving Punta Arenas, Marek Kaminski and I had discussed possible routes from Berkner Island up to the inland plateau. Glaciers often serve as the most sensible corridors to inner Antarctica, but only if you know the nature of the glacier in question. Not all of them move gently. Galloping glaciers, those that advance more than five centimetres a day, can surge with huge power, ice streams shatter, a wave of ice bulges to the front or snout, the surface buckles noisily and becomes no place to travel over. The Columbia Glacier in Alaska was measured advancing at thirty-five metres a day, and the Kutiah Glacier in the Himalaya surged twelve kilometres in just three months, burying forests and villages.

I did not favour the idea of trying to climb on to the plateau south of Berkner Island by way of any unknown glacier, for I remembered the troubles we had had during the Transglobe Expedition on the Scott Glacier. So I had been happy when Marek had shown me a photograph of the mountains with an arrow marking the whereabouts of the Frost Spur, the best route, he reckoned, to climb from Berkner Island's surrounding ice-shelf up to the high polar plateau. I had a mental picture of a hard climb. I was not to be proved wrong. About six hours away from the escarpment three days of poor visibility ended and brilliant sunshine revealed the Frost Spur dead ahead.

I came to an abrupt halt, overcome by disbelief and apprehension. Then I remembered a chance remark by Børge Ousland about Erling Kagge, his fellow Norwegian who had manhauled to the South Pole in 1993. 'I can't understand how Kagge took his gear up the spur without crampons.'

I had no crampons and I had never travelled alone before over a known crevassed zone. My ice-axe had fallen off my sledge during the wild kiting ride, leaving me with only a twelve-inch hammer screw. Ahead lay a crevassed and seemingly impassable barrier, a dark ice-sheathed blue wall rising to an abrupt horizon of blue sky, the rim of the polar plateau. I carried two ice-screws with foot loops and a small ice-hammer in a waistbag. In theory I might be able to rescue myself and perhaps even my sledge after falling into a reasonably shallow crevasse, but crevasses have been measured as deep as forty-five metres.

I am no climber and would not have relished the ascent with a day rucksack on my back, let alone a sledge-load still weighing about 470 pounds. Black clouds promised further bad weather. I began to haul myself up the icy incline, but repeatedly slid backwards. Exhausted, I pitched the tent and decided to split my sledge-load into four. If I could make my first ascent while sunlight still bathed the wall of the spur, showing me the best route, I could descend again, eat and sleep, and complete three more climbs the next day.

My hands were cold, and the ice-wall was about to switch from brilliant sunlight to deep shadow when I was seized by vertigo. Shaking my head to break its mesmeric spell, I gingerly retrieved my ice-hammer from its sledge bag and, using its pick end, started to grope my way up the frozen face of the spur. It was four hours before I could find an even vaguely prominent place to leave my first load. Here, in a wide expanse of nothing, I cached the rations and marked the pile of bags with a single ski.

The journey back down to the tent took just forty minutes and, with relief, I cooked my rehydrated spaghetti bolognese and drank two pints of tea. Ten minutes after I had fallen asleep, a series of katabatic wind-blasts struck the tent. Katabatic winds in Antarctica, the highest, driest, coldest continent on earth, can blow at 190 mph and arrive with just a few minutes warning. I was alarmed, but I waited for an hour before I realised I must move or the tent would be damaged. In a quarter of a century of travel, I had not encountered winds of such ferocious aggression. Sleep was out of the question. Timing the brief lulls between each fresh blast, I dismantled the tent in seconds and tied all my gear together, lashed to a fixed ice-screw. I climbed the spur again, though the wind blew me several times from my fragile holds. Once I slipped thirty feet or more, desperately trying to dig the hammer's pick into the face. Gulping air, I rested, shivering against the ice until I could resume my snail-like ascent.

The third ascent was the worst because I took a wrong route in poor visibility, heading too far to the right. That meant I had to climb twice as high to reach the rock-lined upper rim of the spur. With the clouds to the east now obscuring the escarpment, I immediately made a fourth ascent, but was too tired to manage the last two twenty-five-pound ration bags. That meant I had to descend a fifth time to retrieve them. The final climb, with the fifty-pound load over my shoulders, was easier. However, the storm clouds from the east reached the top of the spur before I did. Light snow began to fall and I could find no trace of my equipment cache. I grew cold as the day's sweat cooled my skin. I knew that twenty days of bagged rations over my shoulders would do me little good if I had lost all the rest of my gear.

I prayed hard and an hour later I stumbled on the dump. Such moments of relief and joy almost make these journeys worthwhile. Hearing the news of winning a lottery jackpot could not even approach the sheer happiness of the instant I found my tent above the Frost Spur.

I could not actually see the Antarctic plateau – in fact, I could see no feature at all in any direction – but I knew I had reached the true gateway to the Pole. The dangers of the ice-shelf and the escarpment were behind me. For the next seventy miles there would be crevasses and wicked moraines, the masses of ice debris that formed difficult barriers. But after that there was nothing but the vast open plain of the polar plateau. Somewhere in this great white land, perhaps halfway between the Pole of Inaccessibility and the isolated Russian base of Vostock, lay the Pole of Cold where winter temperatures can drop to $-100°C$. I ate an extra bar of chocolate and thought again of Børge Ousland's comment to the Chilean film crew: 'Fiennes's competitors are much, much stronger than him.' I might yet prove him wrong. I had caught up more than seventy of the miles he had gained by sailing the east winds. Both Marek Kaminski and the tough little Korean man-haulers were well over a hundred miles behind me after only seventeen days of travel.

I felt elated. To hell with being too old. It's all in the mind. At this stage of our 1993 Antarctic crossing, Mike Stroud and I had already been in a state of semi-starvation and severe physical decline. Yet this time I was still feeling on top form, no more hungry than after a day's training on Exmoor. I was accustomed to the raw skin, poisoned blisters and screaming ligaments which returned on every manhaul trip. The pain in my ankle from the sailing crash was better now, as were the ulcerating blisters on my heels. Life was good and my competitive urge bubbled up as I set out the next morning, the sledge dragging through the soft new snow.

If only the east winds stay absent all the way to the Pole, I would beat Børge, I thought. The harder the manhauling the quicker I will catch him. Then, on the far side of the Pole, the winds will be behind us and my newfound kite skills will cope with his para-wing expertise. After all, in a single day on Berkner Island, my 117 miles were greater even than Ousland's best day's sail. Such were my thoughts.

Only twelve hours later I made radio contact with Morag and my optimism was dashed. Ousland had used his wonderful skill at para-wing control to travel 134 miles in only four days. Ahead of me stretched the Jaberg Glacier and the heavily crevassed snow-fields. This was one of the most wild and beautiful places in Antarctica and, in parts, one of the most dangerous.

On 2 December Morag told me through whining static that our charity, Breakthrough's Expedition Appeal, had already raised over £1 million towards the £3 million needed to fund a London breast cancer research centre. The further I progressed, the more money we would raise. I found this a big help when the going was especially hard. The new snow continued to grip my sledge runners, making every step a battle. For long periods my skis disappeared and often snagged one another, tripping me up. My speed dropped to a mile an hour, sometimes even less. The constant rub and strain reblistered my heels and snapped one of the steel ski bindings. The leather upper halves of my ski boots came away from the plastic foot shells and needed four hours of restitching.

On the twentieth day of my journey, I was already ten days ahead of my previous Antarctic crossing. Not because of faster manhauling, but entirely due to the single day of southerly kiting. I had no major health troubles but various sores. Crutch-rot was an old problem I knew well, caused by trouser-rub. I had treated it as usual with Canestan powder and strips of industrial sticky tape over the raw areas. Sometimes the tape would come unstuck and tear at the sores with each step. Now my morale dipped as the bandages on my privates came unstuck and the new skin on my inner thighs tore with each step. When the sun was out, sweat poured down my face. My forehead and the back of my neck were sun-seared. The ultraviolet light pouring through the ozone hole was far more noticeable than on my 1993 journey with Mike. On previous occasions in Antarctica I had seen mirages of mountains and many strange tricks that rays of light play with ice and vapour, such as moondogs, parahelia and fogbows. But this time the light was mostly too intense, too dazzling, despite my ski goggles, to gaze about at all.

Panic can arise from fear of failure, leading to the sudden collapse of the reservoir of willpower needed to sustain enormous effort and discomfort for long periods. Mike and I had already discovered the best way to keep panic at bay is to have a bank of prepared positive thoughts you can produce on demand. For example, when approaching a crevasse field, it is a great help to conduct a mental rehearsal of exactly what you will do, step by step, should you plunge into the maw of a 100-foot fissure. Thoughts can also be stretched out to help the long hours and slow miles pass by without constantly dwelling on the sheer size of the task ahead and the slow and painful breakdown of your body. Mike's term for getting lost in his thoughts was 'mind-travelling'.

Sometimes I would check my watch only to find to my disgust that a really excellent run of absorbing thoughts had after all only eliminated a few minutes of reality. I often wished to howl like a dog, anything to master my thoughts and banish the insistent desire to halt because the whole task was simply too hard and hurt too much. I would imagine that my grandfather, a pioneer in Canada and Africa, my father and my uncle, both killed in the world wars, and I knew my living family were all right behind me, willing me on. As the last mountain peaks passed by with infinite slowness, I imagined that I was hauling a heavy sledge at a gulag in Siberia, that I was undernourished and poorly clothed, and I would chant, in time to the creak of my sticks, 'Gulag, gulag, gulag.' The extra responsibility of solo travel weighs heavily.

On the night of my twenty-third day, Morag sent me a message from Børge Ousland's base leader at Patriot Hills. Børge had passed the moraine zone in conditions of good visibility and had kindly radioed to warn me of an uncharted crevasse field. By the time I received the information, I had already passed that particular area of danger. But I was grateful for his thoughtfulness. Falling into a crevasse is a bad idea at any time, but doing so alone in Antarctica can lead to a slow and lonely death, for many are mere narrow slits that can trap a human body in a slowly tightening embrace. I was fairly adept at spotting the tell-tale shadowy hollowing of crevasse lids, but many blind crevasses are so well lidded as to be invisible.

On my twenty-fifth day I was sick a few minutes after eating breakfast gruel. I felt faint and started out four hours behind schedule on a fine sunny day, neither too hot nor too cold. In six hours I manhauled six miles, despite a long, steep climb. The improved surface continued but I felt queasy and took two Imodium tablets.

A muffled explosion sounded, vibrating through the snow under my skis. Then two further rumbles in quick succession. Either avalanches or imploding snow-bridges in the great, largely uncharted, crevasse fields to my immediate west. Behind me the deep tracks of my runners disappeared to the north, where countless mountain peaks shimmered as though floating on waves of air. Ahead lay only a blue sky and the gently sloping snowfields leading without further obstruction to the South Pole. I was halfway to the Pole and 125 miles ahead of the point Mike and I had reached in the same time in 1993. I tried not to feel over-optimistic. Things could still go wrong.

To my surprise, I was violently sick again after eating my evening meal, a delicious mixture of ghee milk fat with rehydrated shepherd's pie and Smash mashed potato. I stared at the results on the tent floor and wondered how I could recycle the mess, since I had towed that ration for 400 miles and it represented energy for ten miles of further manhauling. I informed Morag that night that I had been sick, but was uncertain why, since I did not have diarrhoea. She told me to call her at any time if the symptoms persisted so she could relay advice from the camp doctor at Patriot Hill.

Two hours later the first cramps attacked my gut and I recognised at once the symptoms of a kidney stone blockage. The pains of a kidney stone, doctors say, are very similar to those of birth contractions – except that they don't produce such a wonderful result. I knew the pain only too well. In 1990 I had had a similar attack on a floating Soviet scientific sea-ice base 200 miles from the North Pole. Another time I had been working in an office, and the stone had been removed surgically within two days. I lit my cooker and heated water. I would flush the bloody thing out of my system. Drown it with water. Groaning and talking aloud, I wrenched open the medical pack that Mike had meticulously prepared in the knowledge of my 1990 attack which he had treated.

I gulped down morphine substitute tablets, two Buscopan

anti-pain pills and inserted a Voltarol suppository for quick pain relief. Within half an hour the initial pains, which I think I can safely describe as excruciating, had dulled to a background throb. But the relief didn't last.

No living cell can withstand much change to its environment. Even slight changes in acidity will kill a highly developed structure such as a human nerve cell. That's why we have kidneys: to prevent such changes in our bodies. Fifteen gallons of blood flow through the kidneys every hour and a minimum of one pint of water per day is needed to wash away all the harmful waste products that collect there. My doctor had recommended six pints a day. But I had been saving fuel instead of melting snow on my stove for drinking water, and now a chip of calcium in my urinary tract had me writhing on the ground. Had the Gestapo been involved I would have told them anything just to lessen the pain.

For six hours, every hour on the hour, I tried to call Morag. My home-made radio set was the brainchild of her husband, Flo, who had put it together in their Aberdeenshire kitchen. Once I briefly heard Morag calling 'Victor Lima, Victor Lima', my call sign. Then her voice faded into the electronic disturbances that cluttered the ionosphere. Flo had warned us, via the powerful transmitter in his garden, that severe geomagnetic disturbances were likely to cut communication for several days. I feared that, by the time I eventually made contact, bad weather would leave me stranded for further days, without relief.

At the moment the weather was excellent. I yearned to be on my way. Since I was eating nothing and using fuel only to heat snow for water rather than to heat the tent, I was not technically reducing my overall chances of success. True, Ousland was ahead of me and widening the distance, while Kaminski and the Koreans were creeping up from behind. But there was no way I could carry on until I had shifted the stone from my urinary tract. When I finally made brief contact with Morag, the doctor at her camp – a former flying medic from north-west Australia – advised me to take pain-killers every six hours and drink lots of water. For twenty-four hours, possibly the least enjoyable period I can remember ever having spent, I took more pain-killers than the doctor had advised and drank a great deal of water, but the stone failed to shift and the pains from my lower stomach, back and sides stayed with me. For an hour or so after each intake of MST, Voltarol and Buscopan the pain was muted and my desire to continue the journey mounted. Then the dreaded spasms returned with ever-increasing intensity, and I writhed about on the cold floor of the tent clasping my flanks and rolling into a foetal ball incapable of constructive thought processes.

At 11.00 a.m. on 27 December, with two days of tablets left, I decided that the danger of irreparable damage to my kidneys, as well as the risk of running out of pain-killers, was too great a price to pay for the chance of being first to cross the Antarctic solo. I pulled the pin of my emergency beacon which, a few hours later, informed a satellite signal watcher in England, who called Morag, who in turn alerted the Twin Otter ski-plane crew at Patriot Hills as to my exact position.

Nine hours later, with the fine weather beginning to change, the Twin Otter landed by my tent. Throughout the flight back to Patriot Hills, the Australian doctor fed morphine into my blood system through a drip. I was soon completely stoned and in wonderful, painless bliss. Morag recorded: 'I was quite shocked when I saw you, as you were in huge distress. We took you down to the camp after securing you on a stretcher.' My journey had ended almost exactly halfway to the South Pole and a quarter of the way to my destination on the far side of the continent.

Even if I had not been zapped by a kidney stone, Ousland with his superior para-wing skills would have beaten me. He made the crossing in fifty-five days, having sailed for over three-quarters of them. My congratulatory signal was at Scott Base to greet him when he arrived. Kaminski and the SoHos reached the Pole too late to continue.

Morag called my medical insurers, who advised immediate evacuation to a clinic in Punta Arenas. The weather, miraculously, held just long enough for me to fly on a stretcher on a scheduled Hercules flight from Patriot Hills to Punta. After an exhaustive series of x-rays, an enema and fluid injections, the Punta surgeon sent a report to my insurers, who advised that, should I then, or at any time in the future, try such a journey again, they could no longer cover any further stone-related costs. Although the stone had shifted once the morphine had relaxed my nervous system, the condition could return at any time. Any future Antarctic evacuation flight could cost over £100,000 with no insurance cover. I would have to make do with the 1980 and 1993 Antarctic crossings.

Assessing the whole enterprise afterwards, my big mistake, I realised, had been concentrating during training on manhaul fitness rather than on becoming a wind-assistance expert. Using wind assistance with kites or para-wings is very different from using following-wind devices such as parachutes or dinghy sails, employed by Amundsen, Shackleton and Scott. The toil and the suffering is cut to a minimum and that, after all, is what leads to success.

Back at home a month later James Dyson called to say the Breakthrough fundraisers had already raised £1.7 million and that he would personally add £700,000 to that total. He had produced a new 'polar-blue' Dyson model that month, and £10 from the sale of each unit was added to our fund. Many housewives bought his vacuum cleaners and, at the time, one in every twelve British women was being hit by breast cancer. The money raised by the expedition, even though it failed to achieve its physical goal, allowed Breakthrough to help set up Europe's first dedicated breast cancer research centre.

13

Sorry Straits

Trying to plan and organise two expeditions at the same time is something I have usually avoided, but whilst I was training for the solo Antarctic crossing in 1995 I was approached by a Canadian professor in his sixties with an unusual plan which he had named Transglobal. This would involve the first overland crossing of the world on a set of wheels. I met and immediately liked Gordon Thomas, who went by the nickname of Sockeye, and agreed to co-lead Transglobal. I would organise the West European sector of the journey, Dmitry Shparo, who had helped organise our 1990 North Pole bid, would handle the Soviet Union, and Sockeye would deal with North America.

Earth's widest west-east landmass stretches 21,000 miles from Clogher Head in south-west Ireland to St John's in Newfoundland. Various bits of water get in the way en route, including the Irish Sea, the English Channel, the Bering Strait and the Gulf of St Lawrence between the Canadian mainland and Newfoundland. So our vehicles would need to be amphibious. Ford had recently failed in a well-publicised quest to motor across the semi-frozen Bering Strait, but I had a longstanding love for Land Rovers and approached their then owners, BMW, who agreed to sponsor us with three vehicles and a budget of £300,000 to include the cost of rendering them amphibious.

Whilst preparing for the Antarctic expedition, I had also spent time on the Transglobal plans and had visited many vehicle components suppliers, winch manufacturers and design engineers. Eventually a method of making Land Rovers swim emerged, so I asked the Prince of Wales to be patron once again. He agreed and nominated the charity we would work with as the Macmillan Cancer Relief Fund. I called Terry Lloyd and the senior Foreign News Editor at ITN, who agreed to send a team on the expedition. Because I needed to concentrate on Antarctic preparations, I asked Anton Bowring to take over organising the European and the ocean-crossing sections of Transglobal. Flo and Morag Howell agreed to handle all the communications, whilst Charlie Burton and Oliver Shepard dealt with many of the sponsors. They also agreed to run a selection course in Wales to choose suitable individuals for the Land Rover team.

Steve Holland, an old friend from British Aerospace who had helped design my manhaul sledges for many years, joined our team, and we approached a famous yachtsman from Cornwall, Pete Goss, to help design a catamaran-shaped float which could be pulled over sea-ice by a Land Rover. On reaching open sea the vehicle could then push the float into the water, drive up ramps on to the float and provide the motor to power the float.

I went to Antarctica and left the rest of the team to progress with the Transglobal plans. Dmitry in Russia and Sockeye in Canada did various reconnaissance journeys up north to check likely routes through the most difficult regions. Dmitry was by far the most active of Russian explorers and his fame right across Siberia ensured that regional bosses would cause us minimal bureaucratic delays, even in those chaotic post-glasnost and perestroika times.

Dmitry, born in 1941, was a teacher in Moscow who, in the seventies, had risked the wrath of the Politburo by leading a North Pole expedition which they had expressly forbidden. When it proved a success the authorities changed their attitude, Dmitry became a Hero of the Soviet Union with the Order of Lenin and never looked back. Nobody could be better suited to handling the mammoth task of organising our trans-Russia drive.

On hearing that a rival Fiat expedition was making claims that confused the exact goal of what we were attempting, we clarified our precise aim as 'attempting to achieve the first self-propelled journey around earth's horizontal landmass'.

Charlie and Oliver's selection course produced a tough, bossy, highly self-confident and much given to complaining New Zealander who had a superlative record in vehicle maintenance and recovery in extreme regions of the world. Looking at his CV and comparing it with Oliver's second choice, an ex-RAF officer with comparatively little vehicle experience but really good character references, I was surprised and a touch apprehensive. However, Charlie and the other selectors were all in agreement, so I accepted their judgment.

That summer we all assembled at the Royal Marines amphibious testing area at Barnstaple in Devon. There was no public access to Instow Bay so, if our prototype amphibious Land Rover were to sink, the press could not take embarrassing photos. But all went well and our subsequent debrief sent the nine engineers involved in the amphibian's design scurrying off to complete various modifications in readiness for the Alaskan trials we planned for the spring of 1997.

Sockeye had selected the Inuit village of Prince of Wales as our trials site since we would land there after crossing the Bering Strait from Russia on the main journey. It made sense to try the vehicles out in the exact sea-ice conditions that we would encounter and, on the landward side of Prince of Wales, high snowbound mountains would also have to be crossed, using prototype track and winch methods. These too must be tried out.

Even Sockeye knew little about Prince of Wales and its inhabitants. Captain James Cook charted the Bering Strait for the Royal Navy in the 1770s and named it after an efficient but timid Danish navigator, Vitus Bering, who worked for Tsar Peter the Great and, fifty years before Cook, had sailed a Russian ship into the strait but failed to reach the American coast or even to spot it through thick fog. Russia did, however, possess colonies in Alaska with some 600 Russian settlers in the 1860s and, had the Soviet Union still owned the region during the Cold War, President Kennedy might have found things even more troublesome than the Cuban missile crisis. Luckily American dollars in the nineteenth century did good acquisitive work, which would normally have been the task of the military. In 1803 they bought Louisiana from the French, Florida from Spain (for $5 million) and Alaska from the Russians (for $700,000).

Inuit had hunted around Prince of Wales since pre-historic times – the Yupik tribe in the south and the Inupiat in the north. A Royal Navy officer who worked for the Hudson's Bay Company was sent to find copper in 1770 and commented approvingly: 'the women were made for labour; one of them can carry or haul as much as two men do. They also pitch our tents and keep us warm at night . . . Though they can do everything, they are maintained at a trifling expense for, as they always cook, the very licking of their fingers in scarce times is sufficient for their subsistence.' A US government school was set up at Prince of Wales, but the first teacher was murdered there in 1893. In 1900 up to half the community died in a measles and flu epidemic, and an American visitor in 1901, describing Prince of Wales, wrote: 'There is probably no place in the world where the weather is so persistently vile as on this cheerless portion of the earth's surface.'

On arrival at Wales I could see the writer's point, although by 1998 there was the landing strip, a public laundry house, a post office, a grocery store, a schoolhouse and the reasonably neat houses of the 150 Inuit inhabitants. I had flown out with the ex-RAF officer, Andrew 'Mac' Mackenney whose place on the team had gone to the New Zealander. As first reserve, I had asked Mac to become our base camp leader, stores supervisor and, as I grew to trust and like him, chief administrator for Transglobal's Europe sector.

Our rented quarters at Prince of Wales consisted of a large garage with work benches and space enough for both vehicles but not the float. Close by in the same ramshackle building were tiny bedrooms and a cosy kitchen which we shared with Big Dan Richards, the building's owner, a bearded ex-USAF technician with the air of a genial giant hippie. Dan had married a local Inuit lady, left the Air Force and settled down in the village to raise a family. His hobbies included solving complex computer video puzzles and hunting game on a skidoo in the wilderness that stretched east from the village and over a coastal arm of the Rockies to the nearest town of Teller. Dan operated a radio telephone, so I was able to speak daily to Ginny.

Sockeye taught us how to lassoo bucking steers. All his life he had entered steer-roping contests, despite losing a testicle when gored by a bull, and won whatever team event he and his eldest son entered, including at the 'big one', the Calgary Stampede. I went on an outing with Sockeye, towing a couple of days' food and safety gear, to scout out the coastline to the north for a suitable vehicle training area and a bay that was at least partly ice-free. After eight hours Sockeye dropped behind and when at length I lost sight of him, I turned back. He was lying in the snow amidst blood stains from some cut to his leg and not looking at all well. He had lost a glove and the temperature was well below freezing. He spoke with a slurred edge to his consonants and I sensed hypothermia was not far off. We drank tea from a Thermos before turning about and trudging slowly back along our trail. Normally I was the old man on expeditions. It felt good to have a yet more senior citizen along too. I started calling him 'Old Sockeye'.

But watching Sockeye floundering in the Alaskan snow set me thinking. I was, at fifty-three, some ten years younger than he, but I knew he worked out daily in his gym and always kept himself fit. He neither smoked nor drank alcohol. And yet a mere eight hours of gentle trudging in calf-deep snow had rendered him useless for further progress. Soon the ageing process would drag at me, and I too would gasp for breath, hold up colleagues and wonder whether it was time to learn golf or bridge. I glimpsed the future and did not like what I saw. A life without the prospect of any physical challenge would be no life at all.

For many days Arctic storms blasted Dan's hut. Then the weather cleared up. We spent a number of days and quite a few nights working out how best to progress over deep snow and shiny ice. Whenever we met up with deep soft snow we took the wheels off one by one and replaced them with triangular tracked units weighing forty-five kilos apiece. Even with all four of these mini 'tank tracks' in place we often bellied deep into drifts, whereupon someone had to wade ahead, often waist height, and dig deep channels to fix fast points for the winches. We soon became slick at such drills, and during our second month in Alaska we drove right over the York Mountain range and down to Teller, the first road vehicles ever to do so in winter.

We turned our attention in early May to the arrival of the Arctic spring and the break-up of sea-ice in some of the nearby coastal bays. There was a long spell of calm, clear weather so Mac Mackenney and I went jogging in hills where wolf, bear and wolverine prints criss-crossed those of lesser beasts, partridge and moose. Mac, who did most of our cooking and all of our sponsored food rationing, made friends with many of the Inuit and sensibly exchanged our sponsored tinned rations for fresh food and anything else that we were short of. Our New Zealander, who had strident opinions on many topics, complained in surprisingly angry tones that Mac was abusing both Inuit hospitality and the generosity of our sponsors by using barter simply to help our tight Land Rover budget to stretch further. Mac was taken aback by this verbal venom, but we avoided making an issue of the matter since our inter-team relations had been previously untroubled. But I resolved then and there to re-assess the team make-up before the main journey. After thirty years of travel with small groups, I believed I could spot a likely source of trouble fairly quickly.

In early May I found an open bay only a mile from Dan's house, so we towed the catamaran-shaped pontoon, sledge-like, along the coast behind a Land Rover, and on reaching the belt of rough pressure ice that formed a wall up to four metres high and 300 metres wide between land and sea, we cut open a rough lane using axes.

At some point soon this zone of topsyturvy ice chunks would fracture with no warning and float out to sea, so we advanced with the pontoon pushed ahead of the vehicle until it slid down into the sea, where we moored it to two ice-anchors screwed into the seaward edge of the ice. We lowered the ramps and drove up them from ice to pontoon. There was quite a sea swell, so to watch this, our first launching rehearsal, was tense, especially for the driver.

The vehicle was quickly clamped into the correct position atop the catamaran-shaped hull, and the power take-off spindle, a standard device for farmers in Britain, was clipped into a custom-made box unit which allowed us to transfer from mechanical to hydraulic power, which in turn rotated the twin paddle-steamer blades at the rear of the pontoon's twin hulls. Speed and steering functions were controlled by the driver inside the Land Rover's cab. Sockeye, Mac and I watched with pride as our three mechanics 'swam' the Land Rover far out to sea and dodged between ice-floes. These semi sea-ice conditions were, along with the snow flanks of the Rockies, the most severe obstacles we were likely to meet on our 21,000-mile journey. The trials had proved successful and we returned to Britain to announce that we would set out in the autumn of 1998. Two years of solid unpaid work by all the team, the design engineers and sponsors, had finally paid off.

Our contacts at Land Rover from the very top decision-makers to the shop floor had backed us to the hilt all the way. Then, less than three months before our departure BMW's German headquarters decided to cut various Land Rover budgets. Money was needed to launch a new model, the Freelander, so Transglobal was given the chop. So much wasted time and effort to no avail. In nearly forty years of sponsored projects, I have only suffered from last-minute sponsor-withdrawal once, so I suppose I have been lucky overall.

I had failed in Antarctica, and now with Transglobal. I had to recognise the signs. Ginny was, as always, a sympathetic shoulder to nuzzle against. We went skiing in Courcheval, the activity and the place that we both loved best. We made plans to spend much more time together, although I had learned at least twenty years before never to promise Ginny that I would do no more expeditions.

When I was in Antarctica she had been interviewed by *Woman's Weekly*. The reporter, Sue Pilkington, reported her as saying: 'Of course I worry, but I don't sit here with my head in my hands because that's very negative and doesn't do anybody any good . . . I've never said, "Don't go" and I never will. I'm supportive of everything he does.' Any suggestion that she was being brave was dismissed. 'It isn't brave at all. I was brought up in a fairly strict, old-fashioned, stiff upper lip kind of way where you don't show emotions. You don't just sit down and weep. You have to get on with things. If I hadn't been brought up like that, I might find it very difficult.'

She went on to confirm my own memory of our shared Antarctic winter. 'It was one of the happiest winters of my life . . . a crisp, dry cold not like the miserable damp we get here, and our huts were tough and warm.' When asked if she thought I would ever retire and become a pipe-and-slippers man, she replied, 'He wears bedroom slippers most of the time when he's here, but I can't see him ever retiring.'

After twelve years on Exmoor, Ginny had taken on three local people to help run everything. Gina Rawle organised the office and the lectures, Jean Smith helped out in the house, and Pippa Wood on the farm. My accountant suggested I should ask the Inland Revenue if anyone should be treated as fully employed, so I called some tax lady in Taunton who visited the farm.

'Why,' she asked, 'is your company called Westward Ho Adventure Holidays, although you tell me you have never run a commercial holiday?'

'True,' I agreed, 'but when we married nearly thirty years ago we did intend to and so named the company accordingly. Now we make an income through cattle, sheep, writing books and lecturing, but why waste £100 re-registering the company name?'

She gave no immediate response, but I could sense her bristling with suspicion. She called in two more senior Revenue officers who interrogated both of us and suggested to Ginny that she only farmed as a tax dodge. Ginny was furious and told them exactly where to get off. That started a five-year-long 'tax investigation' into our company and our personal affairs, going back ten years through our accounts and files. For five long years my accountant answered constant Revenue questions, for which he naturally charged us.

Since neither the Antarctic nor the Bering Strait projects had succeeded, my normal post-expedition income sources were not available. There was nothing to write or lecture about. At some point I would need another expedition, and it had better be a successful one, to boost the fairly meagre profits accruing from all Ginny's hard work and perseverance with the farm. The only way I knew to stand a fair chance of expedition success was by keeping fit so, rememembering the extreme rigours of Mike Stroud's Eco-Challenge race in Canada three years before, I rang him up. Would he enter a team for another Eco race? And might I join it? Sadly, Mike was too busy, having taken over big responsibilities at Southampton General Hospital, but David Smith, the Exeter cardiologist and good friend of us both who had been with us in Canada, did agree to put together a four-person team and enter the 1998 race which was to take place in Morocco.

We duly arrived in Morocco that summer with a team which included Hélène Diamantides, Britain's fastest female 100 kilo-metre endurance racer, Steven Seaton, an accomplished marathon-runner and the editor of *Runner's World* magazine, David and me. We had trained hard together at weekends over the previous year, but we were up against the world's best endurance racers, fifty-five teams from twenty-seven countries over a race course of 300 rugged, remote miles. There were no official overnight stops and no sleeping areas, for sleep deprivation is a major feature of Eco-Challenge racing. Lack of sleep cuts in with most racers after three days and nights. But if one of the four of us failed to turn up at the finish in eleven days, the whole team would be disqualified.

In Morocco 220 racers on 220 camels lined up along the beach at Agadir. Mark Burnett, the ex-British Paratrooper whose idea the Eco race was, fired the start gun and pandemonium ensued. Our Hélène fell off at once when her mount's girth rope broke. Minutes were lost fixing it but, through the luck of the draw, we had no single camel that held us back and we had made four pairs of light-weight camel stirrups back in Britain so that we could trot in comfort, whereas a stirrupless trot would quickly become too painful on the backside to keep up. So we finished that fourteen-kilometre leg in fifth place. The next seven-kilometre sector involved a fast run along the coastline in between the advancing tide and the rocky shoreline. Slower teams had ever increasing swimming stretches as the sea reached the cliffs. We all carried heavy rucksacks.

We then reached a beach where two two-seater kayaks were awaiting each team. We launched ours through the pounding surf just as we had been taught by Royal Marines off the Cornish coast. The trouble was that the most ferocious surf back then had been two feet high, whereas in Morocco it averaged thirteen feet. Each time over the next eighty kilometres that we had to call in at an obligatory checkpoint, the surf defeated our attempts to reach the beach unscathed. Time and again both our kayaks were rolled and much of our gear was sodden.

Next came 120 kilometres of trekking and canyoning through the Atlas Mountains, burning hot by day and cold by night. When we came to the clifftop above the Taghia Gorge, lying in nine-teenth position, we found nine teams huddled about their camp cookers in a strong, cold wind. They were awaiting their turns to descend a dizzy 200-metre abseil rope to the gorge below, and a backlog of teams had developed. Most teams were using the respite for a brief sleep.

We sat around our cooker pleased with our recent trek, having overtaken eleven teams en route.

'I'm afraid I have to stop here.' We looked up sharply at David, our team captain. I could not believe my ears: he had been going so well.

'What do you mean? Stop?' I breathed.

'I have a health problem. I can't explain, but I really cannot go further.' He was adamant.

Hélène, a highly competitive person, said, 'If you drop out here, David, I will too. I see no point in carrying on if we are unable to gain a qualified place at the Finish. And teams without all four members do not qualify.'

I looked at Steven. He shrugged. 'I would be happy to keep going, but the safety rules forbid teams of less than three continuing.'

I looked around and it struck me that there might be other teams with similar problems. So Steven and I went from group to group and came upon Team California. They had just suffered the withdrawal of half their number from gastroenteritis. Greg, the team leader, was small and cheerful and had recently won the international Camel Trophy Race, a vehicle-borne form of adventure race, with the US Team. He introduced us to Kim, who was very dark-skinned and six feet tall but was of Chinese American parentage. She was a karate champion in California.

'I limp badly from blisters,' Steven told them, 'and Ran here is past his prime, but we always keep going.'

So the four of us set off. The race computers require that each team has a specific title, and we now raced as Team California. We carried on up the Atlas, slowly gaining height, after leaving David and Hélène at the gorge. Six hours later, Kim collapsed, groaning and retching. Greg recognised the trouble at once and broke the seal on his radio beacon to summon a race helicopter.

'Kim has gastro – same as our other two members,' he sighed. 'It was the water we drank on the third day out, from a harmless-looking pool.'

We waited eight hours until dawn when the race helicopter arrived and removed Kim. Five hours later we reached the riding section. Each of us drew a horse, Berber-Arab cross-blood animals of the Moroccan Army. As we mounted two tall men came up. They had lost the female member of their team, thrown off her horse and badly hurt, and their fourth member, her fiancé, had decided to stay with her. Their race title was Team Germany and they asked if they could join us. Greg had no objection even when they said that we must collectively now become Team Germany or their sponsors back home would be angry. The five of us rode the next fifty kilometres fast enough, mostly in the dark, until Greg began to vomit. He too had gastroenteritis, so we left him at a checkpoint along with our horses.

For ten hours we followed the two Germans up Mount M'Goun (4,071 metres), the second highest peak in North Africa. Here we met a team waiting to be airlifted out as one of them had severe symptoms of altitude sickness. Darkness came as we neared the summit ridge, so our German leader decided we should rest for two hours. I snuggled into my thin race-bag against the cold but, moments later it seemed, I was woken by a choking groan and horrid gurgling sounds.

Our leader, over six feet four inches and an ex-swimming Olympian, had for warmth tied up the ties of his six-foot-long sleep-bag, but was then violently sick and started to drown or asphyxiate, unable to untie the knots above his head.

Steven found a knife and cut the knots of the German's bag. The second German, Soren, activated his rescue beacon and, soon after dawn, the helicopter took away our severely ill ex-leader.

We eventually summitted M'Goun and gazed at the stupendous views of the Atlas Mountains all about us.

'Steven,' Soren announced, 'and Ran. I should tell you in confidence that I am actually Danish and only joined Team Germany because we have no national team of our own at present.' We laughed as we realised that we could not alter our team title. There were no Germans in Team Germany. After an exhausting, sleep-deprived, bloody (due to frequent falls) mountain bike ride of 190 kilometres, we arrived in the centre of Marrakesh, unqualified, bruised, 'German', but happy, for we had beaten the eleven-day deadline by twenty-four hours and seen a wild, untamed part of Africa that we could never have glimpsed as mere tourists. We finished in twenty-ninth place, but were 'disqualified' since we had lost two of our original team members.

Apart from the sixteen kayak casualties, fifteen racers were treated for severe altitude sickness, many for gastroenteritis, exhaustion, hypothermia and dehydration.

Steven agreed that we should enter the next Eco-Challenge, wherever in the world it was planned for.

Early in 1999 I was paid a worthwhile amount as a publisher's advance for an expedition book. An expedition I was to pay dearly for.

14

Falling Through

Not long after the Bering Strait project was scuppered by BMW, I heard that plans for the coming millennium year were astir in Norway to knock off the Arctic journey which most polar pundits considered the only true polar challenge that still remained. All others had been achieved during the twentieth century and 99 per cent of them by the Canadians, Russians, British and Norwegians.

Børge Ousland, following his Antarctic crossing success, had tried crossing the Arctic Ocean solo, but had to be airlifted over an especially lethal area. However, he had managed to travel solo and unsupported to the North Pole from Siberia via sea-ice floes that drift slowly towards the Pole. Nobody had as yet completed the final polar grail of reaching the Pole solo and unsupported along the North American or direct route, which involved travel against the prevailing currents.

Norway had at the time at least a dozen powerful cross-country skiers with polar experience, each of whom might be preparing for the solo direct route. The rumour mill favoured one Sjur Mordre but, whoever it might or might not be, it was clear that this last of the great polar challenges was about to be broached.

I approached my literary agent Ed Victor who, despite my recent run of failures, was enthusiastic and quickly gained a good contract. So, with Ginny's blessing, I began the search for a sponsor and struck lucky quite quickly with the giant logistics corporation, Exel. They, in turn, chose the Cancer Research Campaign as our charity and Prince Charles agreed to be patron, as he had for all my expeditions for the past twenty-two years. Mac Mackenney, the linchpin of our Bering Strait project, would be Arctic base leader in Resolute Bay, helped by Morag Howell who had become the Base Manager of First Air in Resolute Bay, the air charter company that would fly me to my Arctic start point at Ward Hunt Island. Morag had by then been involved in the polar journeys for some two decades and seen all the developments in radio communication from remote places. Of that period, she wrote:

> We went from Morse Code, which we used extensively in the beginning, to the most highly advanced technical communications system ever used in any polar environment anywhere. And we succeeded. On my last trip with Terry Lloyd we made communications history by sending the first ever same day news report complete with video from Antarctica to ITN in London. Despite extreme conditions. This was the first ever Inmarsat B data transmission used to send our reports . . . We worked with many journalists and film crews over the years, and most were difficult to look after or very demanding. Or they just found the remoteness, the inaccessibility combined with the cold, just miserable. But our Terry [Lloyd] was great. Very demanding. Extremely difficult at times, and he really didn't enjoy the cold, but in all this he was a laugh! His stories, his humour and his resolve were quite unique and a perfect fit for our team.

Flo Howell dealt with all the communications planning. He is separated from Morag now, and they remain on good terms.

Mike Stroud who, as previously, planned special ration packs for me, was interviewed by the *Daily Express* and explained: 'When we walked across the Antarctic continent together, we both ended up losing more than three stone, despite eating 5,500 calories daily. Ran will start out this time eating 4,000 calories daily and slowly increase to 6,000 calories daily as his hunger mounts. We were burning 11,500 calories on many days. The question is: will he be strong enough in the last month or two to get there?' Mike himself gave me only a 20 per cent chance of success.

I had two amphibious sledges made by Roger Daynes of Snowsled, Europe's top sledge-maker, and began an ambitious fitness schedule in mid-1999, seven months before my Arctic start date. This went alongside a diet of half a pound of complex carbohydrates on top of my normal daily intake, usually pasta, brown rice or potatoes.

I ran over the moors for two hours every second day and entered numerous races. I aimed to do the 1999 London Marathon in 3 hours 30 minutes, and only missed out on this by 29 seconds. This was nonetheless an hour faster than my previous best. Then, with Steven Seaton, I paddled the 125-mile non-stop Devizes to Westminster canoe race in under twenty-six hours. In December Steven and I joined Britain's top male and female adventure racers, Pete James and Sarah Odell, for the 300-mile Eco-Challenge race in Patagonia. At fifty-six, I was the oldest competitor among the fifty-five international teams and was twenty-three years older than my three team-mates. Steven, as was his wont, constantly referred to me as 'the old man'. He still does. I got my own back every now and again, including during the seventy-eight-kilometre Swiss Alpine Marathon that year, which took us nine hours. His subsequent report on that race was disapproving:

We did the first downhill 30 kilometres in three hours. Then we started climbing. Ran isn't great on climbs and struggled a bit, so I waited for him at the top of each climb. The final ascent topped out at 9,500 feet twelve kilometres from the finish and all downhill. Ran took off from the top and I didn't see him again until I finished fifteen minutes behind him and a touch cheesed off that I'd waited for him on so many climbs, only to be run out on the final downhill stretch.

Nonetheless, we continued to team up for many races in various parts of Britain and around the world for many subsequent years.

Pete James, our leader on the 300-mile Patagonian Race, wrote for *Trail* magazine:

The race venue was the Nahuel Huapi National Park, snow-capped peaks, crystal clear lakes, deciduous forests, bamboo groves and dry pampas grassland. The race started with a 90 kilometre canoe paddle. Then horseback across land once owned by Butch Cassidy and the Sundance Kid, then two days of trekking with hours of climbing and traversing fixed rope. We slept as little as possible, perhaps two hours a night. We (Sarah, Steven, Ran and I) had spent months testing and acquiring the best equipment possible, training for at least five different activities (running, horse-riding, sea kayaking, white water canoeing and mountaineering), competing together in shorter races and safe, quick team movement.

One irony of such races is that you pass through the most incredible scenery whilst in a constant hurry, and sometimes in considerable pain and discomfort. We emerged from the bamboo on the morning of our seventh day in 14th place. A good result against a top class field.

I developed big blisters on the balls of both feet. By day five I could only hobble. But by New Year 2000 I felt quite fit. Despite various media innuendoes about my age, I had no qualms, having kept up with world-class athletes in their prime for eight days and nights.

Ginny drove me to Heathrow. A reporter from *Woman and Home* magazine that week asked the same old questions. 'When he's away,' Ginny said, 'I consciously stop if I catch myself worrying . . . I think of Ran as my very closest, dearest friend as well as my husband. It's hell when he's away and he's a wonderful person to be with.'

Each time we parted for such journeys, I hated myself and knew I was guilty of hurting the person I loved most in the world. I was like some smoker, alkie or drug addict who knows he is doing wrong but is too addicted to stop.

Mac and I arrived at Resolute Bay on 5 February, not long after the sun had reappeared there for the first time in five months. Morag met us off the plane and assured us that she had a ski-plane booked to fly me the 600 miles north to uninhabited Ward Hunt Island, the last land before the Pole, from where Mike Stroud and I had made our first foray north in 1986. Meanwhile she had fixed us up with a warm hut with plenty of space to prepare the sledge gear. She drove us through driving snow at −42°C to meet my old friend, Karl Z'berg, the legendary Swiss bush pilot I had first met here some thirty years before. We drank thick Arctic coffee in a canteen where grizzled polar buffs had their own language. 'Jafas with snotsicles', for example, was a suitably derogatory term for the scientific denizen of such a place, jafa standing for Just Another Fucking Academic. A snotsicle, as you might more easily work out, is a long frozen thread of mucus suspended from its owner's nose.

Karl clearly thought I should not set out until early March when the sun would first rise at the latitude of Ward Hunt Island. By my own reasoning that would be too late for me. There are two modes of Arctic Ocean manhauling: very fast or very slow. The Norwegians are the chief proponents of the Speedy Gonzales approach, with light equipment, medium-range calorific intake, superb fitness and, above all, the brilliant skiing technique that comes from cross-country ski-racing since childhood. Such technique becomes useless when towing very heavy sledge-loads, so they keep their loads manageable. At fifty-five I could not hope to reach the Pole in less than the fifty days, which is the sort of time Norwegians aim at. I would take at least eighty-five days and for safety would need ninety days of food. This alone would weigh 230 pounds, with fuel to melt ice to rehydrate it coming to another sixty pounds.

All additional gear – tent, sleep-bag, mat, cook kit, rope, axe, shovel, spare ski, spare clothes, repair kit, medical kit, camera,

radio, lithium batteries, fluorescent marker poles, paddle, etc –
would add up to another 160 pounds, too much for a single sledge
travelling in Arctic rubble ice, so I had to use two sledges. When
walking back along my trail to collect the second sledge, I would
need a gun, and in the past had had a .45 magnum pistol on my
belt. However, thanks to recent Canadian legislation hand guns
were forbidden, so I now would have to lug a heavy shotgun back
and forth. Altogether I would need to haul 510 pounds and relay
two loads which meant every mile gained to the north would
involve three travelled on the ground, with the additional hazard
of white-outs. In such conditions the need to relay sledges involves
a potentially lethal risk – once you have parked the first sledge and
set off for your second load, you may never find it. At some point
you will decide, because of the cold, to return to the first sledge.
But it, too, may be impossible to find. You will then die from the
cold.

I had no option but to take two sledges, so my schedule took the
extra mileage into account. If I could travel north for ten hours
every day for eighty days, with no rest day for injuries, bad
weather or watery obstacles, my best progress would be 500 yards
a day for the first three days, 1.4 miles daily for the next thirty
days, 4.5 miles daily until day fifty-eight and then, with a single
sledge only, eleven miles daily to the Pole.

Many unsupported treks towards the Pole have been scuppered
by stretches of open water blocking the way north without temperatures low enough to refreeze the sea-water. To avoid such
delays I had two buoyancy tubes designed by Snowsled that fastened to either side of my bigger sledge, making it buoyant even
when fully laden with me sitting atop its load wielding a paddle.
At Resolute Bay I spent a week testing equipment and hauling the
sledges over ice-blocks on the sea-ice a mile from the self-catering
hut Mac and I rented.

On 14 February we flew through an ever-darkening sky to the
most northerly of Canada's meteorological stations at Eureka,
where musk oxen and wolves roam the hills around the airstrip.

After refuelling Karl took the plane 300 miles north of Eureka to the edge of the Arctic Ocean and the conical hill at the north end of Ward Hunt Island, starting-point of most North Pole attempts. I threw a 1.4 million watt illuminating flare out of the window, giving Karl four minutes of light in which to spot and land on a flat 400 yards of drift-free snow. With lurching bumps we were down. It sounds simple, but very few pilots in the world could have managed it.

As the door opened I felt the cold of Latitude 84° North in winter. The sun would not show its face here for another three weeks, and then only for thirty minutes on its first twenty-four-hour appearance. Terry Lloyd and cameraman Rob Bowles, friends of so many expeditions, helped Mac unload my gear to the light of three moons. The two false moons, known as moon dogs, were the result of the true and central moon's light being reflected by ice crystals. I shook hands with Karl and the others, gave Mac a note to send Ginny and watched as Karl applied full power. The Twin Otter lurched away in a storm of snow and ice crystals which would remain here as a local dense fog for many hours. I tugged on my dog harness, attached it to the sledge ropes and started to lug the first sledge northwards, not yet on sea-ice, but, for the first few miles over Ward Hunt ice-shelf, land-attached ice jutting out into the Arctic Ocean.

The Twin Otter's lights disappeared, as did the drone of its engines. Silence but for my breath and the sound of my own heartbeat. On my hand compass I set a bearing to geographical north. The compass needle pointed to magnetic north 300 miles west of Resolute Bay and 600 miles south of my position. I had to set a magnetic lay-off of 98°, then wait a minute for the needle to settle in the less than normal viscosity of its alcohol-filled housing. I could not use the North Star as a marker because it was almost directly overhead. Nor, pulling a sledge, could I use my GPS position-finder for direction.

The clothing policy I had evolved over twenty-eight years of polar expeditions was based on non-stop movement and light, breathable clothes. Any halt, however brief, led quickly to hypothermia. Once my metabolism was up and running, pumping blood furiously to my extremities, I took off my duckdown duvet and stuffed it in the sledge next to my Thermos and 12-bore pump shotgun. Now I was wearing only a thin wickaway vest and long johns under a black jacket and trousers made of 100 per cent ventile cotton. Cotton is not windproof so body heat is not sealed in. Alas, no modern clothing is completely breathable so cotton is still in my opinion the best compromise for polar heavy manhaul travel.

My schedule allowed two days to descend the soft snowfields of Ward Hunt Island's ice-shelf to the edge of the sea. But I kept going without a rest and established both sledges at the coastline within seven hours. This boded well, for the sledges were running easily despite their full loads, the low temperature and soft, deep snow.

Geoff Somers, an experienced polar man, had advised me to include a cantilever design in the sledge moulds. Snowsled had done so, and the result was good. After seven hours of hard manhauling, I was cold and tired. I erected the tent in six minutes and started the cooker in four. These two acts, which I had practised thousands of times, are the key to survival, and with two usable hands can be performed easily in extreme temperatures, high winds and blizzards. I got into my sleeping bag, drank energy drink, ate chocolate and set my alarm watch for three hours. The weather was clear when I woke and the sea-ice quiet to the north, a sign that the ice-floes were not on the move.

The moon had vanished behind the hills so I would not be able to differentiate clearly between solid ice and thinly skinned zones, so the overall silence was a bonus. I re-stowed the big sledge, moving rapidly to keep my body core temperature up. I decided to take the smaller sledge first. Its load was 210 pounds, a third less than the eight-foot sledge. The ice-floes that are blown south against this northern coastline of the Canadian Archipelago often shatter against the ice-shelf, and blocks up to thirty-five feet high tumble over one another, often forming huge ramparts that run east-west for miles. Behind them a scene of utter chaos can meet the despairing manhauler, slab upon slab of fractured ice-block as far as the weary eye can see.

Travelling over the past twenty-five years our group had four times broken the current world record for unsupported travel towards the North Pole. Each time the ice conditions north of Ward Hunt Island were invariably bad to horrible. To my joy I saw that, this year, the previous condition of wall-to-wall ice blocks was broken down by a series of crazily laid out but negotiable lanes. The ice 'defences' were split everywhere by recent breakage. In many places, like the cauldrons of witches, thick black fog swirled above new cracks and pools as the 'warmer' water gave up its comparative heat to the supercool air above. This phenomenon is known as frost-smoke or sea-smoke. New ice-floes of twilight grey zigzagged through the stark black outlines of ice obstacles wherever I looked, a fragile highway to the North. My schedule of 500 yards a day for the first three miles from the start began to look pessimistic.

I pressed on over the fissure dividing land from sea and into a broad belt of rubble. One sledge at a time. I took my skis off. For a few hundred yards I would have to haul each sledge over a vista similar to that of post-war Berlin. Between each ice slab soft, deep snow covered the fissures. I often fell into traps, sinking waist-deep into pools of *nilas* slurry, that thin elastic ice crust, a dull grey in colour, which forms on calm sea-water and is easily bent by a wave or mere swell.

I came to a wall of slabs fifteen feet high and, to help haul the sledge over it, I decided to test the simple pulley system devised by Mac. I attached it to the big sledge, which I had hauled first to the wall, and tugged it jerkily up the forty-five-degree slope. With the 300-pound sledge at the top of the wall, I detached the tiny grapnel hook and rolled up the pulley line. Too late I heard movement, and leaped towards the sledge, which quickly gathered momentum in its slide over the edge of the wall. I managed to grab the rear end, but my 200-pound body weight was not enough. The far side of the wall was a sheer fifteen-foot drop on to sharp ice-blocks. I landed hard and was winded but unhurt.

At first the sledge appeared to be undamaged, but closer inspection revealed a thin tear under the bow, presumably where the sharp edge of the ice-block had made contact with the 300-pound falling sledge. I tried pulling the sledge, but snow lodged in the damaged section and dragging it became difficult. Also, the sledge's hull, designed to be 100 per cent watertight, was compromised. There was no course but to head back to the hut on Ward Hunt Island and find suitable materials to effect a repair. In the mid-1980s we had erected a canvas cover over the steel skeleton of a hut long abandoned by scientists and installed a couple of wind-powered generators to provide electricity. With minimal safety gear in a bag, I skied for two hours back up my trail and via the Twin Otter's landing strip about a mile east of the huts. The camp looked ghostly, unchanged over the twelve years since my last visit. After an hour spent digging out the door of our old hut, I gained entry. There were a few tools and canvas materials, so I decided to bring the sledge back to make it watertight and capable of being towed in all conditions. I skied back to the sledges and loaded minimal camping gear on to the smaller one. Then I lashed the damaged sledge on top. Uphill through soft snow was slow going, some several hours back to the hut.

I put my tent up inside the canvas-skinned hut. The temperature had fallen to −49°C and a bitter breeze caressed the frozen canvas. With the cooker on, a hot drink inside me and fully clothed, I began the repairs. Some hours later I was back at the ice edge, happy that my work had made the sledge easy to tow, even in soft snow, and pretty much watertight again.

I found my previous trail easily. I camped on thin ice and woke to hear all manner of noises: cracking and rumbling, then silence. Then a frightening roar that galvanised me into movement from the depths of my four-layer sleeping bag. The moon was full, the scenery startlingly beautiful. Moonshadows played about the upended ice-blocks and the ice shapes took on an uncanny resemblance to animals, castles or giant mushrooms. Fearful of imminent upheaval due to the tidal influence of the full moon, I pressed on northwards. I dared not take either sledge too far because the surface between the rubble fields consisted of very thin ice, through which my probing ski stick sometimes passed with ease into the dark waters below. After eight hours I had moved both sledges more than a mile to the north. My morale was high, for the sledges ran well whatever the surface, far better than any previous design. My mental arithmetic raced ahead and I estimated a Pole arrival in only seventy days.

I kept an eye open for a good campsite. Sea-ice grows at a rate of two to three feet a year. Ice-floes that survive intact for more than two years are easy to identify, for the broken blocks that litter their surfaces will be rounded off by two or more years of summer melt. Floes in this condition are known as multi-year floes. The wind and snow abraid them into hummocks. Such floes can be at least eight feet thick and are more likely to withstand great pressure from neighbouring floes. They can provide good landing strips for ski-planes. Above all, the surface snow will have had most of its original salt content leached away by the sun and so will provide good drinking water. Unfortunately, time passed without the appearance of any floe older than a few months. Indeed, the area began to show increasing signs of recent open water only partially refrozen. My ski stick frequently sank through the surface skin, forcing me to detour to safer ice.

I had been travelling for well over the intended ten hours and making good progress, but was tired and cold. I ate a chocolate bar every two hours to ward off hypothermia, but was still very weary and decided to camp on any surface that looked solid. I came to a zone of interlacing fractures. The moon had vanished and, whenever I stopped, I heard the grumble of ice on the move. I tried to avoid a trench of black water, and mounted a bridge of twelve-inch-thick slabs, buckled by floe pressure. I had the small sledge with me and the big one 500 yards to the south. I clambered over the slabs with my skis on. The sledge followed easily in my wake.

There was no warning. A slab tilted suddenly under the sledge, which responded to gravity and, unbalancing me, pulled me backwards. I fell on my back and slid down the slab. The noise that followed was the one I most hate to hear in the Arctic, a splash as the sledge fell into the sea.

I kicked out with my skis and flailed at the slab with both hands. One ski boot plunged into the sea and one gloved hand found an edge of the slab. Taking a firm grip I pulled my wet foot and ski out of the water. I unfastened the manhaul harness. I was already beginning to shiver. I squirmed around until I could sit on a flatter slab to inspect the sledge in the gloom. It was under water, but afloat. I hauled on the traces, but they were jammed under the slabs. Seventy days' worth of food and thirty of fuel were on that sledge – and the communications gear. Without it, the expedition was over. A nearby slab crashed into the sea: the ice was moving. I had to save the sledge quickly. Soon I would be dangerously cold.

With my feet hooked around a slab, I lay on my stomach and stretched my left arm under the slab to free the sledge trace. I took off my mitt so that I could feel where the rope was snagged. For a minute or so I could not find the underwater snag. Then by jiggling the rope sharply, it came free. I pulled hard and the sodden sledge rose to the surface. My wet hand was numb but I could not replace the mitt until the sledge was out of the sea. Gradually the prow rose on to a slab and water cascaded off its canvas cover. Minutes later the sledge was on 'dry land'. I danced about like a madman. Both my mitts were back on and I used various well-tried cold hands revival techniques to restore life to the numb fingers. Usually they work and my blood returns painfully to all my fingers; this time they did not.

I took the wet mitt off and felt the dead hand. The fingers were ramrod stiff and ivory white. They might as well have been wooden. I knew that if I let my good hand go even partially numb, I would be unable to erect the tent and start the cooker – which I needed to do quickly for I was shivering in my thin manhaul gear. I returned to the big sledge. The next thirty minutes were a nightmare. The cover zip jammed. With only five usable but increasingly numb fingers, precious minutes went by before it was free and I unpacked the tent. By the time I had eased one tent-pole into its sleeve, my teeth were chattering violently and my good hand was numb. I had to get the cooker going in minutes or it would be too late. I crawled into the partially erect tent, closed its doorzip and began a twenty-minute battle to start the cooker. I could not use the petrol lighter with my fingers, but I found some matches I could hold in my teeth.

Starting an extremely cold petrol cooker involves careful priming so that just the right amount of fuel seeps into the pad below the fuel jet. The cold makes washers brittle and the priming plunger sticky. Using my teeth and a numb index finger, I finally worked the pump enough to squirt fuel on to the pad but was slow in shutting the valve; when I applied the match a three-foot flame reached to the roof. Luckily I had had a custom-made flame lining installed, so the tent was undamaged. And the cooker was alight – one of the best moments of my life.

Slowly and painfully some feeling came back into the fingers of my right hand. An hour later with my body warm again, I unlaced my wet boot. Only two toes had been affected. Soon they would exhibit big blood blisters and lose their nails, but they had escaped true frostbite. All around the tent cracking noises sounded above the steady roar of the cooker. I was in no doubt as to the fate of my bad hand. I had seen enough frostbite in others to realise that I was in serious trouble. I had to get quickly to a hospital to save some fingers from the surgeon's knife. I had to turn back.

I hated the thought of leaving the warmth of the tent. Both hands were excruciatingly painful. I battered ice off the smaller sledge, unloaded it and hauled it back to the big sledge. I set out in great trepidation. Twice my earlier tracks had been cut by newly open leads, but fortunately needed only small diversions to detour the open water. Five hours later I was back on the ice-shelf. I erected the tent properly and spent three hours massaging my good hand and wet foot over the cooker.

I drank hot tea and ate chocolate. I felt tired and dizzy, but the wind was showing signs of rising and I knew I should not risk a high wind chill. The journey to the hut took for ever. Once I fell asleep on the move and woke in a trough of soft snow well away from my intended route. Hypothermia is a danger at such times. When I feared its onset I often spoke to myself aloud, trying to enunciate the *My Fair Lady* lines about the rain in Spain, because an un-slurred voice is about the only reliable assurance that I was not on the slippery path to hypothermia and, on a solo expedition, death.

When at length I came to the old hut, I erected the tent on the floor, clumsily started the cooker and prepared the communications gear, which we called a Flobox after Flo Howell. I spoke to Morag in Resolute Bay. She promised to evacuate me the following day on the Twin Otter scheduled flight due to change over the weather men at Eureka.

The fingers on my left hand began to grow great liquid blisters. The pain was bad so I raided my medical stores for drugs. The next day I found an airstrip near the hut and marked its ends in the moonlight with kerosene rags. When I heard the approaching ski-plane I lit the rags and prayed the First Air pilot, not Karl this time, would not funk the landing. He didn't, and some forty-eight hours after my arrival at the hut I was on my way to try to save my left hand. At Resolute Bay Morag did what she could with immediate dressings and took me to a nurse. Morag, who had seen me survive kidney stone cramps and other batterings, understood frostbite at first hand. She later wrote to me: 'I have had some (frostbite) in my time and can relate to the pain. It's awful. All you want is for it to stop. I know that when you froze your hand you bound it tight. I have always believed that you stopped the circulation by that action, and that's what caused you to lose the fingers. There you go, that's my one gripe over twenty years. Mo.'

That night I flew to Iqaluit on Baffin Island where, after intravenous antibiotic therapy, a doctor started to open up the big finger blisters. After transference to the Ottawa Hospital, I was in the hands of frostbite experts, Doctors Conrad Watters and Heather O'Brien. Their initial report stated:

> The left hand demonstrates severe thermal injury to all five digits. The thumb is blistered from the mid portion and the fingers are all edematous throughout the course.
>
> His right foot is remarkable for areas of frostbite covering a coin-sized area of the distal great toe and a corresponding portion of the second toe on the right side. He was unaware of this injury prior to changing his clothing to begin hyperbaric treatment. I am optimistic that he can get some benefit from aggressive and immediate hyperbaric oxygen therapy.

Over the next two weeks I spent sixty hours sitting in a long oxygen tank like a goldfish bowl. A fat Frenchman sat in the far end of the tank facing me. He had diabetes leg damage. We both watched videos (in French) on a roof-screen of our container tube. The Frenchman was constantly and noisily flatulent in the enclosed tank. When the hyperbaric treatment ended, Conrad Watters reckoned a few millimetres of my fingers had been saved. The down side was that I couldn't see properly. Everything remained out of focus and blurred for the next three weeks.

I called Ginny, whose immediate reaction to my being less able to help with the cattle was, 'Typical, and we're already shorthanded on the farm.' To a *Times* reporter she commented, 'We know several people here on Exmoor who have lost bits of fingers or worse in farm machinery or with ferret bites. As long as Ran doesn't leave his finger bits on the edge of the bath, as he once did with a blackened toe, I'll be happy to see him back next week. He did put on a lot of extra weight for the expedition, so now he'll have to take it off again. I might hide the farm machinery and give him a dung fork to clear the cowshed by hand.'

15

Amputations

I returned to Britain with another failure under my belt, a scant amount raised for our charity and a disappointed sponsor. Kidney stones and frostbitten digits are no more acceptable to critics as reasons for failure than are unseasonal polar storms or crevasse accidents. I suppose that, over a twenty-six-year period of polar travel, the frostbite odds were always narrowing. This time they caught up with me, which was a shame because everything was otherwise looking good, the sledge was going well and I was in peak condition.

There is, of course, no point in crying over spilt milk since, if you go for the big ones and you win some in your lifetime, you can be sure you will lose at others on the way. The best course, I've usually found, has been to shrug, note what you've done wrong and apply yourself quickly to trying again. This, my standard policy over the years, sadly did not look like working this time because my damaged fingers were liable to be amputated fairly shortly, which would seriously affect extreme cold projects in the future. One of my firm rules in selecting individuals for polar travel had always been to avoid anyone, however experienced or skilled, who had any history of frostbite damage. Badly bitten noses and ears were okay. Fingers and toes were not.

I also knew that this Arctic failure, coming hot on the heels of the Bering Strait cancellation and the Antarctic solo kidney stones, was asking for trouble from the UK media, who are almost as eager to savage a failed expedition leader as a football manager who has lost a couple of key matches. Most of them enjoyed being witty at my expense. *The Times* offered me solid advice.

> It is a reasonable bet that if Sir Ranulph's frostbitten hand allows it, he will be planning to trudge through the snow again. Doggedness and fortitude saved his life on this occasion, but he was fortunate to survive and time is not on his side. The older someone is, the more they are liable to suffer from hypothermia, frostbite and diseases associated with the cold. The reflexes that come into play to protect skin when its temperature is dangerously lowered are less efficient, so corrections to skin temperature may be slow and frostbite more likely. So Sir Ranulph should opt for holidays in Spain.

Media barbs the week after I returned home from Ottawa were easily kept in perspective by the more immediate worry of what to do about my damaged fingers. They throbbed most of the time and complained loudly with needle-sharp pain when brought into contact, however lightly, with any object, even clothing material. To avoid this, especially when trying to sleep, was often difficult. Two of my friends who were surgeons advised speedy amputation of the damaged fingers to avoid complications such as gangrene. After checking the records of a number of specialists, Ginny found a surgeon in Bristol, Donald Sammut, with a history of brilliant treatment of damaged fingers. The south-west of England produces very few frostbite cases, but so what? Damaged fingers are all the same once cut off, whatever the original reason for the trauma, and I was greatly relieved when Donald agreed to deal with my fingers.

A friend from the Institute of Naval Medicine in Portsmouth, for whom I had previously completed cold water research work in his immersion tank, telephoned out of the blue. Under no circumstances, he warned, should I undergo any amputations until at least five months after the date of the accident.

'Why not?' I asked, perplexed.

The Navy surgeon explained that he had seen many divers with toe and finger damage which had been operated on too early before the semi-traumatised tissue that lies between the dead ends and the undamaged stumps had had time to heal properly.

'This is the tissue,' he stressed, 'that will be needed – after the dead finger ends are cut away – to stretch over the stumps. So it must be strong, elastic, healthy tissue; not severely damaged, as it is now. More fingers have been shortened unnecessarily by premature surgery than by the original damage from the bends or from frostbite. So don't you let them cut you up too early, Ran, or you'll regret it. Your new stump material will simply fail to do its job and you'll end up back on the chopping block with ever shorter fingers.'

Donald's own policy on the best timing for the surgery was similar. He advised me 'The best method is to advance the "frontier" skin, which is immediately adjacent to the frostbite and is inflamed. It is crucial that this skin returns to supple normality before any attempt is made to dissect and advance it.'

Throughout this period I took penicillin to keep gangrene from developing in the open cracks where the damaged but live flesh met the dead and blackened ends. Mary Bromiley, the physiotherapist who had over twenty years dealt with my aches and pains, applied laser treatment and electrical stimulation to the stumps. Every three weeks I also drove to Bristol to Melanie Downs-Wheeler, a specialist physiotherapist, who taught me gripping and bending exercises for each semi-mummified finger, and then, the dreaded moment, out came her debridement tweezers and for the next fifteen minutes, which is all I could stand, she picked away at the dead and damaged tissue in the semi-live areas to 'encourage healing there'.

Most days I tried to help Ginny with the cattle and sheep. I bought her two black alpacas for her birthday. She named them Punto and Mucho and they soon became inseparable companions to the black sheep. After their bi-annual shearing they resembled Spielberg's ET, gangly with huge liquid and appealing black eyes.

The tax investigation into the affairs of our company and

ourselves, sparked off by my enquiring back in 1995 about self-employment rules, had been ongoing ever since, at considerable cost in terms of my accountant's responses to the voluminous questionnaires from the Revenue. Since one of the main lines of attack by the taxman was that all Ginny's farming activities were a mere front to offset or avoid taxation, the five-year-long investigation with its often threatening overtones both worried and depressed her. No farmer worked harder or more meticulously than did Ginny, and in weather conditions that were at best sturdy, at worst foul, for Greenlands is, at 1,300 feet above sea-level, one of the highest – if not the highest – working farm in the south-west. Driving sleet and fog off the adjoining moors and the nearby Atlantic were the norm for much of the year. Midnight calving and difficult deliveries in sodden clothes were common every spring, and snow drifts would cut the farm off from the road over the moors, our only access point, for up to three weeks a year. So Ginny did not need officious taxmen telling her that her only aim in life was to defraud the Revenue. We were referred to as 'Registered Investigation Case F18579'. An old expedition friend who had become a part-time tax commissioner in Northumberland advised us to take the matter to our local commissioners. This we eventually did, and finally the adjudicator at the court concluded that the Revenue had handled our tax affairs very badly, should pay the court costs and close the investigation. There was no compensation or apology after five years of worry and doubt.

Our long-time expedition patron, Prince Charles, asked us to visit him at his Highgrove home. He wished me well with my pending amputations and we joked about old times with Dr Hammer. The Prince had been the active and caring patron of all my expeditions for twenty-five years, during which we had raised millions of pounds for the charities he had nominated.

After four months of living with grotesque, witch-like talons, purple in colour, sticking out of my stumps, I could take it no longer and, with another month to go before Donald Sammut was due to cut them off, I decided to take the matter into my own hands. Each and every time over the previous sixteen weeks that my fingers had hit or merely brushed against anything, never mind something hot, I had sworn at the pain. Ginny suggested that I was becoming irritable.

The answer was obvious. The useless finger ends must be cut off at once, so they could no longer get in the way and hit things. I tried tentatively to cut through the smallest finger with a new pair of secateurs, but it hurt. So I purchased a set of fretsaw blades at the village shop, put the little finger in my Black & Decker folding table's vice and gently sawed through the dead skin and bone just above the live skin line. The moment I felt pain or spotted blood, I moved the saw further into the dead zone. I also turned the finger around several times to cut it from different sides, like sawing a log. This worked well and the little finger's end knuckle finally dropped off after some two hours of work. Over that week I removed the other three longer fingers, one each day, and finally the thumb, which took two days.

My physiotherapist congratulated me on a fine job, but Donald Sammut was not so happy. He later recorded my visit: 'Ran appeared one day on a routine appointment and calmly told me he'd chopped off his fingertips. We had quite a heated exchange over this. He risked making it worse.' I apologised to Donald, but felt secretly pleased with myself since life improved considerably once the gnarled mummified ends no longer got in the way. Ginny agreed that I had done the right thing. She no longer had to tie my tie for me, nor put in my cufflinks before I gave a conference talk.

That summer we received an invitation for the Millennium Year meeting of the Fiennes tribe at the family HQ, Broughton Castle near Banbury, in which the family boss has lived since 1377. This clan coming-together involved 200 of us from all over the world and all descended from Frederick Fiennes, the 16th Lord Saye and Sele. James, the 1st Lord, fought at Agincourt and was Treasurer of England. You can catch up with the rest of them in the family tree on page 360.

At least sixteen of us at the castle that lovely summer's day were the progeny of my mother who, at eighty-eight, was the oldest person present. Our host, Nat, had been a pageboy at her wedding. Ginny and I had a great time meeting my sisters' families, including my American nephews and nieces. The castle is surrounded by a wide moat complete with drawbridge and portcullis, and Ginny provided Nat with iridescent Cayuga ducks from our farm that swam around in the Broughton moat weed, out of reach of foxes. My cousin Joseph Fiennes was at the meeting. He was no stranger at the castle, having recently starred with Gwyneth Paltrow in *Shakespeare in Love*, which was filmed there. His brother, Ralph, was unfortunately away in America.

The very first Fiennes who came to England that we know about was Eustache Fiennes, who came from a village called Fiennes in northern France which is now an industrial suburb of Boulogne. According to the historically accurate picture diary that is the Bayeux Tapestry, Eustache arrived at Hastings in 1066 and, commanding the Norman Army, he personally cut off the English King Harold's head with his axe and was given various castles as a reward. One was Herstmonceux just a few miles from Hastings, but subsequent Fienneses sold it. Today, only Broughton, which is open to the public for most of the year, remains. Oliver Cromwell plotted against the Royalists using Broughton as his local base, since most of the Fiennes family were fervent Parliamentarians. Cromwell's war jacket is still on show in the castle.

Before we left Broughton my sisters and I agreed that we should meet up in Lodsworth as our mother was moving, after forty years in the village, including twenty as president of the football club, to a retirement home in nearby Petworth. She was becoming increasingly forgetful and a little lame, so she had decided to make the move whilst she was still physically able. She wanted us all to decide which items of furniture each of us would like, since in her new one-room home there would be no space for most of it. We all sat around the kitchen table and one by one – starting with Sue, the eldest – listed our choice, little knowing that within three years only two of the five of us would still be alive.

Ginny had for years only been able to go on holiday or on expeditions with me by hiring an Animal Aunt, a sort of experienced animal-babysitter, from a company in Sussex. She had often been sent one particular girl, Pippa Wood, who was excellent with the animals. Eventually Pippa, who was self-employed, agreed to work at Greenlands whenever needed, enabling us to enjoy holidays again with old friends like the Gaults and the Bowrings without Ginny constantly worrying about the farm. That summer, unable to race competitively, I had time on my hands and almost learned to relax. We went for long walks with the Black Dogs, Pingo and Thule, great-grandchildren of the original Black Dog Ginny had brought to England a quarter of a century before. We expanded the farm by thirty-five wilderness acres, bought from our neighbour, mostly a place of wild flowers, jack snipe and a tumbling stream. A good place for picnics and bird spotting, with plenty of shelter for the cattle in winter.

Five months after my Arctic accident, Donald Sammut amputated the remaining bits of dead finger on my left hand and folded the previously semi-damaged skin neatly over the newly gaping stumps. He described the operation in simple terms:

Ran's Do-It-Yourself amputations had rather forced the issue, since the resulting raw surface had opened up the core of the amputated bone to the elements and we no longer had the protection of the mummified dead finger tips. The results of his 'surgery' included the middle finger bone being particularly exposed, protruding free well beyond the skin cover. Nevertheless this did not much compromise the eventual surgery, and I operated on 14 July, removing any residual dead tissue and providing skin cover to the tips. This skin cover consisted of islands of skin dissected virtually free on a stalk of nerve and artery advanced to cover the tip of each digit: this permits one to preserve maximum length (and crucial tendon insertions which preserve maximum power) while providing good quality, sensate skin similar to pulp.

So Donald grafted on extra patches cut from the sole of my left hand. He is a superb surgeon and anything I have been able to do since then which involves intricate finger movement is thanks to his meticulous skill.

I spent a post-operative week in hospital doing nothing in between visits by Ginny, various good friends and my cousin Rosalie Fiennes, who gave me a book which appeared from its cover, to be the Works of Shakespeare but which was in reality the first book about the as yet unknown boy wizard, Harry Potter.

'You may think it is a children's book,' Rosalie told me, 'but don't be embarrassed. Nobody will know it's not Shakespeare. I have read it and, believe me, it's brilliant.'

I whiled away the hours with the book and have been a Potter fan ever since.

Back at Greenlands again with time on my hands – one of them gloved after the operation – I was sorting through some long over-due filing when I came upon a box of documents I had forgotten all about. The papers had come a long way. In 1995 when I was working as a lecturer for an Abercrombie and Kent cruise ship, I had found myself in Antarctica and, because that year was unseasonably warm with lots of loose ice the ship was able to visit a scientists' hut on the coast not previously reachable by cruise ships. Our German skipper asked the chief lecturer, Dr John Reynolds, Europe's top polar geologist, to check out the hut's safety before allowing his shipload of mostly American tourists ashore and John asked me to join him.

We beached the inflatable boat close by the hut. The last scientists to have worked there, some thirty years before, had left everything in place – food, equipment, six bunk beds and a great many books, including notes on the very first studies of what later turned out to be the ozone hole. Many of the scientists' notebooks were damp and stuck together, so John decided they should go back to Britain, and when I flew back to London from Chile I handed them over to Dr John Heap, Director of the Scott Polar Research Institute. Two of the notebooks, unlike the rest, were not on Her Majesty's Stationery and, since John Heap did not want them, I took them home and soon forgot about them.

I now found that the pages of one of the books had, over years of damp summer atmospheres presumably, become largely glued into a pulped mess. The other was in better condition and appeared to be a rambling diary written in biro. I could only access forty-five mostly separated and disjointed pages, but the little that I could read was fascinating.

I called Ed Victor, my literary agent, who agreed to approach a publisher, and I phoned Paul Cook, chief paper conservation expert at the Greenwich Maritime Museum, who gave me detailed advice on, and materials for, un-sticking the pages. Using Gore-Tex slips and an iron, I eventually managed to separate and render legible some 60 per cent of the diary, which turned out to be that of a fifty-five-year-old Canadian welfare worker named Derek Jacobs who, during the 1970s, had learned of his family's massacre at the hands of Nazis in 1945.

Determined to locate his mother's murderer, a policeman escorting the Wallern Death March during the last week of the war, Jacobs joined the Secret Hunters, an organisation dedicated to tracking down perpetrators of war-time atrocities. The diary showed that he had eventually traced the man he believed to be his mother's killer to Bermuda where the former Nazi had chartered a yacht to sail to Antarctica in secret quest for a reputed seam of gold. Jacobs had joined the yacht as crew.

When my application to inspect the records of the 1945 Death Marches drew no response, I asked a German friend, Mike Kobold, to trick his way into the archives at the Zentrale Stelle zur Verfolgung von Nazi Verbrechen and photocopy 400 pages of the relevant documents. I also tracked down Prince Yurka Galitzine, the man who had originally set up the Secret Hunters, and I went to visit him at his Mayfair address.

I spent the next eight months checking out most of the events described in Jacobs' diary and travelling the Sudetenland Death March route in Czechoslovakia and East Germany with Mike before settling down to start writing. I intended to produce the full story of Jacobs' life and the horrors experienced by his parents. But at that stage, Mike and I had failed to track down the whereabouts of Michael Weingärtner, the man Jacobs held responsible for his mother's death.

Travelling in Mike's lethally fast Audi on autobahns with no speed limit gave me a taste of Formula One, so when the *Top Gear* TV programme asked me to have a go on their Surrey race track, I jumped at it. They had an instructor named Stig who taught me the rudiments required and my best time, although bettered by Kate Moss, was several seconds ahead of the socialite Tara Palmer-Tomkinson, which was a great relief for my ego.

At the weekends I took time off to show Ginny's best cattle at agricultural shows. I came home from a show one night, well past midnight, and found Ginny sitting in the kitchen with a man. They were both drinking whisky and both were literally covered in blood – recent blood that was still shiny in the lamplight. The scene resembled that of two killers having a drink after committing a murder, but I soon recognised Donald, our local vet of many years, who Ginny had called in to deal with a difficult birth and prolapse. They had just spent an hour together in rain and darkness trying to force the bloody intestines of the mother cow back through her vulva.

Each of Ginny's hundred or so Aberdeen Angus cows had a name and, that year for the first time, I got to know most of them by sight. Ginny specialised in selling her own brand of bulls and, because few fences can keep randy bulls away from cows on heat, she kept all her bulls at a farm several miles away from Greenlands. Sadly bovine tuberculosis, which is endemic in the south-west, struck in the autumn of 2000 and all Ginny's bulls had to be shot by the Ministry. I remember the night before it happened, I came home from a lecture to find no supper but a note from Ginny saying, 'Not sure when I'll be back. Have joined the blockade. Love you, Gin.' I turned on the television news and learned that there was a national fuel crisis, sparked off by the sudden hike in petrol prices to £0.81 per litre at the pump, and groups of truckers, taxi drivers and farmers, including Ginny, were blockading oil terminals. There were pictures of police breaking up demonstrations. Ginny eventually called me on her mobile, not to explain what she was up to nor with whom, but to announce that she'd left me a rice dish in the Aga.

Only five months later, in February 2001, the foot and mouth epidemic was officially confirmed. I shuddered at the thought of how Ginny would react to the prospect of each and every one of her cattle and sheep being shot. If the virus reached anywhere on Exmoor, it would spread like wildfire across the largely unfenced moorlands of the National Park over which red deer and sheep wandered at will for many miles. For months we exercised maximum movement control on and off our farm. We avoided calling in the vet in case he brought us the dreaded bug on his van tyres or his clothing. All our gates were kept closed at all times and buckets full of disinfectant with a hand spray were left by our cattle grid for use by essential visitors like the postman. Every farmer in the area did likewise and prayed hard.

After the tax investigation and tuberculosis, Ginny needed this foot and mouth threat like a sore foot. She did not look at all well over those long summer months as the virus crept closer and closer to Greenlands, eventually stopping, God knows why, approximately twelve miles away.

Ever since the end of the Transglobe Expedition some twenty years before, Charlie Burton, Oliver Shepard, Ginny and I had met from time to time to chat about all those special years we had spent together. We thought of big, tough Charlie as immortal, but in October 2001 he suffered some form of heart attack whilst crossing a road, and then a few months later he died at home one morning, and Oliver rang to tell us. The three of us joined many more members of the Transglobe team and several hundred others for his memorial service at the Royal Geographical Society. I was lucky to have shared so many trials and tribulations over so many years with such a brave and solid man with a huge spirit and sense of humour.

Ginny and I had always slept with one leg or one arm entwined. When we had an argument by day, increasingly rare as the years fled by, this physical contact – which had become virtually subconscious like puffing up a pillow last thing – stopped any bad feeling spilling over into the next day. It also led to the likelihood of being struck when the other party was having a bad dream. One morning that June, just before dawn, Ginny went rigid and I woke with a shock.

'What's up?' I asked. 'Are you okay?'

Ginny stared down at me. 'Celia,' she said, 'your sister. You must go and see her. Now.'

'Why?'

'I don't know, but I think she's got much worse.'

My middle sister, Celia, living in Augusta, Georgia, had for a year or so been receiving chemotherapy for stomach cancer. That month reports from her husband Bob indicated that things were not too good, but there was no suggestion that she was dying. However, Ginny had never had such psychic intimations of bad news before, so I caught a flight the very next day, rented a car in Charlotte, North Carolina, and arrived at Celia's home at 6.00 p.m. Bob greeted me at their door with a worried look. He and Celia had gone for a quiet walk together the previous day, but on return she had fallen into a deep sleep, her breathing had rapidly become shallow and she was no longer reacting to normal stimuli.

She opened her eyes when I greeted her and seemed to smile. Her fingers lifted momentarily from the quilt and Bob said he was sure that she knew I was there. But I never heard her speak again. We stayed in relays with her through that night. Bob and her son, my nephew Tony, were both doctors and one of her two daughters, Deirdre, was a nurse. They looked after her beautifully and held a bedside communion service, until at 9.00 a.m. the following morning, with her family all about her, she died peacefully – a lovely person, an active and committed Christian and a perfect sister.

When the following week I drove to see my mother, I found her much quieter than usual. We went out to lunch, as we often did, at the Angel Hotel in Midhurst where, as a teenager over forty years before, I had done the washing up for pocket money. For the first time my mother did not recognise members of the hotel staff she had known for many years. She asked why my fingers were bandaged, a question I had answered her in full many times since the accident. She asked me about Celia, and I stressed that I had been with her as she died peacefully. But my mother did not seem able to take in at all that one of her children was dead.

That summer, back in the village hall of her beloved Lodsworth, my remaining two sisters and I arranged a party for her ninetieth birthday with fifty of her best and oldest friends, plus many of her grandchildren. After various toasts were offered and speeches laughed at, my mother spontaneously stood up and, with a lovely smile, thanked everyone there for all the happiness and fun they had given her down the long years. I loved her dearly and knew no mother could ever have been more loving or caring. She had brought up four young children, for much of the time in a foreign land, with no husband and a domineering mother-in-law. Thanks to her I had never felt any parental void as a child, no need for a father figure, for her shoulder was always there to cry on. I wondered on her ninetieth birthday, perhaps for the first time in nearly sixty years, on whose shoulder she had been able to cry since my father's untimely death.

My father, although I never missed him, has always been one of the three people I have in different ways wished to emulate. I was brought up with stories of his bravery. My other two heroes were Wilfred Thesiger and Wally Herbert. That summer I learned that the former, whom I considered the greatest British desert traveller of all time, was living out his old age in a rest home in Surrey. I had met him, only once, to interview him about one of his travel books thirty years before. He was a craggy, imposing figure, even then, with the face of a hawk. I decided it was time I paid him another visit. I found him resting in a deep armchair in a small room that seemed to imprison him. But he was cheerful.

'I've won at last,' he said with his sun-leathered features

creasing into a smile. 'I've escaped from the mixed wing. No more old ladies blocking up the stairways.'

He levered his long frame out of his chair with two sticks and suggested we venture to the local pub for some lunch. He spurned the offer of a lift in my car and we walked down the road for twenty minutes, resting occasionally as he leaned heavily on my shoulder. The pub turned out to be a sandwich bar. His mind, like my mother's, wandered now that he was ninety-two years old, but I listened spellbound to his stories of the great deserts of Oman, Saudi and the Yemen, and especially of his wanderings, some twenty years before I was there, in the wilds of Dhofar. I had met and worked with perhaps a dozen Dhofaris who clearly remembered Thesiger. They had called him by his Arab nickname of Mubarreq bin Miriam, and all remembered him with great respect. After two hours of yarning he began to doze off, so we walked slowly back to the rest home and I left him alone in his room. He had no family any more, but an unrivalled wealth of memories of people and places, of incredible journeys he had dared and endured, and the inner pride in knowing that he had never given up.

A year later I was lecturing in Kenya when Ginny phoned me to say the Prince of Wales had asked me to represent him at Thesiger's memorial service in Eton's magnificent college chapel, as he would be abroad. If I could taste just a mere fraction of the wonders Thesiger experienced, I would die happy, but I never will, for Thesiger was born just in time to be the last of the Marco Polos, a stranger in strange lands marvelling at weird, often savage, rituals in the harsh badlands of Danakil, among the nomad raiders of the Empty Quarter or the biblical marsh-men of the pre-Saddam Hussein Euphrates marshes. Thesiger's powerfully written and photographed books ensure that neither these people as they used to be nor he who travelled then among them will be forgotten.

The other great traveller whose books I had studied and whose journeys I had long coveted was not acquainted with hot deserts at all, for he specialised in the world's coldest places. In Antarctica and on the shifting sea-ice of the Arctic Ocean, Wally Herbert's great journeys were, through the 1950s and 1960s, the stuff of polar travellers' dreams, especially his 1968/69 first true crossing of the Arctic Ocean. On this expedition a news reporter in his radio base camp overheard Wally describe his expedition's London committee, a group including the most senior polar men in the Establishment at that time, as people who 'didn't know what the bloody hell they were talking about'. As a result, thirty years after his monumental success in the Arctic, Wally had still not been honoured in any way, unlike a number of his direct contemporaries, including Chris Bonington, the mountaineer, and Robin Knox-Johnston, the sailor.

For three years I conducted a fierce correspondence with the Cabinet Office and the relevant civil honours bureaucrats. But Wally's file was clearly blacked, and I got nowhere fast. Eventually, after obtaining letters of admiration for Wally's pioneering achievements from all over the world, the Cabinet Office agreed that Wally should be knighted. He died in 2007, our greatest polar traveller since Scott.

Early that autumn, Mike Kobold phoned from Austria to say he had traced the ex-Nazi policeman who had murdered the mother of Derek Jacobs, as well as some 200 other women. Since neither the Secret Hunters nor the Nazi-hunting services of Simon Wiesenthal in Vienna, who had helped us in our Nazi search for over a year, had been able to trace the man, I was amazed at Mike's announcement. Nevertheless I flew out to meet him at Frankfurt Airport, close to his German home, the following day.

An exhausted Mike Stroud surveys his sledge after its 25 feet fall
into a crevasse. Antarctica is bigger than China and
India put together. But with no shops.

Many things go into making an expedition happen: a supportive sponsor like James Dyson, hours of training and a good relationship with the media – on the left is the late Terry Lloyd who was killed in Iraq, believed to be the victim of American so-called 'friendly fire'.

Then there is the assembly of all the necessary supplies – and if you
return safely, a chance to meet interesting characters like Mrs T.
This photo was taken five days after the Brighton hotel IRA bombing.

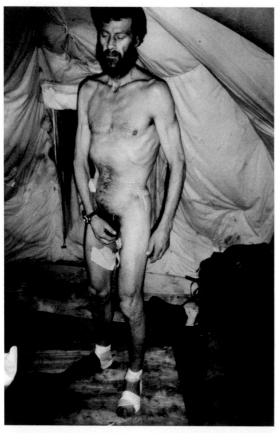

Counting the cost: the author after one of the polar journeys. Such expeditions are hard on the human body, particularly if you don't take in enough calories while you're exerting yourself in what are very unfriendly conditions.

My right hand, photographed (by me) soon after frustration drove me to amputate the mummified ends with a hack-saw.

Over the years I've tried many things to keep in good condition, from camel racing to endurance running – here with Gary Tompsett after winning the Elite Veterans Cup at the two-day Karrimor Mountain Marathon.

Seven marathons in seven consecutive days on seven continents: in the words of *The Times*, 'an inspiration for every runner, every ordinary person, tempted to give up in the face of the impossible'. Clockwise from top left: the first in the Falklands accompanied by penguins, then on to Santiago, Sydney, Singapore, London, Cairo and finally New York (overleaf).

16

Heart Attack

Mike Kobold had trained with the German Traffic Police driving department and as we sped from Frankfurt to Vienna he frequently exceeded 150 mph in his Audi. My feet pressed hard against the footwell, as Mike chattered amiably. I began to understand why Germany produced so many Schumacher-class speedmasters.

Simon Wiesenthal, Mike informed me, had identified the Nazi we were after – Michael Weingärtner – who had never been punished, nor indeed had the vast majority of individuals who had perpetrated acts of cruelty or murder in the name of Hitler. Weingärtner had, according to Wiesenthal's researchers, fled Germany in the sixties, soon after Adolf Eichmann's hanging in Israel and, like many of his ilk, had found sanctuary in Austria. Our discreet enquiries had revealed that he was living in the suburbs of Wels, a prosperous town near Vienna. We drove to Wels and parked close to the house. We both wore suits and carried briefcases. Mike led me up a path through a well-tended garden and knocked on the front door. A small grey-haired woman with tight features stared at us with hostility, if not menace. Mike explained that we had just flown from New York to follow up our newspaper's story about Weingärtner's part in the Wallern Death March of April 1945. We had heard that Weingärtner had somehow saved the lives of three women from murder by his colleagues. Would he please corroborate this?

Frau Weingärtner, for she could be no other, disappeared for a few minutes. An angry male voice sounded from within. Then she returned and told Mike that her husband was watching the F1 Grand Prix, that Michael Schumacher was winning, that it was a Sunday, that we had not deigned to make an appointment and that we should leave their home at once. The door slammed.

We had come a long way, if not from New York, and we conferred on the doorstep. We agreed to wait in the car until the Grand Prix ended. The Audi's radio duly announced that Schumacher had won the event so, assuming that Weingärtner would now be in as good a mood as we would ever be likely to find him, we again knocked on his door. Weingärtner himself answered this time.

He was no bigger than his wife and as unremarkable-looking. His face was certainly hard and his manner ice-cold, but, at first, his tone was polite enough.

'May we come in?' Mike asked.

Weingärtner ignored this. 'You say that I saved the women's lives.' He made a slight shrugging motion. 'Na. Ya. I did my best for them. They were difficult times for us.'

'So,' Mike countered, 'you would disagree with these US 5th Army records resulting from interrogations of the surviving women?' Mike produced a file from his case. 'As you can see, they say that, of the 3,000 women killed or allowed to die on the march, you were personally the killer of at least 200 women, mostly teenage girls, whose photographs are shown here.' Mike pointed at line upon line of women's mugshots.

Weingärtner then clammed up. 'I killed nobody,' he said, and slammed the door in our faces. After a minute, his wife poked her head out and said firmly, '*Das ist alles.*' So ended our attempt at being foot-in-the-door investigative journalists and I was left wondering about such people as Weingärtner who are still to be traced all over the world today, individuals who have caused agony and misery and committed mass murder. To my mind there can be no date nor age beyond which a person guilty of mass murder should become immune to justice. Mike and I sent details of Michael Weingärtner's address to Simon Wiesenthal's office and I subsequently gave talks on our search for the Wallern Death March murderers to groups of Holocaust survivors in Britain. The book about Derek Jacobs and his quest, *The Secret Hunters*, was published in 2001.

My next biography was going to be a very different sort of undertaking. In 1980, when I reached the South Pole Scott-Amundsen Base for the first time, I spent four days there. I helped the inmates with the dishwashing in their canteen and chatted to many of the overwintering scientists. It was interesting to hear their views on various explorers, including Captain Robert Falcon Scott, after whom their polar base was half named. They mentioned to me that the previous year an Englishman named Roland Huntford had published a new book on Scott. Apparently, they said, the whole story about Scott the polar hero was merely old Brit imperialist propaganda which this Huntford guy's book ruthlessly exposed. I meant to buy this book on returning home, but I forgot.

Then, in the mid-1980s, I was reminded about it from an unexpected source – Mrs Raisa Gorbachev, to whom Ginny and I were making a presentation in Moscow on behalf of Dr Hammer. She told me that Stalin had much admired Scott, who had been awarded various Soviet honours, but that more recently Scott had been exposed as a mere fool. I bought the Huntford book and watched a seven-hour ITV documentary film based on it. Both contained much information that my own experiences by then made me find questionable, although I found book and film good entertainment value. The book read like an exciting novel and, not being well versed in polar history at the time, I was impressed by its lengthy acknowledgments and lists of references.

Later, after Mike Stroud and I manhauled across the Antarctic continent in 1993, I saw the ITV film again and this time it rang a very different bell. There were huge inaccuracies and they stemmed from Huntford's book. Over the next decade I read all the books that I could find about Scott, some 112 in all, and I became slowly aware of the magnitude of the change wrought to Scott's reputation by Huntford's book which had by 2003 become the generally accepted view of the explorer. Huntford himself was considered the world's number one polar biographer, although he had never been near either Pole, and his books were treated as reliable history. His fabricated version of Scott would be difficult to expose.

I was not alone in my dismay at the injustice done to Scott. Britain's most senior polar explorer, Sir Vivian Fuchs, dismissed Huntford's book: 'This is one man's interpretation and his inexperience of the conditions he is writing about clearly makes him incompetent to judge them.'

I determined to instigate my own research and reach my own conclusions which were that Huntford had skewed history in his vendetta against Scott and his championing of Amundsen. At least with polar experience on my side I could reinvestigate the facts and contribute something towards restoring historical reality.

As work on my Scott biography was coming to an end I knew I needed a complete break and change of activity. Out of the blue I phoned Mike Stroud and suggested we get involved in another expedition. He was however too busy in Southampton to spare the three months an average expedition would take. His counter-suggestion was that we run seven marathons on each of the world's seven continents in seven days. This was an idea originally proposed by Mary Gadams, his American team-mate on a previous Eco-Challenge race, but she had not managed to get the enterprise off the ground. The idea appealed to me enormously and Mike and I set about getting the sponsorship and logistics in place while training seriously for the running. We would need to start in Antarctica and it would be good to aim to finish by joining an official marathon run somewhere like New York. It was only a case of connecting it all up.

The day after I finished the final corrections to the text of my Scott biography I was due to give a talk to a convention in

Dunblane, so I told Ginny I would see her the following morning and I drove to Bristol Airport, arriving at the departure desk of the no-frills airline, Go, in good time. I boarded the aircraft and settled down to read a magazine. I can remember nothing that happened from that moment for the next three days and nights.

Apparently not more than a few minutes before take off I collapsed noiselessly and was dragged into the aisle, where a passenger with medical training gave me instant mouth-to-mouth cardiac resuscitation. The pilot called the fire service, and the fire engine accelerated across the tarmac to drop off two firemen recently trained in the use of the mobile defibrillator which they carried on board. They applied a powerful 200-joule DC electric shock which passed right across my chest to depolarise every cell in my heart. This caused my natural pacemaker to recover and my heart was once more a regularly beating pump. Deeply unconscious, I was then rushed to a waiting ambulance. Twice more on the journey to Bristol's Royal Infirmary and three more times in the Accident & Emergency unit I lapsed back into fibrillation. The stabilising drugs I was given proved ineffective but the doctors managed in due course to stabilise my condition. Fearful however that I would have further attacks, they sent me to surgery. Within just two hours of my initial collapse, I was on cardiac bypass with a machine artificially pumping and refrigerating my blood.

A consultant cardiologist, Dr Tim Cripps, commented to me much later, 'Out of the hundred thousand people a year in the UK who have a cardiac arrest, the first and only warning they get is the attack itself and only very few are lucky enough to be near a defibrillator and someone who knows how to use it.' After treating me to some examples of others who had not been so lucky, he went on, 'When you arrived in our ICU you were measured at 4 points on the Glasgow Coma Scale. The lowest the scale goes is Level 3, which Richard Hammond of *Top Gear* achieved after his car crash at 260 mph.'

Dr Cripps called the senior Bristol cardiac surgeon, Gianni Angelini, who subsequently wrote:

On arrival RF had a coronary angiography which showed the presence of a large thrombus (blood clot) blocking the left anterior descending and the intermediary arteries, two of the most important arteries of the heart.

He was fully anaesthetised, artificially ventilated and taken at once to the operating theatre. I was informed at my home and when I arrived was told it was quite bad . . . The situation was so urgent that we decided to go ahead and open his chest even prior to the arrival of the perfusion team . . . Two bypass grafts were performed, one using an artery called the internal mammary artery, which is behind the breastbone, the other a long segment of vein from the leg. There was serious concern about his neurological state since we didn't know the extent and duration of his cardiac arrest at the airport and thereafter. He was kept sedated for 24 hours . . . Then woken up . . . From then on it became rather difficult to manage him, since he virtually refused any analgesia, saying he did not have a great deal of pain. And that he wanted the tubes and lines removed as soon as possible because he had to walk up and down the corridor. He was discharged five days after surgery.

Ginny had sat by my bedside day and night and watched my tube-fed, artificially ticking body, blood-smeared in places, lying in front of her for more than three days. Every now and again a nurse would enter and thump my knee or foot for a reaction. None came. This could not have been a good time for Ginny. When I eventually came to, we kissed as best we could and she told me that I had had a heart attack. It took a while to work out what she was saying and where I was. My chest had been opened up from top to bottom and later sewn up with silver wire, the knots of which I can still feel jutting proud just beneath my skin.

Leaning on Ginny's shoulder, once the pipes and tubes had all been removed from various places, I managed to walk a few paces but felt extremely sore. Ginny drove me home the next day and put me to bed with strict instructions not to move. I asked for chocolate, but she said I was never to eat chocolate again.

Why, we both wondered, had I had this attack at all? Some years later Mike Stroud wrote about my attack and his opinion of it in his book *Survival of the Fittest*.

Ran smoked enthusiastically earlier in life and never paid much attention to 'healthy' aspects of his diet. Furthermore, he probably has an inherited metabolic predisposition for heart problems. In many, this would have been recognised from their family history – a mother or father having a heart attack at an early age. In Ran's case, however, this could have been missed. He knew his mother had a healthy heart to great age but his father's medical potential was unknown (he died young in the Second World War). Ran's cumulative risk factors simply overcame even his level of physical-fitness protection. Of course, the newspapers had a field day, for the story of Ran's heart attack was of great appeal. Sir Ranulph Fiennes, the epitome of continued vigorous activity in middle age, declared various columnists, had clearly been overdoing it. This annoyed me intensely. I immediately rang the hospital intensive-care unit to send best wishes to Ran and his wife Ginny. She must have been incredibly distressed, and she now faced a future without the man who had matured from childhood sweetheart into a husband and longstanding expedition partner. But although concern for them both was uppermost in my mind, I have to admit that, for me, Ran's condition also raised practical issues, because with Ran in a coma in intensive care, all thought and planning that had gone into our seven marathons project seemed to have come to nought. This did not, however, reckon with Ran's resilience. On the fourth day after his surgery he rang me.

'Mike?'

I immediately recognised his voice.

'Ran, how are you? How's Ginny? How's – ' My flurry of surprise was swiftly interrupted.

'Mike, I can't chat for long but I'm fine. Don't cancel anything for now.'

I guessed immediately what he was referring to but I needed to be absolutely certain.

'You mean the marathons?'

'Yes,' he replied. 'I've been told there was a little damage so I don't see—'

'What? You mean your doctors say it's okay?' I interrupted.

'No, no,' he responded, whispering. 'I haven't asked them yet.'

Our conversation ran on for a couple more minutes but at the end I was clear. Ran was in cloud-cuckoo-land and his specialist would soon bring him down to earth.

Then five days later he rang again.

'How's it going? When will you be home?' I started.

'Oh, very soon,' he came back, a slight laugh in his voice. 'I'm just walking off the moor.'

When it came to confessing my future marathon intentions, I had hopes that my surgeon Professor Angelini would be sympathetic. After all, he still held the Italian 800 metres record. However I decided to approach the topic cautiously. Here is his account of his response:

I saw RF in my office for the usual post-operative check-up and he told me it was his intention to run a marathon. He asked my opinion and I said, as much as I liked running myself, I have never had a patient who had asked me a question like can I run a marathon after a heart operation. I told him he probably could, given the fact that his coronaries were now pretty well sorted out. However I would advise him not to run in a competitive fashion. What he failed to tell me was that his intention was to run seven marathons in seven days on seven continents. Something which I would strongly advise not to do!

Meanwhile, the cardiologist, Dr Tim Cripps, decided that his colleague, Dr David Smith in Exeter, would be best qualified to decide whether or not I should be allowed to try to run a marathon, since he knew a lot more about sports cardiology. David, who was a frequent running partner and good friend to both Mike Stroud and myself and had been my team leader on the Moroccan Eco-Challenge, checked my post-operative angiograms with care and said it would be okay to run non-competitively provided I kept my heart rate low.

For my own part, I decided to see if the sponsors of our marathon project, Land Rover, would be prepared to postpone everything for a year. They were then owned by Ford who decided that postponement was not on the cards. I must teach myself to run again in three and a half months. The bottom line, I decided, was to give it a go and if I couldn't do it, Mike would have to go solo.

So I started to walk, very slowly, on mostly flat ground, and whenever I became breathless or felt giddy, I lay down on the ground until I felt better. Sometimes, if I tripped on uneven ground, my chest hurt where the rib-cage had been slit open and it felt as though the wire ties had torn.

I took a mobile phone on each outing and kept calling or being called by Ginny. After a while she agreed that I was approaching things in a slower, more controlled manner than she had thought possible and did not seem worried by the marathon plan which, unlike most previous projects with Mike, would only last a week. Our charity, which we chose ourselves this time, was the British Heart Foundation, who support the placement of out-of-hospital defibrillators, like the one that saved me. Mike also decided, with Ginny's enthusiastic approval, to take one with us on each run.

My recovery programme, also carefully planned with Ginny's approval, stated:

3 weeks after op: walk for 5 minutes with stops, lie down when giddy

8 weeks after op: walk for 30 minutes, no stops
12 weeks after op: jog for 60 minutes, no stops
13 weeks after op: jog for 120 minutes, no stops
15 weeks after op: jog gentle (7 hour) marathon
16 weeks after op: start the 7x7x7

A total of 294 kilometres in seven days. The seven marathons would not be at fast race pace but they would not be gentle runs either. We would need to complete each within six hours, including airport customs and security (in and out). Since none of the scheduled jumbo flights could be expected to delay take off by even one minute if we were late, I tried to foresee potential airport security problems by writing to airlines in advance, warning them of Mike's metal detector-alarming medical hand baggage and the defibrillator.

Only eight weeks before departure Mike called me. Bad news. He had been going for a run near his home in Hampshire when his left hip began to complain. He was forced to call his wife Thea to collect him by car to take him home. In a few hours a grapefruit-sized swelling appeared which became a massive, blue-black bruise tracking down his thigh. He had an ultrasound check which showed that a small muscle running from the hip to beyond the knee had torn through. The ripped ends were swimming in a pool of blood. Mike's orthopaedic and sports medicine colleagues' advice was gloomy: he would not be running anywhere for several months, let alone doing a marathon.

Mike said he was not sure he agreed with their negative prognosis and would hope to get training again after a short rest. In fact, he took only twelve days' rest, lots of aspirins, some physio and then a test half-hour outing. His hip was sore, he self-diagnosed, but workable.

Our sponsor Land Rover decided not to announce the event at all unless we could prove we were fit to run at least two full marathons before departure. Mike chose the Cardiff event a fortnight before our start date and a small marathon near Winchester a week later. Land Rover stressed that we must tell nobody at all about the project until after both trial runs were successfully done. So I was extremely worried when the Cardiff organisers sent me my running number to stick on my vest a week before their event. The number was 777! They had obviously found out about our main plan. I called Mike, but he assured me he had not told anyone, and it transpired that the number had been chosen entirely at random. We took this as a good omen.

The Cardiff course turned out to be flat, and Mike, who set the pace, went fast by my standards, finishing in around four hours. I felt drained at the end, but Mike wrote:

In contrast to me, Ran looked pretty fresh at the end . . . despite the ten years' age difference and his enforced, slow training schedule. It was easy to see that he was by far the more natural athlete. But he too had a problem. For many years, his back had been the source of much discomfort, causing considerable grief when he was pulling heavy sledges during some of our polar trips. Sadly, running also made it worse and if one marathon exacerbated the pain, how would it react to the hammering it was going to receive? We were both aware that, determined or not, enough pain could defeat us. I made a mental note to add more pain-killers to the medical kit.

The next marathon, seven days later, took us from Winchester to Salisbury and Mike slowed the pace slightly. We finished in 4 hours 22 minutes. I had taken Ibuprofen tablets and aspirins and felt better than in Cardiff. The Big Seven, we agreed, was at least worth having a go at. We left Heathrow on schedule on 21 October, heading for South America. Land Rover had announced the overall plan of the Challenge the day we left Britain with a simplified summary:

The team will run their first marathon in Antarctica and the 7-day clock will tick from the moment they start. A twin-engine plane will immediately fly them back to Santiago to run the South

American marathon (Number 2). From there to Sydney, Singapore, London, Cairo and finally New York. But they will lose a whole day when they cross the international date line and will have to make this up by running two marathons within one 24-hour period, a morning run in London and another that night in Cairo. If they succeed, the two runners will complete the seven runs in less than 7 x 24 hours and will see only six whole days in terms of sunrises and sunsets.

Put like that it all sounded straightforward enough. We intended to run our first leg, the Antarctic marathon, on the sub-Antarctic King George Island, part of the South Shetlands once administered by the British Antarctic Survey, but now a Chilean airbase. On 25 October we left Punta Arenas and flew over the glaciers and mountains of Tierra del Fuego for two hours. Then our pilot had to turn back due to bad weather. On 26 October, the forecast being better, we again taxied hopefully along the Punta Arenas runway. Rob Hall, our BBC reporter and by now good friend, announced, 'Nothing can stop us now.' A minute later, on sod's cue, the starboard engine coughed, the pilot confirmed engine failure, and our last chance of making the South Shetlands on time was lost.

A rapid conference at the Punta Arenas Airport followed. From long experience I have always believed that if Plan A fails you get going with Plan B. Our Plan B was that we would run our South American leg immediately and here in Punta rather than in Santiago as originally planned. And while we were doing it, our local organiser would try to find another aircraft to take us to another ex-British Antarctic Survey islands group, the Falklands, for the Antarctic leg.

That afternoon we all drove out of town to a long pebble-strewn beach beside the Magellan Strait. At 6.00 p.m. a whistle from a member of our Chilean support team served as our starting gun and off we loped along the coast before, ten miles later, we turned inland and crossed barren moorland where we flushed out startled groups of rhea who galloped off very much faster than we could. I managed to stay close behind Mike's shoulder all the way and our first marathon clocked in at 3 hours 45 minutes. Back in Punta Arenas we were greeted with the news that a twin-engine jet was on hand to take us to the Falklands.

The question has been asked whether the Falklands are genuinely part of the Antarctic continent or not. Well, they aren't part of South America and the *Antarctic Dictionary* assures me Antarctica comprises the continent and its surroundings seas and islands. Support came from quite another direction with the illustrious nineteenth-century botanist Sir Joseph Hooker writing about the flora of the Falklands and South Shetlands in his *Flora Antarctica*. It was good enough for me.

'Look left, Ran.' Mike woke me from sleep on our executive jet and pointed out of one of the portholes. An RAF Jaguar fighter plane cruised a few metres from our starboard wing: the pilot's thumbs-up was clearly visible. We landed at Mount Pleasant Military Base. A giant map of the Falklands hung in the airbase commander's office and we agreed to follow a marathon route he and other officers suggested that led from close to the base to the cathedral in the islands' capital, Port Stanley. We set out with six hours to go before our jet would have to leave in order to connect with the next key flight. We had therefore to run this one in under five hours.

At first we were both painfully stiff. Army vehicles passed by every now and again, the drivers hooting and waving. Our progress was being reported on Falklands Radio. There were long climbs and the pebbly road was uneven. We passed by skull and crossbones signs, warning of twenty-one-year-old minefields beside the track. In dry areas dwarf shrubs known as diddle-dee spread like heather with red berries mixed with an overall dun-coloured grass, white plumed flowerheads and patches of low pig vine. Occasional rook-like birds plunged and soared over the moors. After three hours we passed below Mount Tumbledown, site of fierce fighting during the 1982 conflict, where British paratroops assaulted Argentinian infantry dug into its upper slopes. Mike wrote:

My legs began to demand remission. On the uphills as we climbed hundreds of feet, they begged me to stop. I had reached 'the wall' and the time for gritted teeth . . . Fatigue was not my only concern. As Port Stanley grew closer, I kept getting twinges of cramp. These occurred every time we climbed a hill, and this could be serious. You can choose not to listen when muscles cry 'enough' which is just a matter of exhaustion, but the body does have other means of making you stop. Cramp in both legs can't be ignored: it simply takes you down . . . My legs were lead when we crossed the finish line after four and a half hours to be met by Stanley's children, half of the adult population and the Governor of the Islands.

The Governor had laid on tea and sandwiches for us at Government House but there was, unfortunately, no time to observe the diplomatic civilities as an army Land Rover rushed us back to Mount Pleasant and hasty goodbyes to the commandant. We made it to Santiago Airport in the nick of time to catch the scheduled BA flight to Sydney with two marathons under our belt and not yet down and out, just tired and aching all over. Before we left Chile we had pared our luggage down to a single item of hand baggage. As the schedule became tighter, we would have no time to wait for baggage carousels at airports.

We reached Sydney on the morning of 29 October, raced through the airport formalities to face a barrage of questions from a curious but sympathetic media, Australians being keen on any form of sporting activity. Then we changed speedily into our running gear. Land Rover Australia had thoughtfully arranged for members of the Sydney Striders running club to run with us in a pack, which was a big help. They included the Australian Iron Man champion who made sure we did not get lost. The route began near the Opera House, transited the Botanic Gardens and climbed up and then down the impressive Harbour Bridge, a near nine-mile course that we were to repeat three times, thus ascending and descending the bridge's 104 steps six times. Marathons are meant to be flat. So far none of ours had been. I remember feeling drained.

But Mike was feeling much worse. It had started for him in the previous race but now his legs were becoming tighter and stiffer in a way he could not at first understand, and the competitive edge which we used to spur each other on had not kicked in for him this time. The first signs that Mike's problems were not just fatigue appeared before we left Sydney. His urine was mixed with blood and he suffered persistent diarrhoea. This in turn led to the likelihood of dehydration. But when he weighed himself, anticipating severe weight loss, he was shocked to find that he weighed six kilos more than in Patagonia three days earlier. This explained to him that the tightness in his legs was because of the build up of fluid in his muscles caused by damage to the muscle cell membranes due to extreme mechanical overwork. What was going on in Mike's body was the result of the abuse to which he was subjecting it, the actual breaking down of his muscles. Not a happy state of affairs given the fact that he had only run three out of the seven marathons and the worst part of the schedule lay immediately ahead. The hottest, most humid run would be in Singapore. And then two marathons within twenty-four hours and ever increasing jet lag.

We arrived half-asleep and confused at Singapore Airport, and were whisked by our hosts, the Singapore Heart Foundation, to a hotel for one hour's sleep before the press conference they had fixed for 4.00 a.m. We awoke like zombies, stiff as boards all over. I really did not feel like getting up or walking to the bathroom, never mind trying to run somewhere. Failure, I now perceived, was eminently likely. However, a cold shower, a cup of black coffee and a well-attended press conference, at which we were reminded that we represented the UK, made me realise that withdrawal from the nightmare, at least at this stage, was not an option.

So, to the hooting of horns and the cheering of the sixty Singapore runners who were to accompany us, we set out at dawn to thread our tortured way for the next six hours through the parks and skyscrapers of Singapore. The sun rose all too quickly, as did the roar of the rush-hour traffic.

Singapore was a marathon too far for poor Mike. He was peeing blood and reduced to walking the last third on jellied legs. His diary recorded:

> Within an hour of starting the Singapore run I realised that this was the marathon too far. I felt sick and my legs, although still painless, had become utterly useless as the first few miles flew by. The heat was stupefying . . . We had managed little more than a quarter of the course before I drew up beside Ran and told him of my predicament. However much I wanted to go on, it was not within my capability and I explained that for me there was no choice but to give in. I urged him to go on running every step if he possibly could. Feeling pretty dismal I cut back and watched as he and most of our accompanying runners drew slowly away.

I was not much better. After four hours I felt faint, nauseous and could not run in a straight line. A Singaporean Army major from their Special Forces clung to my running vest to steer me. Another runner kept dousing me with water and shouting constant encouragement. He must have said 'Nearly there' a hundred times. But we never were.

My back ached. My neck was shot through with sharp pain from the weight of my hung head. I drank copiously from my camelback container of Science-in-Sport drink. I fought against the ever increasing desire to stop running. I counted my steps. One to a hundred. One to a hundred. Again and again and again. I tried to think of home and Ginny, of the Dhofar war, of Charlie Burton, Ollie Shepard and Anton Bowring on the bridge of the *Benjamin Bowring* in a South Atlantic storm. Of anything that could even briefly take my mind away from the torture of Singapore that morning.

Mike's diary:

Towards the end of our run, the course made a short loop of about three miles with outward and backward paths along the same sector of road. Struggling along, I suddenly realised that Ran was coming the other way. He crossed over and as we approached one another we both raised our hands, which met in passing as the briefest of high-fives. It was a privilege to witness this supreme performance by a man ten years my senior, a man whom so many had recently written off.

Ran went on to finish having run every single step, although he still took five hours and twenty-four minutes. I ended up running about two-thirds of the course and walking the remainder, coming in more than half an hour behind him at just over six hours. I was disappointed, but at least I had done the job.

When the end finally came (on the parade ground where Lord Mountbatten had received the Japanese surrender fifty-eight years before), I simply fell over under the FINISH banner. The time was over five hours, but the time was immaterial. (The results of all seven marathons are in Appendix 3) Paramedics supported me to an ambulance, shoved needles into me and gave me various drinks. A BBC Singapore man with a tape recorder came in and sat on the ambulance bunk. 'Are you giving up?' he asked. He looked blurred to me. 'Yes,' I whispered. 'It would be stupid for me to carry on. But Mike will keep going. I know he will. If one of us can do it, that will be enough.'

Mike said that run was the hardest thing he had ever done. 'I felt like shit from the word go. The prospect of doing this again in London tomorrow is really appalling.'

Three hours later and just before our next intercontinental British Airways flight, we were feted at a Singapore Heart Foundation dinner. A doctor gave Mike the report on our body checks, done at the end of the run. Mike believed we were suffering from something called rhabdomyolysis, which simple tests would confirm by measuring the level in our blood of creatine kinase (CK), which plays an important role in fuelling muscle function. The Singapore report showed that my CK level was fifty times above the norm. I was suffering from significant muscle damage. My disappointment in learning this was soon overshadowed by Mike's exclamation as he studied the report. His own CK level was nigh on 500 times the norm, surpassing by far anything he had feared and indicating massive muscle loss. Mike was still up and running through sheer mental willpower alone.

His reaction to the news was typical.

Boarding the plane from Singapore, I seriously considered giving up. If things got much worse, I would be in real danger. The blood test results offered me a get-out, a chance to listen to my body's injuries with little loss of face. But I knew inside that there was another way. The risks were manageable if I had further tests with each subsequent race. Giving up is fine if you really have no choice. But if I stopped when I could have done better, I would regret it for the rest of my life.

We flew on to our next continent, Europe, where London, or rather Heathrow's immediate surroundings, had been the only choice for our fifth run if we were to fit Africa and North America into our remaining forty-eight hours. Even this thought was stressful, and I had been warned 'not to get stressed'.

Our main marathon organiser, Steven Seaton, also our Eco-Challenge companion in years gone by, had arranged for some fifty runners to accompany us on the European leg and our race leader was Hugh Jones, one of the best marathon runners Britain has ever produced and a previous London Marathon winner. He had researched for us the exact route of the original 1908 London Olympics marathon, which began at Windsor Castle and ended at the White City Stadium. Things had changed since 1908 and the morning rush-hour traffic was in full tortoise-like flow when we set out from the castle gates at 7.30 a.m. My thoughts as my back, hips, neck and legs creaked into action were centred around the ghastly proposition that, if we managed to complete this run, we would need to begin our next marathon in Africa that same night.

The Independent newspaper was clearly wary of our challenge. They quoted a Loughborough University sports science professor: 'RF and MS are risking permanent damage and even death by trying to complete their challenge. They could suffer potentially fatal kidney failure because their bodies will have no time to recover between each of their 26 mile runs. They are really punishing their bodies, possibly even to the point of death. We could never get approval from an ethics committee to conduct an experiment on people like this.'

Bruce Tulloch, another racing legend, led the way. We passed by Eton College, where groups of boys in tailcoats cheered us on. I glanced up at the high dome of School Hall and remembered the long ago thrill of night-climbing. Mike, who should have been recovering in a hospital bed, somehow ran for two and a half hours before having to walk intermittently. Friends and relations from all over the UK greeted our arrival at White City before Land Rovers rushed us to Heathrow for our flight to Cairo. Mike had lost a torn toe nail and was hobbling, but somehow he had completed the twenty-six miles ten minutes faster than I had finished in Singapore the previous day.

The wife of President Mubarak of Egypt was hosting our African run and using it to raise funds for one of her charities, Women for Peace. She had organised a press conference at Giza immediately below the floodlit Pyramids, so I answered the press queries in Omani-accented Arabic, which is perfectly understood in Egypt. We set out at midnight, passing the Sphinx and running alongside some sixty local runners through clamorous crowds of residents busy feasting after their Ramadan daytime fasting. There was an atmosphere everywhere of carnival and chaos, but we ran behind a hooting phalanx of police vans and two ambulances. 'One each,' Mike shouted at me.

The roadside crowds cheered and cat-called as we passed, and the route was flat tarmac all the way to the airport. We recorded our speediest time since our first Patagonian run, which completely mystified Mike from a medical point of view. We had just run, after all, two complete marathons in a single day. Circadian rhythm, Mike pondered, might be involved.

We had, by the time we finished in Cairo, chased the sun three-quarters of the way around the globe, creating about eighteen hours of jet lag. In general, Mike knew, the body can recover about one hour a day so, on our sixth day, we were twelve hours out of phase. He theorised that our time-confused bodies, during the London run, must have thought it was midnight when all hormone support is at a low ebb, whereas in Cairo we had woken up and our systems were firing on all cylinders.

We arrived at JFK Airport, New York, on time on 2 November and, with the help of a British Airways special assistant, passed rapidly through immigration and customs. My German friend, Mike Kobold, and Steven Seaton had organised things with great efficiency and we joined some 35,000 other runners at the Verrazano Narrows Bridge for the start of the New York Marathon, a far cry from our first run six and a half long, long days ago in Tierra del Fuego. There, the only other runners in sight had been the odd group of rhea.

Knowing that we would, if still going by New York, be physical wrecks, we had taken the precaution of assigning two strong helpers to each of us for this the last of our seven runs. Mike Kobold would stay with Mike, and so would my American nephew, my late sister Celia's son, who was a doctor and extremely fit. Steven Seaton and a runner friend of his would, if necessary, physically push me for the twenty-six miles through the streets of the Bronx, the concrete canyons of Manhattan, and finally the green acres of Central Park. The excitement of the great human pack surging forward to the boom of a cannon at the start momentarily made us both forget our delicate states of health, but not for long. My own main memories of the day are of fighting off the desire to stop running, bad but not as bad as in Singapore, and Steven was always there with his depth of endurance knowledge and calm encouragement.

I knew that Mike was suffering mental torture to keep going in his physical state, but I remembered many, many days on the ice at both ends of the world and over many years when he had been in dire straits and yet kept going. I felt certain he would make this last run within the rapidly dwindling time reservoir of our seven-day limit, and I was determined that this time we should cross the final line together. So I started running back to find him which other runners must have thought quite mad.

Mike wrote:

Ran was still forging ahead but he soon hit a generous (if painful for him) solution. Unlike previously, he had determined we should cross the line together. Every few hundred yards he would turn round and drift slowly back towards me. Other participants, spotting this figure moving in the wrong direction, must have questioned his sanity. Had they known that this was now his seventh marathon in seven days, he might have been committed.

Even with intermittent walking, I began to wonder if I could finish. My legs at times were literally buckling beneath me and this led to an intermittent sudden stagger. Worse, when I did so, I could not help but yelp with pain.

Central Park was a scene of wonder. Each side of the road was lined with tens of thousands of well-wishers and although we had ended up going slowly there were still thousands of other runners around us. For me, its gentle hills were still utmost tests of resolution, but now there was a difference. From the moment I entered the park gates, I knew for sure that it was all over. Even if I had to crawl, I would cover those final two miles in the two hours that were still left before our clock hit seven full days. I had not done as well as I had wished, for I had not run every single step. But at the outset I did not really think that I would make it at all. Now I was about to complete the undertaking.

And then there was Ran. He had never stopped running, not even for a single step, in any one of the seven marathons. As I saw him waiting, trotting on the spot, a few hundred yards from the finish, I was so grateful. When we finally crossed that seventh line together, it was a moment to cherish. I cannot thank him enough.

We finished 28,362nd out of 35,000 runners. Mike went on to make a very important point:

When, following our success, many experts in both the USA and Britain expressed disbelief at what we had achieved, they did not realise that they could have done it too. The difference is only one of perception. Whereas most people look at very big challenges, whatever the field or their walk of life, and start from the position 'I can't', Ran and I make a simple word substitution and say 'Why can't I?' 'I can't run seven marathons' easily transforms into the question, 'Why can't I run seven marathons?' Once it was asked, we felt obliged to find the answer.

The Times editorial the following day said: 'Both men are supposed to be too old to be running so far and so often. Both ignored medical scares and both kept going not by coddling or psychological bonding but by the abrasive competitive spirit that has marked their friendship and rivalry. Their triumph against all odds is not only a magnificent publicity boost for the charities that they are supporting, it is also an inspiration for every runner, every ordinary person, tempted to give up in the face of the impossible.'

17

Ginny

The day we returned to England, a press conference was held by the British Heart Foundation. I said goodbye to Mike and his family and was given a lift back to Exmoor by a friend. On reaching Exford village, just over a mile from home, I saw a big banner flying high over the road by the village green, and, below it, a crowd of people. We stopped as local folk, many of whom I knew well, surrounded the car and cheered and clapped. The banner was a 'Welcome Home, Ran' sign. I looked around for Ginny and spotted her with our two dogs. She wore her lovely warm smile of welcome, but looked both tired and thin. Later that evening, sitting by the log fire at Greenlands as we had so often done over the past twenty years, she told me her news and my stomach churned with dread. She might have stomach cancer.

The days, weeks and months that followed were the worst of my life. I cancelled everything in the diary except a handful of contracted conference lectures, and I called their organisers with the warning that, should my wife's condition deteriorate, I might not be there. Because we had both paid for private health care insurance for over thirty years, I drove Ginny to the top cancer-care hospital in London the following day, having booked her into a room there and requested an urgent appointment with a relevant specialist.

Ginny had, over many years, had sudden stomach pains at no particular time and for no known or obvious reason. We had both put this down to twisted Fallopian tubes, or some other birth-connected condition. We had seen our doctor and specialists about the pain intermittently after especially bad attacks, but these were thankfully rare, to the point that sometimes a year would pass without one. Or so I assumed. Maybe Ginny did not always tell me when it happened. The doctors never found anything specifically wrong with her. Ginny had suffered two especially bad pains in the lower stomach area whilst I was away on the seven marathons and she had been driven to Taunton Hospital, an hour from home, for a check-up and pain-killers.

Now, at a major London hospital, a place rich in millionaire patients from many countries, with doctors and nurses of similar ethnic diversity buzzing around the plush corridors like white or blue-coated flies, we could find nobody able to deal with the sudden attack of stomach pains that convulsed Ginny in the waiting room. There was no warning. One moment we were quietly chatting; the next she was in agony, clawing at her bowels and moaning aloud, a sound which wrenched at my heart. I rushed into the corridor and approached the first nurse I could find.

'Please come at once. My wife is in extreme pain.'

'I will get someone for you.' She trotted off.

'Somebody is coming,' I told Ginny.

Five hellish minutes later nobody had come.

Ginny, the bravest of people, wept tears of pain, fear and desperation. I ran again down different corridors. I begged four different nurses to come to the waiting room. Ginny looked at me in confusion, hurt that I was doing nothing to help her in her hour of greatest need. I swore to myself that I would never leave her alone here, however magnificent the decor.

A doctor arrived some twenty minutes after Ginny's pains began. He looked impatient at this detour from his programme and gave me a prescription for some form of morphine. I rushed to the basement in-house pharmacy and asked the waiting queue if I could go to the front as my wife was in great pain. A pharmacist took my proffered prescription and returned, after an interminable pause, to tell me that the doctor had not signed the correct spot.

She was obdurate when I begged her for the pain-killers. So I rushed upstairs again and luckily found the doctor who, without apology, scribbled another signature on my docket. Back to the pharmacy and, after some forty minutes of hell and suffering by Ginny, eventually found a nurse who administered the tablets.

Our lifelong friends, William Knight (who had in 1965 been with me at the 'bombing' of Castle Combe) and his wife Sylvia, were true friends to us during that nightmare time, and I spent the next week in London, by day at Ginny's bedside, and by night letting myself into the nearby Regent's Park home of my literary agent and kind friend, Ed Victor.

The specialists confirmed that Ginny had a virulent form of stomach cancer which was spreading fast. She must have chemotherapy sessions every week for at least three months and starting at once. In between them we could live at home.

We spent Christmas on Exmoor with Ginny's family and many of our best friends visiting from time to time. But mostly we just stayed together. I tried always to be in the same room. When we cooked, we both moved to the kitchen. As Ginny became weaker, we made up two beds downstairs. Ginny spoke often to Neil and Ruth, who looked after the sheep and cattle for her. We went for walks and, when the pain attacks came, our doctor or the local nurses made sure Ginny had sufficient morphine. She did not want her family, apart from her sister Abby, told of her illness until the last moment, to shield them from worry.

I will never forget that time. I cannot believe that any human has ever loved another as much as I loved and still love Ginny. I could not remember any time in my adult life when she was not the reason for the glow in my heart when we were together, and the longed-for safe haven during my wanderings without her. I was desperate not to lose her and thankful for any tiny spark of hope that our doctor might murmur.

By the second month, January 2004, Ginny was seldom able to leave the house, other than by ambulance for treatment. We were assigned a doctor in Exeter Hospital who specialised in cancer treatment. But the various chemotherapy treatments did not work and the disease spread. Later that month Ginny moved into an NHS cancer ward shared with some seven other ladies. She made friends quickly with many of them and with many of the nurses. I spent every day at her bedside or wheeling her about in a chair. At night I slept in a spare upstairs room in the hospital. Abby would drive down from Liverpool as often as she could and many friends were frequent visitors, but Ginny's health diminished inexorably as the disease spread into her key organs. She had emergency operations and I sat outside the theatres startled by every unusual noise from within.

Three months after her diagnosis, Ginny was moved to the hospice close to the hospital, and I think she took this as a sign that the end could not be far away. I was allowed to sleep in a spare room in the hospice. Our lifelong friends the Bowrings and the Gaults drove from Suffolk and Kent respectively to visit us. Just before writing this book, I received a note from Anton Bowring taken from his diary of those sad times:

Many years ago, soon after we finished the Transglobe Expedition, I went to hospital with a suspect lump in my throat. I was sitting in bed in the lung cancer ward awaiting surgery the next day and surrounded by very ill people when Ginny arrived out of the blue and announced she was taking me out to supper. We had a wonderful evening and I completely forgot all my woes. Later my lump was found to be benign, but I never forgot Ginny's warmth and thoughtfulness. Nearly twenty years later, Jill and I arrived at the Exeter hospice knowing full well we might not see your Ginny again. The four of us had supper in nearby Topsham, Ginny in a wheelchair, but otherwise just as though we were on holiday at your home or ours. She was so alive and full of her usual fun that it was hard to believe anything was wrong. I remember she had a morphine drip in a floral pattern bag around her neck which alone showed what she was going through. We talked that evening of all the wonderful times we had had

together, of Namibia, France, Scotland, and we planned new outings too. We played cards by the fire there and we were together.

The excitement of our outing was maybe too much and Ginny
could not see us the next day, so Jill and I bought bird feeders which
we hung in the hospice garden outside Ginny's room. You told us
then that the specialist had said Ginny's chances were very slim.

The next day, our last down south, we drove Ginny to
Teignmouth and you pushed her chair about the crowded town
until we found a pub overlooking a small boat harbour at low
water. We sat outside and watched the seagulls. After a lovely day
we returned to Exeter and said our goodbyes, believing we'd meet
up again before long. That was the Sunday evening. The following Friday you phoned us in the evening and told me that dear
Ginny had died just fifteen minutes earlier and that she was still
in your arms. It makes me tearful, even now, just remembering
that moment.

Many friends and Ginny's family came on her last day alive to
show their love for her. But her pain became ever worse, and
towards evening the nurses had to increase her morphine drip
above the previous levels. Abby and my niece Beelie were with me
as Ginny faded slowly. I could not control my misery. She died and
escaped further pain.

Over the previous week we had sometimes prayed together with
the friendly and sincere hospice chaplain. Once Ginny held me
tightly and thanked me for our life together, using wonderful
words that I will never forget.

Anton and Abby came back to Greenlands and stayed with me.
Together we planned Ginny's funeral, memorial service and,
months later, a gathering of her friends, over 700 people, at a cele-
bration of her life at the Royal Geographical Society, the place where
she had spent many long hours in the dusty archives with maps and
books researching for our expeditions. Three of the Black Dogs
Ginny had bred were there and a film of her life was shown, put
together by her old friend Alex Leger, the long-time producer of

television's *Blue Peter* who had, in the 1970s and eighties, often featured Ginny and her Jack Russell, Bothie, on the programme.

Abby was ten years younger than Ginny. She later wrote of her inner thoughts.

What wasn't easy was watching my sister die, too fast and too slowly, of an aggressive cancer that gave her months of excruciating pain. She was fifty-six, fit, strong, tough, and it was Ran who'd had a major heart attack less than a year before. He was the one at risk, not Ginny.

I'd known she wasn't well, but we all thought she needed a hysterectomy, nothing more. Then she phoned me when I was walking into a restaurant one evening in October 2003. She never phoned my mobile; so I knew before she spoke that it was bad news.

I didn't realise she was in hospital till New Year 2004, because she hadn't wanted to worry me. In the end Ran rang, because Ginny couldn't. Her body was packing up and she was in constant pain.

I shot down to Exeter hospital. Ginny was thin and pale, but undiminished: still my big sister. The days I spent with her from then until her death will be some of the most prized of my life. And the hardest. In those few weeks the patina of sibling squabbles was scrubbed away and all that was left was love. In February, after three days at home, I got back to find she'd been moved to the hospice. I got there at 2 a.m., and Ran was asleep in the camp bed, gripping his beloved wife's hand. He didn't wake, but Ginny opened her eyes. Her smile terrified me because it was a really lovely, joyful welcome and there was no worry or pain on her face. I just hope she couldn't see the shock on mine. This was the first time I'd been so close to someone who was going to die very soon, and this was the person I loved most in the world. There were black circles round her eyes and her lips were shrivelled in gaunt, waxy cheeks. This change from my big sister, ill but alive, to this shadow creature on the fraying hem of life undid something in me which hasn't been repaired.

Seeing Ran and Ginny together in their last two days you'd think they'd only been married a week, instead of thirty-four years. It hurt badly to watch a true marriage being ripped apart.

I started life without Ginny. At Greenlands, the urn containing her ashes was buried in a garden beside the earlier graves of all the dogs she had owned and Fingal, her cat. Set in a glade of trees she had planted and overlooking the hills and fields where her cattle still grazed, it is my most special place.

On weekdays I busied myself in the office, where Gina and Jill and Joyce were kind and understanding, and on the farm, where Neil and Ruth continued to deal with the cattle and the sheep. Jean tidied the house three times a week, as she always had, and often left a saucepan of rice mixed with sweetcorn, which became my staple diet. At night, alone, I would wander around the cows, especially Ginny's favourites, talking to them and at times crying aloud. Three months after Ginny died I could bear things no more. I was becoming morose, inactive and full of self-pity. I knew I must break out of my own cage of misery and I remembered the Everest climb invitation I had received a year before from Sibusiso Vilane in Swaziland, the first black person ever to summit Everest. I needed a sharp jolt and what could provide one better than facing my greatest, lifelong fear – vertigo. If I went with Sibu to Everest that would surely drag me out of the dark void of my current existence. The highest mountain on earth would surely test my irrational terror of heights.

I wrote to Sibu. He was delighted and accepted the fact that I would first have to learn how to climb. He suggested doing so through a UK mountain tours company called Jagged Globe. I called them at once, but their boss, Simon Lowe, explained they could not take anybody and everybody up Everest and, with due respect, I was 'sixty, cardiac-challenged and missing some digits'. He drove to Greenlands later that week and suggested that I join two of Jagged Globe's mountaineering courses. First there was a ten-day Alpine peaks instructional tour to see if I could cope with the basics of snow and ice climbing. Then, if I received a reasonable report from the Alps guide, I should progress to their Ecuador Volcanoes tour, involving climbs up to 20,000 feet, which would introduce me to the effects of high altitude on my system. This was especially important because of my cardiac history.

Since none of the relevant Alpine or Ecuadorean mountains needed actual technical climbing skills, I assumed that no big drops would be involved.

Many years ago Ginny and I had gone to the Alps with Monty Don, the gardener, and other friends, including Simon Gault and Geoff Newman. We had walked up Mont Blanc, the Matterhorn and the Jungfrau with a guide and had a good time. So I invited Simon and Geoff to join me on the Jagged Globe Alpine fortnight. Both accepted. There were fifteen students on the course, mostly men at least thirty years younger than us, but we all passed the guides' report easily enough. The basic skills we learned involved use of ice-axes and crampons and long snowy trudges. But no actual climbing.

Back home my sister, Susan, ten years older than me, was ill with mesothelioma or asbestosis. Her husband of over forty years, John Scott, called me, and I joined him and my two nieces, Beelie and Neesh, at the Wiltshire hospital where Sue had been assigned to the cancer ward. She died three months after Ginny, and I lost another wonderful, caring member of the family. My last remaining sister, Gill, and I went to see our mother in the Sussex rest home. Usually we visited her once every month on different dates. She had been getting increasingly forgetful and confused, which was just as well in a way since the news of Celia's death, then Ginny's and now Susan's never really sank in. She kept asking us how they all were long after we had gently told her that they had died.

After her ninetieth birthday party in July 2002, my mother slowly became less interested in the world outside her own little room. Early in 2003 she had a stroke. The last time I took her outside the home, on one of my monthly visits, was soon after

Ginny's death in the spring of 2004. Thereafter we stayed in her room or sat holding hands and saying little on a bench in the garden outside her room. Her best and oldest friend from Lodsworth, Betty Simmonds, visited her every week, as did Judy Tarring, who had once been her professional carer.

In August, when I returned from the Alps, my sister Gill warned me that our mother was fading away and unable to leave her bed. We took it in turns to visit her daily. I stayed in a bed and breakfast near the home and one evening arrived in her room after dark. The nurse said she had been sleeping most of that day. I found her fast asleep and sat by her bed, whispering that I loved her and that she was the best mother in the world. Which she was. Her breathing was shallow. I am not sure if she heard me or not. I fell asleep on the carpet beside her bed and woke some time later towards midnight. I have no idea what woke me, but I held her hand and some minutes later she stopped breathing.

Gill and I followed our mother's wishes and made sure her grave was beside those of her many old friends and fellow parishioners in the village of Lodsworth. Within a stone's throw of our old house, the graveyard overlooked the fields and woods and the River Lod where I had spent so many happy teenage holidays with my sisters and with Ginny.

I tried to lift my head above the deep ache of Ginny's death and tell myself that she would be wanting me to attack life again, to 'get on with it', to 'be dangerous': all her little catch phrases. I still keep a short pencilled note she left me about six months before she died. I can't remember the exact context, but it reads:

My poor, mad, bad, darling man, I didn't realise you were giving a lecture there. PLEASE stay the night with Charles or John. You'll be so tired – and dangerous to drive home. Everything will be OK here and you'll be back on Saturday for a lovely evening. I love you so much and hate to be so worried about you and see you so tired. Please be good.
Your Ginny.

She often, remembering her father's description of me before we married, called me 'mad, bad and dangerous to know'. I found boxes of all the notes and letters she had sent me down the years since long before we married. I read them all again when alone in our bedroom. Then I filed them in boxes and sent them to Abby for safe-keeping because, at the time, I felt and wished that I would die.

Sometimes I would say to myself that everybody will sooner or later lose or be lost by their loved ones, but life has to go on. I would argue to myself that every one of the billions of people who have ever lived has been sad to some degree at some time. I remembered walking with Ginny and Anton and Jill Bowring down the 1.5-kilometre-long death tunnels of the Paris catacombs. We passed by six million neatly stacked skulls. Each and every one had had, during their brief lifespan, the chance to spend time in sadness or in joy. I thought, too, of how lucky I was to have known such love and to have been with Ginny during the last months when she needed me. Now, with Ginny gone, and my mother, and Susan, and Celia, in so short a time, I was still alive, if only just, cardiac-wise, so I must get on with life. Not vegetate for even a moment.

I took on as much work as I could and averaged four conference lectures a week. I loved Greenlands, but the sadness and loneliness returned each time I went back. Ginny had told me many times over the years that, should she die before me, I was to remarry as soon as possible. I had said the same to her. She had also told me that I was to sell her sheep and cattle only to people with whom she had done previous business. Over that summer I sold the majority of the sheep and cows to individuals from Ginny's contact list. A friend and neighbour who had bought many of her cattle took over the rest of the herd and continues to run them, many at Greenlands, to this day.

I flew to Quito in Ecuador and met Jagged Globe's chief guide there. For a week he took our group up minor volcanoes which overlooked the polluted pall of Quito. Then we moved further afield to tackle the two 'big ones'. Cotopaxi is 19,000 feet above sea-level, and the effects of the altitude slowed me down alarmingly. But we reached the top and, being by then the only remaining 'student' on the course, I travelled in guide Pepe Landazuri's car for the four-hour drive south-west from Quito to Mount Chimborazo. I was aware that, if I summitted this last volcano, I would be cleared for Everest with Jagged Globe the following year. We spent the early part of the night in the Carrel Hut at 4,800 metres and immediately below the volcano's steep ascent route. Pepe regaled me with strong coffee and stories of the hut's ghosts. One of his own experiences included a night when a guide friend of his, with a famous Norwegian climber client, briefly met him in the hut but went on up soon after midnight. The next day, some hours after the two men should have come back down, Pepe phoned the local rescue team and went with them to the summit, where they found both men lying dead near the crater rim. The Norwegian's head had a neat round burn hole drilled in it by a lightning strike. His ice-axe and crampons were mere molten metal and the bolt had passed down the frozen rope to kill the guide for good measure.

'Never climb,' Pepe warned me, 'if you have any reason to think there may be an electric storm coming. If you are caught in the open, never lie down. Just kneel with your head low and your hands on the ground. Avoid shallow depressions in the ground, all forms of water or damp ground where you can, and, if it has a metal frame, keep out of your tent. Many people die on our volcanoes from lightning strikes.'

He also warned me that we had to cross a highly dangerous rockfall zone on our imminent climb, so we must ascend in the darkness and reach the summit by a predetermined turnround time. If we had not reached the top by that time, we *must* turn around or risk death by rockfall on the return journey, since the heat of the sun always loosened the rocks. We left the hut at 3.00 a.m.

Pepe climbed slowly but surely over the next ten hours. I lagged behind feeling the altitude and, despite having taken pills, my head throbbed with a dull persistent ache. The Cinderella-hour of Pepe's turnround time arrived when we were an hour from the top, but he was lenient and let me slog on tortoise-like and breathing heavily to the summit itself. I felt nauseous and my heartbeat was well over the 130 beats per minute that Gianni Angelini had warned me to respect. But, once we had descended 1,000 feet, I recovered and thereafter speeded up to cross the rockfall region whilst the cliff faces above were still in shadow.

A week later Pepe's report reached Jagged Globe's UK office, and Simon Lowe officially accepted me for their projected 2005 attempt on Everest via the Tibetan north side.

At that time everything seemed fine with my health, but I had earlier agreed a week's climb on Kilimanjaro with Simon Gault and a friend, Nick Holder, who had been on the Norway and Nile expeditions in the 1960s. A Masai guide took us along the Lemosho trail for four days, climbing slowly to acclimatise. If we tried to quicken the pace, he would sensibly intone, '*Poley, poley*', meaning 'Slow down', but on the last night he speeded up in competition with another group under a rival guide. At one point, not long before dawn, I asked if we could halt briefly so I could take off my fleece. This was not popular. Seemingly I was the only one finding the pace too fast. This was strange since I was normally fitter and faster than Simon. The last 500 feet were unpleasant. My chest grew ever tighter, as though squeezed by an invisible sumo wrestler, and the resulting constriction made my breathing difficult just when I needed maximum lung power.

Simon taunted my slowness in a good-natured way, as was his wont. We had done a great many walks together since first meeting at school forty years before, so I tried hard to keep up with him. I reached the summit ridge, but only just. I was incoherent and could hardly walk straight. Our guide, worried, tried to say I should go back down at once. He knew of my cardiac history from the client forms we had had to sign. I refused, hardly knowing what was going on except that the true summit was further along the rim of the crater. Some time later we arrived there and I rested with my head held low between my knees. Only when we had descended some 500 feet to about 5,486 metres (18,000 feet) did the feeling, by then like a tight band wrapped around my chest, disappear and I immediately felt normal. We walked back down to the base camp in good time where other guides were swapping gossip about their groups. Ours translated for us that two clients from separate groups had died of heart attacks that night on the mountain.

Back in London I had an ECG which recorded no new cardiac damage, so I thought no more about the incident. The British Heart Foundation took on my Everest project as a charity-raising tool, calling it the Ran Fiennes Healthy Hearts Appeal. The aim was to raise £2 million specifically for a new scanner unit for children with heart trouble at the Great Ormond Street Children's Hospital.

I gave a talk after a fund-raising dinner for twelve well-heeled businessmen in a North Yorkshire castle, and the host, Paul Sykes, a fiery Yorkshireman, asked if I was planning any more expeditions. I told him about Everest, and he agreed to sponsor the project financially as he approved of the plan and the charity aim. He had a long history of donating to charities, he liked to keep fit, and we were the same age. Paul was fiercely opposed to the EU and Brussels government, and largely funded the campaign against the single currency and the UK Independence Party election success. He would leave the climbing to me, but would do his best to keep the Heart Foundation working hard to reach our target figure of £2 million.

Late in the winter of 2004 I found myself high up on the Empire State Building, having given a talk at a New York conference. I tried to look down but, in seconds, felt the familiar nausea, the quickly rising terror of vertigo, and had to look away immediately to recover my composure. Vertigo is, I knew, an irrational problem, a mental sickness that is purely psychological. Some people are born afflicted by a deep-seated fear of wide open spaces, and that is just as unreasonable. I did not like living in the knowledge that, aged sixty, I had still not outgrown this problem, but I felt confident that if I could climb the highest mountain in the world, I would gain sufficient self-confidence to lose all fear of lesser heights.

18
Almost

The Ecuador volcanoes and Kilimanjaro were reasonable teasers for Everest but did not help my overall aerobic fitness, so I entered one or two team races in 2004 including, with Steven Seaton from *Runner's World*, the North Pole Marathon in the Arctic spring that year. This was organised by the Irishman, Richard Donovan, the first person to run a marathon at both Poles, and took place at 89.5° North on a floating Russian ice station. The temperature was –28°C and the surface was firm and icy. Due to the usual moving canals of open water between floes, the course consisted of a five-kilometre circuit to be completed eight and a half times.

Entries for the marathon from all over the world were restricted to sixteen, since the two Russian helicopters Donovan had hired each had a capacity for eight passengers. Many of the other runners had very respectable marathon records. Steven and I set out together wearing snowshoes, but after two laps Steven removed his and dropped behind. I gradually moved up the field over the next three hours until, with two laps to go, I was lying second. The leader was a tall, thin American, Sean Burch, martial arts expert and mountaineer, who went on to claim a world speed record, climbing Kilimanjaro in 5 hours 28 minutes.

I tried hard to catch him but failed, and finished a good thirteen minutes behind him in just under four hours. Having run the twenty-six miles with my legs forced apart by the snowshoes, my groin muscles took several weeks to stop aching.

The UK media portrayed the race in a way which must have muddled the minds of quite a few young readers because, in a *Yellow Pages/Daily Mail* survey a few months later, only 30 per cent of the young adults questioned recognised Robert Falcon Scott as the first British explorer to reach the South Pole, with 28 per cent wrongly crediting me. Similarly, only 29 per cent correctly named Sir Francis Drake as the first Britisher to sail round the world, with 36 per cent naming Dame Ellen MacArthur. However, 80 per cent answered correctly when asked the names of the recent winners of *Big Brother* and other celebrity television shows. (I was invited to participate in *I'm a Celebrity, Get Me Out of Here* in a jungle setting somewhere. I said no with alacrity for various reasons, including horror at the thought of having to lunch on live maggots.)

A year to the day after Ginny's death, her sister Abby and I sat together at Greenlands on the hill where Ginny's headstone stands. We remembered our times together with her.

At a lecture I had given to the Chester branch of the Royal Geographical Society the previous summer I had met one of their members, Louise Millington, and had since taken her out when she was not busy with the horse transporting company she had built up based from her Cheshire home. She was thirty-six years old, full of life, mercurial, had a ten-year-old son Alexander, and she jolted me out of my miserable state. We agreed to marry in March 2005 and honeymoon at the Everest Base Camp in Tibet.

Abby, Ginny's closest relative, said to the press:

Ran has been a much-loved member of our family for nearly fifty years and always will be. He and Ginny had an exceptionally happy marriage and were in love with each other for all their adult lives. Ran was devastated by Ginny's illness and death and he has had a desperately long, lonely year without her. To see him happy again with Louise is wonderful. He still grieves for Ginny and nothing will change or diminish his feelings for my sister. But

Ginny wouldn't want Ran to be sad or lonely. She urged him to marry again and everyone in the family is one hundred per cent supportive of his decision. We all wish Ran and Louise every happiness.

Abby's mother Janet had collapsed on her way to Ginny's funeral over a year before and had never really recovered. We went to see her that spring at a rest home in Liverpool, close to Abby's own home, and I sensed that she did not have long to live. A month before I was due to leave for Everest, I joined Abby in fulfilling a promise I had made to Ginny two years before. Her father, who had fought our teenage love for so long, had been buried in a churchyard close by the family chalk quarry in the South Downs of West Sussex. But no headstone had ever been erected at his grave due, in a roundabout way, to a nationwide gravediggers' strike at the time of his death. We had contacted the relevant vicar and, on a cold clear February morning with a group of Tom Pepper's old friends and relations, we prayed by his newly erected headstone.

During the last month before going to Everest, I discovered that I could not properly hold a standard ice-axe in my frost-damaged left hand. So we went to DMM, a climbing gear factory in Wales, where they sponsored me with a special axe with a thin shaft as well as a steel hook for, hopefully, gripping those tiny holds that my half-fingers could not manage. Whilst in Wales we also went with an old SAS friend to the Cardiff Millennium Stadium to watch Wales defeat England at rugby.

No football fan, I had recently acquired a definite appetite for watching the fifteen-man sport at national level after meeting the Irish team in Dublin. Ten days before they were due to fly to Australia for the 2003 World Cup, their manager Eddie O'Sullivan and former captain Keith Woods had me flown out at the last minute to lecture the squad on 'team morale when the odds look bad'. I had talked to the forty-strong group for an hour in a small closely packed hotel room. No smiles. No laughter. Just intense frowns that looked to me like glares. I don't remember ever feeling so much concentrated human *power* in one place before. But when I stopped talking, their enthusiastic questioning went on for a second hour, and Eddie sent me emails of their subsequent excellent progress down under.

My own power during the run-up weeks to Everest was not improved by a severe bout of bronchitis. Louise was worried and booked me to see various lung, chest and heart specialists, starting with my own cardiac surgeon Gianni Angelini in Bristol and progressing to Dr John Costello, a lung expert, in London. An altitude test chamber simulated up to 15,000 feet above sea-level where I had to perform various lung function tests, and then have blood taken. The results, which were quickly available, were disappointing. They showed a limitation of flow in my airways, presumably due to my previous smoking. The flow was 80 per cent of what it should have been for a man of my age and height and, in John Costello's professional opinion, 'would be an important limiting factor in my ability to carry on at 7,000 metres and above'. Additionally, my ability to saturate my bloodstream with oxygen, a key function when exerting yourself at high altitude, was badly impaired. Coupled with my cardiac status which dictated never getting badly out of breath, I was not an ideal candidate for an Everest attempt. Better news was that the organisers of our Everest fundraiser, the Ran Fiennes Healthy Hearts Appeal, had already raised, prior to our departure, more than the entire £70,000 the charity had managed to total following our 7x7x7 marathons.

7 March was my sixty-first birthday. Five days later Louise and I were married, and a fortnight after that we left Heathrow bound for Kathmandu in Nepal. At the airport a reporter from *The Times* interviewed Louise and asked her all the usual questions. She admitted she was worried about the altitude and the strain on my heart. This reminded me of Sherpa Tenzing's account of his wife's reaction when told he was joining John Hunt's attempt on Everest. 'You are too weak,' she said. 'You will get ill again, or you will slip on the ice and fall and kill yourself.' 'No, I will look out

for myself,' he told her. 'Just like I always have.' Adventuring husbands have always been having these prior-to-departure conversations.

Those members of our team we did not meet at Heathrow we caught up with in Kathmandu where we were introduced to our group leader. He was a tall Scotsman named David Hall. His number two, Neal Short from Liverpool, was small and mild-mannered. The rest of the group included my South African friend, Sibusiso, at whose suggestion I had become involved in the first place, and Ian Parnell, a professional freelance climbing photographer, who was covering my climb for *The Times* and, with minimal equipment training, was organising live TV coverage for BBC Breakfast TV.

Ian later wrote:

My first introduction to Ran was when I received a phone call from him pretty much out of the blue in February 2005. 'Ian, would you like to go to Everest with me?' 'Er . . . um . . . well, maybe . . . when?' 'We leave in two weeks, it'll be a ten-week trip.' 'Well I was meant to be travelling to the States to see my girlfriend.' 'Ian, I'm sure she'll understand. If you have any problems, let me have a word. I tell you what, I'll give you twenty-four hours to talk it over with her.' So within two minutes of talking to Ran for the first time, I'd been invited to spend three months with him on the world's highest mountain and had twenty-four hours to make a choice.

My job on the expedition was to facilitate live broadcasts and send back film and still pictures to be used by the BBC and *The Times* newspaper. The fact that over ten weeks this probably only amounted to twenty minutes of footage makes this task seem pretty trivial. However, the reality proved pretty challenging. My first inklings of this reality gap came when I went to Broadcasting House to pick up all the equipment I would be using. The conversation with one technical guy started with, 'Can you get power on the summit?' I wasn't sure how to answer. Was he wondering if there was a mains plug, or something? 'Well, how about getting a generator up there?' he asked. Considering that most people could barely walk at over 29,000 feet and the Sherpas were pushed carrying enough oxygen for everyone, there was no chance. We eventually settled for a relatively lightweight battery-operated set-up. When I say relatively lightweight, I'm talking about an extra twenty-five pounds of equipment.

Problems started early. The laptop computer's hard disk drive gave up the ghost only a week into the trip, while other parts of the set-up needed constant nursing to keep operating. A typical broadcast would involve an hour or so spent locating satellites for the two sat phones in series. Of course, with one sat phone locked in, the other phone would drop its connection, and vice versa – it was a constant plate-juggling trick. Having finally got both phones talking to Broadcasting House, I'd have to fire up the video phone, which unfortunately developed an alarming syndrome of cutting out every five minutes. Each live interview lasted about three minutes, so the timing when to crank up the video phone was crucial. To top it all, I discovered the batteries had a warning that they shouldn't be used below +5°C. Considering that the average temperature at Everest Advance Base Camp hovered around −10°C, we had a constant battle on our hands. The trick, I found, was to get in my sleeping bag and put the batteries on my belly minutes before transmission.

But, as with most things in life, the more effort you have to put in, the greater the reward. So, despite the struggles, we managed not to miss a single broadcast, and the feeling as you listen to a live interview broadcasting from the slopes of Everest all the way back to the UK is one that rivals the feelings I have when I reach mountain summits.

Two other South Africans in our group, Alex Harris and Mark Campbell, were both experienced climbers and good friends of Sibusiso. Tore Rasmussen was a Norwegian businessman, hobby climber and black belt karate instructor. Fred Ziel from California was our doctor. Like Sibu, and indeed with Sibu, he had been on a previous Jagged Globe Everest climb, on the south side, but he had failed, where Sibu had succeeded, and he had suffered frostbite damage to his fingers and nose. Jens Bojen, born in Norway, was now a Grimsby businessman with a lifelong experience of North Sea fishing. Although a year older than me, he was twice as fit and the proud possessor of an abnormally slow heart rate. Rosalind Buckton had once very nearly been the first British woman to climb Everest and, although now in her late fifties, was keen to succeed on this her second attempt.

The general opinion of the more experienced climbers in our group was that our Tibetan northern route was a bigger challenge than the Nepalese southern route, pioneered by John Hunt's British expedition of 1953 which made the first ascent. This was because our route involved more time spent higher than 8,400 metres, in the notorious 'Death Zone'. The twin words 'altitude' and 'acclimatisation' were on our group's lips much of the time. Sensible application of the latter, the old hands constantly assured us, would be our main way of defeating the potentially lethal effects of the former.

The next day we started our drive towards Everest Base Camp 400 kilometres (250 miles) away and at an elevation of 5,200 metres (17,000 feet). We would drive there in stages because we must not rush our acclimatisation process. At Base Camp there would already be just half the oxygen available at sea-level. We travelled north-east towards the Nepalese/Tibetan border in jeeps, our gear on high-back lorries, and we all attempted to drink four litres (eight pints) daily, as advised by David, our leader. The border town of Zhangmu, a place of shabby wood huts on the Nepalese side and ugly concrete blockhouses in Tibet, buzzed with groups similar to ours and all with the same thing on their minds . . . the summit. As we joined various queues in the complex process of passing through Chinese customs, security and immigration, I met nine climbers of different nationalities, some aiming to climb Everest solo but most with commercial groups and street-wise handlers adept at dealing with Chinese bureaucracy.

From Zhangmu the scenery changed from relatively bland to spectacular as our road, evilly potholed and often edged with sheer drops to our immediate left and cliff walls to the right, fought its tortuous way up the sheer and rugged gorge of the Bhote Kosi. A thousand feet below, often immediately below us, roiled and roared the fearsome rapids of the Bhote Kosi heading back south to Nepal. Neal assured us we had already been lucky on two counts when our convoy reached our overnight stop, the raggedy town of Nyalam. Not only had we avoided ambush by Maoist terrorists in Nepal who shot up tourists or merely stopped them and demanded cash, but, secondly, we had to date been spared the avalanches and mud slides which most years plague the Nyalam road. What we could not avoid were the rat-infested, filth-encrusted rooms in Zhangmu and Nyalam. I itched like hell. Louise was fairly stoical but, a migraine-sufferer since her teens, her headaches were exacerbated by the ever increasing altitude. Others in our group also began to complain of lethargy, appetite loss and splitting headaches, and Dr Fred offered us all the altitude sickness prevention drug Diamox.

An hour or so north of Nyalam, our convoy eased into the main Himalayan range between India and Asia, the mightiest geo-graphical feature on the earth's surface. It boasts more than a hundred peaks in excess of 24,000 feet (7,315 metres) above sea-level, and includes all the famed fourteen 8,000ers, the trophy peaks over 8,000 metres (26,247 feet) whose summits are 'collected' by many dedicated high altitude climbers, the first of whom was Reinhold Messner. For hours we travelled on up over the high dusty plateau until we came to a couple of passes, the higher being the Lalung La at 5,125 metres (16,810 feet).

The Tibetan Plateau stretches across south-west China, bounded by the deserts of the Tarim and Qaidam to the north and the Himalayan, Karakoram, and Pamir mountain chains to the south and west. With an elevation of nearly five kilometres above sea-level, this desolate, dry, windswept landscape is the world's highest plateau. Wild yaks were once abundant on the plateau, but they were mostly killed off for meat from the 1950s, when new roads made the area more accessible to hunters.

After Nyalam's concrete scenery, we passed isolated villages the same orange-brown hue as the wide country vistas that rolled away beneath the great clear blue sky. The wind was always blowing when we stopped to leg-stretch, and the spring weather seemed always cold and dry. Our average height now, on these panoramic plains between high crumbly hills, was some 4,300 metres (14,000 feet). The Tibetan herders and farmers were clearly a hard bunch. Their squat adobe huts, isolated or in hamlet clusters, were often close by stone-built ruins of ancient Buddhist monasteries destroyed in the Chinese Cultural Revolution, often along with their inmates. Potato and barley crops showed between intricate irrigation ditches, whilst scraggy sheep, goats and yaks roamed free.

After many hours our road began to turn east and we came to the village of Tingri, built on a hillside with an impressive view looking back to the south of a distant array of snow-clad peaks floating on cloud. This was the great Himalayan range that reached east and west from Everest, mother of all mountains. Our convoy hove to in a dusty football field-sized courtyard with low dormitory blocks on three sides. A canteen and office provided the only facilities, and rooftop squat toilets awaited the growing number of our group with uneasy stomachs. From this fly-ridden base we trudged out of town and climbed local hills to find our feet at our new altitude of 4,390 metres (14,400 feet). I discovered that I could keep up with or ahead of most of the others without undue effort or breathlessness. So far, so good.

From Tingri our group headed east on a switchback drive over the 5,120-metre (16,800 feet) Pang La pass. We stopped at the highest point to take photographs, for the view was impressive. Everest was now clearly visible, crested by a plume of ice crystal 'smoke', indicating violent winds on the summit ridge. The highest mountain on earth was certainly no visual let-down.

The onward road took us through moon scenery with wide river beds now dry but ready conduits for awesome melt-floods. Towering glacial moraines loomed above and twisted spires of rock supported boulders, big as churches, which teetered on the highest ledges and threatened imminent freefall. Some four hours after the Pang La, we came to the Rongbuk Monastery, close to the original Base Camp used by the pioneering British expeditions of the 1920s. It was from here that Mallory and Irvine set out in 1924 never to return. Then we climbed sharply up a narrow valley, the Rongbuk Gorge, which widened quite suddenly to become a bleak, flat plain some 500 metres wide between high hills with Everest dead ahead. This plain, home to the modern Everest Base Camp, was dotted with the colourful tents of at least a dozen expedition groups and was swept by a bitter cold wind from the glaciers above. Everest herself, now only twelve miles away, rose impressively above us, black rock streaked with ice and crowned with snow.

Louise and I shared a two-man tent which was hardly a honeymoon suite. There was a fairly cramped communal tent for meals and various stores tents. David introduced us to our Sherpas, small powerful men with affable features, and we settled down for the night.

Due largely to a Nepalese government clampdown on the number of climbers they allowed annually on Everest, more and more groups and individuals were switching to our Tibetan approach. We learned that at least 400 individuals would be hoping to climb the northern route over the next few weeks. Some years there was enough good weather to allow climbers to sneak briefly on to the summit, other years nobody made it at all, however great their skill and their strength. Most years people died trying. The current death rate was estimated at one in every ten attempts.

We spent two weeks in Base Camp at 5,200 metres (17,060 feet), sometimes trudging a few miles upwards on the Everest trail or back downhill to the Rongbuk Monastery. Acclimatisation was the main aim of our existence. Louise still suffered severe headaches but stayed with me for a fortnight before returning to England just before David decided we were ready to try our first trek up to the Advance Base Camp. Our gear was taken by sixty-five yaks with drivers who whistled and yelled at their animals when the trail was especially narrow or slippery.

The morning before we left Base Camp, a Belfast police friend of mine, Noel Hanna, visited our group tent. I knew Noel from adventure racing in New Zealand. He was one of the fittest men in Britain and had been planning to marry his long-time fiancée on the Everest summit. His group had trudged up to the Advance Base Camp (ABC) a few days earlier, but Noel's eyesight began to trouble him. His group leader diagnosed tunnel vision, but a doctor with an ophthalmoscope later discovered 'pools of blood' behind his retinas where blood vessels had burst. He was now due to head back to Ireland for treatment as soon as possible or, he had been warned, he would risk permanent eye damage and possible blindness.

Following behind Sibu and Alex I began the walk up the Rongbuk Valley from Base Camp on 12 April, often moving off the well-trodden but narrow path to make way for yaks coming back down from the ABC with loads of rubbish or barrels of latrine soil which is sold for crop manure in the valley. Past ecological outcry had resulted in a system of payment to yak drivers for this litter removal service, which was becoming ever more necessary as the annual numbers of climbers increased exponentially.

As we moved up the glacial valley, banks of hardened mud and rock pinnacles, some as high as thirty metres, flanked our progress. Rocks rain down regularly from these walls on to the path below but, thankfully, not while we were passing. After some four kilometres we trudged up a steep scree slope and into a side valley. This, after a few hours, widened out into the corridor of the East Rongbuk Glacier, our highway to Everest.

I knew that all 2005 summit bids had to be completed by the first week of June because that was the annual date for the arrival of the monsoon winds which would make Everest lethal to climbers. I still had about fifty days in which to reach the top and thereby, I hoped, enable the Heart Foundation to raise our £2 million target. I also had a personal pet hope. For twenty-three years I had competed with Norwegians for polar firsts. Now I had a chance of going for another. Only a handful of individuals had managed to cross both Antarctica and the Arctic Ocean. Børge Ousland was one of them, and he had tried to add Everest to his trophy list. Sibu and Dr Fred had been with him when he had decided to turn round not far short of the summit. So I hoped that my heart, my lungs and, remembering Noel Hanna, my retinas would behave themselves for the next fifty days. Weather permitting, I might then raise my £2 million *and* beat the Norwegians. Wishful thinking, I realised, but there was no harm in hoping.

I slept well that night at the first interim camp at 5,500 metres (18,045 feet) en route to Advance Base. I had taken three hours to get there at a slow trudge with a light rucksack, and still had no headache, no sickness and no loss of appetite. Sibu kept telling me to drink more water, and I had done so, mostly to keep him happy as I'm not normally a water drinker despite knowing (and indeed preaching) all the standard dictums on the blessings to be had from H_2O.

Next morning our group moved on up the glacial valley, an ascent of 950 metres with sharkfin pinnacles of ice towering above each side of the trail, known as the Magic Highway. We crossed or skirted lakes of frozen melt-water, great glaciers curved down from high valleys to join ours, but all, we knew, were shrinking, the main glacier by over 100 vertical feet in the past ten years alone. I kept up with the others without trouble, and after five hours came to the tents of the second interim camp at 6,088 metres (approximately 20,000 feet).

I slotted my sleeping bag, boots and rucksack between the two other Brits, Ian and Jens – by chance, not chauvinistic intention – and welcomed a cup of tea proffered by Ian. We were all dog-tired and most of us had headaches since, despite our cautious acclimatisation to date, we were for the first time living and working well above 17,000 feet where the human body starts to deteriorate, indeed to rot. It literally consumes itself for energy. Sleeping becomes a problem, muscle wasting and weight loss take place, and this process of deterioration continues more quickly the higher the altitude. Scientific advice by 2005 strongly recommended that nobody stay at that height for more than an absolute maximum of ten days and that, at or above 26,000 feet, the so-called Death Zone, acclimatisation is not possible.

Ian asked me if I'd like to take over the cooking, for he was dog-tired, having a far heavier backpack than mine due to all his delicate photographic and TV gear. I declined as I was struggling with my first bad headache and felt nauseous, and so did Jens. This naturally irritated Ian who felt he was doing all the work, as though he were a paid Sherpa or guide. In such close quarters when tired, sick, wet and uncomfortable, folk can get easily irritable or offended. Ian did well to hide his annoyance at that time, and I only learned about it two years later in another cramped and difficult night spot.

I lay awake for a while listening to water dripping on to sleeping bags, the distant crackle of moving glacier ice and the muted rumble of some snoring neighbour. Then, with no warning at all and a nasty shock, I jerked up gasping for air with a terrible sensation of suffocation. My heart beat wildly. The phenomenon passed as quickly as it came, and I felt drowsy again. Within minutes, or maybe mere seconds, I was again jumping up in a panic. Again I felt as though I had been throttled. The instant the shock awoke me, my breathing reverted to normal, but as soon as I drowsed off again, the gasping for air routine was back. There was no way I could get any sleep.

Next day, after a sleepless, worried night, I learned from Fred Ziel exactly what my problem was – an ailment known as Cheyne-Stokes periodic breathing which occurs when the system which regulates breathing gets out of sync. The would-be sleeper responds involuntarily to a build-up in carbon dioxide by hyper-ventilating which in turn leads to the breathing centre responding by shutting off respiration. CO_2 levels then increase and the unfortunate cycle repeats. A standard cure is for the victim to take Diamox tablets just before going to bed. Diamox blocks an enzyme in the kidney and makes the blood acidic, which is interpreted by the brain as a signal to breathe more. Diamox, therefore, enhances the physiological response to altitude by increasing the rate and depth of breathing. However, with my lung problem, I was already taking the maximum advised dose of two 250mg tablets daily. The only answer therefore, Fred advised, was to use oxygen whenever I needed to sleep at or above the height of that camp at 20,000 feet.

Early next day our group pushed on up the Magic Highway until we came to a great bowl of polished blue ice nearly a mile wide and rimmed by steep ridges. The trail then veered farther east, climbed abruptly over rough ground and, rounding a sharpish bend, revealed, all of a sudden, the stupendous mass of Everest's North-East Ridge ever ascending to the wind-driven streamer that raged along the impossibly high summit ridge at a height of 8,850 metres (29,029 feet) where jumbo jets fly.

After an hour I clambered up scree and loose boulders, over small melt pools and past the first outlying tents of the waiting congregation of aspirant summiteers, climbers of varying skills or, like me, none at all, from all over the world. This was Advance Base Camp (ABC), splattered like some multi-coloured rash up the rock-strewn moraine that lies in the eastern shadow of Changtse, a giant feature in her own right but a mere dwarf satellite to her neighbour Chomolungma, the Goddess Mother of the Snows to all Tibetans, Everest to us foreigners.

I caught up with Sibu after a three-hour trudge somewhere in the hugger-mugger labyrinth of tents large and small which stretched for at least 600 metres up the moraine, perched wherever a flat platform could be found or prepared by Sherpas smoothing out rock jumbles.

I was now at 6,460 metres (21,200 feet), higher than I had ever been. So far, I thanked God for small mercies, I appeared to have escaped retinal damage, severe headaches, heart pains, cerebral and pulmonary oedema, tensions with my fellow climbers, and even the hacking Khumbu cough that racked many climbers even down at Base Camp. Periodic breathing or Cheyne-Stokes syndrome would only affect me if I slept or dozed without oxygen, so my summit chances were still intact.

David's plan, now that all the Jagged Globe group, apart from a badly coughing Rosalind, had reached ABC in good condition, was to have us sleep only one night there, then descend all the way back to Base Camp. This was part of the generally accepted acclimatisation policy of 'climb high, sleep low'. We would recuperate for a while at Base Camp, then come back up (in a single day next time) to ABC *and* climb the formidable ice slopes which give access to the North Col. Then back down. And so on until we and the weather were ready for a final four- or five-day push from ABC to the summit. It was the yo-yo principle of bouncing up and down. This is how the body and the brain learn to cope with inadequate oxygen. By pushing the limits, then retreating to safety, repeatedly, human beings can gradually acclimate to the thin air of the high Himalaya. The thicker, more oxygen-rich air down below allows the body to sleep better and recover faster than at the debilitating altitude of ABC. The body's metabolism begins to work more effectively. On returning to ABC, the body is as strong as it will ever be.

David and Neal were sympathetic about my Cheyne-Stokes problem and agreed that I could use oxygen from their precious supply of canisters, but I was to control the usage or flow rate to as low a setting as would allow me to sleep. Later, thanks to a satphone facility at Base Camp, I was able to ask Louise to organise an additional supply.

I slept hardly at all that night, finding it difficult to fit the oxygen mask so that it stayed tight when I moved in my sleep. Saliva slowly blocked up the inlet pipe and mouthpiece, which impeded the breathing process and produced a gurgling snore which my tent companion, Ian Parnell, found so distracting, he eventually banished me to sleep by myself. I was not alone in finding control of my oxygen mask difficult to master. No less a climber than Ed Hillary had described the same salivatory problems, I was pleased to discover later.

I was relieved to leave ABC after an early breakfast of cereal. I turned down the Sherpa chef's kind offer of yak stew and set out downhill at a good pace. Alex was the only member of the group faster at descents, and he was a long-time adventure racer for a top South African team. The only obstacles that day, since the trail was obvious enough to preclude any chance of getting lost, were the intermittent traffic jams of yak caravans hogging the narrow mountain paths. The yak drivers were a wild-looking bunch with deeply wrinkled features and sleek black hair of which they were clearly proud, plaited beautifully and braided with precious gems and shiny bones.

My first night back down at Base Camp was blissful now that I knew how unpleasant it was to sleep or even doze using oxygen. On subsequent days I heard the faraway muffled thud of avalanches. Over on the south Nepalese side we heard that Kenton Cool, my erstwhile Alpine instructor and Jagged Globe Everest guide, was doing well with his client group, the mirror image of our own gang. An avalanche had, however, struck at one of the tented camps over there and injured some of the climbers. I knew that avalanches are one of the main reasons for Everest deaths.

Before we left Base Camp for our next upward sortie, David and Neal arranged for a lama from the Rongbuk Monastery to conduct a *puja* or blessing ceremony for our climbers. Prayer flags were strung in long lines from a makeshift stone altar on a hillock, and the ensuing rituals lasted almost an hour with much chanting, hand drum-thumping, bell-ringing, throwing about of tsampa flour and rice, and the eventual handouts of good-symbol-necklaces to help protect us. I took mine but decided not to wear it, since I trusted that my own bog-standard Church of England beliefs would sort out whatever fate had in store for me.

By the time we left Base Camp for the second time, there were few folk still there other than temporary acclimatisers like us, the sick and wounded, and the camp guardians. There were also a few unlucky souls whose arrival had been delayed along the road from Kathmandu by the haphazard ambushes of the heavily armed Maoist rebels whose fight had begun in 1996, killing since then over 3,000 Nepalese and a few tourists.

My second return journey to ABC took a full day with no halts en route and far fewer yak jams to cause delays. After resting for forty-eight hours, I joined David and the others for my first trip from ABC to the North Col. We were starting out from a point already 1,600 feet higher than Mont Blanc (where twenty years before I had been violently sick from altitude) and, within ten minutes of climbing into what Tibetans call 'the poison gas' – the thin air of high altitude – I was already feeling geriatric. It seemed as though, at 21,000 feet, my personal tree-line was broached.

I could never match Alex for speed, but had previously kept up with all the others uphill and well ahead downhill. Now, all of a sudden, I lagged behind everyone, constantly needing to rest my lungs and my legs. It was a novel experience for I normally prized my ability not to need a rest for many hours of adventure racing and ultra marathons in wild country. I felt wretched and, when David dropped back to check on me, I apologised and felt ashamed. He was kind and stayed close as I trudged on for an hour over rocks, ice and snow to the base of the North Col ascent. Fixed ropes were in place all the way from this point to the summit of Everest, put there and maintained by Sherpas from all the groups.

Using a simple hand device called an ascendeur (to grip the rope when tugged downwards but to slide along the rope when pulled upwards), I followed David up a succession of very steep snow slopes. In my free hand I grasped my ice-axe. Everybody climbed in this manner, pretty much all the way up the mountain. You do not need to be a 'proper' technical climber for Everest. But you do need to be altitude-fit, which I clearly wasn't. All the others in the group (except Rosalind who was back in Kathmandu seeing a lung doctor) made it to the North Col that day and spent the night there.

David saw me back down to ABC and gave me a gentle but not too subtle warning that my current form would not see me much higher than the North Col. My speed must improve.

Various other sorties followed, then it was back once more to Base Camp. With time on my hands I took a lift in a jeep down to Tingri, where I stayed for four days at a spa-cum-bed-and-breakfast. I went for a long walk every day and met up with an American climber in Tingri village. In the high street he pointed out two climbers striding past us.

'Those guys,' he muttered, 'are both big US climbers. I mean Number One dudes. Ed Viesturs and David Breashears. Both have been up the Big E several times with and without oxygen. And all the other big peaks too. Hey! Isn't that something?'

I agreed that it was, wishing only that I could make it up the North Col, using plenty of oxygen all the way. A few days later, on 27 April, I did manage the North Col, extremely slowly, but in time to make it in daylight and to spend the night there at 7,066 metres and using oxygen before heading back down to ABC.

After one more spell in Base Camp, we all (except poor Rosalind who had had to return home due to her lung trouble) made our last ascent to ABC by the third week of May and stayed there, with small local excursions from time to time, eagerly awaiting our chance for the final push. We were truly acclimatised, but were also in danger of general deterioration due to spending far too long above the 17,000 feet marker. We were living on borrowed time, according to every high-altitude book on the market.

David allocated a Sherpa to each climber. I was matched with Nima Dorje Sherpa (or Boca Lama), the smallest and most humorous ever-grinning dwarf of a Nepali. He was also a lay-lama which, I mused, must be a plus point in these Buddhist mountains for whoever he worked with. More than half of all Sherpas live entirely off their seasonal tourism and mountaineering incomes. Whether high-altitude guides, cooks or camp staff, they are among the best paid people in Nepal, earning up to eight times the average annual income.

Whilst our group yo-yoed up and down between Base Camp and the North Col, our Sherpas were moving heavy loads up to and establishing the higher camps, often without oxygen. I could imagine the frustration of the many Sherpas whose clients fall by the wayside long before they reach the high camps, never mind the summit. Then their poor Sherpas have to bring down all the heavy gear they have just sweated blood to position at risk to life and limb. In 2005 on our side of Everest only sixty of the 400 climbers who reached ABC actually went on up to reach the summit, so there must have been a good many irritated Sherpas.

The high 2005 failure rate was due to many causes. The weather was average to bad, but altitude sickness, diarrhoea and the Khumbu cough took their regular toll. The dry air at altitude can wreak havoc with even the toughest climber's prospects. Also known as high altitude hack, the Khumbu cough can be bad enough to cause broken ribs. One of the early British attempts to pioneer the northern route involved climber Howard Somervell in 1924. When a coughing fit wracked him just above the North Col, he found his throat was obstructed. He could neither breathe nor call for help, so he sat down to die. Then in desperation, 'I pressed my chest with both hands, gave one last almighty push and the obstruction came up. Though the pain was intense, I was a new man.' He had coughed up the desiccated mucous membrane of his throat.

The two main high-altitude sickness killers, cerebral and pulmonary oedema, are both caused by the body's reactions to lack of oxygen. Many people who travel from sea-level to over 8,000 feet report symptoms ranging from headache to loss of appetite and nausea. Why? As the available oxygen falls, the body responds by increasing the blood flow to the brain, but it can overcompensate, whereupon fluid leaks from the blood vessels into the brain causing it to swell. The victim is then suffering cerebral oedema.

Not surprisingly, the greater the elevation gain, the more severe the swelling. In severe cases the brain can get squeezed down the spinal cord, which results in death. The way to avoid falling victim is to ascend gradually, about 1,000 feet per day over 8,000 feet, which gives your body time to acclimatise properly.

As the body tries to get as much oxygen from the air as it can, pulmonary oedema can result from the greatly increased blood flow through the lungs. The heart increases the flow by increasing the pressure, causing leakage from the blood vessels into the air sacs. It usually takes a few days to develop, and is exacerbated by overexertion. In bad cases, you can hear a gurgling of fluid in the lungs, and the victim brings up bloody sputum. This is a serious condition which can kill in only a matter of hours and again is best avoided by gradual ascent. Treatment is by an immediate descent of several thousand feet and use of oxygen if available.

The body also responds to the lower oxygen levels by putting more red blood cells into circulation. Up to a point, this is a good thing. However, if it goes too far, the blood becomes thick and prone to clotting. Clots which get dislodged float around and can cause strokes, heart attacks and pulmonary embolisms. Due to my own cardiac state, Professor Angelini had upped my daily blood-thinning aspirin intake from 75mg to 300mg whilst I was at high altitude.

The Times journalist who had been sent out to cover the entire climb, wrote cynical articles, humorous in a caustic sort of way, that covered most aspects of life at ABC:

There are normal people on Everest, but the proportion of glory-hunters is abnormally high when compared with that at sea level. As a BBC compère might say: if you liked 'Fame Academy', then you'll LOVE 'Advance Base Camp'. They're all here, the star-struck and the fame-chasers, with their promotional stickers and funny logo'ed hats, their business cards and Americanised pidgin English, and for a journalist there is just nowhere to hide from these people – all want front-page coverage, preferably in *The Times*. So far I have met the sirdar who is to guide Tom Cruise up the mountain next year, the prospective first Punjabi woman and the first Bhutanese man to climb Everest. There is the bloke from

Australia whose aim is to be the first one-armed Australian on the summit and another man who claims that he will be the first asthmatic to have reached the top.

Why do these trophy-hunters annoy me so much? And doesn't Ranulph Fiennes fall into the same category? In answer to question two: absolutely not. Fiennes is one of the most self-effacing, focused people here and is climbing Everest only to raise £2 million for charity: he talks about almost nothing else.

The Times journalist was less enthusiastic about the ABC lavatory facilities, one of which was very close to *The Times* tent. I have experienced many such way-out facilities all over the world. In order of dreadfulness, I would rate the long communal muddy trench with a sit-on-pole down its length, as dug for the annual Karrimor Mountain Marathon in the UK, as winner, a short head in front of the Soviet military bucket squat galley in Sredniy, Siberia. Then came the Everest loos. Rosalind was unlucky enough one night to lose her spectacles (and her head torch, if the camp gossip was to be believed) down one of our loos. As deputy boss, the task of locating and retrieving both items fell to Neal, who did so successfully and without complaining.

On 30 May we were still ensconsed at ABC and still waiting for the high roar of the jet stream winds, up to 200 mph on Everest's upper reaches, to die away and stay away for the five-day period of calm, clear weather that we would need to attempt the climb. Such a break in the jet streams usually comes just before the onslaught of the annual monsoon storms which arrive most years in the first few days of June. Some years the break never comes, and nobody summits Everest. And some years the break only lasts a day or two, catches people out in the Death Zone and kills them.

The group leader has the often extremely difficult task of assessing from met forecasts whether or not to risk the lives of his clients, all of whom will be raring to go, especially if they can see the fatal date of the monsoon's dreaded arrival fast approaching. Many clients will have spent some US$65,000 of their savings and will know they are unlikely to have another chance, so they champ at the bit at the ongoing wimpishness, as they see it, of any group leader who is still refusing to try for the summit with only five or six days left till the monsoon is likely to be due.

At last, on 31 May, half of our group left ABC for their summit attempt. David had sensibly divided us into a fast-moving greyhound group of Sibu, Tore, Alex and Fred, led by him, while group two, led by Neal, would be Mark, Jens, Ian and me.

On the other side of Everest, only a single day of less strong winds is needed to climb from the South Col to the summit and back. Jagged Globe's group on that side, led by Kenton, summitted on 31 May. That same day I made it up to the North Col camp with the rest of group two. Group one were, by then, two camps ahead of us and experiencing high winds. The North Col camp, in the lee of a great snow wall, was the last haven of shelter all the way to the summit, so our group, sleeping with oxygen, stayed there awaiting orders from David to come on up once his group had vacated our tents. This leapfrog shuffle would involve the three camps between the North Col and the summit, positioned at 7,500 metres (Camp Two), 7,900 metres (Camp Three), and 8,400 metres (Death Camp).

We had set out from ABC much later than would have been possible in a normal monsoon year. But in 2005 it was running late, so we just squeezed in. Of the 400 would-be climbers in ABC, about one-third had been forced to give up during the ongoing bad weather in May, due to ill-health, homesickness, flight dates, or visa restrictions.

I was happy to have made it to the North Col Camp at a reasonable rate; slower than the rest, but not by much. I was feeling far better physically than at any time over the past month. The Col is hard grind. I had read descriptions of it by experienced climbers. One, Andy Politz, was part of an earlier group who located Mallory's body. He wrote simply, 'The entire lower half of the Col was an exercise in surviving torture.'

Scaling the Col involves a series of short, nearly vertical steps interspersed with steep snow slopes and twisting crevasse detours. The relief when reaching the last ladders over a wide crevasse, just a few metres from the first tent at the Col Camp, is huge. I tottered into one of the four tents our Sherpas had erected for us, fairly near to the great snow wall that gives protection from the violent west winds and surrounded by some ninety or more other tents. The toilet arrangements were simple. You squatted as near as was safely possible to the edge of the ice precipice on the far side of the encampment. Slipping on the ice there would be a bad idea, for the resulting fall would be over 1,000 feet.

At the Col Camp I spent a lot of time in the tent fiddling with my oxygen system in the knowledge that most deaths on the upper reaches of Everest are the result of oxygen shortage, and the oxygen regulator is the key to survival. New Zealander Russell Bryce, generally accepted as head honcho on the north side, had kindly lent me a spare regulator as all the Jagged Globe spares were already in use. The oxygen systems we used were made by Poisk in Russia, and they had been in use for many years but were prone to failed seals and valves due to grit particles and ice. The smaller orange cylinders most in use gave five or six hours of oxygen if you set a flow rate on the regulator dial of 2.5 litres a minute. The larger 1,000-litre canisters gave ten hours on this setting.

Eventually our number two group set out from Col Camp. The sky was clear and the winds manageable, so we all made good time up the long steep snow ramps to where shattered shale underfoot gradually replaced the snow, and the fixed ropes edged to the right, at first gently then, for the last hour, at quite a steep gradient. This 7,500-metre camp was much smaller than the Col Camp and the few dozen tents there were tattered, in some cases completely shredded. Our own two tents had survived well and we all slept on oxygen. Each time I woke to knock frozen dribble from my mask, I intoned, 'Only two days to the top and two million quid in the kitty.'

From 7,300 to 7,500 metres the wind had picked up and made life quite unpleasant. My oxygen mask kept needing adjustment, my frost-damaged feet spent a good deal of time complaining that my Kathmandu-purchased boots were too tight, and my frostbitten hand needed many halts to force blood back into the fingers during those stretches where I needed to keep the fixed rope on my right-hand side. Let me explain to anyone who is not a climber how Everest hopefuls who are upwards-trudgers like me haul themselves up the many thousands of feet from the base of the North Col, where the fixed rope starts, to the summit where it stops.

You have a climbing harness around your waist and crutch and to a strong point on the belt's front just above your tummy button there is attached a steel karabiner (or krab). A loop or sling is attached to this krab. Another detachable device, also on your sling, is clipped on to the fixed ropes that lead you up the mountain. This is called a jumar (or ascendeur), and has metal teeth. Slide the jumar up the rope and it runs along smoothly, but any downwards pull and the jumar's teeth will clench the rope and stop you falling.

Because there are hundreds of knots and fixed points along the rope line, you always use two of these slings and never unclip one until the other is attached to the rope beyond the obstacle. Many of the bodies lying along the rope line and below it are there because they slipped and fell when briefly unattached to the mountain or a rope. You can't add to the number of corpses who died from that particular fate so long as you always use the two-sling system – *and* so long as the fixed rope does not break or come loose. The older ropes are often cut by falling rocks or chafed through by rubbing on sharp points, so Sherpas assess and, where necessary, renew them most years. But it still pays to keep checking every rope that you intend to rely on.

The 7,500-metre 'camp' was in reality a raggedy series of ledges, anywhere big enough for a tiny tent to be pitched with guy ropes tied mostly around rocks in lieu of tent pegs. The recent big winds that had held up David's group had rendered many of the tents I passed mere skeletal tent-pole hoops attached to wildly fluttering bits of material. Cylinders and food packs and bric-a-brac lay all around. Every so often a couple of climbers would slowly descend, and I would unclip myself to let them pass down the rope. They often moved like zombies and were unrecognisable in their hooded, goggled sameness. One of them was our doctor, Fred Ziel, who had sensibly turned round too sick to continue.

Between the 7,500- and the 7,900-metre camps the going became harder, with many slippery rocks and icy runnels to negotiate. A strong cold wind from one flank had the effect, I am not sure why, of blocking off oxygen, at least partially, somewhere between the cylinder in my rucksack and my mask. This caused constant halts to turn away from the wind and breathe deeply. My hooded down jacket covered parts of the system to stop them freezing up, but in order to reach them or to alter the flow setting, I needed to undo the jacket's main zip. Dribble from the mask often landed on the zip and froze it solid. Should my goggles mist up or move out of place, I again needed to unzip. Whereas these sorts of clothing problems had often occurred on polar expeditions in far colder circumstances, they had not involved the added complications of an oxygen system, nor being attached to a mountainside, nor feeling below par due to the altitude. In the Arctic most travel was at three or four feet above sea-level, and in Antarctica we had suffered from altitude sickness at a mere 11,000 feet up.

I kept checking that my system's pipes were not snagged, nor the mask workings frozen, but I never managed to discover why, every so often in strong winds, the oxygen stopped coming and I had to tear my mouth from the mask and try to gulp in air. I had set out from 7,500 metres an hour earlier than Ian, Jens, Mark and Neal in order to reach the next camp at the same time as them. My driving aim as I toiled up the mountain was to keep ahead as long as possible, growing to dread the moment I heard the crunch of their boots just below me. Halfway through the morning, Mark caught up with me. We lifted tired arms in greeting. There was no point in trying to communicate verbally as the wind tore away the words.

At 7,900 metres the camp was perched on tiny tilted ledges and felt, I thought, unpleasantly exposed. But I also enjoyed a new feeling of anticipation because the summit ridge that, for the past seventy days had seemed so far away and so high as to be unobtainable, now for the first time looked within reasonable grasp. How many other hopeful folk had reached this point and likewise felt they could make it, only to die within forty-eight hours? A good many. At least one out of every ten. The most famous were, of course, Mallory and Irvine.

In 1924 Mallory was on the mountain for a third time. The British were gradually pushing the northern route, experimenting with oxygen, and Mallory was their best climber. That year their colleagues far below spotted Mallory and Irvine on the summit ridge through binoculars, but neither man ever made it back down. To this day it is uncertain if they reached the summit, but in 1999 a group of top US climbers searched for Mallory and Irvine's bodies in the area around and above the 7,900-metre camp, especially the snow basins beneath the steeper rock faces. Bodies dressed in brightly-coloured Gore-Tex jackets were not hard to find. The climbers recorded, 'We found ourselves in a kind of collection zone for fallen climbers . . . Just seeing these twisted, broken bodies was a pretty stark reminder of our own mortality.' Then one of the Americans, Conrad Anker, spotted something different. He thought he had discovered the remains of Andrew Irvine: 'We were looking at a man who had been clinging to the mountain for seventy-five years. The clothing was blasted from most of his body, and his skin was bleached white. I felt like I was viewing a Greek or Roman marble statue.'

Soon the five searchers were crouched around the body in awed silence.

The body itself did the speaking. For here was a body unlike the others crumpled in crannies elsewhere on the terrace. This body was lying fully extended, facedown and pointing uphill, frozen in a position of self-arrest, as if the fall had happened only moments earlier. The head and upper torso were frozen into the rubble that had gathered around them over the decades, but the arms, powerfully muscular still, extended above the head to strong hands that gripped the mountainside, flexed fingertips dug deep into the frozen gravel. The legs were extended downhill. One was broken and the other had been gently crossed over it for protection. Here too, the musculature was still pronounced and powerful. The entire body had about it the strength and grace of a dancer. This body, this man, had once been a splendid specimen of humankind.

Name-tags on the tattered clothing remnants established that this was Mallory, not Irvine. The searchers concluded that:

George Mallory fell to his death from a spot well down the face of the Yellow Band, tantalizingly close to Camp VI and safety; his injuries are too mild, his body too unmarred, for there to be any other explanation. And he did not fall alone; at the critical moment, he appears to have been roped to his partner, Andrew Irvine. Irvine fell too and was injured, though not as profoundly as Mallory. They did not fall far. They did not fall from the dangerous Northeast Ridge, as had the many badly twisted bodies frozen in agonized death in the great catch-basin of the 'snow terrace'.

The searchers' conclusion was open-ended, but one wrote:

The route they pioneered to the Northeast Ridge in the 1920s is the one most climbed today on the north side. For the two of them to have gotten as high as they did with the resources they had is truly amazing. Whether or not they made the summit, they will forever hold a place as heroes on the world's highest peak.

If Mallory and Irvine did not summit, it is certain that nobody else did until, twenty-nine years later, a British Commonwealth expedition under John Hunt, an Army colonel, finally placed two of its climbers, Ed Hillary from New Zealand and Sherpa Tenzing Norgay from Nepal, on the summit from the southern side on 29 May 1953. By then, ten expeditions had tried for the summit and failed, and thirteen men had died. The previous year Tenzing himself, with a Swiss climber, had been forced to turn back not far short of the summit. News of Hillary and Tenzing's success was flashed to London just before the coronation of Queen Elizabeth II.

By the end of 2006, records showed that, in the seventy-six years since Mallory's death not far from my 7,900 metres tent, 2,062 climbers had reached the summit and 203 of them died on the mountain. Since there were ten climbers in our two groups, I wondered if any would succumb to this Everest law of decimation. Five climbers had died on the mountain already during the past month, I knew, and maybe more, since there were a number of lone climbers as yet unaccounted for at ABC.

The good weather spell was still with us at dawn on 3 June. Today we would move into the so-called Death Zone, above which the majority of North Ridge climber fatalities take place. Our next camp lay, at 8,400 metres, higher than all but five of the world's mountain summits.

Two hours later, above 8,000 metres (26,246 feet), I was preoccupied with not slipping off the shale and ice, aware of, but studiously avoiding, any glimpse of the sharp drop to my right and focusing on slow but continuous movement to keep ahead of the others in my group. I had, as usual, set out an hour ahead of them and was determined to keep that lead. Luckily I felt stronger than before, probably because the oxygen system was working better because there was less wind.

One of America's most famed modern-day climbers, David Breashears, described the act of upwards movement of the route. 'Our bodies were dehydrated. Our fingers and toes went numb as precious oxygen was diverted to our brains, hearts and other vital organs. Climbing above 26,000 feet, even with bottled oxygen, is like running on a treadmill and breathing through a straw. Your body screams at you to turn around. Everything says: this is cold. This is impossible.'

There were some very steep sections where I had a problem passing other climbers descending in a dazed, clumsy state. I tried speaking to one who knocked his pack hard against me as he slipped down past me, but there was no reply. He looked exhausted. I passed by a climber curled up on a tiny ledge. As I cautiously unclipped to get by him, I asked if he was okay. There was no reply, but his hooded, masked head nodded slowly. It struck me that, if he was dying, I might well be accused of being one of those callous climbers who pass by the near dead without offering aid. But I had passed several such inert individuals and I myself had been passed as I rested, completely winded, on some tiny perch, too tired even to acknowledge a passing greeting.

The media point fingers of guilt in such cases. The following year a Kiwi amputee climber, Mark Ingliss, was interviewed and agreed that, after he had talked to fellow climber, David Sharp, in a bad way some 1,300 feet below the summit and sheltering under a rock, he had moved on upwards, as had others in his group. All agreed that any rescue attempt would only cause more deaths. Many of the forty climbers who passed Sharp by assumed that his own group would save him, whereas in fact he was not with any group. His condition slowly deteriorated as climbers went by him on their way up and, later, back down. His chances of rescue diminished through the day. His legs, feet and fingers became frost-bitten and dead, so he could no longer walk or use his hands. His oxygen gave out and he died, as some people do on this stretch of this mountain. When a climber near the summit of Mount Everest reaches a stage of exhaustion and oxygen starvation so severe that he can no longer move on his own initiative, he is typically left to die. It is simply impossible for one climber to descend such treach-erous terrain carrying or dragging the inert body of another. The mountain is littered with the bodies of climbers who have simply sat down and died of exposure. Sibu nearly joined their ranks.

Five days after our wedding, Louise and I were in Nepal.

Below the Advance Base Camp: many climbers were already seriously affected by altitude by this point.

My second attempt to follow David up the North Col without oxygen: 20% of my lung capacity was shot.

At the North Col camp: from here I used oxygen all the way to the 'Death Camp'.

With my friend Sibusiso, the first black person ever to climb Everest and the man who inspired me to make this attempt.

Recreating the last few days of Doctor Livingstone's journey to Victoria Falls with a team of Zimbabweans and Zambians in 2005.

With Louise at the very edge of the Victoria Falls.

One hundred and fifty years to the day after he reached the Falls, we unveiled this plaque honouring the great explorer.

The North Face of the Eiger, Tuesday 13 March 2007, day 1.

There's a drop of 3,000 feet from the overnight ledge at Death Bivouac, so sleep-walking is to be avoided.

For five days I tried to avoid looking down.

The Summit Ice Field, where Ian began his fall.

The summit in sight.

On the summit of the Eiger, 10.30am, Saturday 17 March, 2007.

I came at last to the exposed series of ledges at 8,400 metres on which perched a few battered tents. I saw Sibu sitting outside one. I waved to him and he waved back slowly. He looked tired. I assumed he was on his way down from the summit with David and the others. The last fifty metres up to one of the two colour-coded Jagged Globe tents took me twenty minutes, for my oxygen pipe kept snagging on my rucksack but, for the first time, I arrived within a few minutes of Ian, Jens, Neal and Mark. We crawled into our tents tired but exhilarated. After seventy days we were nearly there. The tent was pitched on a slope. The Sherpas had done their best to find a flat spot, but there were none. Ian, my own Sherpa, Boca Lama, and I tried to get ready for our night in the Death Camp, unpacking our rucksacks and checking our oxygen systems without upsetting each other's space, all in a tiny two-man tent pitched on rocks and ice. Any item that escaped through the entry door was liable to slide, then fall for many thousands of feet to the snow terraces and glaciers below. Various dead bodies had been found in the tents here, including an Indian climber the previous week.

Sibu nearly died that day when his oxygen ran out, although we did not know this until the following morning when one of our Sherpas found him slouched beside the ropes an hour or two below the tents. Various stories of recent happenings reached us on the walkie-talkie system or through other climbers. A few days earlier, when a Slovenian died on the summit ridge, a solo climber from Bhutan, close by him, ran out of oxygen and began to hallucinate due to hypoxia. He wandered by one of the old corpses near to the fixed rope, probably the one with green boots that most climbers remember, and thought he saw the corpse pointing at an object nearby. This turned out to be a half-snow-buried orange oxygen cylinder. The Bhutani, to his joy, found that there was still oxygen in it, clipped it to his system and survived to tell his tale to everyone in ABC.

From the Death Camp, the final climb ascends and traverses a steep stretch of striated limestone, known as the Yellow Band, mostly by way of a part-snow-filled gulley where many old ropes can cause confusion, especially since this section must be done at night. However, the great motivating thought is that from the tents to the summit ridge is a mere 300 metres in height.

So why on earth do people want to risk their lives on Everest year after year? George Mallory wrote:

> If one should ask me what 'use' there was in climbing, or attempting to climb the world's highest peak, I would be compelled to answer 'none'. There is no scientific end to be served; simply the gratification of the impulse of achievement, the indomitable desire to see what lies beyond that ever beats within the heart of man. With both poles conquered, the mighty peak of the Himalayas remains as the greatest conquest available to the explorer.

Mallory, in fact, had a very reasonable motive for his Everest trials. Curiosity. Nobody had yet reached the summit. Nobody knew if the human body could survive at that altitude. On a more cynical level another British climber, Stephen Venables, observed, 'Everest is prime *Guinness Book of Records* territory.'

In 2004 150 climbers had summitted Everest in a batch and, had the weather turned nasty at the wrong moment, there would have been dead people all over the Death Zone. Back in 1996 it did and there were. Two world-famous professional guides were among them. Questions were asked about Everest tourism. One amateur climber who survived was journalist John Krakauer who went on to write a bestselling book about the debacle, *Into Thin Air*. In it he apportioned blame and particularly criticised Anatoli Boukreev, an immensely experienced Russian guide who had rescued three people. Boukreev hit back with his own book, and was then killed climbing on Annapurna. The American television talk shows were packed with journalists and with survivors. Discussion forums sprang up on the web, filled with speculation by people who knew very little about it all. It began to rival the assassination of J.F. Kennedy for conspiracy theories. Everest had become a spectator sport.

I struggled into my boots, pack and oxygen system, said good-bye to Ian and the other three and, with Boca Lama a few yards behind, grinning as usual, began the fairly steep climb up the fixed ropes with new batteries in my head torch. The others would start out in an hour at 11.00 p.m. In seven or eight hours, on a fixed rope the whole way, I hoped to be on the summit of Everest. We moved off into the night, pitch black beyond the cone of our torch lights. There were slippery rocks, snow patches and a bewildering choice of upwards-leading ropes, some frayed almost through, others brand new. In the torch light it paid to take time. I found myself panting far more than on the previous climb, despite taking it slowly, perhaps because of the gradient. I felt cold despite the exertion, and I felt dizzy, too. Something was wrong but nothing I could identify, so I kept going in a stop-start way, gasping for breath every few metres. Then, some forty minutes after setting out, my world caved in.

Somebody, it seemed, had clamped powerful arms around my chest and was squeezing the life out of me. And the surgical wire that held my ribs together felt as though it was tearing through my chest. My thoughts were simple: I am having another heart attack. I will be dead in minutes. No defibrillator on hand this time. Then I remembered that Louise had pestered me to carry special pills with me – Glycerine Tri-Nitrate (GTN). You put one under your tongue where it fizzes and causes your system to dilate in all the right places. I tore at my jacket pocket and, removing my mitts, crammed at least six tablets under my tongue before swallowing.

I clung to the rope, hanging out over the great drop and waiting to die. My one glimpse of Boca Lama, who said nothing, was of his usual big grin as my torch light lit up his features. Five minutes later I was still alive. The tablets, I knew, could, if you were lucky, stave off a heart attack and give you time to get to a cardiac unit. They are *not* a means of avoiding an attack in order to allow you to continue climbing. This might not be my own end, but it *was* definitely the signal to descend to lower altitudes at once.

Some twenty minutes later we were back down in the Death

Camp. There was no tent to enter as our group were in the act of booting and kitting up, using all available tent space. So I waited outside with Boca Lama until Ian and the others had disappeared up into the night.

'I must go down quickly,' I told Boca Lama. He shook his head and the grin disappeared. It would, he explained, be too dangerous to descend until we could 'see our feet'. That meant dawn in five hours' time. I knew my best hope of survival, as had been the case on Kilimanjaro, was to lose height rapidly. The tightness had gone from my chest, but the sharp discomfort around the stitch-wires was still there. I contemplated going on down without Boca Lama, but decided against it. Going up an icy, slippery, steep slope in the darkness is a lot safer than descending one. Statistically, the vast majority of accidents happen on the descent. The concentration of going up seems to disappear to be replaced by a weary nonchalance. Nothing matters apart from a longing for warmth and comfort. Lost in these thoughts you become careless. The focus gone and the mind weary, it is all too easy to lose your footing or clip carelessly into a rope. Three thousand metres of void waited directly below our tent.

Nine times Everest climber, Ed Viesturs, has two favourite sayings: 'Just because you love the mountains doesn't mean the mountains love you' and 'Getting to the top is optional. Getting down is mandatory.'

Dawn came eventually and we descended without a break to the North Col, where we rested for two hours, then on down to ABC for the night. My Everest was over. If I had feared a scathing reaction from our *Times* correspondent, I was pleasantly surprised: 'Aborting his climb will be seen by the mountain community as a wise and courageous decision. Duncan Chessell, who has led thirty-five Himalayan expeditions, said, "For a 60-year-old man to make it even this far is extraordinary. You would expect only fifty per cent of climbers to reach anywhere near this high, especially during this season."'

I congratulated my fellow Jagged Globe climbers, especially Sibu, who was the first black person to climb Everest from both sides, and Jens, who was a year older than me. Fred, who had recovered from his illness but still looked weak, assured me that he would be having another go, his third, in a year or so. I thanked David, Neal and our wonderful team of Sherpas, especially Boca Lama, for what had truly been a great experience. Would I try again? Not for a while. Maybe never, but I hate saying 'Never again'.

Within a day, with Tore, Alex and Sibu, I was back down in Base Camp, and forty-eight hours after that I was checked out in Harley Street for new cardiac damage. None was evident, so it is likely that, on Everest and previously on Kilimanjaro, I had mere angina warnings. What would have happened if I had not heeded them or had not had the GTN tablets, it is impossible to know. I learnt later that, on the other side of the mountain a Scottish climber, 49-year-old Robert Milne, died of a heart attack on the same night and at the same height as I had my attack. I assume he had no GTN pills with him.

The tangible declared aim of my Everest attempt, all costs of which were sponsored by the generosity of Paul Sykes, had been to raise £2 million for an MRI Scanner Unit and Catheter Laboratory in the Great Ormond Street Hospital for Children in London. The British Heart Foundation eventually raised the £2 million through the Ran Fiennes Healthy Hearts Appeal, despite my failure on the mountain, and I cut the ribbon to officially open the gleaming new clinic. Its purpose is purely for heart research, and it will enable BHF medical professionals to explore the heart disease that affects children, helping them to develop new interventional techniques with the aim of saving young lives.

Since our 'honeymoon' at the Everest Base Camp had been a non-event, Louise and I took up the kind offer of John Costello, who had checked out my lungs prior to Everest, to stay for a week in his family villa in southern Spain. A couple of months later, Louise told me that she was pregnant and, on Easter Day 2006, our daughter Elizabeth gave her first yell. A month later I was sixty-two years old and changed my first nappy.

19

Vertigo

The Everest experience and the advent of my new family extracted me from my period of misery and hopelessness following Ginny's death. But my irrational fear of heights (or rather drops) was never put to the test on Everest, since the seventy-two days I spent moving up and down that mountain's north side at no time involved any vertigo-inducing moves.

A couple of months after returning to England, I had a letter from Neal Short, who had led our ascent group two. He wrote: 'As you were so close, I often wonder whether you are tempted to give it another go. Maybe you could go from the south side, with Kenton Cool, where they spend far less time above 5,300 metres and where dropping down the valley to lower altitudes for recuperation is an easier option.' Kenton Cool had been one of four mountain guide instructors on my Jagged Globe pre-Everest course in the Alps. He had mentioned during that course that Everest was not a particularly scary feature in terms of sheer exposure, and he should know, as he was to become the first Briton to scale Everest five times. But I had assumed that his definition of scary was light years away from mine and that, since Everest was, after all, the highest mountain on earth, with a menacing casualty rate, it would prove a truly vertiginous experience for a person like me. Perhaps if I had completed the last few hours of traverse along Everest's summit ridge, I would have experienced the 'fearful voids' I had looked for. But, as it was, my seventy-two Everest days had merely provided a long, toilsome trudge along fixed ropes up endless snow slopes with some rocky zones thrown in, plus a huge slice of boredom in high-altitude tents. My vertigo remained unchallenged, apart from by crevasses and school roofs.

Back on that Alpine course, it had been suggested that anyone looking for a *real* test of exposed climbing would be a lot better off in the Alps rather than in the Himalaya, since the daddy of all nasties was ready and waiting a mere three-hour drive from Geneva Airport: the North Face of the Eiger, the notorious Nordwand, the North Wall. In German *mordwand* means 'murder wall' and that is what the face is often called. I had heard various horror stories of this face, and some twenty years before, together with Simon Gault and Geoff Newman, had planned to walk up one of the easier ridges over a weekend with a guide. Those plans had never materialised for Geoff and me, although Simon had managed it and had never since let us forget the fact.

At some point I had tentatively approached Kenton with the suggestion that, if the Eiger was indeed to be a tougher challenge exposure-wise than Everest, would he guide me up it? And, if so, when? I knew that Kenton had climbed the North Wall of the Eiger with two friends and had taken three days and nights to do so. I also knew that he was held in huge respect by Britain's mountaineering community. He was thirty-three years old and supremely fit. He lived and worked in Chamonix, the mecca of Alpine climbers, and did not suffer fools, especially climbing fools, gladly. In response to my Eiger query, he was forthright. He would not even consider climbing the Eiger with me unless he first taught me how to climb to a standard where he was sure he would not be risking his own life.

How long would such an instructional period last, I asked him. 'As long,' he replied, 'as a piece of string. It depends on your ability, determination, strength and how long you're prepared to spend training in the Alps. Have you read *The White Spider*?'

'No,' I replied.

'Well, you probably should. It may put you off before you even think of going anywhere near the Eiger.'

I found a copy of the book, by the Austrian, Heinrich Harrer, one of the team who made the first ascent back in 1938, and noted his comments on some possible motives of a would-be Eiger North Face climber.

> With the best will in the world no one could suggest any usefulness to mankind in such a climb. Nor could any material advantages be worth the risks, the indescribable labours and difficulties which demand the uttermost physical, spiritual and mental resistance merely to win fame at the expense of that horrific wall. To do the climb as compensation for an inferiority complex? Any climber who dares to tackle the North Face must have examined and proved himself a hundred times in advance. And how about a climb of the North Face as a counterbalance to hysteria? A hysteric, an unstable character, would go to pieces at the very sight of the Wall, just as surely as any mask would fall away in the face of this menacing bastion of rock and ice.

The White Spider made harrowing reading and explained in detail the reasons for many of the deaths of the highly capable climbers who perished on the North Face. I was impressed and not a little disturbed. Harrer was doing nothing to put my mind at rest, no doubt as Kenton hoped.

> The North Wall of the Eiger remains one of the most perilous in the Alps, as every man who has ever joined battle with it knows. Other climbs, the North face of the Grandes Jorasses for one, may be technically more difficult, but nowhere else is there such appalling danger from the purely fortuitous hazards of avalanches, stone-falls and sudden deterioration of the weather as on the Eiger . . . The North Face of the Eiger demands the uttermost of skill, stamina and courage, nor can it be climbed without the most exhaustive preparations . . . The Eiger's Face is an irrefutable touchstone of a climber's stature as a mountaineer and as a man . . . Anyone who makes headway on the North Face of

the Eiger and survives there for several days has achieved and overcome so much – whatever mistakes he may have committed – that his performance is well above the comprehension of the average climber.

I assumed that Kenton would, given time, be able to turn me into an 'average climber'. Was that going to be enough? I moved on, depressed, from *The White Spider* in order to find more optimistic advice from equally famous but more contemporary climbers.

Joe Simpson, of *Touching the Void* fame, had written: 'It wasn't the hardest or the highest. It was simply "The Eiger". The very mention of the name made my heart beat faster. The seminal mountain, a metaphorical mountain that represented everything that defines mountaineering – a route I had dreamed of climbing for my entire adult life.' This, from the man famed for rescuing himself from the depths of an Andean crevasse after his partner had thought him lost and cut the rope, was less offputting than Harrer but hardly reassuring.

Jon Krakauer, who had stirred up the Everest '96 hornet's nest, wrote:

The problem with climbing the North Face of the Eiger is that in addition to getting up 6,000 vertical feet of crumbling limestone and black ice, one must climb over some formidable mythology. The trickiest moves on any climb are the mental ones, the psychological gymnastics that keep terror in check, and the Eiger's grim aura is intimidating enough to rattle anyone's poise . . .

The history of the mountain resonates with the struggles of such larger-than-life figures as Buhl, Bonatti, Messner, Rébuffat, Terray, Haston, and Harlin, not to mention Eastwood. The names of the landmarks on the face – the Hinterstoisser Traverse, the Ice Hose, the Death Bivouac, the White Spider – are household words among both active and armchair Alpinists from Tokyo to Buenos Aires; the very mention of these places is enough to make any climber's hands turn clammy. The rockfall and avalanches that rain continuously down the Nordwand are legendary. So is the heavy weather. Even when the skies over the rest of Europe are cloudless, violent storms brew over the Eiger, like those dark clouds that hover eternally above Transylvanian castles in vampire movies . . . Needless to say, all this makes the Eiger North Face one of the most widely coveted climbs in the world.

All this and more in the same vein by other Eiger climbers put me off the whole idea in terms of treating it as a reasonable project. But from the point of view of a worthy vertigo-testing challenge, the mountain seemed perfect.

So I went back to Kenton, who agreed to have a go at teaching me how to climb on mixed rock and ice in the Alps. But because there would be a good deal of plain rock as well as ice on the Eiger, I needed to learn simple rock-climbing as well, which I could do near home on Exmoor, my finger stumps well strapped for protection. A Welsh climber from Cardiff, Haydn Griffiths, started me off on sea cliffs on the Gower Peninsula, various quarry-type cliffs near Cardiff, and the Avon Gorge near Bristol. Whenever I fell off, which was often, he held my fall from above and was always patient. Under his tutelage, I passed from climbs graded as DIFFICULT (meaning Easy) to those graded HARD VERY SEVERE (HVS), but never managed to complete the latter without considerable shouted advice from Haydn en route.

Paul Sykes from Yorkshire had underwritten the Everest project, so I put the Eiger idea to him. This time he was not happy. It all sounded a lot more dangerous and if anything happened to me he, as sponsor, would feel partially responsible. But he did agree to meet up with and quiz Kenton, who talked him round, even if Paul was still dubious about my chances of success.

I looked at various UK charities and ended up deciding on Marie Curie Cancer Care. This was an easy choice for when I had been with Ginny in Exeter Hospital's cancer care ward, we had noticed other terminally ill patients who were never visited by friends or family and, when we went to their bedsides, they confided that they pined for the familiar surroundings of their own home, the friendly face of some pet or other and the memories they associated with their own pictures, ornaments and furniture. But they couldn't afford to pay carers, so they must die, lonely, in an NHS cancer ward. Macmillan and Marie Curie nurses are the best answer to this very real problem and, because I had done some work ten years before for Marie Curie, I called them first. They were enthusiastic and their committee decided that, using my Eiger attempt, they could and would raise at least £1.5 million, and maybe double that figure.

My literary agent Ed Victor signed up *The Sunday Times* to cover the climb exclusively, and I approached old friends at ITV News (the new name for ITN). Sadly, their veteran reporter, Terry Lloyd, who had been on so many of our expeditions in the past, had been killed whilst on ITN duty near Basra in 2003. An investigation was still going on as to the exact circumstances of Terry's death, but the official version was 'caught up in a fire fight between US and Iraqi forces near the Shatt Al Basra Bridge'. However, the Leader of the Liberal Democrats, three and a half years after Terry's death, was still pushing Parliament for justice. 'When,' he asked, 'may we expect the Attorney-General to make an application for the extradition and trial in Britain of those American soldiers against whom there is a *prima facie* case for the unlawful killing in Iraq of the ITN journalist Terry Lloyd?'

ITV News agreed to send a two-man team to record the Eiger attempt and to make clear how viewers could donate to Marie Curie. The new Terry Lloyd was reporter Philip Reay-Smith and his cameraman was Rob Turner. ITV subsequently agreed, with Paul Sykes' help, to produce a sixty-minute documentary film in addition to their sequences for the national news.

Once ITV and *The Sunday Times* were on board, I approached Mountain Equipment, the mountain and polar clothing company I had worked with since 1972, and they agreed to full equipment sponsorship, and the UK Met Office in Exeter and the Swiss equivalent in Berne also agreed to sponsor us. Met forecasts are key to any successful attempt on the North Face of the Eiger, which Kenton assured me would best be made in March when winter temperatures should freeze loose rubble in place and minimise the likelihood of rockfalls.

'Which March?' I asked Kenton.

He smiled. 'That depends on when, if ever, you become sufficiently proficient for me not to consider you the lethal liability that you are right now.'

So month after month through 2006 I flew out to Geneva for five-day training sessions in the Alps, trying to imbibe a basic understanding of the principles of rope-work and how to use an ice-axe (or two) in conjunction with crampon spikes, in order to head in an upwards direction on vertical ice sheets. Not just to help plod up slopes, as on Everest.

The nursery slopes that Kenton initially used were mostly close to Argentière, near Chamonix, but, when the weather was bad, he drove us through the Mont Blanc tunnel to the Italian valley of Cogne, a place of many frozen waterfalls. The basics of ice-climbing, as far as I could see, involved hacking one or both of your axes into the ice-wall above your head, kicking the front-facing spikes on your boots into the ice at about knee-level, then hauling your weight up. You then keep repeating this process until you reach the top of the waterfall.

As we progressed slowly to more difficult waterfalls, variations on this basic theme were introduced, some fairly dicey. When the ice was a mere transparent coating, as though painted on to the rock, bludgeoning your axe into it was useless. In such places it was better to try to be incredibly patient and place your axes' tips with surgical precision into the tiniest indents. That sounds easy, but it's not when your arms are burning or cramping with muscle pain.

Joe Simpson wrote, 'Climbing frozen waterfalls appears to the uninformed observer to be a complicated if somewhat novel form of suicide, and quite often this very same thought worms itself uneasily into the mind of the hapless climber.'

An American climbing journal sent a freelance journalist, Greg

Child, out to Chamonix to record a typical Kenton training day. Greg had himself been a world-renowned mountaineer for many years. He wrote:

We're all clammy with sweat when we reach the frozen waterfall. Ropes uncoiled, ice axes leashed to wrists and crampons clamped to boots. 'Baron von Cool', Ran's pet name for his guide, leads us up a swathe of vertical ice. Ran hacks with his ice axes and Cool pulls the rope in on his waist. Despite his mangled hand and awkward grip, Ran swings his ice tool true and confidently, and judging by our relaxed banter, he's well on his way to conquering his lifelong fear of heights. Cool then belays me up. I find that the cold air has rendered the ice so brittle that grapefruit-size chunks of it are exploding all around me as I hack my ice axes into the cascade. Halfway up to the ledge where Cool and Ran are seated I notice a trail of blood. The droplets lead straight to Ran's nose, which an ice shard has neatly slit. He's unperturbed, and he sits on his perch with a bloody grin.

With Cool in the lead, we start up a rambling ice floe near Italy's Cogne Valley, a grade 4+ named Patri. Mini tornadoes of powder snow sting us whenever the wind feels angry. On a low-angled stretch of the route, Ran steps on the rope in his spiked boots – a climbing no-no.

'Get off that bloody thing, Ran,' Cool barks like a rabid drill sergeant.

Ran smiles at me, and steps aside. For an alpha male accustomed to unconditional authority over his expeditions, his deference to Cool is quaint. It's also pragmatic: he knows he's on a learning curve as a climber, and he's soaking up everything Cool can teach.

That day we completed my first Grade Five waterfall, aptly named the Cascade Difficile.

I got to know the mountains above Chamonix quite well through my training with Kenton. The town is possibly the greatest mecca in the world for mountaineers and is dominated by the great rounded summit of Mont Blanc. On average, one climber dies each and every day in and around Chamonix during the summer climbing season. Helicopters fly overhead on rescue missions, and sometimes come back with a bodybag dangling beneath them.

In November 2006 Kenton finally agreed that I could, if I continued my improvement, set a date of 1 March 2007 for the Eiger climb. Meanwhile there were times when he was busy with other clients in the Alps or Himalaya, so he appointed alternative guides for my tuition. One such was Jon Bracey, another Chamonix-based Brit, who led me to my most difficult ascent at that time, the great tooth-shaped block called La Dent du Géant (the Giant's Tooth), a true Alpine aiguille or needle. We only reached the base of the final 600-foot cliff at dusk, so we dug a bivouac into the snow slope at the very base of the rock and carried on the climb after dawn the next day. I didn't relish the unbroken nature of that stark wall and was extremely thankful for the thick rope which some thoughtful soul had fixed all the way up the cliff face to the vertiginous summit.

Climbing guides like Jon, who live in Chamonix and depend upon the Alpine snows for their livelihood, are worried, as is everyone in the winter sports industry, that the Alps are running out of snow. It is true that during Roman times the Alps were warmer even than they are today, but the current speed of warming is what worries French and Swiss scientists. They estimate that the Alps have lost half their glacier ice in the past century, and 20 per cent of that since the 1980s. Swiss glaciers have lost one-fifth of their surface area in just fifteen years. One side effect is an increased incidence of huge rockfalls and avalanches.

Kenton introduced me to various other individuals who are cult figures in the large expatriate British community in the Chamonix area who pay French taxes. One was the Alpine guide and artist Andy Parkin who had suffered appalling fall injuries on some Swiss rockface. He received surgery to his heart, spleen, liver, hip and elbows but, within months of leaving hospital, he was climbing again on highly demanding routes.

By the end of 2006 Kenton professed himself satisfied that there had been 'improvement'. He was a hard taskmaster, which I liked, especially since I am forgetful and inclined to be vague. I need to be shouted at in circumstances where a single absent-minded action (or lack of action) can kill someone. On two occasions over the months I received a major Kenton bollocking for putting my helmet down during rests between climbs with its rounded top on the ground. That way it could slide the more easily down a mountainside.

One day at the base of the Tournier Spur of the Aiguille du Midi, we stopped to take our crampons off, when Kenton yelled, 'Get down', and flung himself sideways. A rock, slightly bigger than a rugby ball, screamed through the air directly towards us from some distant cliff. I copied Kenton's evasive action with less than a second to spare, and the missile thrummed past the point where our heads would have been.

Five minutes later we had to stop to put our crampons on again, and whilst doing so Kenton took his helmet off. To my amazement and great delight he put it down on the snow *the wrong way up*. I screamed at him, 'KENTON!!' Quick as a flash and thinking another flying rock was about to arrive, he crashed to the ground.

'Kenton,' I said, when he had picked himself up warily, 'you put your helmet down the wrong way up. You should never, ever do that. You might lose it on a slope.'

I cannot remember now whether he said 'You bastard' or not, but he was considerably less bossy than usual for an hour or so afterwards.

Most of my climbing back at home had to be squeezed in between lectures and family activities so, since Bristol was a lot closer than Cardiff, Haydn gave me some pointers to instructors there, and by good fortune I ended up in the capable hands of Paul Twomey, the supremo instructor-cum-manager of Undercover Rock, a former parish church taken over as a climbing school for the young and old of Bristol (including, I noticed, the very young and the very old). The atmosphere was happy, excited and frenetic.

It was fun to watch as well as to participate. Each and every wall and nook of the entire church, including the belfry, was crammed with artificial climbing routes, colour-coded for degrees of severity. Paul taught me many excellent rock-climbing tips in the church, and then drove us out to the Avon or Cheddar Gorge for real climbs whenever the rock there was dry.

One hot summer's day, Ian Parnell took me to Cheddar. I watched every move Ian made in order to copy it when he was ready to belay me. One difficult section was only negotiable by holding a rock bulge from below whilst traversing round it. When I reached this rock, aping Ian's every handhold, the entire rock, all 200 pounds of it, came away, knocking me into space. Ian held my fall and the rock landed several metres away from our car in which Louise, Alexander and Elizabeth were sitting. The same face higher up proved too much for me. A key grip, tiny and all but smoothed away by weather, defeated my stumps. Since I could not use my good right hand anywhere useful and my arms ran out of strength, I fell off again.

'Pull me up, please,' I yelled at Ian, unseen but somewhere high above. Either he couldn't or he wouldn't. I tried again and again to find a way up the tricky bit and kept shouting at Ian. He continued to ignore my pleas. I swore (silently) at him. He was Kenton's climbing partner of many years. Between them they had achieved great new climbs on many sheer remote faces. They were the best in Britain, and Ian had agreed to join Kenton and me on our Eiger attempt. Now, I assumed, he was testing me out in cahoots with Kenton. They had plotted this between them. Damn them. With all my strength virtually gone, I was forced to *think* about the bit of rock that was defying my every effort. I spotted a side hold and two finger-holes that I had previously missed but which made all the difference. On my seventh attempt, I made it. I said nothing to a grinning Ian when I reached him, but made up my mind to learn how to ascend the rope itself in case I again came across rock I couldn't manage.

I knew that Ian's opinions of my ability, or lack of it, would be reported to Kenton, who, despite our tentative March 2007 date, had yet to make up his mind finally about the wisdom of taking me up the Eiger Nordwand. I did later see Ian's summary of the climbing.

His hand, damaged by frostbite, of course proved a real hindrance, and at times his 'stumps' would prove completely ineffective at gripping the rock. I'm sure for Ran this was a real frustration, but he didn't let it show. The real big issue, however, was Ran's vertigo. Again, he would say very little and at times you could forget that he was battling a constant fear of heights, but when things got tricky and he became flustered, his vertigo would begin to spiral out of control. During these moments he'd seemingly lose sight of any alternative foot- or handholds other than those right under his nose. Scrabbling for purchase, his feet would start pedalling as though riding a bike over slippery cobbles and his knuckles would be white as he gripped harder and harder. But he wouldn't give up until his arms were so drained of energy that the holds would just melt through his fingers. I did wonder if Ran's proposed ascent of the Eiger would ever happen.

In order to work on overcoming this Kenton introduced me to a Scottish climbing instructor, Sandy Ogilvie, who took me to Swanage one day on the Dorset coast. Halfway across a sea cliff route called the Traverse of the Gods, I lost a key hold and fell in a long pendulum swing, just missing the tide-free rocks below by a metre. I was left dangling free some twelve feet below the nearest point of the rockface. Fortunately, Sandy had explained how to use prussik loops, small cord slings which form rope grips, and clumsily but successfully, I managed to scale the taut rope itself in order to get back up to the rock and continued the climb.

Soon afterwards Sandy took me and the family to the Orkneys to climb the famous Old Man of Hoy. This sea stack was my first truly exposed climb, with a near 400-foot drop to the sea. What helped me considerably was the presence, as third man on the rope, of the freelance reporter sent by *The Sunday Times*, himself a famous climber and author. Stephen Venables had a great sense of humour and was completely unfazed by the exposure. There were two especially nasty places, both of which Sandy from above and Stephen from below talked me over with clear and patient shouted instructions.

But I did it. Stephen later wrote,

Ran shoved and grunted, trouser seat scraping one wall, knees the other. It was all brute strength with little finesse, but the cussed determination was impressive. I also had a struggle getting out of the chimney and round the roof, conscious that there was nothing but fresh air between my feet and the sea-washed boulders over a hundred feet below . . . The accident happened on our way back down from the top, during an abseil. 'Keep to the right,' I shouted, as Ran walked backwards down the cliff, over the big ledge. But he didn't move in time. I heard the throaty rattle of a defiant bird standing its ground, then a violent splatter as the aspiring mountaineer was showered with fulmar bile.

The smell was horrible but at least I had a helmet on, though as Sandy reminded me, it was a helmet with ventilation holes. People steered clear of me for a while that day.

Louise had watched the climb from the mainland clifftop. She confessed to Stephen Venables. 'He's away almost continuously. So either I'm left holding the baby or I have to go everywhere with him.' She hadn't developed a very high opinion of my ability to look after myself either. 'On Everest,' she said, 'I had to stick Ran's heart pills up all over the Base Camp mess tent to make sure he took them.'

Louise, Alexander and Elizabeth flew out to Geneva with me a month after the Hoy climb and Stephen came too. This time our goal was to reconnoitre the Nordwand so that I could actually look at the great wall close up for the first time and, if I realised that it would be folly to have a go at such a climb, I could still cancel things without embarrassing our charity. I knew that on his first attempt Joe Simpson had turned back after climbing part way up. If somebody like Simpson could make such a decision, I realised that I must face up to the unpalatable fact that I might be way out of my league. A lot of the problem, I know, would be entirely caused by my over-active imagination. Jon Krakauer, the famous climber journalist, who once managed to climb halfway up the North face, summed up this tendency well: 'The problem with climbing the North Face of the Eiger is that in addition to getting up 6,000 vertical feet of crumbling limestone and black ice, one must climb over some formidable mythology. The trickiest moves on any climb are the mental ones, the psychological gymnastics that keep terror in check, and the Eiger's grim aura is intimidating enough to ruin anyone's poise.'

At Grindelwald Jon Morgan, one of Kenton's guide friends, took charge and Stephen, Jon and I travelled to the base of the Eiger by train, the amazing legacy of nineteenth-century Swiss railway fever which tunnelled into the North Face itself. We got out at the Eigergletscher station and started walking up the gentle south-west flank of the mountain. Stephen takes up the story:

We were still in shadow, following Jon up scree slopes and occasional little rock steps. When it got steeper he stopped to put Ran on a 'short rope', leading him on a 10-foot tether up hard frozen snow, then a little rock overhang, which got us onto classic Eiger territory – downward sloping tiles of grey limestone, littered with rock debris.

Then suddenly it all changed as we emerged onto the crest of the west ridge proper, where the sloping tiles reached a knife-edge between two utterly different worlds – on one side our rambling sunny slope, and on the other an immense sombre abyss.

Jon lobbed off a rock and counted 15 seconds before hearing its distant clatter. The bottom of the north face was 2,500 feet below.

Ran said nothing. Jon got him to crawl along the edge. Then he made him stand up and walk along the edge. Then he anchored the rope, paying it out slowly as he told Ran to lean right out over the abyss.

Like the well-trained former soldier that he is, Ran obeyed orders, brown eyes still inscrutable beneath bushy eyebrows. Then he admitted: 'That is horrible!'

We dangled him there for about ten minutes, then let him back onto the gentle side where he and I sat in the sun, sharing a sandwich. I asked him why he needed this challenge, and he insisted that he just had to overcome his 'irritating' fear of heights.

Somehow that bluff quip didn't quite account convincingly for this non-mountaineer's ambition to attempt the climb which one of the first ascentionists described as the mountaineer's 'supreme test of stamina, skill and courage'.

Dangling over that 2,000-foot sheer void would, I am certain, have made me realise I could not face climbing up to such a place (nor the other 4,000 feet above) *if* I had actually dared to look down. As it was, I had spent the entire ten minutes focusing as hard as I could on watching Stephen and Jon on the cliff edge just *above* me. On reflection, this rendered pointless the whole rationale of the reconnaissance which was to learn whether or not I could stomach full-scale exposure. I had merely put off the day of reckoning.

Back in France, Kenton drove me to a cliff face known as La Fayet, an hour or so from Chamonix, and introduced me to a climbing technique known as dry tooling, which he advised me would be especially useful for the mixed rock and ice conditions he reckoned we would face on the Eiger. He headed up the cliff with only the very tips of his axes hooked into tiny rock holes or over fractional rock ledges. Sometimes just one axe's tip. His legs often hung in space where there was an overhang or the vertical rock offered no purchase point at all for his crampon spikes. I grew really attached to this, to me, new system because it meant virtually no requirement for me to use my stubby left hand to hold and haul up my bodyweight. This gave me the much needed confidence to decide irrevocably to try the Eiger in March 2007. Both Kenton and Ian Parnell wrote off that entire month in their diaries, and the fundraising machine of Marie Curie clicked into action.

Throughout the post-Everest, pre-Eiger months, I had needed to make a living and accepted lectures to business conferences all over the place. We flew everywhere as a family. One lecture, to 9,000 individuals, all members of the Million Dollar Round Table, in a huge theatre in New Orleans, allowed us a spare day in town. So we walked to the banks of the Mississippi and watched the paddle steamers moored close by. Later that week, after we had left, Hurricane Katrina struck the city, and the conference organisers must have thanked the Lord that they had just got rid of their 9,000 millionaire attendees.

We flew all the way to Sioux Falls via Chicago to lecture to just thirty crop-spray manufacturers in the middle of the prairies. My US-based German friend, Mike Kobold, who had so helped me research the Nazi horrors of the Death Marches, joined us there for a three-day drive to the Black Hills of Dakota and the high sculptures of Mount Rushmore.

We went to Cape Town for a forty-minute presentation and, wanting to show Louise my old home in nearby Constantia, took a taxi there. The entire area had altered beyond recognition. Gone were the open vineyards and the dusty roads. Instead, acres of high security fences and tall dense undergrowth lined both sides of the smart tarmac lanes, and this time I failed even to find the home of my childhood. In between the lectures, we managed to slot in brief holidays, including a week in Transylvania with Abby who had bravely bought a derelict cottage in the mountains close by Castle Bran, the original home of the mythical Count Dracula. We trekked along high ridges and saw wolves and bears, but no vampires.

The Allied Joint Force Command in Naples, part of the United Nations force there, asked me to be guest speaker for their Trafalgar Night Dinner, and a Scottish colonel, Jim Hutton, kindly spent the following day in a jeep tracing from archive material he had researched the exact route along which my father and his tanks of the Royal Scots Greys had advanced in 1944 between their landing at Salerno and his death from a German anti-personnel mine just before the relief of Naples. I was sixty-one years old when I stood for the first time in the leafy Italian lane where my father had been mortally wounded, aged forty-four. I would have loved to have told my mother about that day, reliving his last few months, but, as I have mentioned, she had died the previous year, as had two of his four children. I hope there is an afterlife, as I would love to meet my father for the first time.

On our last day in Naples, I joined two bus-loads of soldiers, sailors and airmen for the annual Vesuvius Half Marathon, uphill all the way to just below the crater and won by a very fit Frenchman. At the prizegiving he was reminded in a (half) joking sort of way that the French hadn't done too well at Trafalgar.

The trouble with being post-middle-aged, I found, was that I needed to spend a lot more time trying to keep fit. The most time-effective way of maintaining basic all-round fitness was jogging but, as the years went by, the number of hours needed per week pounding out the miles kept on increasing if I was still to do things that involved fairly strenuous activity. Added to this, I did not really enjoy the training runs as I once had and was often too busy or travelling when I most needed to put in all those boring jogging hours. My old friend Mike Stroud pinpointed my problem:

> Why is exercise so hard to undertake? Boredom, discomfort, fatigue and lack of time must all be contributory, but there is an additional problem. Goals such as good health in old age are far too nebulous to provide the motivation. For that reason, it is often only those with a more definite short-term goal that succeed. People who need to lose weight, for example, are more likely to continue to put in time and effort than those who are not too fat. If you give yourself a definite aim, exercise acquires a purpose. You need to set yourself a challenge.

This is what saw me, especially in my post heart-attack years, entering the succession of races itemised in Appendix 5.

My old nanny from South African days had been a loving

correspondent ever since I was eight, but she finally died aged ninety-five, having driven until she was ninety. Ginny's mother, Janet, died whilst I was on Everest, and my late sister Sue's husband, John, who I had known for over forty years, died suddenly of a heart attack in March 2006. My family and friends had begun to disperse in an upwards direction, which is what can happen with alarming frequency when you pass by the magic year of sixty.

I reacted by passing all my old photos, maps, polar documents and gear from the 1970s and 1980s to the Royal Geographical Society and the Scott Polar Research Institute. To our regimental museum in Edinburgh Castle, I gave my own medals from the seventies for fighting Marxists, my father's 1940s medals for fighting Nazis, and my grandad's (he had by far the greatest number) for extending the Empire and then defending it in the late nineteenth and early twentieth centuries.

In the African summer of 2005, Louise and I interrupted lectures and climbing training to join a team of white Zimbabweans and Zambians on the Zambezi River to recreate the last few days of Doctor Livingstone's journey to the Victoria Falls. We paddled traditional dugout canoes with steersmen from the same tribe as had accompanied Livingstone exactly 150 years before to the day. We passed a great many hippopotami, an unknown number of crocodiles and, on our arrival at the falls, unveiled a commemorative plaque to the great doctor beside the Zambian edge of the mighty waterfall, which truly deserves its position as one of the seven natural wonders of the world.

After this enjoyable journey to honour a great Scottish explorer, I contemplated switching future activities from the cold regions of the world, whether the Poles, the Himalaya or the Alps, to places where cool breezes, eggshell-blue skies and verdant valleys can be savoured. It was a nice idea, but my more pressing concern was the North Face of the Eiger.

20
Murder Wall

O n 1 March 2007 I flew to Geneva with the family and drove a rental car to Grindelwald, where we stayed at a family-run hotel, the Grand Regina, with a reputation among British tourists of being the best in all Switzerland. The owner, Hans Krebs, had kindly given us accommodation free of charge because he approved of and wanted to help our Marie Curie aims. The hotel manager, Ingo Schmoll, warned us of the consequences of the mountains not being as stable as they should normally be in mid-winter. The rate of retreat of glaciers throughout the Alps, together with the thawing of the permafrost layer, had created temporary barrages of fallen rock blocking high ravines and creating lakes. Increasingly torrential summer rains then burst the feeble dams of rubble, causing flash floods, mudslides and more loosened rock. The previous autumn the Eiger itself had suffered a major rockfall, a chunk bigger than two Empire State Buildings.

Kenton, in Chamonix, was in touch with Ralph Rickli, the famous Swiss met forecaster in Berne, and with the top European weather bureau, the Met Office in Exeter. We needed a clear good weather window of at least five days and nights on the North Face if a non-skilled climber like me was to reach the summit. Kenton and I cleared the whole of March in our diaries and waited. The ITV crew, led by Philip Reay-Smith, installed themselves in a suite with a balcony looking directly opposite the Eiger which was swiftly transformed into a studio resembling a CIA electronic snooper room, with the intention of transmitting the first ever live news footage from the Nordwand. Philip warned me that, once his team was in Grindelwald, we must start the climb. ITV could make no open-ended commitment, since their team had to be on permanent call to go anywhere in the world at short notice. Indeed, Philip sent me an email warning me not to do the climb during the week starting 19 March, because that was ITV's 'Iraq Week' and there would be much less space on the News for non-Iraq-related items.

When I told Kenton this, he snorted, 'If the weather's good for the week of 19 March, and we haven't gone by then, we will set out at once, ITV crew or no ITV crew.' I relayed this back to Philip.

The March days slowly ticked by in Grindelwald, Louise having to return to Britain to take Alexander back to school. I began to find the bulk of the Eiger, looming over the hotel, a touch oppressive. I tried to keep busy. I went for a daily two-hour run out of the village, along hilly lanes and up the glacial ravines. As I ran I heard the intermittent explosions of avalanches from the heights of the Alpine giants all around. After six days of evil weather forecasts, I was padding about Grindelwald increasingly worried that we would never get a five-day clear period in March. Every time I looked out of the window or trudged through the village streets, I found myself looking up at that great black wall, the upper limits obscured in thick fog. One night I couldn't sleep and spotted a single pinprick of light high up on the bulk of the North Face. The very sight of it made my stomach muscles tighten as I imagined having to try to sleep anywhere on that hideous cliff.

I went for a walk to a mountain coffee house and paid £3 in Swiss francs for a 'Rockslide' (coffee spiked with schnapps) named in honour of the recent big Eiger rockfall. I sat there for three hours and frightened myself reading Joe Simpson's Eiger experience in 2002. But at last, our friendly met-experts in Berne and Exeter concurred and a five-day window was forecast for the middle of the month.

Louise and our baby Elizabeth, eleven months old with blonde hair, large blue eyes and a sunny nature, were back in Grindelwald when Kenton confirmed our imminent departure. I tried to hide the fear, almost panic, that surged with the knowledge that we were about to start the climb. Until then there was always the doubt about the weather, the chance that we might not be able to try the climb at least until the following September. But now the die was cast. I did my best not to reveal my wobbly state of mind, especially at the Grindelwald rail station when saying goodbye to my wife and daughter. And later that day, in the hostel at the foot of the Eiger, I needed to work hard to appear unfazed in the boisterous company of Kenton, Ian, the ITV crew and Stephen Venables, who was back reporting for *The Sunday Times*.

We were to leave the hostel for the hour-long snow traverse to the base of the North Face at 4.00 a.m. the next morning and I found sleep elusive that night. I remembered a hundred similar sleepless nights before big moments, but polar fears were something I knew how to handle. Mountain fears were different. I feared my own inadequacies, of being revealed as a coward or, at best, as a wimp. Would the North Face trigger uncontrollable vertigo? Would I freeze to some cliff, unable to move, thereby risking Ian's and Kenton's lives, as well as my own? Never mind the ridicule. And what of a fall? I had by now read all the accounts by far better climbers than myself.

Joe Simpson, survivor extraordinary, wrote about how he felt *as* he fell, apparently towards certain death.

Deprived of the ability to imagine the future, you are fearless; suddenly there is nothing to be scared about. You have no time to ponder on death's significance or fear what it may feel like. In the cataclysmic violence of the accident you lose not only the future but the past as well. You lose all possible reasons for fear, unable as you are to understand the loss of what you once were or what you could become. Time is frozen for you into the present events and sensations, the knocks, and bumps from which you can draw no emotional conclusions. 'I'm crashing. I'm falling fast. I'm about to die. This is it.' In truth you have far too much on your mind for such frivolous luxuries as fear.

One set of fears I had fought against in the 1960s, which had nothing to do with crevasses or frostbite or falling through weak sea-ice, was that of being shot when fighting Marxist terrorists in Dhofar. It was not so much the fear of being killed outright as the thought of some bullet, shrapnel shard or mine blast ripping out my genitals or blinding me. These were the terror images in the mind. To cope, I learned to keep a ruthlessly tight clamp on my imagination. With fear, you must prevent, not cure. Fear must not be let in in the first place. If you are in a canoe, never listen to the roar of the rapid ahead before you let go of the river bank. Just do it! Keep your eyes closed and let go. If the fear then rushes at you, it will not be able to get a grip, because your mind will by then be focusing on the technical matter of survival.

That was all very well when coping with rational fears about what *might* happen. But vertigo is not rational and the trigger likely to set it off was the all too real sight beneath my feet of a great beckoning sickening void. Exactly what would it feel like to spend time cartwheeling, rushing downwards for several thousand feet?

I have been asked, since Elizabeth was born, if I felt guilty risking my life on the Eiger. Perhaps I should, but being aware I could have another heart attack at any moment militates against such guilt feelings. Additionally, I know that Louise is a truly wonderful mother, as mine was, and I grew up without a father. To this day, although I hugely respect his memory, I have never emotionally missed him, for I never knew him, and Elizabeth, not yet one year old at the time of the Eiger, would certainly not remember me. Both Ginny and Louise married me in the full knowledge that I make a living through expeditions and intend to do so as long as I can. So I could feel no more guilt than would, say, a miner or truck driver, both professions with far higher death rates than mine.

Once my alarm went off and I began to check all my gear before a rushed breakfast, the dread thoughts and fears of the night did indeed disperse. We left on time in pitch darkness with Kenton leading. Ian's diary of the week recorded: 'For Ran, although he hid it well, Everest had been a failure. This time round we were to attempt the Eiger North Face, and while we didn't have the barrier of altitude, in my mind this was a much tougher challenge.'

Ian's backpack was heavier than mine, due to all the camera gear, as he was to document the climb and attempt the live ITV News broadcasts. Kenton's pack, also heavier than mine, was festooned with climbing paraphernalia, but I still felt dubious about climbing with a pack that restricted my movement, cramped my arms and limited my ability to look upwards. Dawn crept over the Alps and the mountain tops were tipped with an orange alpenglow. The stars disappeared and the great wall above us came alive. I thought of its German nickname *Mordwand*, or Murder Wall.

Half an hour of trudging along a line of boot prints in deep snow took us to the spot Kenton decided to climb from. We said our goodbyes to Philip and Rob of ITV and to Stephen Venables. They should be able to watch our every move over the next few days, providing bad weather stayed away, through their powerful camera lenses. And at night they should be able to spot the pinpricks of our head torches from wherever we slept.

We fixed on our crampons beneath a feature known as the First Pillar. Many climbers lose the route in this area, but Kenton seemed confident as he stared up at our first obstacle, some 2,000 feet of mixed snow gulleys, loose scree, shiny ledges of smooth, compact limestone and temporarily lodged boulders. Looking away to the flanks of the face, the lofty silhouettes of the peaks of the Wetterhorn and Mittelhorn seemed dwarfed by our own monster.

Few of the infamous Eiger tragedies occurred on this first 2,000-foot climb, but the fallen detritus of many an Eiger incident lay all around us. I remember, from one of the Eiger books, a photograph of climber Edi Rainer's body lying smashed in the scree of this catchment zone. And Chris Bonington, on his Eiger ascent, had among these rubble-strewn lower reaches passed by blood trails and a piece of flesh attached to some bone.

I knew that the world's top soloists, acrobats of the top league, could climb the Nordwand in hours, not days, without ropes, in their sticky-soled rock-shoes, as light as woollen socks. A single slip or false move would see them dead, crushed on the rock, but they survive on the confidence born of their expertise. The mere thought of climbing a single rock pitch unroped made me flinch.

In a few hours, with constant encouragement from Kenton and Ian, I had blundered my way up 1,000 feet or more of the initial rubble slopes. I felt much comforted by the thought that, if my nerve failed as the drop below grew far greater than any climb I had done before, there was a nearby escape hatch, the Eiger tunnel's gallery window or porthole which allows tourists to look out and gasp at the airy void immediately below them.

We must have climbed some 2,000 feet up the mountain when we reached the next recognisable feature, the aptly named Shattered Pillar. I was feeling tired and my neck muscles were aching from the tug of my rucksack harness. But the weather was, as prophesied by the met offices of Berne and Exeter, holding good and clear. Every few hours I tore open a new hand-warmer bag with my teeth and inserted the two tiny pouches into my mitts. They worked well and whenever the sensitive stumps of my amputated fingers began to feel numb with cold, I positioned the hand-warmer pouch over their ends for a while.

I had never climbed on similar rock before, smooth like slate with almost nowhere to provide even the tiniest holding point for the tips of my ice-axes and crampon spikes. At times I had to remove one or other of my mitts with my teeth and use my bare hand to clasp some rock bulge or slight surface imperfection to avoid a fall. This I hated to do, for my fingers, once cold, took for ever to re-warm, even with my heat pouches.

Every now and again I glanced below me without thinking and felt that shock of terror I knew so well which presages the first wave of vertigo. I instantly forced my mind to concentrate on something of interest above me, usually Kenton's progress. On that first day this process worked well for me. I was, due to vanity, keen to prevent Ian and Kenton from glimpsing my fear. With Kenton I may have succeeded, but Ian was a sharp cookie and zealous in his film-making responsibilities. Philip had especially instructed him to record personal emotions and such points of human interest as discord within the group.

At some point on a steep icy slope, to my considerable alarm and dismay, one of my boots skidded off a nub of protruding rock and my left crampon swung away from my boot. Although still attached by a strap, the crampon was useless. Luckily the same crampon had come loose once before, on a frozen waterfall with Kenton a month ago. So I reined in my rising panic and, hanging from one axe and a tiny foothold, I managed, with much silent swearing, to reattach the crampon to the boot.

We came, over 2,000 feet up, to an eighty-foot-high rockface known as the Difficult Crack, which I found virtually impossible, far more technically demanding than any of my previous training ascents, and extremely testing on my puny biceps. To be more precise, my arms felt as though they were being torn from their sockets since, in the almost total absence of any reasonable footholds, I had literally to haul my body and rucksack upwards by arm-power alone. I wished I had spent more time obeying Paul Twomey's instructions to train hard at obtaining some upper body strength. By the time I heaved myself up the last steep and glass-smooth boulder of the Crack, I was on my very last ounce of willpower and wanted only to stop for the day and sleep. Not that there was anywhere remotely suitable in sight to lie down or even sit.

Ian recorded my ascent of the Difficult Crack through the eyes of a top-flight mountaineer who knew I was facing my first big test on the North Face.

Through Ran's two years of training for the route, he proved himself to be a competent and efficient ice and mixed climber, but steep rock tended to bring out his weaknesses. In particular, his ineffectual stumps for fingers on his left hand . . . Ran's worst fear was that he might be forced to climb bare-handed. Luckily he had one big advantage. Whereas Kenton and I spent valuable time fretting and testing the security of the meagre hooks we'd uncovered, Ran, to put it bluntly, was clueless. His technique basically involved dragging his tools down the rock until they somehow snagged, then he would blindly pull for glory. His footwork on rock was similarly polished: a wild peddalling technique that for all its dry tooling naivety was surprisingly effective.

From the top of the Difficult Crack we could look immediately above us at an immense sheer wall, known as the Rote Fluh, smooth, red and infamous for its propensity to shower loose rock-falls on to the face below. A natural desire of all climbers at this point is to ascend as quickly as possible towards the base of this lethal feature, since proximity minimises the danger of being hit. With a bulky backpack, however, speed is not too easy. Balancing like a dainty gymnast in rock-shoes is a far cry from climbing heavily laden with the weight on your back ever threatening to pull your body away from the rock and out into space. From the Crack we still had more than 8,000 feet of climbing, including traverses, on the North Face, much of which, I knew, would be a lot harder and more exposed than had been the eighty-foot-high Crack.

Kenton had planned for us to bivouac the first night at a ledge known as the Swallows Nest. Between the Difficult Crack and this refuge was the infamous Hinterstoisser Traverse, the key passage, unlocking access to the centre of the wall. It was a passage won at considerable cost by its pioneers, two German guides, Andreas Hinterstoisser and Toni Kurz, and two Austrian guides, Willy Angerer and Edi Rainer.

Their story forms a part of the forbidding history of this section of the face. In 1935 a couple of Germans, Sedlmayer and Mehringer, had climbed a record distance up the mountain, but at 3,300 metres they had frozen to death on a ledge. A year later Hinterstoisser and his companions, hoping to set a new record, if not to reach the summit, had reached the ledge of the frozen bodies which with climbers' macabre humour they named Death

Bivouac, only to be themselves turned back by the weather and falling rocks. But fatally they had left no rope in place across their key traverse, and their desperate attempts to reverse their route over this slippery, vertical cliffside all failed. So they tried to rope down to reach the railway's porthole in the rock but disaster overtook them. One fell and dropped free to the valley below, one was strangled by the rope, and a third froze to death. The youngest German, Toni Kurz, dangled from the rope-end a mere 100 metres above the porthole, just out of reach of and conversing with his would-be rescuers. His was a slow, unenviable death.

When we reached their traverse, a relatively new-looking rope, clipped to the rock, disappeared round a bulge at the top of the great slab. My mouth felt dry and my hands weak. This was a moment of truth, and the only way I knew how to face it was by attacking the obstacle in a rush, desperate to keep my mind busy with no tiny chink into which sheer terror could claw, then spread incubus-like and render me a gibbering fool, an embarrassment to myself and to the others. This was my nightmare as I tried to find successive nicks in the glistening rock to place the steel points on my crampons. I gripped the black rope where I had watched Kenton hold it, and edged down around the bulge – and into space. Suddenly, and with a visual impact that took my breath away, there was a panoramic view of the world below. For 2,500 feet under my boots, only the wind touched the plunging rock. My crampons skidded out of their tenuous holds. I gripped the black rope dangling from the rock as my feet scrabbled desperately to find a hold. Into my brain, unbidden, came the picture of my heavy body tearing Kenton off the cliff, and then the deadweight of us both pulling Ian away, and the rush of air as we cartwheeled through space. *Will I scream*, was my main worry, strangely enough.

The first team to climb the North Face had used this same route, and the author of their story, Heinrich Harrer, wrote, 'The rocks across which we now had to traverse were almost vertical, plunging away beneath into thin air. We were full of admiration for Hinterstoisser's brave achievement.'

My own memory of that traverse is thankfully confused. I know that I swore to myself again and again that this was my last climb. I also recall, at some point during that fearful move, focusing on a sudden whiteness in the black rope, the rope upon which I was, in my mind, utterly dependent each time my crampons slipped away from the face. Somehow the rope had become frayed at this point to a single fragile strand.

When I eventually came to the far side of the traverse, Ian recorded:

> Ran emerged near the end looking by his standards pretty nervous – not one to shout his complaints, his eyes which were wide open and out on stalks betrayed what he was really thinking. I kept the ropes tight but couldn't pull him up the final few feet. So, when he started slipping down, his cramponned feet pedalling for purchase on blank rocks, sparks flying, I think he felt desperate measures were needed. The nearest thing at hand to assist him was his ice-axe, so he took an almighty lunge up at the ropes and pulled himself to safety. The only problem was that his 'safety' was reliant on the one centimetre thick cord of nylon he had snagged with his razor sharp axe blade and which secured *me* to the belay.

I clambered past Ian's body and savoured the blessed relief of a solid six-inch ledge under one crampon. I rested on it and felt a wave of exhaustion pass through me. So had I conquered my fear of heights? Had I vanquished my sixty-two-year-old bogeyman of vertigo? I *had* crossed the Hinterstoisser Traverse on the great North Face of the Eiger, so surely I *must* have become a 'proper climber'. And proper climbers surely don't fear heights. Yet I suspected that nothing had really changed. There had been no actual confrontation within myself. No fearful struggle I had bravely and finally won. My only victory thus far had been to prevent the creeping angst getting a grip on me. Day one on the Eiger was almost over without a disaster. Three or four more days, ever higher, lay ahead.

From the end of the traverse, we inched up a seventy-foot

vertical crack to an eighteen-inch-wide ledge beneath an overhang, the Swallows Nest. A scab of frozen snow was stuck to the ledge and we used our axes to flatten this out, giving us some four feet of width and almost standing up space. Ian clipped my waist harness to a rock bolt, and Kenton melted snow over a tiny gas stove. Our bivouac was comfortable but, for me, ruined by the knowledge that, as I lay with my nose up against the rock wall and my knees curled up for warmth in the lightweight sleeping bag, my backside protruded over the edge of our ledge and over the void below.

The world-famous climber, Walter Bonatti, pioneer of some of the hardest cliffs in the Alps, wrote of his own Swallows Nest visit in the 1960s:

> I was not the first man to tackle the Eigerwand alone. Two others had tried in recent years, but both had died in the attempt. The aura of fatality and blood that hangs over this killer mountain seemed painfully distinct to the eyes of a solo climber, restoring it to the atmosphere of the early years.
>
> I appeared on the first snowfield simultaneously with the first thundering salvo of boulders, and I just had time to dodge smartly back into the Swallows Nest before they came shooting by. The incident did not surprise me; it is natural on a face like this that as soon as the upper snow slopes are touched by the sun they should start to unload their wares, and it was by chance that with the whole wide face available they had fallen exactly where I happened to be.

When Joe Simpson and Ray Delaney had bivouacked here seven years before us, two other climbers (Matthew Hayes from Hampshire and Phillip O'Sullivan from New Zealand) had fallen off, roped together, from an icy slope higher up and dropped past this ledge. Simpson had written: 'I thought of their endless, frictionless fall, numbed in their last moments of consciousness by the full enormity of what was happening . . . I stared down thinking of them lying there tangled in their ropes, side by side . . . We didn't hear them go. They didn't scream.'

That could have been their epitaph, I thought. 'They didn't scream.'

During the night a breeze blew ice-dust down the neck of my jacket, and small stones clattered by. I resisted the temptation of rolling over to sleep facing outwards. The clear night sky was crammed with stars, mirrored by the pinprick lights of Grindelwald in the dark valley below. Kenton woke us before dawn. He passed me an empty cloth bag which I filled with snow blocks that I cut, reluctantly, from the end of my sleeping platform. Ian asked me for some item and, unthinkingly, I threw it along the ledge to him, forgetting for an instant where we were. This deserved and got a mouthful of abuse from the others. '*Never*,' they cried in unison, 'throw anything. Pass it over with care.' Ian went on to warn me about my boots and crampons. 'Put them on carefully. It's all too easy with cold hands trying to force a cold foot into a rigid boot to lose your grip and then, before you know it, a boot is gone – a long way. Then you are in *serious* trouble.'

Answering the call of nature during the first day's climb was something I had successfully postponed, but the moment of truth arrived on the narrow ledge. There was a sharp breeze and I felt cold. Squatting between the rock face and the void, I was thankful for the small mercy that I was up one end of the ledge and not, like Ian, in the middle. Luckily I had an empty polythene bag to hand as a receptacle. Nonetheless, I did begin to wonder how climbers cope on big mountain faces having to drink water from the soiled snow floors of oft-used ledges. But then I remembered that the London sewage system provides Londoners with oft-recycled drinking water without even the safeguard of its being boiled on Kenton's gas stove.

Shortly before sunrise, Kenton disappeared upwards from the Swallows Nest. Soon after I followed his lead on to the ice slope above our bivouac, there came an awkward leaning move over the face of a smooth rock. For a while I was flummoxed, but, stretching the axe in my good hand fully upwards, I felt its spike lodge in some unseen nook. Such moments require a blind hope that your sole hold on life will be a reliable one when you make the next move. If it isn't and your sudden bodyweight dislodges the axe's placement, you will plummet downwards hoping not to drag your colleagues with you.

Once over the rock I was on to a long steep icy slope known as the First Ice-Field, and here I heard the whistling thrum of solid matter falling past us, whether ice or rock, I'm not sure. The day before, a small stone had struck Kenton's helmet, and at the base of this First Ice-Field, arrowing upwards at some 55°, a largish lump of ice caught Ian on the helmet.

With careful axe work, I crawled up two steep slopes of mixed rock and ice with extreme caution, for there was a deal of loose rubble just itching to respond to the call of Isaac Newton. After 200 feet negotiating this unstable zone, we scaled the first real ice-field, which I found less difficult than anything to date. It ended all too quickly at the bottom end of a 300-foot-high near-vertical gulley of part-iced rock known as the Ice Hose. I definitely disliked this section which, as an amateur, I find difficult to describe. But I took some comfort from Harrer agreeing with me: 'there isn't a cranny anywhere for a reliable piton, and there aren't any natural holds. Moreover, the rock is scoured smooth by falling stones, bread-crumbed with snow, ice and rubble. It isn't an invitation to cheerful climbing, it offers no spur to one's courage; it simply threatens hard work and danger.'

More stones whistled by as I inched up the Hose but, although I found myself flinching and ducking, none made contact, and the next time I reached Kenton's belay position, he looked happy, clearly pleased we had reached the Second Ice-Field intact. This was the great white sheet easily identifiable from Grindelwald. At some point as we axed our way up it, Kenton saw an ice-axe whistle by us on its way down the face. We never did identify its owner. I shivered at the thought of trying to climb any distance at all on such a mountain with only one axe. The wind picked up on the wide open flank of the ice-field. An explosion sounding further down the face, as we learned later from Philip and his film crew, came from an avalanche of rock and ice roaring down the Ice Hose that we had earlier scaled. The ice climb seemed to go on and on and our ropes were usually slack between each other to the extent that I felt as though I was almost free climbing un-roped. On the many soft snow patches, I took special care to dig in my spikes and axes as deep as I could.

Philip had hired a helicopter to film our ascent of the ice-fields, and he needed to collect all the film Ian had taken with the hand-held videocam. The helicopter dropped a steel hawser down towards us with a black bag on its hook. But the angle of our slope was too steep, so Ian cramponned down and then out towards the centre of the ice-field. Perched on a rock, with no apparent regard for the huge drop below, he attached his film container to the swinging hook. Simply watching him made my blood run cold.

The helicopter disappeared way below us, and we finally reached the upper edge of the ice slope, following it to the left. At this point a difficult rock pitch leads up on to a triangular rock buttress called the Flat Iron. In 1961 two British climbers, Brian Nally and Barry Brewster, were progressing below the buttress when Brewster was hit by a rock and injured. Chris Bonington and Don Whillans abandoned their own ascent to attempt a rescue, but the already unconscious Brewster was swept to his death by rockfall before they could reach him, so they led a seriously disoriented Nally to safety.

Kenton, seeing that I was flagging badly on a difficult section to access the Flat Iron, had pointed upwards. 'Only two or three pitches to Death Bivouac,' he assured me. The name of the place was hardly reassuring. Just then, however, Kenton's promise of its proximity did make it sound a very welcome spot. Again we dug away at a snow-clogged ledge and cleared enough space for the three of us to lie head to toe. I slept well at Death Bivouac for I was tired, but some climbers have found its atmosphere oppressive. The legendary French climber, Gaston Rébuffat, wrote of his time there: 'On this sinister, murderous face, the rusty pitons and rotten ropes dating from the early attempts, the stone wall which surrounded us as we ate, and which sheltered Sedlmayer and

Mehringer before they died, all combined to remind us that the moment you cease climbing toward the summit, success and safety itself are compromised.'

That night my right arm rested on the very edge of a 3,500-foot drop, and Kenton's pan of breakfast muesli tasted none the worse for his half-joking warning that some previous climber had used his end of the ledge, from where he had scooped our brew-up snow, as the Gents.

As before, Kenton set out at dawn. He led some pitches and handed over to Ian for others. I remained always in the middle. Since I was by far the most likely to fall, this system would hopefully minimise the chances of my body dragging both the others off the mountain with me. That, of course, assumed that neither of *them* were knocked off by a rock first.

That day, our third on the Eiger, began badly for my mental state because, expecting to continue heading in an upwards direction, we actually had to move diagonally downwards across an extremely steep slope, known as the Third Ice-Field, to the base of a crucial feature known as the Ramp. This 700-foot-high left-slanting gash overhung by walls of limestone contains many nasty surprises, and was graded in 1997 by two skilled Irish climbers as 'a solid VI.6', a grade more difficult than I could climb without a number of falls when attempted during my British climbing outings. However, I had not used axes or crampons in Britain, so I hoped that they would make a key difference. (For comments on the severity of grading the North Face, see Appendix 4.)

I had read much about the Ramp, which some Eiger pundits describe as the most technically difficult section on the wall. Harrer, one of the first group to try it, wrote, 'The "Ramp" – well, it fits that Face, on which everything is more difficult than it looks. You cannot run up it, for there are no rough slabs, no good foot- or hand-holds. Here too the rock-strata slope outwards and downwards, and the crannies into which a piton can be driven can be counted on one hand.'

Twice over the next few hours, inching up the central chimney of the Ramp, I came within an ace of falling, but on each occasion, my axes caught hold on some tiny unseen nub and halted my downwards rush. There were icy chimneys, awkward rock slabs, tricky and frightening overhangs, side-pulls, hand-palming off sloping holds, and the occasional hand-jamb, all techniques I had been taught by Paul Twomey on his Bristol church climbing walls. Near the upper reaches of the great gully there were two or three stretches of rock that nearly defeated my every attempt. Looking down at any point during the Ramp climb would have been a big mistake, as the airy ice-fields immediately below had a hypnotic effect. Looking up was not to be recommended either in the Ramp's narrower reaches, for then my rucksack lid's contents would jab the back of my neck.

Somewhere on the Ramp in 1961, an Austrian climber with a brilliant repertoire of ultra severe Alpine ascents, the twenty-two-year-old Adolf Mayr, came to grief attempting the first ever solo ascent of the face. Down in Grindelwald, queues of tourists waited their turn to gawp at 'Adi' through the hotel telescopes. Somewhere in the mid-section, at a spot named the Waterfall Chimney, he needed to traverse across wet rock. Watchers below saw him hack at a foothold with his axe. Then he stepped sideways, missed his footing and fell 4,000 feet to his death.

Above the Ramp there were sections of slippery ice and treacherous patches of soft snow into which neither my axes nor my crampons could be trusted to hold firm. By always checking I had three reasonable holds before advancing a leg or arm to a fourth higher hold, none of the many slips that I made proved disastrous, merely heart-stopping at the time.

Unbeknown to me, both my companions had been concerned that the Ramp might prove too technically difficult for my meagre rock-ability and that the expedition would end there. Ian recorded on his camera tape that evening:

> The Ramp is about three pitches high, or three rope lengths high, and the most difficult bit is the final rope length. There is no ice which would give good purchase for the axes, it's only rock. It's

very steep in places and it's also overhanging. That pushes you out and, with the rucksack, all the weight is on your arms. You're looking for features either side on the wall and they are pretty smooth in places, so you are scratching on tiny holds to get up. Ran is doing excellently; today was probably the point at which he could have failed. He managed to do it very well, so we were very pleased.

At one belay I met up with Ian just below a single boulder the size of half a standard UK red postbox. As we conversed a rock struck the boulder and shattered into shards, one of which struck me hard on the helmet. The rest passed harmlessly over our heads. Just above the boulder, Kenton traversed to the right of the straight-to-heaven route we had been following for 700 feet up the gulley of the Ramp. Here we ran out of ice at a place of much loose slate aptly named the Brittle Ledges.

For a while I could find no way up one layer of slate, for every rock I tried to use for a hold simply broke off. My axes were no help. Eventually I had to remove my mitts and bury my bad hand deep into a vertical cleft to achieve the needed purchase. This move coincided with the failure of my last available hand-warmer pouch. Resupplies were unobtainable deep in my rucksack, and my hand soon grew numb with cold. This was bad timing because, above the Brittle Ledges, Ian led up a vertical wall of slate about ninety feet high. Maybe I was too tired to think clearly, or perhaps my cold, numb left hand, incapable of gripping anything but my ice-axe (and that thanks only to the crutch of its wrist loop), left me pretty much one-armed at the time.

Whatever the reason, I worked harder and with greater desperation on that single ninety-foot wall than on any previous part of the North Face. Despite the brittle nature of the rock, the first few metres up from a little snow-covered ledge on to the Brittle Crack are really overhanging. The upper twelve feet involved an appallingly exposed traverse around a corner with space shouting at you from every direction. The tiny cracks and sparse piton placements available for my axes disappeared as I neared the top.

All apparent handhold bulges were smooth and sloped downwards, and my bare fingers simply slid off them. My arms and my legs began to shake, my biceps to burn. Pure luck got me to the ice patch that capped the wall, into which I sank an axe with great relief and hauled myself up, a wreck, to the tiny snow ledge where a grinning Ian was belayed.

'This is it,' he said. 'We spend the night here. Lovely view.'

A bit of axe burrowing formed a fairly comfortable ledge for the three of us, and again the mental stress and physical toil of the day overcame my worries about that drop a few inches away from my sleeping position. I lost a mitt off the ledge during the night, but I had a spare immediately available. The stumps of my left-hand fingers ached, but far less than all ten fingers had hurt on most polar trips. I felt fine as I fell asleep, worried only by tales I had heard of two of the obstacles to be faced the next day, the hugely exposed Traverse of the Gods and the technical problems of the final Exit Cracks, rated more difficult than the Ramp. I had just spent hours ascending by far the most difficult climbing of my admittedly short climbing life, and yet, by repute, the worst lay ahead.

Ian recorded his night perched above the Brittle Crack, during which he was scheduled to conduct a live interview. This, according to our ITV friends, would – if it worked – be the first time ever that anyone had managed a live interview on the national news from somewhere as remote as the Eiger Nordwand. A digilink was used in order to achieve this, utilising microwaves to send high-quality television images through the air so that Philip and the ITV crew at the base of the mountain could see and talk to me. Ian recorded:

I knew the film crew were getting my footage from the helicopter long line pick-ups of my tapes, but I really wanted to make a breakthrough and manage a live broadcast with Ran being interviewed on the face. I'd painstakingly shivered through the hour of preparation and tested both previous evenings, but first communication problems scuppered things and then a breaking story of a stabbed Welsh vicar knocked us off the News roster. This time, as I knelt on the edge of the drop, camera held out in one hand and the broadcast antennae in the other, I felt a muscle begin to spasm in cramp. 'Three minutes to go', and the cramp starts an inexorable rise up my back. 'Two minutes, could you hold the camera steady, Ian', and my neck has joined the knot. I try to meditate and breathe through pain. 'Thirty seconds, keep the light on Ran', and I'm gasping for air now. Must try to stop breathing. 'So, Ran, could you tell us how you keep your spirits up in such hostile terrain?' It's happening, we're live! 'Excellent, chaps, you can relax now. London says it's some of the best footage they've seen all week.'

On the morning of our fourth day on the face, I woke with a dry mouth and butterflies fluttering about in my stomach. Joe Simpson's professional description of the Traverse of the Gods was clear in my mind. 'For 400 feet the points of protection – weak, damaged pitons, battered into shattered downward-sloping cracks – are marginal to say the least. Most climbers would prefer not to weight such pitons statically, let alone fall onto them . . . and the drop beneath the climber's feet is 5,000 feet of clear air . . . The hardest climbing comes right at the end of the traverse around a protruding prow of rock and close to the edge of the Spider.'

In the valley below, Stephen Venables, who had climbed the North Face over twenty years before, watched our every move through binoculars. He wrote: 'Taking crampons repeatedly on and off is not an option, so Ran had to tread with steel points on snow, ice and bare rock. Terrified of damaging the shortened fingers of his left hand, he kept his mitts on, gripping as best he could. He knew that if he fell, he would go for a huge swing over the void before the rope held him.'

Stephen was assuming that the rope would hold me, but, having just come away from the unreliable region of the Brittle Crack, I envisaged the scenario of a pendulum plunge with my full weight tearing out the feeble flaky placements, together with both Kenton and Ian who were attached to them.

The Irish climber, Paul Harrington, who had climbed the Traverse of the Gods at exactly this time of year, had observed: 'Everything revolved around balancing crampon points on snow-covered ledges. There were no positive handholds. Only rock that could be pushed down upon to take some weight off the feet. It was a psychological passage.' Ian was behind me as I stepped out along this hellish cliffside. He described his thoughts. 'It's dramatic, nervy climbing for experienced climbers, but for someone like Ran who suffers from vertigo, it can easily become a complete nightmare. The rock here is loose, covered in verglas in winter and frighteningly exposed. In fact, at one point your heels overhang the whole drop of the wall to the snows of Kleine Scheidegg below.'

Suddenly, well ahead of me and appearing to be glued to the sheer wall merely by his fingertips and booted toes, Kenton disappeared around an abrupt corner. For no good reason this unsettled me badly. Behind me, Ian observed my reactions:

He is no drama queen, so I didn't expect him to break down sobbing, but by the methodical and calm way he worked across the first half of the traverse, he looked to be in complete control. Once he'd disappeared out of sight, I packed up my cameras and began climbing. It soon became evident that all wasn't as well as it seemed on the surface. I can't repeat Kenton's comments here, but it was a classic example of what is known in British alpine circles as a 'Kentrum' – the toys were well outside the pram. The issue seemed to be that, caught out of rope, Kenton had been forced to take a belay on two pathetic rotting bits of tat. Ran, swinging round to the second half of the traverse, felt the full impact of the sickening exposure and suffered an attack of the vertigo he'd so far successfully kept at bay. Reeling in their own worlds, a frank exchange of views followed.

Ian's interpretation of events was close to the mark. Something snapped as soon as I rounded the sharp bend in the wall. I may have inadvertently allowed myself a glimpse downwards beyond my normal carefully regimented focus point – my crampon points and not an inch beyond them. The onrush of sheer terror that this error sparked coincided with a tightening of the rope between me and the still invisible Kenton.

'Give me slack,' I shouted.

I had the rope back to Ian jammed behind me round an ice nub. I had to retreat a metre to loosen it. I was teetering on my front points on a mere rock scratch. I was terrified. My voice rose to a bellow.

'GIVE ME SLACK!'

This brought a furious response from my unseen leader. Furious, but to me unintelligible, so I had no idea what his problem was, no idea that his position was precarious. He knew that, if I fell at that moment, he was unlikely to be able to maintain a hold on the mountain. He was desperately doing his best to screw ice-screws in to improve his belay point. The last thing he wanted to do was to give me slack.

Fortunately, my instant reaction to the angry tone of his voice was to get angry myself, and that eclipsed the power of the vertigo attack. I controlled myself, closed my eyes, thought of a huge plate of steaming porridge laced with maple syrup and clung to the miserable rock face. After an age, or so it seemed, I felt slack rope from Kenton, reached back to flick Ian's rope free, and crept onwards above that sickening drop until I could see the still muttering Kenton perched on a patch of naked ice. I joined him and stayed silent as he berated me for my impatience, knowing that his moods of thunder never lasted long and were usually well deserved. There was nobody, not even Ian, who I trusted so completely in what, to me, was the most frightening environment on earth. Without Kenton, I could never have even contemplated setting foot on the Eiger's North Face.

'Lighten up,' Ian advised Kenton. They knew each other well.

We moved fairly quickly up the steep hard ice of the White Spider, so called due to its shape – a blob of white ice with white gulleys stretching up and down from its centre for hundreds of feet. In bad weather detritus from above can turn the Spider into a death zone for any climber caught on its face. Above and just to the right of the Spider was another, smaller ice-field, the Fly.

I crawled up the Spider. I felt really tired; perhaps due to the stress of the Traverse of the Gods or because the previous three days of climbing had slowly taken their toll on my reserves of fitness. I was also getting clumsy in a place where this was inadvisable. The sun beat down from a clear sky and the extreme exertion of hauling myself and my rucksack ever upwards made me sweat. Kenton, at a belay, helped me take off my windproof jacket, but I fumbled and lost my grip on it. A breeze grabbed it and, in an instant, it slid away down the slope, gathering speed. A bad item to lose at that height on the Eiger. We still had 1,000 feet to go straight up a maze of intricate gulleys, the notorious Exit Cracks, the final chimney of which included two rope-lengths up a near vertical ice staircase with the treads all sloping the wrong way.

From the White Spider on there were many obstacles that would, back in the Avon Gorge or on the Welsh sea cliffs, have been too much for my inadequate technical skills and lack of upper body strength. But this was the last rock problem I would face. The summit was tantalisingly close, so I attacked each new problem as though my life depended on it. Perhaps it did. The walls on both sides of various grooves and chimneys were smooth, featureless and often at eighty degrees. I remember a whitish wall called the Quartz Crack which looked evil but turned out to be merely nasty. And a smooth walled runnel which nearly stopped me and where Kenton pointed to a tiny ledge. 'Corti Bivouac,' he said, and I remembered Harrer's tale of this Italian wrongly accused of cutting his companions' rope.

Corti and Longhi had joined up with two top German climbers in 1957 down near the Hinterstoisser Traverse. They later missed the Traverse of the Gods altogether and tried to reach the Spider by a far more perilous route. Longhi fell 100 feet on to a ledge, where he sat for five days before he died. His body dangled on the rope for two years, ogled by telescope tourists. High in the Exit

Cracks Corti took a bad fall, so the Germans gave him their tent and key supplies and climbed on, hoping to raise help. Corti camped on a tiny ledge, the one Kenton showed me, until he was eventually rescued by the pioneering use of a winch cable from the summit. Longhi was too far below to be saved. The Germans disappeared and Corti was suspected of being responsible for their deaths until, four years later, their bodies were found. They had reached the summit, but died of exposure on their subsequent descent down the western flank.

I had reflected more than once on our climb how often Ian and Kenton must secretly have dreamt of cutting their ponderous client off their rope, since I knew they could both move like ballerinas over ice or rock as a team of two. Mountaineering was their passion and their profession and they had reached the pinnacle amongst their brilliant international peers.

The nightmare of the Exit Cracks ended with a great pendulum traverse, way to the left of our previous axis of ascent, a long icy shute and a treacherous bulge of mixed shale and snow, both ingredients being unpleasantly loose underfoot. The evening sun was welcoming as we emerged from the last of the gullies. I craned my neck, arching my back, and saw a wonderful swathe of open sky where for four long days I had seen only the ever-rising, dark wall of the Eiger. Above us now was only a steep wall of snow and ice leading up to a knife-edge, the summit ridge. This sharply angled snow wall was the reservoir, the source of the avalanches that sweep down the North Face. New, often wet, snow that settles here frequently fails to cohere firmly with the névé and ice beneath and sloughs away in lethal waves down the Exit Cracks, out over the Spider and beyond.

Ian led up this last steep climb, taking his time with care and caution. From an ice-screw belay I paid out Ian's rope. I could see the outline of his rucksack high above as he fixed another screw into the snow. He straightened up to move off and I felt the rope go taut. I obviously had him on too tight a leash. I quickly paid out more rope, looking down at the coils to check against knots forming. At the same moment, Ian, caught off balance by the taut rope, had slipped, fallen over on to his back and begun to slide head first down the Eiger.

He wrote later: 'I began to head down towards Grindelwald. Kenton luckily heard my screams, saw that Ran was paying *out* the rope and yelled at him. This seemed to reawaken Ran to the appropriate rope procedures and, thankfully, my downwards journey was brought to an abrupt halt.'

By dusk we had reached the knife-edge snow cornice of the summit ridge, but were still some thirty minutes and 300 metres below the actual summit further along the Mittellegi Ridge. So Kenton selected a nook on the far, southern side of the cornice, where we spent an hour digging out a platform for the sleeping bags. Ian's notes recorded: 'We had an awful night. There was no reception on the mobiles, so we couldn't communicate with anyone or do the live broadcast. Then I dropped the ITV camera over the edge – but we were so knackered and it was so cold. It was a spectacular ridge to the summit, so it was a really nice finish. I'm pretty proud of what we had done. Particularly for Ran.'

We spent eleven hours in the snow dugout, and I remembered, nearly two years before, thinking I had a good chance of summitting Everest because Ian and I had spent that last pre-summit night at some 400 metres below Everest's summit ridge. Almost there. And I never made the summit. Now here we were again, a mere 300 metres below another summit. Ian considered the Eiger North Face a far more difficult ascent than Everest's North Ridge, but this time I had no cardiac troubles lying in wait, for we were at a mere 14,000, not 28,000 feet.

We left the bivouac at 9.30 a.m. and threaded our way towards the summit along a classic knife-edge ridge. Ian wrote: 'Kenton led us with Ran in the middle and myself last in our little line. I was acutely aware that if Ran began sliding down one side of the ridge, it was my job to throw myself off the opposite side of the mountain, arresting our fall in a seesaw effect.'

At 10.00 a.m. on the fifth day of our climb we reached the

summit. Thanks entirely to the brilliance and the patience (usually!) of Kenton and Ian. Within half an hour of our arrival there, an evil-looking cloud bank raced over the mountain ranges to the south, soon to envelop the Eiger. Our weather forecasters had got it dead right. As we descended down the easy side of the ridge I felt deliriously happy to be back on comparative *terra firma*. I made up my mind to steer clear of all mountains in the future . . . probably. It was great to learn that within a week of our return, our friends at Marie Curie Cancer Care had already raised £1.4 million towards our £1.5 million target, with hopes that our Marie Curie Eiger Challenge Appeal would top out at well over £3 million before it closed down.

The climbing training over the last two years has resulted in a lot less running, so I must try to get fit again. And expeditions, whether polar, archaeological or up mountains, do not provide any personal income, so I need to get back on the lecture circuit, along with the US ex-presidents and failed *Big Brother* contestants. As for the next expedition, that depends on who comes up with what suggestion, who agrees to sponsor it and which charity wants to benefit from its proceeds, should it succeed. I would love to reach the figure of £15 million raised for charities before I die, for that is a good sounding round figure to aim for, and I am two-thirds of the way there to date.

For a great many years I have been lucky with the very best of families, friends and good fortune at dicey moments. The future may still hold interesting times. Only yesterday, on 20 July as I finished writing this book, I received an email from Mike Stroud . . . 'Any wild ideas for a trip together would be very much welcome.' I do have an idea or two to put to him.

Appendix 1

I believe we are each very much congenital victims or beneficiaries. Of course there are twists of fate whereby the occasional house-painter's bastard becomes a Führer or a grocer's daughter an Iron Lady, but in the main we run life's course the way we do because of our hereditary make-up. We are each the sum total of a chain of ghostly sires, generation upon generation of evolving characters, of actions good or evil, the vibrations of which pass silently on, foetus to foetus, until there is you and there is me.

On the pages that follow is a family tree of my ancestors. They have owned land in southern England since the days of an Ingelram Fiennes who lived around AD 1100. His family became anglicised and have lived here continuously since 1260. Earlier they were based in the village of Fiennes, which lies between Calais and Boulogne in France.

There are, of course, many members of the family, dead and still alive, not included on this simplified family tree.

KING CHARLES the GREAT
AD 800
(EMPEROR CHARLEMAGNE)

His daughter, BERTHE

The Dukes of PONTHIEU

EUSTACHE FIENNES
(died 1144)

Fought for the Normans at Battle of
Hastings, 1066, but other Fiennes family
members fought on the English side.
Eustache was given English land by William
the Conqueror. His brother-in-law founded
Beaulieu Abbey.

INGELRAM FIENNES — married SYBIL de TINGRIES, heiress to the Dukes of Ponthieu.
Through Sybil's dowry, the Fiennes family inherited English manors
at Martock, Wendover and Carshalton, all of which they lost in the
Hundred Years' War. Ingelram was killed at the Battle of Acre in
1189, as was his cousin Tougebrand Fiennes, close companion to
King Richard Coeur de Lion. Another cousin killed in the Crusades,
John Fiennes, donated his heart to the citizens of London along with
a burial plot, still known as Finsbury Square.

WILLIAM de SAYE I
(died 1144)

Moved from Saye, Normandy, to England.
Fought with the Earl of Essex against King
Stephen.
Killed at Burwell.

WILLIAM de SAYE II
(died 1177)

Captured seven knights single-handed at the
Battle of Saintes. At the Battle of Lewes, he
fought with King Henry III against the
barons.

His brother
GEOFFREY de SAYE I
(died 1214)

Helped ransom King Richard I from the
Germans. He was one of the twenty-five
barons to sign Magna Carta.

GEOFFREY de SAYE III
(died 1321)

Fought for King Edward II vs. the Scots and
the Earl of Lancaster. In 1318 he was jailed for
consorting with the outlaw Robert Coleman.

ENGUERRAND FIENNES

Married the daughter of King Alexander of Scotland. Enguerrand,
Lord of the Fiennes clan in Artois, was responsible for the Wars of the
Roses since his direct descendants included the main protagonists,
Edward IV, Richard III, Henry IV and Henry V, Henry Stafford, Duke
of Buckingham.

ENGUERRAND FIENNES

Married Isobel, daughter of King Edward III.

GEOFFREY DE SAYE I
(died 1359)
Fought at Crecy, 1346. In 1339 as Admiral of the Fleet, he captured the French fleet at the battle of Sluys.

JEHAN FIENNES
Fought against King Edward III's English. Jehan was one of the five famous 'Burghers of Calais' who offered their lives in exchange for a promise not to massacre the citizens.

His son, an MP, married MAUDE MONCEUX.
Fiennes family inherit Herstmonceux.

ROGER FIENNES
A constable of the Tower of London. He married the heiress of the Dacre family, so this branch became the Lord Dacres of Herstmonceux.

THOMAS FIENNES, LORD DACRE
Imprisoned for collusion with thieves.

THOMAS FIENNES, LORD DACRE
Courtier of King Henry VIII. On jury of Anne Boleyn's trial. Bore canopy at Jane Seymour's funeral. Hanged at Tyburn for poaching neighbour's deer.

JOAN SAYE married WILLIAM FIENNES

JAMES FIENNES, 1st LORD SAYE AND SELE
Because the male descendants of the Sayes died out, their grandson James inherited. He was born in 1395 at the dawn of the Civil War. Created a baron in 1447, he chose the title Saye and Sele after a Benedictine Priory which he owned. He became Lord High Treasurer but, in 1459, things went sour. For years, with his son-in-law the Sheriff of Kent, he had practised large-scale extortion in Sussex and Kent, to the fury of the locals, including various Fiennes cousins. Now, an angry mob of southern gentry and clerics, including several Fiennes cousins, went to London and demanded retribution from King Henry VI. Their leader, Jack Cade, lived at Herstmonceux and may even have been a member of the Fiennes family, since Cade is known to have been an alias. Cade had James Fiennes beheaded in 1450.

WILLIAM 2nd LORD SAYE AND SELE
Married the heiress of William of Wykeham and inherited Broughton Castle near Banbury. As a soldier in France he was twice taken prisoner and ransoms forced him to sell the Knole estates in Kent. During the Wars of the Roses he fought for Earl Warwick, the King Maker, at the Battle of Northampton, where King Henry VI was deposed. At the Battle of Towton in 1471 he fought for the Yorkists while his cousin, Ranulph Fiennes, a Lord Dacre, was killed fighting for the Lancastrians at the Battle of Barnet.

GREGORY FIENNES, LORD DACRE
Queen Elizabeth I
restored the Dacres' lands confiscated
after his father's disgrace.

(This branch of the family died out.)

NATHANIEL FIENNES
Roundhead Colonel.

CELIA FIENNES
Famous traveller who rode around England on horseback
annotating everything she saw. A nursery rhyme about her
survives to this day: 'Ride a cockhorse to Banbury Cross to
see a Fiennes (fine) lady upon a white horse . . .'

WILLIAM FIENNES, 8th LORD SAYE AND SELE
Founded a settlement along the Connecticut River which he called Saybrook. With Hampden and
Pym he plotted against King Charles I, although he was not in favour of regicide. When war broke
out in 1641, William and his four sons raised a cavalry regiment. Prince Rupert's Royalists routed
the Fiennes troops at Edgehill and King Charles's troops captured Broughton Castle. William
became known as 'Old Subtlety', for he managed to retain the trust of both sides throughout the
Civil War. After the restoration, Charles II elevated William to Lord Privy Seal.

JAMES FIENNES, 9th LORD SAYE AND SELE
Hero of Baroness Orczy's novel *The Honourable Jim.*

Daughter CECIL TWISLETON, BARONESS
married COLONEL TWISLETON

Daughter CECIL TWISLETON, BARONESS
SAYE AND SELE eloped, aged fifteen, with her cousin GEORGE TWISLETON

GEORGE FIENNES TWISLETON, 11th BARON SAYE AND SELE
Fought with Duke of Marlborough. Adjutant-General during Quebec Campaign.

JOHN FIENNES, 12th BARON SAYE AND SELE
Constable of Dover Castle.

GREGORY TWISLETON FIENNES, 14th BARON SAYE AND SELE
Lived to be the 'Oldest Whig in the House of Lords'.

WILLIAM FIENNES, 15th BARON SAYE AND SELE
Friend of the Prince Regent. He once left a note to his valet: 'Put 6 bottles of port by my bedside and call me the day after tomorrow.'

FREDERICK FIENNES, 16th BARON SAYE AND SELE
Archdeacon of Hereford. His mother's second cousin was Jane Austen. By Royal Licence, this Baron restored the old family name to make him Twisleton-Wykeham-Fiennes.

JOHN TWISLETON-WYKEHAM-FIENNES, 17th LORD SAYE AND SELE
His horse Placida won the Oaks.

EUSTACE TWISLETON-WYKEHAM-FIENNES
After three years as a fur-trapper and later as a Canadian Mountie, he travelled widely in Africa and fought in the Boer War. Became Private Secretary to Winston Churchill and served in Gallipoli during the First World War. Was later created Baronet of Banbury. Governor of the Seychelles and, later, the Leeward Islands.

GEOFFREY TWISLETON-WYKEHAM-FIENNES, 18th LORD SAYE AND SELE

IVO TWISLETON-WYKEHAM-FIENNES, 20th LORD SAYE AND SELE

LT. COL. SIR RANULPH TWISLETON-WYKEHAM-FIENNES, BARONET
Commanded Royal Scots Greys 1942–3. Died of wounds in Italy 1943.

OLIVER TWISLETON-WYKEHAM-FIENNES
Dean of Lincoln. Rtd.

THE AUTHOR married Virginia Pepper 1970. She died in 2004.

NATHANIEL FIENNES, 21st LORD SAYE AND SELE
Current incumbent of Broughton Castle, open to the public.

Appendix 2

The individuals involved with the travels I have enjoyed over the years include:

Norway 1961
Simon Gault, Maggie Raynor

Pyrenees Crossing by Mule 1962/63
Hamish Macrae, Pat Offord, Maggie Raynor

Norway 1967
Peter Loyd, Simon Gault, Nick Holder, Don Hughes, Martin Grant-Peterkin, Vanda Allfrey

Nile 1969
Peter Loyd, Nick Holder, Charles Westmorland, Mike Broome, Anthony Brockhouse; UK: Ginny Pepper

Norway 1970
Roger Chapman, Patrick Brook, Geoff Holder, Peter Booth, Brendan O'Brien, Bob Powell, Henrik Forss, David Murray-Wells, Vanda Allfrey, Rosemary Alhusen, Jane Moncreiff, Johnnie Muir, Gillie Kennard; UK: George Greenfield

Canada 1971
Jack McConnell, Joe Skibinski, Stanley Cribbett, Ginny Fiennes, Sarah Salt, Bryn Campbell, Ben Usher, Richard Robinson, Paul Berriff, Wally Wallace; UK: Mike Gannon, Spencer Eade

Greenland/North Pole 1976/78
Oliver Shepard, Charlie Burton, Ginny Fiennes, Geoff Newman, Mary Gibbs; UK: Mike Wingate Gray, Andrew Croft, Peter Booth

Transglobe 1979/82
Oliver Shepard, Charlie Burton, Ginny Fiennes, Simon Grimes, Anton Bowring, Les Davis, Ken Cameron, Cyrus Balaporia, Howard Willson, Mark Williams, Dave Hicks, Dave Peck, Jill McNicol, Ed Pike, Paul Anderson, Terry Kenchington, Martin Weymouth, Annie Weymouth, Jim Young, Geoff Lee, Nigel Cox, Paul Clark, Admiral Otto Steiner, Mick Hart, Commander Ramsey, Nick Wade, Anthony Birkbeck, Giles Kershaw, Gerry Nicholson, Karl Z'berg, Chris McQuaid, Lesley Rickett, Laurence Howell, Edwyn Martin, John Parsloe, Peter Polley and others; UK: Anthony Preston, David Mason, Janet Cox, Sue Klugman, Roger Tench, Joan Cox, Margaret Davidson, Colin Eales, Elizabeth Martin, Sir Edmund Irving, Sir Vivian Fuchs, Mike Wingate Gray, Andrew Croft, George Greenfield, Sir Alexander Durie, Peter Martin, Simon Gault, Tommy Macpherson, Peter Windeler, Peter Bowring, Lord Hayter, Dominic Harrod, George Capon, Anthony Macauley, Tom Woodfield, Sir Campbell Adamson, Jim Peevey, Eddie Hawkins, Eddie Carey, Peter Cook, Trevor Davies, Bill Hibbert, Gordon Swain, Captain Tom Pitt, Alan Tritton, Jack Willies, Graham Standing, Muriel Dunton, Edward Doherty, Bob Hampton, Arthur Hogan-Fleming, Dorothy Royle, Annie Seymour, Kevin and Sally Travers-Healy, Jan Fraser, Gay Preston, Jane Morgan, Jack Willes

North Pole 1986/90
Oliver Shepard, Mike Stroud, Laurence Howell, Paul Cleary, Beverly Johnson; UK: Ginny Fiennes, Alex Blake-Milton, Andrew Croft, George Greenfield, Perry Mason, Dmitry Shparo, Steve Holland

Ubar 1991
Juris Zarins and team, Nick and Kay Clapp, Ginny Fiennes, Ali Ahmed Ali Mahash, Ron and Kristine Blom, Trevor Henry, Andy Dunsire and team

Alaska, Arctic and Antarctica 1993/2000
Gordon Thomas, Dmitry Shparo, Laurence Howell, Morag Nicolls, David Fulker, Bill Baker, Graham Archer, Charles Whitaker, Granville Baylis, Steve Signal, 'Mac' Mackenney, Steve Holland, Mike Stroud, Oliver Shepard, Charlie Burton

Seven Marathons/Seven Days/Seven Continents 2003
Mike Stroud, Steven Seaton, Mike Kobold, Tony Brown, Giles Whittell, Gill Allen, Robert Hall, Julie Ritson. UK: Ginny Fiennes

Everest 2005
Paul Sykes, Sibusiso Vilane, Ian Parnell, Neal Short, Jens Bojen, Mark Campbell, 'Boca' Lama (Nima Dorje), Louise Fiennes

Eiger North Face 2007
Paul Sykes, Kenton Cool, Ian Parnell, Louise Fiennes

Major Financial Sponsors
Pentland, Damart, Dyson, British Aerospace, British Airways/ Terry Beuacqua, Occidental Oil, Land Rover, Excel, Paul Sykes

Charity Beneficiaries
The Multiple Sclerosis Society, Breakthrough Breast Cancer, Cancer Research Campaign, British Heart Foundation, Marie Curie Cancer Care
(Total raised by 2007: £10 million plus)

Note

A book about the *M.V. Benjamin Bowring* by Anton Bowring, telling the full story of the Transglobe voyage, is expected to be in bookshops in 2008/09.

The original film of the Transglobe Expedition is now available on DVD. The three-year, 52,000-mile journey across deserts, oceans, the North West Passage and both Poles was recorded on film by Armand Hammer Productions. Written, produced and directed by William Kronick, the film is narrated by Richard Burton, with a music score by John Scott. It is available (on DVD region 2, UK & Europe only) for £20 from the Transglobe Expedition Trust, c/o 30a Broad Street, Bungay, Suffolk NR35 1EE (Tel. 01728 604434). For further information and details about the Transglobe Expedition Trust, see the expedition website www.transglobe-expedition.org or email TGExpedition@aol.com.

Appendix 3
Land Rover 7x7x7 Challenge
(Route as planned by British Airways)

The results of the challenge raised large sums for our charities in the relevant countries and by 2007 had not been successfully repeated. The timings were all under 5 hours, except for Singapore and New York. The schedule was in outline:

Date	Location	Completion
27 Oct	Patagonia, S. America Through the Passage of the Great Explorer	3 hrs, 45 mins
28 Oct	Falklands, S. Antarctica Islands Through the hinterlands of Castle Falklands, past mine fields, to Government House	4 hrs, 41 mins
29 Oct	Sydney, Australia, Australasia Over Sydney Harbour Bridge, past the Opera House and through the Botanical Gardens – six times	4 hrs, 41 mins

30 Oct	Singapore, Asia Cordoned off route through the parks of Singapore and the central business district	5 hrs, 24 mins
31 Oct	London, Europe The Olympic marathon route of 1908 from Windsor Castle to White City	4 hrs, 40 mins
1 Nov	Egypt, Africa From the Sphinx to the Pyramids from midnight till dawn	4 hrs, 19 mins
2 Nov	New York, North America Through the streets of New York finishing at Central Park as part of the annual New York City marathon (we finished 28,362 out of 35,000 runners)	5 hrs, 23 mins

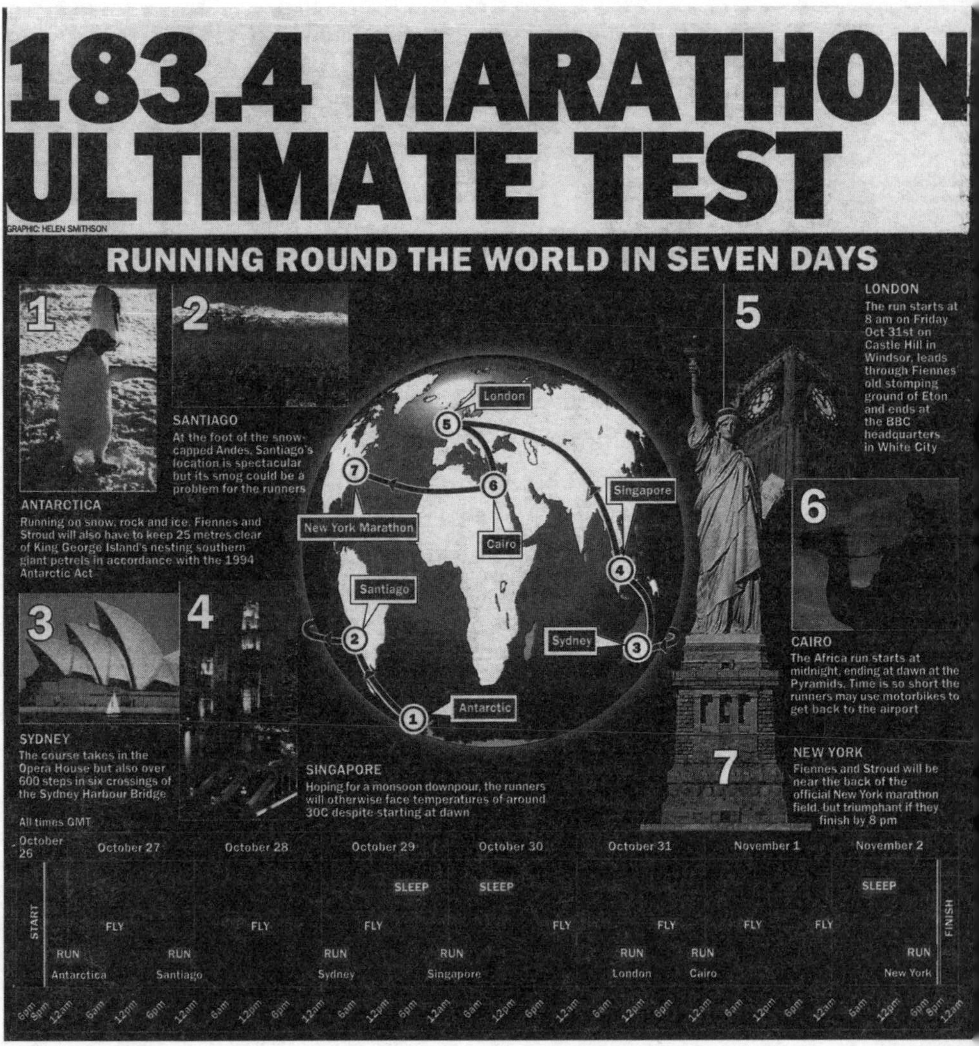

© The Times/Helen Smithson (graphic) 21 October 2003

Appendix 4
Endurance Running

The last year when I can remember feeling reasonably fit was the year after my finger amputations in 2000. I was fifty-seven and averaging three 2½-hour runs most weeks of the year. I ran the London Marathon in 3 hours 39 minutes, some nine minutes slower than my best time in 1999, and, after many years of failing to complete either the Karrimor or the Lowe Mountain Marathons, I entered both with a top adventure racer, Gary Tompsett from Edinburgh. His memories of the Karrimor 2001 were: 'We surprised everyone and ourselves as we survived the attrition of the terrain with our diesel-powered legs and good navigation, whilst the Ferraris around us fell apart, including the Swedish teams who made good scalps. We were 12th in the Elite. This dispelled the myth that you couldn't complete these events.'

Later in 2001 we teamed up again for the Lowe Mountain Marathon, targeting the Veterans' Trophy in the Elite grade. We had to overcome the age handicap system by a long chalk. We did, coming 12th overall in the Elite and first in the Vets.

In the winter of 2002, with top British endurance racers Ski Sharp, Steven Seaton and Anna McCormack, I entered the Southern Traverse adventure race based from Queenstown in New Zealand. Steven and Anna had to drop out for health reasons three days into the race, so Ski and I joined up with the remnants of another team. Together we ended up in 14th place. This race was extremely demanding, with long stretches of cross-country running, high mountains, bogs, devilish mountain biking, and lots of rough water for the canoe stretches. Ski and I agreed to try again the next year, and to that end I trained hard throughout 2002. An outline timetable was:

January	In the UK Mud Race, seven miles of mud and sweat and obstacles, I came 238th out of 2,500
March	The High Peak Marathon: a 40-mile night race in a team of four. Peter James led. We came 4th out of 40. Gary Tompsett's team beat us by a short head
March	The Grizzly 2002: I came 334th out of 1,306. If I had been 9 minutes quicker, I would have come in 208th! The 20 rough miles took 2 hours 49 minutes
April	London Marathon: 3 hours 38 minutes
May	ACE Race, Thetford Forest: 10th out of 72 teams, with Sean Fishpool
May	Devizes–Westminster Canoe Race: 125 miles and 76 locks. 48th out of 88 teams in 25 hours 28 minutes, with Steven Seaton
July	Alpine Marathon: 78 kilometres. 297th out of 780 men in 9 hours 10 minutes, with Steven Seaton
September	ACE Race, Ullswater with Ski Sharp. 1st in '2 males class', and 6th overall out of 189
October	The Southern Traverse 2002, back in New Zealand, was by far the toughest adventure race I've taken part in. Ski Sharp was leader. We were in 10th position when a checkpoint error caused us a 5-hour delay, and we ended up 13th

I entered the High Peak Marathon again in March 2003, this time with Yiannis Tridimas, a top UK veteran endurance runner, and two others. We came in 3rd overall in 11 hours 25 minutes. That year I had the heart attack and ran the seven marathons, but twelve months later I was back with Yiannis and his team. This time (2004) we came in 3rd in 10 hours 51 minutes and won the Veterans Prize.

Ginny died that February and, in a kind attempt to help keep my mind occupied, Steven Seaton entered me for the 26-mile North Pole Marathon, which I have already described.

In June with Yiannis we won the Veterans Elite at the Lowe Mountain Marathon, and came in 10th Elite overall in 11 hours 7 minutes.

In July, in John Houlihan's team of three, we came 5th out of 110 teams in the 100-kilometre two-day Edinburgh Rat Race, the first urban adventure race in Britain.

In December, to pay back the Singapore Heart Association for their help during the 7x7x7 Marathons, I ran in the Singapore 2004 Marathon, being crewed by Louise, and completed the course in 4 hours 29 minutes. Slow in the humid heat, but an hour quicker than the previous year.

In August 2005, again crewed by Louise, I ran the Tour du Mont Blanc Ultra Marathon, taking 38 hours to complete the 158 kilometres of mountain trails, including 8,500 metres of climbing. I was 358th out of 2,000 runners.

In March 2006, crewed by Louise and running once more with Yiannis and his usual team in the High Peak Marathon, we again won the Veterans Trophy and came in 6th overall in 12 hours 14 minutes. The temperature en route dropped to −13°C.

In June 2006, Yiannis and I dropped out of the Lowe Alpine Marathon on Mull, having failed to find a checkpoint.

My last race prior to attempting the Eiger was the Karrimor Mountain Marathon (renamed the Original Mountain Marathon) in October 2006, aged sixty-two years. My team-mate and leader was Jon Brooke. We missed the last checkpoint on Day One, but completed the whole two-day course and came in 23rd in the Elite class, five places behind Gary Tompsett's team. Jon was honest at the end of this race. He needed to race with somebody a lot faster than I now was. I was racing in Britain's top endurance grade and had kept up after a fashion for quite a few years, but in 2005 and 2006 I had spent too much time trying to learn how to climb, at the expense of keeping up my running hours.

By the summer of 2007 I was struggling to jog for more than three hours non-stop and failed to complete a single long-distance race. So, I was happily surprised to be nominated Great British Sportsman of the Year 2007 by the ITV awards against the likes of the boxer Joe Calzaghe and Formula One driver Lewis Hamilton. At 63 years old I felt a bit of a fraud. At the awards Louise sat immediately behind David Beckham and was fascinated by the butterfly tattoo that she said was to be found on the back of his neck.

At the time of writing, I have entered the 2008 40-mile High Peak Marathon with the Yiannis team and will see how things go. But even if I continue to drop down the endurance race rankings, I will still take on team challenge events of some sort, just to keep my feet out of the grave as long as possible.

I have found the ageing process can be slowed down by running for at least two hours every other day or, at worst, every third day. A route including reasonably demanding uphill stretches is important. Entering a team race at least once every three months gives a solid purpose to keep the mind focused. Any period of 'no running' causes ever increased difficulties when you get back in your trainers. At sixty-three I find I have to accept that I'm slower than at sixty, but I can still compete at a slightly lower level.

Appendix 5
The Eiger North Face – 1938 Route

Grading any climb for difficulty is always a controversial issue, so I have chosen a fairly typical assessment of this route by the Irishman Paul Harrington, who led a two-man rope up the standard route at more or less the same time of year (i.e. late February/early to mid-March) in 1997.

Both Paul Harrington and Russian climbing instructor Andrey Kosenko (who led the route in late February 2007) have considerable experience of Scottish Grading. Andrey summarised his Eiger climb as, 'I have onsited various Scottish Grade VII climbs and found some parts of the Eiger route as demanding as them, when in poor condition.'

The Harrington Grading was given when the 1938 route was 'less ice than normal, but with no fresh snow lying around and perfect weather'.

The Entry Chimney: (IV,4)

From the triangular snow slope up to the fixed ropes below the Difficult Crack: (V,4)

Fixed ropes below the Difficult Crack on the Hinterstoisser Traverse and between the First and Second Ice-Fields: Ungradable, but if the ropes were not there, you can be sure that in typical winter conditions you would be talking about no less than Scottish winter Grade VI

Difficult Crack: (V,5)

The first pitch off the end of the Second Ice-Field: (V,5)

The Ramp from the bottom up to the snow slope before the Brittle Ledges: (VI,6) and A1

Brittle Ledges: (IV,3)

The eighteen-metre vertical access pitch to the Traverse of the Gods: (V,6) and A1

Traverse of the Gods: (V,4)

Exit Cracks: (VI,5) and A1. This is assuming the easiest route is taken and it is possible to tension traverse into the middle gully. If one of the other variations had to be climbed, you're probably talking about (VI,6), or maybe even (VI,7)

Appendix 6
Organizing a Polar Expedition – Some Outline Tips

Antarctica is expensive and difficult to reach, which is why, blocked by the roughest seas in the world, nobody penetrated its interior until just over 100 years ago. Scott, Amundsen and Shackleton struggled over the Ross Ice-shelf and on to the vast inland plateau; while the Arctic Ocean, peopled by the Inuit who, for centuries, have survived along its coastlines, is infinitely more accessible to travellers. Sledgers who cross Greenland, the Canadian north and Svalbard often describe themselves as polar travellers, using the Arctic Circle as their yardstick. Thus there are a great many more veterans of the Arctic than of Antarctica.

Travel in the remote polar reaches of the Arctic Ocean itself and the high plateaux of Antarctica demands careful preparation and constant wariness due to unpredictable weather and local hazards which can rapidly prove lethal. On the other hand, during the summer season, polar travel can be easy and almost temperate on windless days and away from problem areas. I have travelled to both poles, often without suffering unduly from the cold, yet I lost part of a toe from frostbite during a weekend Army exercise in Norfolk. A need for wariness is not a uniquely polar prerogative but, due to the remoteness of many polar objectives and the potential hazards involved, the organisation for any polar expedition must be especially meticulous.

You may travel by a wide variety of methods and there is not room here to cover all of these. Dog teams, microlights, snow machines, hot air balloons or even motorbikes have been used, but the most common form of travel at the time of writing, and for adventurous activities, is that of manhaul sledging.

In 1993 Mike Stroud and I suffered considerable physical damage crossing the Antarctic continent by manhaul and minimal use of old-style sails that could only use following winds. Our sledge loads, each in excess of 215 kilograms, required brute force to shift, and 16 kilometres a day was a fair average manhaul stint, costing a daily deficit of 8,000 calories and leading to slow starvation.

In 1996, again towing a load of nigh on 225 kilograms, I deployed a 4.5-kilogram kite and managed up to 190 kilometres a day with minimal physical effort and correspondingly less calorific expenditure. My sledge load could be halved in terms of fuel and food. What had previously proved remarkably difficult was now comparatively simple and, in my opinion, could hardly be described as 'unsupported'.

Polar travel has been truly revolutionised by such wind devices. It is now possible to cross Antarctica in under two months. Of course the element of luck can still play tricks. Broken equipment, unusually bad weather, sudden illness and well-hidden crevasses can all prevent a successful outcome, but at least the reality of polar travel is now within the grasp of the many, not just the few.

To give any practical advice on the organisation of a polar journey would be difficult without lists. Those that follow are the result of a dozen polar journeys in many regions and with differing purposes. I have spent more days and nights out on the Arctic pack and Antarctic plateau than anyone alive, but my kit lists and general tips are by no means infallible. They will not prevent you falling into the sea or an ice crack. You may still become hypothermic, snow blind or lost or be eaten by a polar bear, but I hope they will at least help you get started as a polar traveller of reasonable competence.

First of all, read as much available literature by previous travellers in the area of your chosen trip as you can. Study the annexes at the rear of expedition books. Lists of sponsors and manufacturers are often quoted and can save you time.

Then apply, ideally through the Royal Geographical Society's Expedition Advisory Office, for information on expeditions currently planning to go into your area of interest. It will help if you have a skill to offer (cook, communications, photographer, mechanic, etc).

Go on other people's trips to Greenland, Svalbard, Iceland, Norway, anywhere with snow and ice, to gain experience before progressing to the deep south or north and to leading your own projects, eventually to and across the poles if that strikes your fancy.

Here are some guidelines. Feel free to ignore or alter them wherever you can garner more appropriate updated advice.

Equipment

Clothing

1 Fleece jacket with hood.
2 Ventile outer trousers with braces and long-length hooded anorak (baggy).
3 Down duvet jacket with hood attached (for periods when not manhauling).
4 Wick-away underwear (long sleeves and legs).
5 Meraklon headcover.
6 Duofold balaclava with mouth hole.
7 Separate lip protector mouthpiece with elastic to hold in place
8 Ski goggles and ski glacier glasses with nose-protecting felt pad glued in place.
9 1 pair thick wool socks.
10 1 pair thin Helly Hansen socks.
11 1 pair vapour barrier socks.
12 1 pair Dachstein mitts.
13 1 pair Northern Outfitters heavy gauntlets.

14 1 peaked cap, kepi-style and with under-neck strap.
15 1 pair thin working gloves.
16 1 pair vapour barrier mitts (optional). Some folk swear by them.
17 Footwear, as advised by polar travellers of your acquaintance (or from their books!). There are too many alternatives to be specific here. Correctly fitting boots are of great importance.
18 For polar work when using snow machines, skis or dogs, shops specialising in the relevant sports gear will be able to advise you best.

Note: The heavier the weight you tow when manhauling with no wind support, the more difficult the selection of clothing, as you will sweat, despite the cold, when working and various parts of your body, especially feet and crutch, will suffer if your clothing choice is not excellent. Ensure your initials are clearly printed on each item unless you travel alone.

General Items
1 Geodesic dome tents are best (two- or three-man), but beware of the elastic holding the poles together. When cold it loses elasticity so, if you have room on a sledge, keep as many of the pole sections permanently inserted together as possible. Black tents make the most of the sun's heat and can be seen nearly as well as fluorescent colours.
2 Sledge harness and traces (solid traces are best for crevassed areas). In the Arctic Ocean pack-ice, your sledge should be amphibious. Dry suits can be used to swim over open leads.
3 Skis, skins, ski sticks and relevant spares. (Make sure your ski bindings mate well with your boots.)
4 With your sleeping bag and tent, use stuff sacs that don't need too much effort to squeeze in. The best custom-made down gear in the UK comes from Peter Hutchinson Designs in Stalybridge.
5 MSR (Mountain Safety Research) cooker. Coleman fuel is best in extreme cold. (Be sure to get a secure cooker fitting

fixed to the lid of the box you carry your cook gear in.) Clip the MSR fuel bottle into it firmly before priming. You need a firm base. Take a spare MSR and bag of spares, especially a pricker. (Ensure your MSR fuel bottle tops have winterised washers if you intend to use them in extreme temperatures.)

6 Brush to clear snow (hard bristles).
7 Insulated mug and spoon. Set of cooking pots and pot holder.
8 Zippo lighter and spare flints. Use Coleman fuel.
9 Spare lighter. (Keep warm in trouser pocket.)
10 Silva (balanced) compass and spare compass.
11 Reliable watch and spare.
12 Optional: a light rucksack.
13 Optional: windsail kit and spares in bag (unless travelling 'unsupported by wind').
14 2 ice-screws, 1 pair jumars with loops.
15 Ice-axe (very small, light model).
16 16-metre length of para cord.
17 30 metres of thinnest relevant climbing rope.
18 Optional: foldaway snow shovel.
19 Karabiners.
20 Karrimat.
21 Sleeping bag with inner (and optional outer) vapour barriers.
22 Pee bottle (Nalgene or Rubbermaid).
23 PLB (Personal Locator Beacon) and spare lithium battery.
24 GPS (Global Positioning System) and spare lithium battery.
25 Optional: HF radio and ancillaries (or Global Satellite mobile phone).
26 Video and still camera kit. Polythene bags to avoid misting up.
27 Steel Thermos.
28 Rations (high-calorie and low-weight). Pack as for a twenty-four-hour day per tent.
29 Personal bag. This may contain: small adjustable spanner, pin-nose pliers, dental floss, needles, thin cord, Superglue, wire, diary and pencil, Velcro, charts and maps, Swiss Army knife (with all necessary tools) and spare underwear (optional).

Medical Kit
This should include all that polar travellers advise, and may well include:

- *Pain*: paracetamol for mild pain. For more severe pain and when inflammation is involved, use Ibuprofen. For severe pain, mst tablets or Buprenorphine or morphine (on prescription). Voltarol suppositories are a good additional pain-killer. Be sure to study the instruction paper that comes with each of the above.
- *Infections/Antibiotics*: Augmentin for dental and chest infections. Ciproxin is excellent for severe spreading infections of skin or gut or anything non-responsive to Augmentin. Cicatrin powder for dressing superficial cuts and rashes. Chloromycetin for eye infections. Flucloxacillin is powerful. Good for painful frostbitten toe areas.
- *Wounds*: for deeper wounds, take threaded surgical needles. Take Lignocaine for self-injection for local anaesthetic. Use Steristrips for smaller wounds. For open blisters, burns and frost injuries, Flamazine cream is effective. Take alcohol swabs to clean wounds. Tegaderm second-skin dressings are useful. Granuflex dressings are good for open blisters and frostbite areas. Canesten powder for crutch fungal infection.
- *Sickness*: Immodium is best for diarrhoea. If not effective, use Ciproxin. Buccastem is good for nausea (absorb in mouth, don't swallow).
- *Sunblindness*: take Amethocaine drops.
- *Teeth*: take oil of cloves. Also dental cement pack.
- *Other*: Jelonet dressings for burns/scalds. Rolls of sticky plaster and gauze dressings. Bonjela for mouth ulcers. Neutrogena for hand sores. Anusol for haemorrhoids. Compeed for smaller blisters.
- Treatment for your own personal health needs.

Other Considerations
Remember that insurance, fully comprehensive and including possible search and rescue costs, is mandatory and always sensible.

In Antarctica the best air charter company, Adventure Network International, will give you all the necessary advice on every side of your expedition. In the Canadian Arctic, First Air is the best (based at Resolute Bay, NWT). Remember that your cargo will cost a great deal at both ends. (In Antarctica, count on an extremely large cost per kilogram above your basic allowance to get you there from Chile.)

You can usually locate the very cheapest but suitable flights to Santiago or Cape Town (if Antarctic-bound) or various Canadian/Russian airports (if headed to the Arctic) through the London offices of WEXAS (World Expeditionary Association).

Final Advice

Always train hard and, where possible, with your prospective expedition colleagues to ensure that everybody involved has as much experience as possible. (It is best to be sure that first-time members of your team really are as good as their CVs state, since you will only progress as fast as your slowest member.)

Don't go to Greenland, Iceland, the Arctic or Antarctica to do difficult journeys with folk you don't really know. They should be reliable, easy-going and experienced. You can get to both poles by paying expert guides to help you there. Some are to be avoided. Others are excellent. All are expensive. Pay more and an aircraft will take you all the way to either pole and allow you an hour or two there, before whisking you back to warmer climes.

Never leave litter nor harm life in any form while you are there. Some Everest climbers have polluted their grail. Keep our poles clean.

Plan with great care and never rely on gizmos working, plbs and gpss for instance, or count on immediate rescue, since storms can keep search planes away for days, even weeks, so play safe.

If you aim to join the 'way-out' section by bicycling across Ellesmereland or 'collecting' different poles (geomagnetic, magnospheric, lesser accessibility, etc) then plan accordingly. For example, if you intend doing the South Pole on a pogo-stick, don't forget lots of low-temperature grease and your haemorrhoid cream. Have fun and stay cool.

Picture acknowledgements

Colour inserts, pages 1 – 32

Author's collection: 1 – 7, 9, 10 above, 11 below, 12 above, 13, 18 above left, 20 below, 21 above, 22 above, 23 centre and below. Additional sources: © Ian Bannister 28. © Neil Barnes 15. © Alex Blake-Milton 14 above. © Anthony Bowring 12 below. © Bryn Campbell 8, 11 above. © John Cleare 18 above right, 19 above. © Fiennes/Stroud/Howell 16, 17, 20 above. © Mike Hoover 10 below. © Rob Howard 21 below. © Morag Howell 18 below. © NI Syndication/The Times 22 centre and below, 23 above, 24. © George Ollen 14 below. © Ian Parnell 25, 26, 27, 29, 30, 31, 32. © John Whitbourne 19 below.

Index

Figures in italics indicate maps.

Index

World About Us film team 49, 52, 54–5, 57, 59
World Service 84
Be-Well Foods, Lincoln 185
Beardmore Glacier, Antarctic 174
Beaufort Gyral 70, 123
Beckham, David 374
Beevers, Jonathan 185
Benjamin Bowring, M.V. 71, 72, 74, 75, 94, 96–9, 118, 124, 127–31, 132, 262, 367
Bering, Vitus 206
Bering Strait 96, 97, 204, 206, 212, 232
Berkner Island 159, 160, 165, 191, 194, 197
Berlin 18
Birkbeck, Anto 85
Black Sash (anti-apartheid movement) 2
Blue Peter (television programme) 274
Blunt, Anthony 5
Blunt, Wilfrid 5
BMW 204, 210, 217
Boca Lama (Nima Dorje Sherpa) 299, 311, 313, 314, 315
Bojen, Jens 288, 293, 294, 303, 306, 311, 315
Bomberry, Russ 111–12
Bonatti, Walter 319, 344
Bonington, Chris 246, 338, 347
Boukreev, Anatoli 312
bovine tuberculosis 241, 242
Bowers, Lieutenant Henry 'Birdie' 156
Bowles, Rob 150, 158, 223
Bowring, Anton 71, 73, 74, 78, 128, 132, 205, 272–3, 278, 367

Bowring, Jill (née McNicol) 74, 96, 132, 278
Bowring family 238, 272
Bracey, Jon 324
Bradbury Lines, Hereford 20
Brasher, Chris 183
Breakthrough 187, 198, 203
Breashears, David 299, 309–310
Brewster, Barry 347
Bridge Water Rapids, Canada 59
Briksdalsbre Glacier, Norway 43, 44
Bristol Royal Infirmary 251
British Antarctic Survey 63, 71, 80, 81, 163, 258
British Army 29, 31
  Regular Commissions Board 15
  and the Transglobe Expedition 71
British Columbia 47, 48, 54
British Heart Foundation 255, 269, 281, 293, 315
Broccoli, Cubby 46, 47
Bromiley, Mary 186, 234
Brook, Patrick 42, 44
Brooke, Jon 373
Broughton (family house in South Africa) 75–6
Broughton Castle, near Banbury 236, 237
Bryce, Russell 304
Buckton, Rosalind 288, 296, 298, 299, 302
Buhl, Hermann 319
Burch, Sean 282
Burnett, Staff Sergeant Brummy 23, 40–41
Burnett, Mark 213

387